SUNBURNT COUNTRY

SUNBURNT COUNTRY

THE HISTORY AND FUTURE OF CLIMATE CHANGE IN AUSTRALIA

JOËLLE GERGIS

MELBOURNE UNIVERSITY PRESS
An imprint of Melbourne University Publishing Limited
Level 1, 715 Swanston Street, Carlton, Victoria 3053, Australia
mup-contact@unimelb.edu.au
www.mup.com.au

First published 2018
Text © Joëlle Gergis, 2018
Design and typography © Melbourne University Publishing Limited, 2018

This book is copyright. Apart from any use permitted under the *Copyright Act 1968* and subsequent amendments, no part may be reproduced, stored in a retrieval system or transmitted by any means or process whatsoever without the prior written permission of the publishers.

An excerpt from chapter 18 was originally published in *Cosmos* magazine in 2007.

Every attempt has been made to locate the copyright holders for material quoted in this book. Any person or organisation that may have been overlooked or misattributed may contact the publisher.

Typeset in 11/13.5 pt Bembo by Cannon Typesetting
Cover design by Design by Committee
Printed in China by 1010 Printing International

 A catalogue record for this book is available from the National Library of Australia

9780522871548 (paperback)
9780522871555 (ebook)

A book must be the axe for the frozen sea within us.
Franz Kafka

Contents

Foreword ix

PART I Colonial Calamities 1
1 The Start of a Rocky Relationship 3
2 Unearthing Australia's Climate History 8
3 Life in Sodden Isolation 12
4 Australia's Climatic Tug of War 23
5 Twin Blows 33
6 Rescued from the Rooftops 37
7 Scarcely a Passing Shower 43
8 'The Changes Are Truly Astonishing' 46

PART II Weather Watchers 51
9 What Does 'on Record' Actually Mean? 53
10 The Weatherman 60
11 Australia's Early Climate Records 67
12 Frost and Fire 74
13 Bursting Bubbles of Optimism 79
14 Dust and Desolation 91
15 Gumboot Weather 103
16 Wisdom of the Elders 116

PART III Time Travellers 121
17 Sentinels of Deep Time 123
18 Old-growth Records 126
19 Tales from the Tropics 132
20 Frozen in Time 138
21 Ebbs and Flows 144
22 Piecing Together the Climate Jigsaw 149
23 Taking the Temperature of the Southern Hemisphere 156
24 The Saga of the Millennium 160
25 Welcome to the Anthropocene 166

PART IV History Repeating?   **169**
26   What about the Ice Ages?   171
27   Natural Variability Versus Human Influence   175
28   Life in a Shifting Climate   182
29   Human Fingerprints on Our Climate   187
30   Up in Flames   192
31   Vanishing Snow   197
32   Flooding Rains   201
33   Girt by Rising Seas   208

PART V The Age of Consequences   **213**
34   The 'New Normal'   215
35   Redrawing Our Maps   220
36   Silent Killers   227
37   The Living Dead   236
38   A Symbolic Start   245
39   Our Political Hot Potato   250
40   The Clean Energy Revolution   255
41   We Are All in This Together   264

Acknowledgements   271
References   274
Index   300

Foreword

We are all interested in the weather because it affects everything we do, our lives and our livelihoods. We want to know what clothes to wear, whether to take an umbrella or a coat, when to watch out for frost or heatwaves, thunderstorms or bushfires, extremes of any kind—wet or dry, hot or cold.

In Australia, we know the weather never stays the same for long. It changes from hour to hour, day to day, week to week, with the seasons, and from year to year. Our highly changeable weather and climate have entered our literature and our folklore, from Dorothea Mackellar's famous poem describing Australia varying from drought to floods, to John O'Brien's Hanrahan telling us that we'll all be ruined by too little rain, or too much rain, or bushfires or …

In 2008, a young researcher, Dr Joëlle Gergis, contacted me about a proposal to reconstruct Australia's climate history for as much of the last thousand years as possible. She had completed her PhD on reconstructing a global history of El Niño two years earlier and had just submitted her proposal for funding to the Australian Research Council. We met in my office at the University of Melbourne and she told me how she now wanted to study Australia's climate history by combining early weather observations from the colonies of New South Wales, Victoria and Van Diemen's Land with diary entries, newspaper stories and government reports from the nineteenth century and climate information for the last millennium extracted from tree rings, corals and ice cores. It was a massive task that hadn't been attempted before.

I was impressed by Joëlle's passion and by her proposal, as I had already compared global temperature reconstructions for the last thousand years with observations and climate model simulations for the last century. I was trying to extend the observational record further into the past to provide a better assessment of the range of natural climate variability over longer periods. I knew that no such climate reconstruction existed for Australia as a whole or for south-eastern Australia, which had the highest concentration of early weather observations and written records from colonists.

Unfortunately, I had to tell Joëlle that her proposal was very unlikely to be funded in its form at the time, because she was an early career researcher and she was trying to do it mainly on her own. However, I liked her proposal so much that I offered her a one-year research position, during which she rewrote the proposal, scaling up the research team to include some of Australia's leading experts in the field and linking it with the major state libraries in Sydney, Melbourne and Canberra, the Bureau of Meteorology, and several other agencies interested in the climate history of south-eastern Australia. The SEARCH (South Eastern Australian Recent Climate History) project was born, resubmitted to the Australian Research Council, and funded in 2009. It was a tremendous success and was awarded the Eureka Prize for Excellence in Interdisciplinary Scientific Research in 2014.

This book, *Sunburnt Country*, has arisen from that project and is complemented by Joëlle's personal insights and experiences as she pieced together Australia's climate history. It tells many stories about how Australia's weather and climate has varied over the last thousand years and is likely to change over the next century, affecting the environment and people, including Indigenous communities, colonial settlers from the First Fleet to Federation, current Australian society and future generations. This powerful book fills a crucial gap in public understanding.

It is critically important that we become more climate-literate so that we can better manage and adapt to the impacts of future weather and climate extremes. Our understanding of the weather and its variations is coloured by our local experience and our short memories. The very large natural variability of Australia's climate helps to explain why some people find it difficult to recognise the different climate we are experiencing now. In some ways, this is much like the decades that it took for the early settlers and the colonial government in Sydney to accept that the weather and climate they experienced in New South Wales was different from what they knew from their earlier lives in England.

Sunburnt Country helps us to better understand Australia's climate history and future; the droughts, flooding rains and bushfires, and how they affect people. It sets the current and future climate change caused by human activity on the solid foundation of history.

David Karoly
Professor of Atmospheric Science,
University of Melbourne

PART I
COLONIAL CALAMITIES

1
THE START OF A ROCKY RELATIONSHIP

The women screamed as the huge waves crashed loudly on the wooden deck. Horrified, they watched the foaming torrent wash away their blankets. Many dropped to their knees, praying for the violent rocking to stop. The sea raged around them as the wind whipped up into a frenzy, damaging all but one of the heavily loaded ships.

The severe storm was yet another taste of the ferocious weather that slammed the First Fleet as it made its way across the Southern Ocean in December 1787. Now, after an eight-month journey from England in a ship riddled with death and disease, the passengers' introduction to Australia was also far from idyllic. The unforgiving weather that greeted the First Fleet was a sign of things to come. More than once, intense storms would threaten the arrival of the ships and bring the new colony close to collapse.

So how did the early arrivals to Australia deal with such extreme weather? Have we always had a volatile climate? To answer these questions, we need to follow Australia's colonial settlers back beyond their graves and trace through centuries-old documents to uncover what the climate was like from the very beginning of European settlement. By poking around in the settlers' old diaries, letters and newspaper clippings, we can begin to piece together an idea of what the country's climate was like long before official weather measurements began.

When the British sailed into Australian waters, they had no idea of what awaited them. Eighteen years before the arrival of the First Fleet, Captain James Cook had barely spent a week in Botany Bay. He didn't even stop in for a quick stickybeak at Port Jackson, the settlement site that eventually came to be known as Sydney Cove. HMS *Endeavour* had only briefly skirted past modern-day Sydney Harbour in May 1770, so the British knew next to nothing of the land, its climate or its people. Perhaps they expected that life would resemble their other colonial outposts like India, or an undeveloped version of England. With enough hard work, surely the land could be tamed to support their needs. But when the First Fleet sailed into Sydney Cove, they unknowingly entered an ancient landscape with an unforgiving climate.

Even before Governor Arthur Phillip set foot in Botany Bay, violent storms had battered the overcrowded ships of the First Fleet. During the final eight-week leg of the journey from Cape Town to Botany Bay, the ships had sailed into the westerly winds and tremendous swells of the Southern Ocean. Ferocious weather hit the First Fleet as it made its way through the roaring forties in November–December 1787. Although the strong westerlies were ideal for sailing, conditions on the ships were miserable. Lieutenant Philip Gidley King described the difficult circumstances on board HMS *Supply*: 'Very strong gales ... with a very heavy sea running which keeps this vessel almost constantly under water and renders the situation of everyone on board her, truly uncomfortable'. Unable to surface on deck in the rough seas, the convicts remained cold and wet in the cramped holds.

As Christmas approached, King noted the surprisingly chilly conditions off the south-western coast of Western Australia: 'The cold is in the extreme here as in England at this time of year, although it is the height of summer here'. Aboard HMS *Sirius*, Judge David Collins wrote about how the crew tried to celebrate in 'mountains high' seas, to no avail. On New Year's Day 1788, Arthur Bowes Smyth, a surgeon aboard the *Lady Penrhyn*, described how the sea poured into his cabin:

> Just as we had dined, a most tremendous sea broke in at the weather scuttle of the great cabin and ran with a great stream all across the cabin, and as the door of my cabin happened not to be quite closed shut the water half filled it, the sheets and the blankets being all on a flow. The water ran from the quarterdeck nearly into the great cabin, and struck against the main and missen chains with such a force as at first alarmed us all greatly, but particularly me, as I believed [the] ship was drove in pieces. No sleep this night.

In a letter to his father, *Sirius* crew member Newton Fowell described the terrible weather that greeted the new year: 'This year began with very bad tempestuous weather, it blew much harder than any wind we have had since our leaving England'. As the atrocious conditions continued, the First Fleet was forced to slow down to prevent the ships' sails from tearing. Earlier in December 1787, the *Prince of Wales* had lost its topsail and a man washed overboard in what a sailor on the *Scarborough* described as 'the heaviest sea as ever I saw'.

Captain John Hunter described how the rough seas made life on the *Sirius* very difficult for the animals on board:

> The rolling and labouring of our ship exceedingly distressed the cattle, which were now in a very weak state, and the great quantities of water which we shipped during the gale, very much aggravated their distress. The poor animals were frequently thrown with much violence off their legs and exceedingly bruised by their falls.

It wasn't until the first week of January 1788 that the majority of the First Fleet sailed past the south-eastern corner of Van Diemen's Land, modern-day Tasmania. As his boat navigated the coast, surgeon John White noted: 'We were surprised to see, at this season of the year, some small patches of snow'. The fleet then began the 1000-kilometre struggle up the coast of what would soon be called New South Wales, against a strong headwind and the East Australian Current. Newton Fowell wrote:

> The wind variable and weather dark and gloomy, with a very troublesome high sea. About two o'clock p.m. we had one of the most sudden gusts of wind I ever remember to have known. In an instant it split our main-sail; and but for the activity shewn by the sailors, in letting fly the sheets and lowering the top-sails, the masts must have gone over the side … Fortunately for us the squall was of short duration, otherwise the ships must have suffered considerably from the uncommon cross sea that was running; which we had found to be the case ever since we reached this coast.

According to Bowes Smyth, faced with a 'greater swell than at any other period during the voyage', many of the ships were damaged, as were seedlings needed to supply the new colony with food. Bowes Smyth continued:

> The sky blackened, the wind arose and in half an hour more it blew a perfect hurricane, accompanied with thunder, lightening and rain … I never before saw a sea in such a rage, it was all over as white as snow …

every other ship in the fleet except the *Sirius* sustained some damage … during the storm the convict women in our ship were so terrified that most of them were down on their knees at prayers.

Finally, on 19 January, the last ships of the First Fleet arrived in Botany Bay. But after just three days there, Phillip realised that the site was unfit for settlement. It had poor soil, insufficient freshwater supplies, and was exposed to strong southerly and easterly winds. With all the cargo and 1400 starving convicts still anchored in Botany Bay, Phillip and a small party, including Hunter, quickly set off in three boats to find an alternative place to settle. Twelve kilometres to the north they found Port Jackson.

When the *Endeavour* had sailed past the location eighteen years earlier, Cook had simply noted: 'About two or three miles from the land and abreast of a bay or harbour wherein there appeared to be safe anchorage, which I called Port Jackson'. Early in the afternoon of the second day of their exploration, Phillip and his party discovered a large sheltered bay with a freshwater stream flowing into it. As Phillip later relayed to England, they 'had the satisfaction of finding the finest harbour in the world'. It was decided that their new home would be here, not Botany Bay. It was named Sydney Cove after Lord Sydney, the home secretary of England at that time. John White was even more blown away by Port Jackson, gushing that it was 'without exception, the finest and most extensive harbour in the universe'.

On 23 January 1788, Phillip and his party returned to Botany Bay and gave orders for the entire fleet to immediately set sail for Port Jackson. But the next morning, strong headwinds blew, preventing the ships from leaving the harbour. On 25 January, King wrote: 'The wind blowing strong from the NNE prevented … our [the *Supply*] going out', adding that they were obliged 'to wait for the ebb tide and at noon we weighed and turned out of the harbour'. In the meantime, the rest of the fleet was still trying to sail out of Botany Bay. A surgeon, George Worgan, wrote about 'the wind coming to blow hard, right in to the bay, the *Sirius* and the transports could not possibly get out'. A huge sea rolling into the bay caused ripped sails and a lost boom as the ships drifted dangerously close to the rocky coastline. According to Lieutenant Ralph Clark:

> If it had not been by the greatest good luck, we should have been both on the shore [and] on the rocks, and the ships must have been all lost, and the greater part, if not the whole on board drowned, for we should have gone to pieces in less than half of an hour.

Finally, as Bowes Smyth described, the ships left the bay: 'With the utmost difficulty and danger [and] with many hairbreadth escapes [we] got out of the harbour's mouth … it was next to a miracle that some of the ships were not lost, the danger was so very great'. By 3 p.m. on 26 January 1788, all eleven ships of the First Fleet had safely arrived in Port Jackson. Meanwhile, while waiting for the others to arrive, Phillip and a small party from the *Supply* had rowed ashore and planted a Union Jack, marking the beginning of European settlement in Australia.

After such an epic journey, the whole ordeal was washed away with swigs of rum. Unknowingly, it marked the start of our rocky relationship with one of the most volatile climates on Earth.

2
UNEARTHING AUSTRALIA'S CLIMATE HISTORY

Australia is a country defined by dramatic extremes: erratic climate influences virtually every aspect of our lives. Once the early European settlers had arrived, it didn't take them too long to realise how freakish Australia's weather can be. In his 1793 *Narrative of the Expedition to Botany Bay*, Watkin Tench, a marine officer with the First Fleet, remarked that the weather 'is changeable beyond any other I ever heard of … clouds, storms and sunshine pass in rapid succession'. Buried deep in our historical archives are countless other early stories of Australia's dramatic climate variability that Dorothea Mackellar, in her iconic poem 'My Country' captures so beautifully. Historical documents provide an incredible record of the societal impact of climate extremes in areas of Australia where observational climate records are still limited or yet to be uncovered.

From the early days of European settlement there are accounts of 'fearfully dry' conditions described as 'lamentable to look at', backed by torrential rains when the quantity of farming stock lost was considered 'prodigious'. A rummage through old colonial documents reveals a fascinating history of floods, droughts, bushfires and heatwaves. For example, in 1859 William Stanley Jevons collated the first detailed description of the Australian climate from first settlement to the mid-nineteenth century. His seminal account of the events experienced in the colony of New South Wales noted how 'the extraordinary irregularity of the rainfall escapes no one's observations'. Yet despite the serious threats posed by extreme climate variability throughout our history, a new understanding of Australia's past climate has only recently emerged.

Although there is a long tradition in places like Europe of using historical documents to reconstruct centuries of past climate conditions, until recently Australia's colonial records remained virtually unexplored by scientists for climate information. The major works on Australia's historical climate were written by nineteenth-century polymaths like Jevons and Henry Chamberlain (HC) Russell, who grappled with the nature of the new climate they found themselves in. During the twentieth century, limited work was done to consolidate the amazing amount of climate information recorded in First Fleet logbooks, explorer journals, newspapers, government records and the diaries of early settlers. Aside from a few pioneering efforts by renowned Australian climatologists like Neville Nicholls and James Foley, geographer Robert McAfee, and environmental historians such as Don Garden, little was done to piece together our pre-twentieth-century climate. It wasn't until my research team at the University of Melbourne chose to take up the monumental challenge that we had a consolidated long-term history of Australian droughts and floods that drew on a huge range of historical and scientific records.

In 2008 I developed the South Eastern Australian Recent Climate History (SEARCH) initiative to extend our region's climate record to before the start of official weather records in 1900, using an approach that spanned the traditional physical sciences and the humanities. The aim of the SEARCH project was to fill a critical gap in Australian climate science, to better understand the range of natural climate variability recorded in our history. We were also interested in seeing how extremes of drought, flood and bushfire have shaped the development of Australian society. Like all research projects, we had limited time, funding and personnel, so we mainly focused on the earliest colony of New South Wales, where the lion's share of historical material is available. While we also used many records from Victoria, Tasmania, South Australia and Queensland, still there is huge potential to extend the approach and recover more colonial-era data from other parts of the country.

The SEARCH project involved assembling a team of experts to develop climate reconstructions of south-eastern Australia that extended back from 1900 to the start of European settlement in 1788. The landmark initiative brought together a group of Australia's leading climate scientists, water managers and historians. We also partnered with ten scientific and cultural organisations: the National Library of Australia, State Library of New South Wales, State Library Victoria, Bureau of Meteorology, UK Met Office, National and State Libraries Australasia, Victorian Government, Melbourne Water, Murray–Darling Basin Authority and Sydney's

Powerhouse Museum. It was an incredibly rare opportunity to have such a diversity and depth of expertise at the table, covering Australian history, meteorology, palaeoclimatology, water resource management and archive technology.

To help us sift through immense amounts of historical information, we also enlisted the help of community volunteers to populate a 'citizen science' web portal called OzDocs. This became Australia's first publicly accessible historical database containing information about past droughts, floods, bushfires and other events going back to 1788.

The SEARCH project was the first of its kind in our region to use such a diverse range of sources to reconstruct Australia's past rainfall and temperature history. Importantly, it allowed us to set recent climate extremes against a longer record of natural variability than ever before. In 2014, we were lucky enough to win the Eureka Prize for Excellence in Interdisciplinary Scientific Research, part of a national award scheme informally known as the 'Oscars of Australian Science'. As we were up against pioneering medical and biotechnology research, we really weren't expecting to get the gong. Perhaps it was because of a growing realisation of the serious threat that climate change poses to our region, and the urgent need to compile as much historical information as possible to get a more complete view of the range of our climate variability.

One of our team's main goals was to gather together early accounts of weather and climate conditions buried in documents dating back to the First Fleet days. We started by using previous compilations developed during the nineteenth century and expanded during the twentieth century by the Bureau of Meteorology, and a modest list of other research efforts by Australian scientists and historians. These records proved to be an invaluable springboard for diving deeper into key collections.

However, while historical records are a fascinating way of reconstructing the past, it's important that they are interpreted carefully, as human memory is short, imperfect and subjective. It's an issue that historians worldwide grapple with. People also usually report on very specific local conditions, which may not represent the broader picture. For example, in her research on Australia's early colonial climate, historian Claire Fenby cautioned that a newspaper report describing a flood in Sydney as the highest 'ever experienced in the colony' could only ever signal that a major flood had occurred and did not mean that New South Wales as a whole was flooding. What is more powerful is when several accounts from different people in the same region describe the event in a similarly unusual way. Only if multiple people in many locations simultaneously recall unusual or severe weather conditions can we confidently conclude that the event was widespread. In the end, only solid numbers can ever determine something as precise as the exact height of a past flood or the amount of rainfall that fell during a storm. But sometimes, eyewitness accounts are the best we've got.

Perhaps most importantly, historical records are able to provide us with unparalleled insights into how people were personally impacted by past climatic extremes. Early newspapers commonly reported on the state of water supplies, crops, livestock and infrastructure, and the general prosperity and wellbeing of society at that time. It is information that is not contained in instrumental weather observations, so these records provide us with a separate way of counting the human cost of past climate extremes.

Sunburnt Country is the story of my team's quest to gather up the tales of Australia's climate history for the first time. The story begins in the summer of 1788 and journeys through the previously unknown droughts and floods that shaped our nation, taking us beyond the well-known twentieth-century weather events that define the 'on record' understanding of Australian climate. By combining a range of historical and scientific records going back hundreds of years before official meteorological records began, we gain an unparalleled perspective on our past. Only by listening to the howling winds scattered throughout the pages of our history can we hear the clues needed to face future challenges.

3
LIFE IN SODDEN ISOLATION

So what was the weather actually like when the First Fleet finally made it to Sydney Cove? Despite arriving in the height of summer, Governor Arthur Phillip noted: 'This country is subject to very heavy storms of thunder and lightening, several trees have been set on fire and some sheep and hogs killed in the camp since we landed'. George Worgan, surgeon on HMS *Sirius*, wrote:

> The thunder and lightening are astonishingly awful here, and by the heavy gloom that hangs over the woods at the time these elements are in commotion and from the nature and violence done to many trees we have reason to apprehend that much mischief can be done by lightening here.

Marine Lieutenant Ralph Clark described a turbulent summer storm: 'What a terrible night it was … thunder, lightening and rain. Was obliged to get out of my tent with nothing on but my shirt to slacken the tent poles'. The stormy weather continued as the convicts finally disembarked on 6 February 1788. Arthur Bowes Smyth wrote about landing during the startling intensity of the summer storm:

> They had not been landed more than an hour, before they had all got their tents pitched or anything in order to receive them, but there came on the most violent storm of lightening and rain I ever saw. The lightening was incessant during the whole night and I never heard it rain faster. About 12 o'clock in the night one severe flash of lightening struck a very large tree in the centre of the Camp, under which some

places were constructed to keep the sheep and hogs in. It split the tree from top to bottom, killed five sheep ... and one pig.

But not even a raging storm could stop the celebration that erupted after the last of the convicts finally reached land, as Bowes Smyth described:

> It is beyond my abilities to give a just description of the scene of debauchery and riot that ensued during the night ... some swearing, others quarrelling, others singing not in the least regarding the tempest, though so violent that the thunder shook the ship ... I never before experienced so uncomfortable a night, expecting every moment the ship would be struck with the lightening. The sailors almost all drunk, and incapable of rendering much assistance had an accident happened.

Perhaps the most detailed records of Sydney's early days were kept by the colony's chief bureaucrat, David Collins. He meticulously recorded all the activities of the young settlement, including convict deaths, legal hearings and agricultural production. Collins also made regular mention of weather conditions, the first of which reads: 'The weather during the latter end of January and the month of February [1788] was very cold, with rain, at times very heavy, and attended with much thunder and lightening, by which some sheep, lambs and pigs were destroyed'. It's interesting that the British, used to the frigid conditions of the Northern Hemisphere, found the height of the Australian summer cold and wet.

From the outset, the settlement was plagued by problems. Very few convicts knew how to farm the poor soil around Sydney Cove. Marine officer Watkin Tench had an enthusiastic first impression of Australian soil, writing that 'there seems no reason to doubt that many tracts of land around us will bring to perfection whatever shall be sown in them'. Perhaps he was echoing the optimism of the naturalist Joseph Banks, who had sailed with Captain Cook's first voyage to Australia in 1770. Giving evidence before a House of Commons committee in 1779, Banks had stated that the best location for a convict settlement was Botany Bay, where due to 'the fertility of the soil, they might be enabled to maintain themselves after the first year with little or no aid from the mother country'. But after experiencing repeated crop failures in Sydney first-hand, Tench soon changed his tune, declaring that much of the land seemed 'cursed with everlasting and unconquerable sterility'.

The infertile country and unpredictable weather prevented the settlement from being agriculturally self-sufficient. Most of the food had to be imported, with everyone from the convicts to Governor Phillip surviving on rationed food shipped from as far afield as South Africa, Batavia (Indonesia) and China. While the Aboriginal people survived on local plants and fish, the new settlers, still unaccustomed to this strange new land, found few of the plants appetising. In later years, on the brink of starvation, the settlers used rats, dogs, crows, kangaroo and emu to supplement the inadequate food supply.

Although the colony was clearly struggling, positive accounts of the new settlement were still relayed back to England. Phillip enthused that the climate of Sydney Cove was 'equal to the finest of Europe'. Tench echoed this sentiment, saying that 'no climate hitherto known is more generally salubrious, or affords more days on which those pleasures which depend on the state of the atmosphere can be enjoyed, than that of New South Wales'.

Meanwhile, the difficulty of life on the ground escaped no-one. By July, most of the First Fleet ships had left and the settlement became isolated. More 'inclement, tempestuous weather' persisted throughout the winter of 1788, making life in the new colony difficult, as Collins wrote:

> During the beginning of August much heavy rain fell, and not only prevented the carrying on of labour, but rendered the work of much time fruitless by its effects; the brick-kiln fell in more than once, and bricks to a large amount were destroyed; the roads about the settlement were rendered impassable; and some of the huts were so far injured as to require nearly as much time to repair them as to build them anew.

Tench recalled:

> We were eager to escape from tents, where a fold of canvas, only, interposed to check the vertic beams of the sun in summer, and the chilling blasts of the south in winter ... under wretched covers of thatch lay our provisions and stores, exposed to destruction from every flash of lightning.

After crop failures and the destruction of precious grains and seeds, the colony began to suffer from serious food shortages. So on 2 October, the *Sirius* was despatched to the Cape of Good Hope in South Africa to fetch provisions. To avoid the impossible headwind caused by the mid-latitude westerlies, they had to sail via Cape Horn, on the southern tip of South America. On their way, they were met with what Captain John Hunter described as 'a piercing degree of cold' and a sea strewn with icebergs that were 'in general … the size of a country church, to the magnitude of one, two or three miles in circumference, and proportionately high'.

Tench reported the relayed news of frosty weather in his journal: 'The weather proved intolerably cold. Ice, in great quantity, was seen for many days; and in the middle of December [the Southern Hemisphere summer] … water froze in open casks upon the deck in the latitude of forty-four degrees south'. That's just a bit further south than Tasmania's South East Cape and the city of Christchurch on New Zealand's South Island.

While the *Sirius* was off getting fresh food supplies, rations were cut back, reducing productivity in the hunger-weakened colony. The *Golden Grove* took a small contingent of convicts and marines to the recently established penal colony on Norfolk Island, 1600 kilometres north-east of Sydney. The land there was more fertile than Sydney Cove and the local trees of better quality. But the rocky cliffs surrounding the island meant that the timber could not be easily loaded onto the ship. Green turtles were found there, so the *Golden Grove* brought a few back to supplement Sydney's food supply.

Figure 1. HMS *Sirius* passes icebergs in the Southern Ocean off Cape Horn, South America, on 14 December 1788.

Source: Bradley, W (1802). *A Voyage to New South Wales, December 1786–May 1792.* Reproduced courtesy of the Mitchell Library, State Library of New South Wales.

By the second year of settlement, the foreign landscape and erratic weather were still wreaking havoc on the establishment of agriculture in Sydney. In February 1789, the young colony was continuing to experience wet conditions, making life increasingly desperate. Collins reported:

> The weather was extremely unfavourable; heavy rains, with gales of wind, prevailing nearly the whole time. The rain came down in torrents, filling up every trench and cavity which had been dug about the settlement, and causing much damage to the miserable mud tenements which were occupied by the convicts.

Life in sodden isolation was becoming hard to bear.

Meanwhile, on Norfolk Island, life was about to get a lot more difficult that stormy summer. On 25 February 1789 a cyclonic storm slammed into the fledgling colony, causing widespread devastation. The island's newly appointed governor, Philip Gidley King, vividly described how

> from four in the morning until noon, the wind increased to a very severe hurricane ... Pines, and oak trees of the largest size, were blown down every instant; the roots were torn up together with rocks that surrounded them, frequently leaving pits at least ten feet [3 metres] deep.
>
> Some of the very large trees, which measured 180 feet [55 metres] in length, and four feet [1.2 metres] diameter, were thrown by the violence of the tempest to a considerable distance from the place where they grew; and others, whose roots were too deep in the earth to be torn up, bent their tops nearly to the ground. In addition to the horror of this scene, a very large tree fell across the granary and dashed it to pieces ... whole forests seemed, as it were, swept away by the roots ...

Relentlessly, the unsettled conditions continued into 1790. To make matters worse, supplies in the colony were running drastically low. An extract from a letter by a surgeon's mate from 13 January explained the situation: 'It is now so long since we have heard from home that our clothes are worn threadbare. We begin to think the mother country has entirely forsaken us'.

Watkin Tench wrote:

> The distress of the lower classes for clothes was almost equal to their other wants. The stores have been long exhausted, and winter was at

hand. Nothing more ludicrous can be conceived than the expedients of substituting, shifting, and patching … to eke out wretchedness, and preserve the remains of decency …

As Sydney endured more flooding, the settlement learned of the devastating loss of the *Sirius*, flagship of the First Fleet, on Norfolk Island on 19 March 1790. David Collins reported that

the *Supply* returned from Norfolk Island, with an account of a disaster which depressed even the unthinking part of the inhabitants, and occasioned universal dismay. A load of accumulated evils seemed bursting upon their heads. The ships that had so long been expected with supplies were still anxiously looked for; and the *Sirius*, which was to have gone in quest of relief to their distress, was lost upon the reef at Norfolk Island … bad weather immediately ensued, and, continuing for several days, the provisions could not be landed, so high was the surf occasioned by it.

The loss of the *Sirius* brought Sydney Cove to the brink of famine, as drastic rationing was enforced. Collins wrote:

It was unanimously determined, that martial law should be proclaimed; that all private stock (poultry excepted) should be considered as property of the state … the general melancholy which prevailed in the settlement when the above unwelcome intelligence was made public, need not be described; and when the *Supply* came to an anchor in the cove everyone looked up to her as to their only remaining hope … it was determined to reduce still lower what was already too low … very little labour could be expected from men who had nothing to eat.

A surgeon's mate also described the desperate conditions:

In this deplorable situation famine is staring us in the face … happy is the man that can kill a rat or crow to make him a dainty meal … but such food … does not supply strength but keeps us lax and weakly. I dined most heartily the other day on a fine dog, and I hope I shall soon again have an invitation to a similar repast.

Cold, wet and hungry, the weakened colony was in danger of collapse.

According to Watkin Tench, by June 1790 'the clouds of misfortune began to separate' with the approach of a large ship with 'English colours flying'. After nearly eleven months at sea, the *Lady Juliana*, with 226 female convicts on board, was the first ship to arrive since those of the First Fleet almost two and a half years earlier. Tench described rowing out to meet the ship in 'wet and tempestuous weather', and the elation after boarding:

> We continued to ask a thousand questions on a breath. Stimulated by curiosity, they inquired in turn; but the right of being first answered, we thought, lay on our side. 'Letters! Letters!' was the cry. They were produced, and torn open in trembling agitation. News burst upon us like meridian splendour on a blind man. We were overwhelmed with it; public, private, general and particular … the French Revolution of 1789, with all the attendant circumstances of that wonderful and unexpected event, succeeded to amaze us.

These letters contained the first news of events in Europe the settlers had heard since setting sail for Australia in May 1787. Two weeks later, the storeship *Justinian* arrived in a colony now in frantic need of provisions, followed a week later by the three ships of the Second Fleet with their cargo of convicts.

With the dawn of spring came new hope. By September 1790, the weather had started to improve, lifting the settlers' spirits. But it wasn't long before they got a proper taste of just how extreme Australian temperatures can be. On 27 December, Tench gave the first European account of a summer heatwave in Sydney. He likened the north-west wind to the 'blast of a heated oven', recording the temperature in impressive detail, including up to nine temperature readings on 28 December. Most of us know what oppressive summer nights are like, when the heat is so stifling that there's nothing you can do but restlessly toss and turn the night away.

No doubt the early settlers were stunned as the temperature then plummeted 8.6°C in under an hour on 28 December. Such rapid and enormous swings in summer temperature are common in Australia, but they would have come as a shock to those used to milder English conditions. And just imagine trying to cope with the intense heat in the stiff finery of the era! In those days, the fashionable suit for a gentleman consisted of a coat, a waistcoat, a white shirt with lace ruffles at the neck and wrists, breeches or pantaloons, embroidered silk stockings and high-heeled shoes. Suits were highly decorated and made of rich velvets, silks and satins.

To make matters worse, the trousers were skin-tight, as during this period, close-fitting pantaloons were a key indicator of status. Looser-cut trousers and drop fronts were the sign of a labourer. If this wasn't enough, upper-class men wore wigs and soft fabric cravats tied at the neck on formal occasions. Alexander Harris' 1847 publication *Settlers and Convicts* includes a scene in a Sydney pub in 1830 highlighting the cultural shock of seeing bare skin in public: 'And not a shin in the room that displayed itself to my eyes had on either stocking or sock. Of course I speak here only of the very lowest class'. It boggles the mind to think of the heat stress they must have endured.

And so the long hot summer of 1790–91 rolled on. Watkin Tench described the impact of the drought on the food supply:

> Vegetables are scarce ... owing to want of rain. I do not think that all the showers of the last four months put together, would make twenty-four hours rain. Our farms, what with this and a poor soil, are in wretched condition. My winter crop of potatoes, which I planted in days of despair (March and April last), turned out very badly when I dug them about two months back. Wheat returned so poorly last harvest.

Early in 1791, Governor Phillip wrote: 'the dry weather still continued, and many runs of water which were considerable at this season the last year, were now dried up ... at Sydney, the run of water was now very small'. Tench reflected:

> Even this heat [of December 1790] was judged to be far exceeded in the latter end of the following February [1791], when the north-west wind again set in, and blew with great violence for three days. At Sydney, it fell short by one degree of [December 1790] but at Rose Hill [Parramatta], it was allowed, by every person, to surpass all that they had before felt, either there or in any other part of the world ... It must, however, have been intense, from the effects it produced. An immense flight of bats driven before the wind, covered all the trees around the settlement, whence they every moment dropped dead or in a dying state, unable longer to endure the burning state of the atmosphere. Nor did the 'perroquettes', though tropical birds, bear it better. The ground was strewn with them in the same condition as the bats.

David Collins also documented the extraordinary effect of the heat on the local wildlife:

> Fresh water was indeed everywhere very scarce, most of the streams or runs about the cove being dried up. At Rose Hill, the heat on the tenth

and eleventh of the month, on which days at Sydney the thermometer stood in the shade at 105°F [40.6°C], was so excessive (being much increased by the fires in the adjoining woods), that immense numbers of the large fox bat were seen hanging at the boughs of trees, and dropping into the water ... in several parts of the harbour the ground was covered with different sorts of small birds, some dead, and others gasping for water.

Imagine strolling through Sydney's Botanic Gardens to be met by a writhing carpet of bats and birds dying of heat stress! Phillip elaborated on the staggering scale of the scene: 'From the numbers that fell into the brook at Rose Hill, the water was tainted for several days, and it was supposed that more than twenty thousand of them were seen within the space of one mile'.

Mass mortality of wildlife from heat stress hasn't been unheard of in more recent times. On 12 January 2002, temperatures in excess of 42°C killed more than 1300 grey-headed flying foxes in Dallis Park in northern New South Wales. State-wide, more than 3500 flying foxes reportedly fell due to the soaring temperatures on that single day. Similarly, at least 1000 grey-headed flying foxes from Melbourne's Yarra Bend colony died during the February 2009 heatwave that culminated in the devastating Victorian Black Saturday bushfires. Although the event may not be unprecedented, the number of bats killed in the summer of 1791 may have been higher due to the denser population that would have been supported by Sydney's bushland before large-scale urbanisation.

In a letter dated 4 March 1791, Phillip commented on the emerging drought:

From June until the present time so little rain has fallen that most of the runs of water in the different parts of the harbour have been dried up for several months ... I do not think it probable that so dry a season often occurs. Our crops of corn have suffered greatly from the dry weather.

But little did he realise that erratic rainfall is perhaps the most defining characteristic of the Australian climate. In modern-day Sydney, the autumn and winter rains are important for recharging reservoirs and rejuvenating parched land. The failure of these rains can have as devastating an effect on agriculture today as it did over two centuries ago. In April 1791, Phillip wrote:

The dry weather continued ... the quantity of rain which fell in the month of April, was not sufficient to bring the dry ground into proper order for sowing the grain ... this continuance of dry weather, not only hurt their crops of corn very much, but the gardens likewise suffered greatly; many being sown a second and a third time as the seed never vegetated, from want of moisture in the soil.

As a result of the drought, Phillip tightened rations as the food supply of the struggling colony began to dwindle: 'Little more than twelve months back, hogs and poultry were in great abundance, and were increasing very rapidly ... but at this time [April 1791] there was seldom any to sell'. Tench lamented: 'I scarcely pass a week in summer without seeing it rise to 100 degrees [37.8°C]; sometimes to 105 [40.6°C]'.

David Collins described the dry conditions that persisted into June 1791: 'The ground was so dry, hard and literally burnt up, that it was almost impossible to break it with a hoe; and until this time there has been no hope or probability of the grain vegetating'. On returning from Norfolk Island, John Hunter, former captain of the doomed *Sirius*, described the scene at Sydney Cove: 'All the streams from which we

Figure 2. Reservoirs were carved into the sandstone surrounding the freshwater Tank Stream in 1791 to help regulate Sydney's erratic water supply.

Source: Henderson, JB (c. 1852). *Old Tank Stream Sydney*. Reproduced courtesy of the Mitchell Library, State Library of New South Wales.

were formerly supplied ... were entirely dried up, so great had been the drought; a circumstance, which from the very intense heat of summer, I think it probable we shall be frequently subject to'. Indeed, the boom–bust rainfall cycle still defines life in Australia.

The irregularity of the freshwater stream and the worsening drought led to the first documented account of water restrictions imposed on Sydney. To try to control the amount of water flowing out of the colony, holding tanks were cut into the stream's sandstone banks. In November 1791, Collins wrote that 'the Governor had employed the stone-mason's gang to cut tanks out of the rock, which would be reservoirs for the water large enough to supply the settlement for some time'. These chiselled basins led to the small freshwater creek flowing into Sydney Cove becoming known as the 'Tank Stream', and is probably the earliest example of water regulation in Australia's European history. It certainly wasn't to be the last.

4
AUSTRALIA'S CLIMATIC TUG OF WAR

Viewed through the eyes of Australia's colonial settlers, life 'Down Under' often seemed like an all-stations journey through the Apocalypse. So what are the factors that create our erratic weather? Why is our climate so extreme?

To start with, Australia is a huge island surrounded by vast oceans. Our landmass stretches from the tropics to the mid-latitudes, generating an enormous range of climate zones that support tropical rainforest, coral reefs, immense deserts and even alpine environments. We are also the flattest continent on Earth, meaning that weather systems can travel huge distances very quickly without being tripped up by rugged terrain. The main geographical feature that moderates climate on the east coast is the Great Dividing Range; a mountain chain that stretches 3500 kilometres south from the northern tip of Queensland, running the entire length of the east coast before finally fading into the central plains beyond the Grampians in western Victoria. In a nutshell, away from the eastern seaboard, Australia is mostly a flat, dry desert with wet coastal fringes that house all of our capital cities.

Essentially, Australia's climate is a tug of war between warm tropical influences from the north and cool temperate systems from the south. The weather experienced during each season is driven by differences between the rate of warming of the land and sea as the Earth rotates around the sun. These contrasting temperature and atmospheric pressure gradients set the scene for the complex atmospheric and ocean cycles that drive Australian climate.

So what causes the seasonal weather conditions we experience every year? During summer, the sun heats up the land and, to a lesser degree, the surrounding seas. The land surface becomes hottest in northern tropics, where the sun is directly overhead. Cooling sea breezes can't reach very far inland, allowing the land to heat up even more. As northern Australia warms up, the surrounding oceans also warm, losing a lot of moisture through evaporation. The hot air generated over northern land areas rises and warm humid air flows in from the surrounding tropical Pacific and Indian oceans, eventually falling as the torrential rains of the summer monsoon.

This hot, humid air rises over the tropical north and starts flowing towards Antarctica and the South Pole. As it drifts over the hot Australian landmass, it begins to cool and sink, creating a band of high atmospheric pressure over the country. This creates the very dry conditions that form the subtropical deserts that dominate our country. Nearly all of the great deserts of the world are found within these zones of high pressure around 20–30 degrees south and north of the equator. It is because Australia sits directly underneath this high-pressure band that we are the driest inhabited continent on Earth.

Like migratory birds, wind systems in the Southern Hemisphere follow the sun, moving north in winter and south in summer. When the belt of high pressure is at its most southerly location during summer, the subtropical high-pressure zone, known as the subtropical ridge, lies in the Southern Ocean. The westerly winds that whip around the South Pole contract towards Antarctica. The dominance of the subtropical ridge over much of the southern half of the country generates the hot and dry conditions that occur in areas outside of the tropics during the summer months. Tropical cyclones are the most dramatic weather events that develop over the warm seas off northern Australia between November and April. The accompanying high winds and storm surges can bring catastrophic damage to coastal communities and ecosystems during these times.

In winter, the westerly winds generated around Antarctica expand northward towards Australia, picking up moisture from the Southern Ocean. This shift generates the westerly storm tracks that sweep across southern Australia, bringing regular rain to the southern fringes of the mainland, and snow in Tasmania and the alpine areas of the south-east. This interplay between the high pressure of the mid-latitudes and the low pressure of the polar region around Antarctica is what sets up the seasonal weather patterns we experience each year.

Against the backdrop of these seasonal conditions, Australia also experiences major year-to-year and even decade-to-decade fluctuations in its climate, further amplifying our variability. Aside from the seasons, the planet's largest natural climate cycle, the El Niño–Southern Oscillation (ENSO), is the main source of natural year-to-year climate variability in our region. ENSO is an interaction of ocean and atmosphere processes that influences changes in global circulation, causing massive redistributions of major rainfall-producing systems. The ENSO system causes extremes like droughts, floods, bushfires and cyclones that affect around 60 per cent of the Earth. Here in Australia, ENSO is the culprit responsible for our climatic bipolar disorder—it's what makes us the land of droughts and flooding rains. We swing wildly from one rainfall extreme to the other—El Niño dries to La Niña deluges—as the warm waters of the western Pacific spill out from Indonesia to the South American coastline, dragging our rain clouds with them. After pounding into the Peruvian coastline, the waters bounce back with a vengeance, unleashing torrential drought-breaking rains on their return.

'El Niño' refers to the ocean warming component of the ENSO phenomenon, while the 'Southern Oscillation' is a measure of the seesawing of atmospheric pressure across the Pacific basin between Darwin and Tahiti. The Southern Oscillation Index (SOI) is a metric used to monitor differences in the pressure between the eastern and western Pacific. In its strongly negative phase, the SOI generates El Niño events, indicative of high pressure that brings hot and dry conditions to our region. By contrast, highly positive SOI values indicate La Niña events that form with a background of dominant low-pressure conditions that bring cool and wet conditions to Australia.

Initially generated in the equatorial Pacific, ENSO events create a far-reaching system of climate impacts on society. The climate variability associated with ENSO episodes outside of the tropics are referred to as 'teleconnections'. This is experienced through climatic extremes including drought, flooding, bushfires and tropical cyclone activity across vast areas of the Earth. These episodes are commonly associated with social and economic hardship for the millions of people living in areas where agricultural productivity is influenced by the Australasian, African and American monsoon systems.

To understand how ENSO influences Australia's regional climate, we need to think about how changes in ocean temperatures and atmospheric winds shift across the Southern Hemisphere. During normal conditions, strong trade winds blow from east to west across the Pacific Ocean over the equator. The winds push warm surface ocean water from South America towards Asia and Australia. Cold water upwells from along the

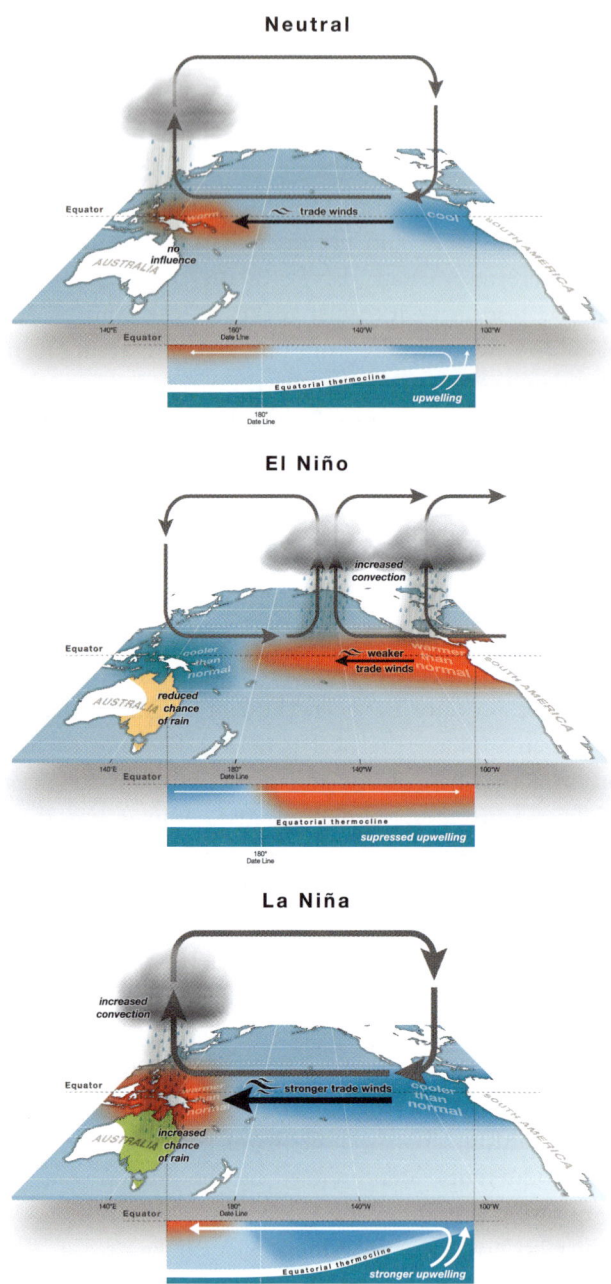

Figure 3. Ocean and atmospheric circulation associated with the El Niño–Southern Oscillation (ENSO) conditions. Neutral (top), El Niño (middle) and La Niña (bottom) phases are characterised by changes in atmospheric pressure and ocean temperatures across the Pacific.

Source: Reproduced courtesy of the Bureau of Meteorology.

South American coastline, creating a temperature gradient across the Pacific—that is, warmer water in the western Pacific north of Australia, and cooler water in the east. This in turn keeps the trade winds blowing, as the temperature difference and the easterly trade winds reinforce each other. The accumulation of warm water in the western Pacific adds heat to the air, causing it to rise and create the warm and rainy weather that characterises the tropical rain belt of the Indo-Pacific region. This pattern is known as the Walker circulation.

During an El Niño year, the trade winds associated with the usual Walker circulation weaken or break down. The warm water that is normally pushed towards the western Pacific flows back across the Pacific, piling up on the eastern Pacific coastline from California to Chile, increasing rain and stormy weather. Although El Niño's strongest impacts are felt around the equatorial Pacific, they can affect weather all over the world by influencing the position of high and low pressure systems, winds and rainfall patterns. As warmer ocean waters release excess heat into the atmosphere, global temperatures rise.

Typical El Niño events in our region generate a weaker than normal summer monsoon, resulting in reduced rainfall and river flow and fewer of the tropical cyclones that batter Australia's coast. Historically, many of the worst droughts in eastern Australia have coincided with El Niño events, and the southern parts of the country experience more hot days than usual. The combination of drier conditions and extreme temperatures means that high-fire-risk days are more common during El Niño years.

Sometimes after an El Niño year, the pendulum swings back in the other direction to create La Niña conditions, essentially an intensification of the normal Walker circulation pattern. The trade winds blow harder from east to west, upwelling more cold water around the South American coastline. This pushes warm water from South America west towards Australia, resulting in weather patterns that are the reverse of El Niño. When the western Pacific becomes rainier, flooding can be severe if following El Niño–induced droughts, and northern Australia often experiences more cyclones.

During typical La Niña events in Australia, the summer monsoon is more active than normal, leading to greater flooding due to increased tropical cyclone and storm activity. The majority of the wettest years in Australian history have generally taken place against a background of La Niña conditions. The number of tropical cyclones that hit the Queensland coast roughly doubles during La Niña summers, causing widespread flooding, especially along the eastern seaboard.

The tricky thing about ENSO is that it does not have a reliable pattern, with events developing erratically every 3–7 years. Each event tends to last 12–24 months, peaking in summer. Sometimes ENSO conditions can last for many years in a row, causing major headaches for communities. Unfortunately, most of our understanding of ENSO comes from relatively short instrumental weather records of the SOI that date back to 1876. To extend our understanding of the long-term ENSO cycle, during my PhD research I used a range of centuries-long tree-ring, coral, ice-core and documentary records to reconstruct the phenomenon back to 1525. This year-by-year list of El Niño and La Niña events has been helpful for historians and scientists interested in determining if and how past episodes impacted local communities around the world, including Australia's early settlers. For example, this allows us to know that the first European colonists probably experienced wet conditions associated with a very strong La Niña event that spanned 1788–90, followed by a severe El Niño event in 1791–93.

While ENSO is the main factor influencing Australia's climate variability, especially between June and February, it isn't the only cause of major swings in rainfall and temperature across our region. From late autumn to early spring, Australian rainfall is also influenced by changes in the Indian Ocean. A little bit like ENSO, there is a seesawing of ocean temperatures and atmospheric pressure over a large part of the Southern Hemisphere, but this time between the western Indian Ocean near Africa and the eastern Indian Ocean around Indonesia. Sustained changes in the difference between sea surface temperatures and atmospheric pressure between the tropical western and eastern Indian Ocean give rise to what's known as Indian Ocean Dipole (IOD) events. These episodes usually start around May and peak between August and October, before rapidly decaying when the monsoon arrives around the end of spring. IOD events are one of the key drivers of Australia's climate and can have a big impact on agriculture, as these conditions generally coincide with the winter cropping season.

During negative IOD events, warmer than average temperatures in the Timor Sea pool off the north-western Australian coastline. Westerly winds also intensify along the equator, allowing warmer waters from the coast of Africa to pile up to the north of Australia. Increased convection favours the formation of north-west cloud bands—large areas of cloud that can extend from the Indian Ocean, sucking moisture across virtually the whole country to its south-eastern corner. Negative IOD conditions typically result in above-average winter–spring rainfall over parts of southern Australia as the warmer waters off north-western Australia provide more moisture to weather systems crossing the country.

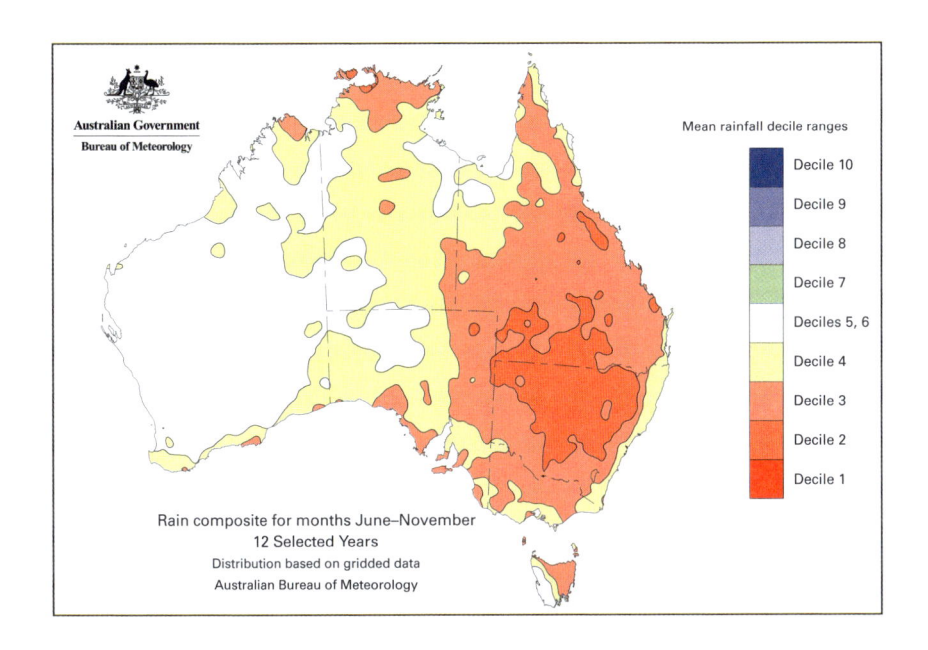

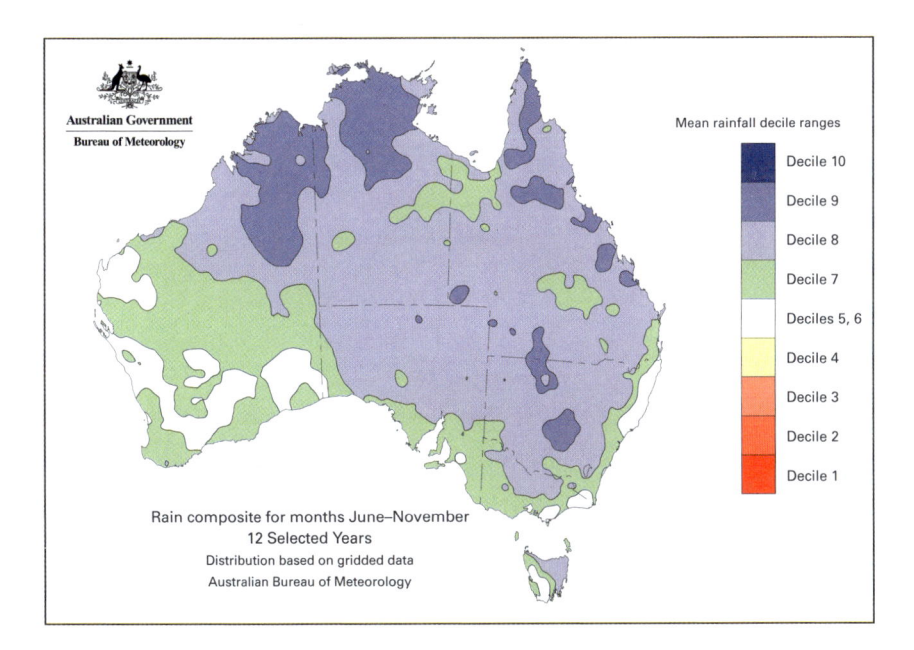

Figure 4. Typical Australian rainfall patterns associated with dry El Niño (top) and wet La Niña (bottom) conditions.

Source: Reproduced courtesy of the Bureau of Meteorology.

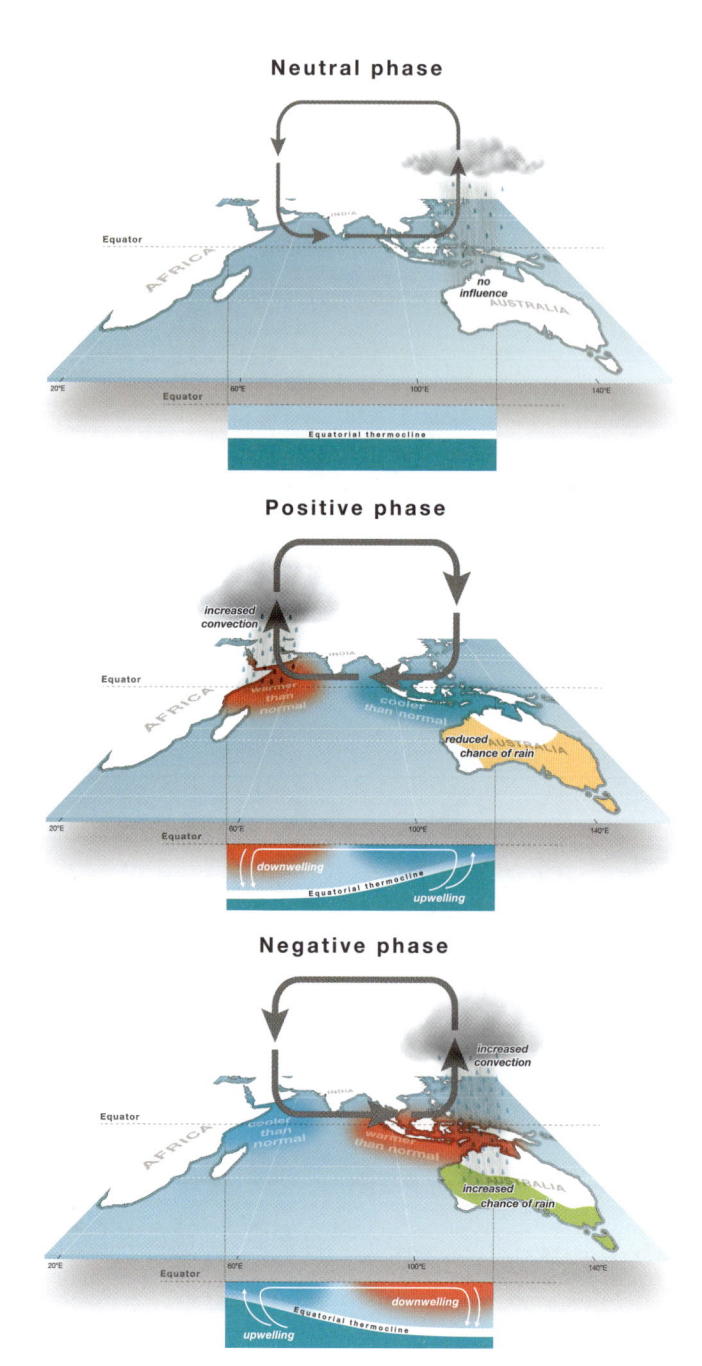

Figure 5. Ocean and atmospheric circulation associated with Indian Ocean Dipole (IOD) conditions. Neutral (top), Positive IOD (middle) and Negative IOD (bottom) phases are characterised by changes in the atmospheric circulation and temperatures across the Indian Ocean.

Source: Reproduced courtesy of the Bureau of Meteorology.

During positive IOD events, essentially the reverse occurs. Cooler than normal water off Australia's north-western coast leads to less moisture than normal in the atmosphere. Westerly winds weaken along the equator, allowing the warm water around Indonesia to spill out towards Africa. Under these conditions, north-west cloud bands are less likely to form, removing a major source of rainfall over inland and south-eastern Australia. Cooler ocean water alters the path of weather systems coming from Australia's west, often resulting in less rainfall and higher than normal temperatures over parts of the country during winter and spring.

Outside of the tropical heat engine of the Indo–Pacific region, the Southern Ocean exerts an important influence on the climate experienced in the coastal regions of southern Australia. The interplay between the high pressure of the mid-latitudes and the low pressure of the South Pole is referred to as the Southern Annular Mode (SAM). Essentially, the SAM describes the north–south movement of the westerly wind belt that circles Antarctica and how it influences the climate of the middle to high latitudes of the Southern Hemisphere between 40 and 60 degrees south. The changing position of the westerly wind belt influences the strength and position of cold fronts and mid-latitude storm tracks, making it an important driver of rainfall variability in southern Australia.

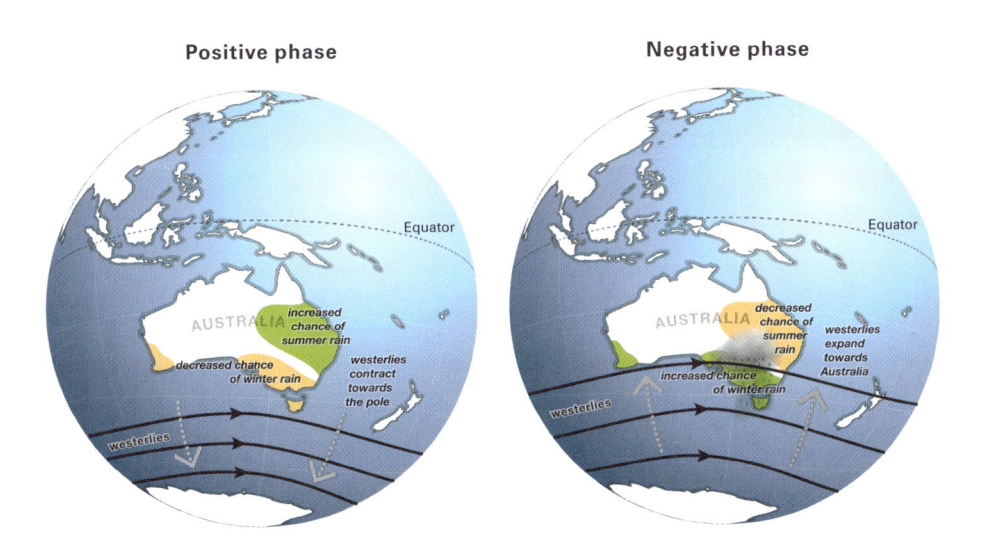

Figure 6. Atmospheric circulation associated with the Southern Annular Mode (SAM) and its influence on Australian rainfall. Positive SAM (left) and Negative SAM (right) phases are characterised by changes in the atmospheric circulation over the Southern Ocean.

Source: Reproduced courtesy of the Bureau of Meteorology.

In the negative phase of the SAM, there is an expansion of the belt of strong westerly winds towards the equator. This northward shift in the westerly winds results in more low-pressure systems over southern Australia. During extremely negative phases, the SAM can cause increased rainfall and more cold air outbreaks in southern Australia, sometimes resulting in snowfall. During its positive phase, the SAM is associated with weaker than normal westerly winds and higher pressures over southern Australia. This means that cold fronts and storm systems slide further south, depriving southern Australia of some of its precious rainfall.

So along with the shift in the seasons, these major modes of climate variability in the Pacific, Indian and Southern oceans drive variations of the climate conditions experienced in Australia from year to year. Without the benefit of vast amounts of scientific data and modern computer processing power, there was no way the first European settlers could have ever imagined the complexity of the Australian climate. Instead, they found themselves in a land that was unrecognisable from that of England. They were soon to find out just how extreme life on the other side of the planet could really get.

5
TWIN BLOWS

Following the drought of 1791–93, good rains associated with La Niña conditions during the mid-1790s and the opening up of richer agricultural land around Parramatta, about 25 kilometres to the west of Sydney, kept the colony afloat until another major drought hit in 1798–99. The initial survey of the Australian coastline conducted by explorers Matthew Flinders and George Bass revealed that Batemans Bay, some 300 kilometres south of Sydney, and Western Port near Melbourne showed signs of drought from as early as 1797. William Stanley Jevons' compilation reported that 'the water holes were all dried up, and the Aboriginals who usually resorted to them were not seen'. By 1798, dry conditions were taking their toll on Sydney's agriculture, which had only begun expanding out to the Hawkesbury River region four years earlier. Barely any rain fell for ten months, damaging wheat, corn and potato crops.

On 25 September 1798, Arthur Phillip's replacement as governor of New South Wales, John Hunter, reported back to the Duke of Portland that the ample crop they

> had every reason to expect would have furnished a supply of wheat for at least twenty months to come, exclusive of considerable crops of maize, is at present in a very precarious state from an uncommon and tedious drought … there is now a great probability of wheat being scarce during the ensuing season.

To make matters worse, in December bushfires blazed through the Sydney region. David Collins reported that

> the heat of the sun was so intense that every substance became a combustible, and a single spark, if exposed to the air, in a moment became a flame, much evil was to be dreaded from fire. On the east side of the town of Sydney, a fire, the effect of intoxication or carelessness, broke out among the convicts' houses, when three of them were quickly destroyed; and three miles from the town another house was burnt by some run-away wretches, who, being displeased with the owner, took this diabolical method of showing it.

This is one of the earliest descriptions of Australian bushfire conditions, and perhaps the first recorded account of deliberate arson in our history.

By January 1799, strong El Niño conditions had set in, prompting Collins to remark:

> Agricultural concerns at this time wore a most unpromising appearance. The wheat proved little better than straw or chaff, and the maize was burnt up in the ground for want of rain. From the establishment of the settlement, so much continued drought and suffocating heat had not been experienced. The country was now in flames; the wind northerly and parching; and some showers of rain, which fell on the 7th, were of no advantage, being immediately taken up again by the excessive heat of the sun.

In February, Collins described the impact the drought was having on the colony's water supplies: 'Such ponds as still retained any [water] were reduced to very low, that most of them became brackish, and scarcely drinkable ... the woods between Sydney and Parramatta were completely on fire, the trees being burnt to the tops; and every blade of grass was destroyed'.

Relief finally came to the settlers in early March when heavy rains began to fall. Collins wrote: 'The dry weather which had so long prevailed, to the great detriment of the cultivated and pasture lands, was succeeded by rain for two or three days, which greatly refreshed the gardens that were nearly wholly burnt up, and everywhere revived the perishing vegetation'.

Unfortunately, the respite was short-lived, as the much-needed showers progressed into torrential downpours. Heavy rainfall battered the region, causing widespread flooding on the Hawkesbury River from 3–19 March.

The river is reported to have risen by over 15 metres above its usual level within the space of a few hours, though the accuracy of this estimate is unknown. It broke its banks with such ferocity that the torrent swept away everything in its path. Collins told the story of what happened as the Hawkesbury spilled over:

> The government store-house ... was not out of the reach of this inundation, and was swept away, with all the provisions that it contained. Many of the inhabitants were taken off from the ridges of their houses, by a few boats which they fortunately had among them, just in time to save their lives; for most of the dwellings were inundated, and the whole country appeared like an extensive lake. Many hogs, other live stock, poultry, with much of the produce of the last unfortunate harvest, and the domestic effects of the people, were hurried away by the torrent.

Collins also reflected on the origin of the flooding:

> It was said, that the natives foresaw it, and advised the inhabitants; but this wanted confirmation. If true, the trait was a favourable one. There could, however, be no doubt, that, unperceived by our people, a heavy fall of rain had taken place in the interior of the country, among the mountains, and which, from the parched state of the land for such a length of time, had in no part been absorbed, but ran down the sides of the hills, as from mountains of solid rock, filling all the low grounds, and branches of the river, which, being in form suddenly serpentine, could not give vent so fast as the waters descended.

According to Collins, the very wet conditions saw an outbreak of caterpillars that was reported to have 'commenced its ravages wherever it found any young grain just shooting out of the earth'. Then, in June 1799, strong southerly winds brought incessant deluges that saturated the colony, destroying the church tower and damaging the new Government House that was in the process of being built at Parramatta. Collins reported:

> The ravages of this storm were so great, that the settlement was thrown back nearly twelve months in those works which at the time were expected very shortly to be completed. The weather, from the beginning of this month, had never since the establishment of the colony been observed to be so severe. The settlement had indeed, between

the fires of the summer, and the floods and gales of the winter, suffered very considerably. Added to these, at this time, were the inconveniences arising from an unproductive harvest, from an exhausted store in the very essential articles of clothing and bedding, from the hostile disposition of many of the natives, and from the annihilation of morality, honesty, and industry in the major part of the colonists.

It had been a hugely demanding time for a colony trying desperately to get on its feet. As the eighteenth century came to a close, it was clear that the challenges of life in Australia were more than the new settlers had bargained for. They were still struggling to gain a foothold in subsistence agriculture with limited equipment in a land so foreign to their own. The colony was on life support: food imported from England was the only thing preventing starvation. There was little clothing or bedding, and general provisions had been depleted since the last shipment in November 1796.

And there was more to come. The colony was still far from recovered from the twin blows of severe drought and flood when disaster struck again.

6
RESCUED FROM THE ROOFTOPS

On 20 March 1800, six months before the end of his stint as New South Wales governor, John Hunter reported that 'now at the time we are about to gather in our maize … the River Hawkesbury has again overflown its banks and has had the whole crops under water—has swept away some of the savings of our last wheat harvest there, with a considerable number of hogs and poultry'.

By the turn of the century, the population of New South Wales had risen to just under 5000, and following the 1799 flood, Hunter had expressed his concerns about the growing number of people settling along the Hawkesbury:

> It is much to be lamented that in establishing themselves on the banks of the Hawkesbury, the settlers had not with more attention considered the manifest signs of the floods to which the river appeared to the first discoverers to be liable, and erected their dwellings upon the higher grounds; or that the inundations which had lately happened had not occurred at an earlier period, when there were but few settlers. These, indeed, had been such as formerly no one had any conception of and exceeded in horror and destruction anything that could have been imagined.

But in 1800, the lure of exploiting the region's rich soils to generate Sydney's food supply was too strong. It was too late to abandon the riverside settlement—people would have to learn to live with the constant threat of flooding.

In March 1800, weeks of wet weather and two subsequent floods occurred in the Hawkesbury and Georges rivers districts. David Collins described the conditions:

> The weather had, unfortunately for the maize, now ripe, been uncommonly bad for three weeks, the wind blowing a heavy gale, accompanied with torrents of rain that very soon swelled the river Hawkesbury, and the creeks in George's river beyond their banks: laying all the adjacent flat country, with the corn on it, under water. Much damage, of course, followed the desolation which this ill-timed flood spread over the cultivated grounds: and, although fewer than could have been expected, some lives were lost. The prospect of an abundant maize harvest was wholly destroyed: and every other work was suspended to prepare the ground a second time that season for wheat.

Feeling the mounting stress of the situation, Collins continued: 'The settlement was too young to be able to endure such a succession of ill-fortune without it being felt, in some degree, an inconvenience and expense to the mother country'. These comments reflected the compounding effects of the weather, limited supplies and a growing population settling in floodplain areas.

The new governor, Philip Gidley King, had hoped to put an end to the suffering caused by the flooding of the Hawkesbury, but on 10 March 1801 he informed the Duke of Portland of

> one of those calamities with which it pleases God sometimes to afflict mankind, and which no human foresight can avoid ... Fair prospects by some settlers had been defeated by three successive inundations of the Hawkesbury since last December [1800]; the last of which happened the 2nd and 3rd instant, had swept away half the stacks of wheat and destroyed nearly the whole of the corn and swine at the place.

Governor King elaborated on the difficulties caused by successive floods and limited supplies: 'Thrice in four months have they been drove from their habitations to save their lives in trees and pieces of floating wood, until the floods subsided, when they found themselves deprived of every comfort, clothing, or shelter ...' In May 1801, in response to the threat to the colony's food supply, he ordered HMS *Porpoise* to sail to Tahiti to buy as much salt and pork as the ship could hold. Armed with James Cook's salted pork recipe, the crew set off, desperate to secure the settlement's meat supply.

From July 1802 to May 1803, the region experienced a mild drought. But despite some reports of water shortages that caused 'much loss to the gardener', other historical accounts say that conditions were not as severe as those in 1790–91 and 1798–99, and the colony still managed to harvest a decent wheat crop. The good conditions continued into 1804, with months of heavy rain resulting in bumper harvests. The wealthy landowner William Wentworth noted that 'the harvest of the year 1804 was so abundant, and the surplus grain so extensive that no sale could be had for more than half the crop'. Good seasons at the Hawkesbury freed up barley and wheat for use in a newly established government brewery set up at Parramatta in 1803. Hops were in short supply, but the brewers realised that other ingredients could do the trick. Governor King hoped that making beer commercially available would put a dent in the sale of grog, a dodgy mix of rum and water that was fuelling rampant alcoholism in the colony, and divert much-needed funds into government coffers.

In her seminal PhD research on Australian climate history, Claire Fenby discussed how, in the absence of quantitative weather records, human memory was used as a benchmark of climate conditions experienced in the early days of the colony. The memories of the 'oldest colonist' were often all that was available to settlers to take a long-term perspective on unusual events. This explains the reporting in July 1804 by the recently created *Sydney Gazette* that 'the extreme mildness of the present season excites the surprise of the oldest colonist. The grain at Hawkesbury was scarcely ever known to be in so forward a state at this time of year'. Long-term settlers had become more used to the fluctuations in the Australian climate, and so were now able to benchmark events against sixteen years of life in the colony.

Conditions turned again early in 1805, when *The Sydney Gazette* reported on the 'very heavy and incessant rains' that continued to threaten floodplain settlements. By March, torrential rain had caused the Hawkesbury River to rise and submerge the low-lying farms around South Creek. Wet conditions rotted most of the maize crop before it could be saved. As the end of the year approached, there was fresh concern at the state of crops now ravaged by the blight, smut and rust that thrived in the damp conditions.

Wet weather persisted throughout the strong La Niña summer of 1805–06, culminating in the 'great and memorable flood' of the Hawkesbury River from 20–26 March—one of the most dramatic in our colonial history. The meteorologist HC Russell described it as the 'heaviest flood that up to that time had visited the Hawkesbury'. A study by historian JCH Gill provided further historical accounts from *The Sydney Gazette* about the shocking impact of the floods:

> The incessant rains on Friday and Saturday night gave a new turn to expectation; and by day-light on Saturday morning [22 March] a scene of horror presented itself in every quarter. It [the Hawkesbury] was by this time nearly as high as on the 2nd of March 1801; many farms were then under water; the rain continued without intermission, and a rapid rise was in consequence observable.

William Stanley Jevons collated vivid accounts of the horrific scene:

> In the course of one dreadful day upwards of 200 wheat stacks were swept into the stream. Nearly 300 persons were placed in situations of more or less imminent danger, but [through] great exertions were mostly rescued from the tops of houses or trees to which they had climbed. Five or seven persons were drowned. Cries for help, and reports of muskets, the signals of distress, were heard both day and night, and added greatly to the confusion of a scene which was throughout strange and terrible ... An immense expanse of which the eye cannot in many directions discover the limits, everywhere interspersed with growing timber and crowded with poultry, pigs, horses, cattle, stacks, and houses, having frequently men, women and children clinging to them for protection and shrieking out in agony of despair for assistance.

Gill's work featured a fascinating account of the rescuing of people stranded by the floodwaters:

> The measures adopted by Thomas Arndell Esq., for the preservation of lives, were actively carried into execution by Mr. Thompson, Chief Constable, who, in one of his boats, saved the lives of a hundred persons, whom he took from the tops of houses and rafts of straw floating on the deluge. He had two more boats employed in the same humane work, and by means of this also a number of lives were saved. Mr. Thomas Biggers, often at the risque of his own life, saved upwards of 150 men, women and children; and others who possessed boats, particularly the District Constables, were very active in this benevolent duty.

Like the modern-day State Emergency Service (SES), rescue operations in the early 1800s were coordinated by volunteers dedicated to helping their local communities.

Figure 7. A stylistic impression of the dramatic flooding that impacted the colony in New South Wales, particularly during the early nineteenth century.

Source: Artist unknown (c. 1870s). *A Flood in New South Wales.* Reproduced courtesy of the National Library of Australia.

The enormous scale of the losses made the 1806 flood the most destructive the settlers had experienced since their arrival in 1788. An area of over 14 500 hectares was covered by water 3.5–4.5 metres deep. According to newspaper reports of the time, many people 'lost every thing they possessed'. The extensive inundation also caused damage to houses, farming equipment and other infrastructure, and resulted in seven deaths. In an assessment of the flood damage, the government estimated that the 'Great Flood' had destroyed £35 000 worth of property, crops and livestock. Such extensive crop losses in the colony's food bowl once again reduced it to 'a state little short of starvation'.

Following the disaster, the government moved quickly to impose food restrictions to avoid famine. *The Sydney Gazette* reported that rations were reduced throughout the colony and limitations placed on the use of wheat. Governor King directed a bench of magistrates to consider 'the most equitable method of restricting the consumption of bread', to stretch out the wheat provisions in store. HC Russell reported that 'No flour was allowed to be used in biscuits, cakes or any pastry whatever, and those who had saved their grains were compelled to part with a portion of it to those who had not been so fortunate'.

In 1809 and 1816, similarly destructive floods occurred on the Hawkesbury River that were major blows to the colony. By then, Hawkesbury settlers were starting to read the signs of impending flooding, and were now well and truly aware of the potential for widespread damage to low-lying farms. But the temptation of productive agricultural land proved too great and people continued to rely on flood-prone areas—and still do to this day.

Figure 8. Example of the extensive flooding of the Hawkesbury River in New South Wales that repeatedly impacted the young colony during the early nineteenth century.

Source: Artist unknown (June 1816). *Flood on the Hawkesbury River.* Reproduced courtesy of the Mitchell Library, State Library of New South Wales.

7
SCARCELY A PASSING SHOWER

Following the very wet La Niña conditions of the early 1800s, one of the longest droughts in Australia's colonial history gripped New South Wales from 1809 to 1815. Dry weather was reported in *The Sydney Gazette* from as early as January 1809, with reports of 'little short of total failure of the maize crop' by April. Variable conditions prevailed during 1810, and by March 1811 the water tanks at Sydney were nearly empty, resulting in major water shortages. It was the first time the storage basins of the Tank Stream had been empty since they were constructed during the 1791–93 drought.

On 2 March, *The Sydney Gazette* reported: 'The long prevailing drought has destroyed every hope of a maize crop. In Sydney the tanks have been for several weeks empty, and water is sold from 4d to 6d [pence] the pailful'. Historian Claire Fenby's research into this drought period noted that the wheat crop was promising but anxiety about sustained drought conditions compelled Governor Lachlan Macquarie to order a precautionary supply of wheat from Bengal to avoid possible food shortages in the colony.

On 11 October 1811, *The Sydney Gazette* reported:

> The long succession of dry weather at the present season has heretofore been unexampled, and the field and garden languish for want of rain. The last refreshing shower was upon 27th August; it was very general throughout the various settlements, and lasted twenty-four hours, since which period we have scarcely had one passing shower. From the best information we can get, so intense a drought at this time of year has not been witnessed since the year 1789 when the new colonists suffered a parching thirst for several months, the springs from which they had before been supplied either failing entirely, or yielding scarcely

sufficient to support nature. Numbers of flying foxes, squirrels, and birds of various kinds flocked from the interior to the coast and perished as they flew. A visitation of such a calamity now that stock is so numerous would be dreadful.

The newspaper then referred to the hot summer of 1790–91, benchmarking the event against the very worst effects of the major 1791–93 drought.

Towards the end of 1812, HC Russell reported that 'heavy rains counterbalanced the drought of the previous year', but dry conditions set in again during 1813. By October that year, approximately 5000 cattle and 3000 sheep had died because of major pasture and water shortages. Russell later described how drought influenced the push to open up new land in the west: 'The prevalence of a drought during the years of 1812 and 1813 compelled the settlers to seek new pastures for their flocks and herds, and in May 1813 Messrs. Wentworth, Blaxland and Lawson made a successful attempt to cross the Dividing Range'. The explorers crossed the Blue Mountains in New South Wales in 1813 'in the hope of finding pasture and water for the exhausted cattle of the colony'. There were also reports that 'scarcely a drop of rain fell on the east coast of NSW; and when the country about Bathurst was visited, it bore marks of being similarly affected by drought'.

Drought conditions persisted into 1814, when *The Sydney Gazette* reported:

> The long subsisting droughts of the present season are very severely felt throughout the country. The wheat fields are in a universal state of languor, while the grazing stock are hourly falling off from the poverty of the pastures. The grub caterpillar is very much complained of, in many fields of wheat it appears in prodigious numbers, but we trust it will vanish with the first heavy showers.

Although it is clear from newspaper accounts that agriculture was hit hard by the drought, Fenby noted that major food shortages were not experienced this time around because of proactive government policy. As soon as the signs of drought appeared, Governor Macquarie issued a public notice encouraging farmers to sell as much grain as possible to the government stores. According to a government and general order published in 1814, settlers withheld their produce 'to give them an opportunity of exacting a most exorbitant price for their grain, knowing that it must be submitted from the necessities of the times'. Macquarie eventually caved in to paying inflated wheat and maize prices, finally encouraging farmers to sell

Figure 9. Arrival of the water train in drought-stricken Broken Hill, western New South Wales, in 1892. Like in the drought conditions of 1811, water was sold by the pailful to manage the severe shortages.

Source: David Syme and Co. (1 February 1892). 'Broken Hill—the Water Famine.' Reproduced courtesy of the State Library Victoria.

six months' worth of grain to avoid major food shortages. In October 1814, the colony's food supply was further bolstered by the arrival of 250 tonnes of wheat from Bengal. As water shortages took their toll on livestock numbers, preserved meat was once again imported into the colony.

Fenby's research has suggested that the local Aboriginal people also felt the impacts of the 1813–15 drought. She discussed Grace Karskens' book *The Colony*, which describes the death of an Aboriginal boy shot while raiding a maize field in May 1814. Karskens questions the motivation for the attack, stating: 'Had the violence really flared suddenly from nothing, out of years of peace and good relations?' She then mentions the food shortages caused by the drought, quoting Governor Macquarie's comment that the farm raids 'had not been carried on to an alarming extent, or even in serious Prejudice to any one individual settler'. Fenby further explored the possible role drought played in frontier violence, suggesting that Aboriginal people were probably driven to desperate acts like crop raids during a time of food and water shortages as the colony expanded further, marginalising the First Australians.

By October 1815, there were increasing newspaper reports of good rain, finally ending one of the longest periods of drought experienced by the young colony. The brutally dry conditions of 1809–15 made the settlers fully aware of the impact drought could have on their settlement, yet not much really changed. Instead of adapting their farming practices to better suit the volatility of Australian rainfall cycles, the inhabitants of the colony spread further into the surrounding regions in search of new pastures, avoiding facing reality for a little longer.

8
'THE CHANGES ARE TRULY ASTONISHING'

During the 1820s and 1830s, human memory was still the main source of climate knowledge, as long-term weather observations were rare or unavailable during this period. Having experienced life in the colony for over 40 years, early settlers were starting to realise that droughts and floods were a defining feature of the climate in New South Wales. They were still trying to shoehorn British farming practices into the new landscape, and still had a lot to learn about the weather and climate of Australia.

Royal Commissioner John Thomas Bigge's 1823 report on agriculture and trade summed up the frustration of trying to farm the land:

> Independent of the effects of an uncertain climate, that is not generally favourable to the growth of European grains, and of a degree of heat that either too suddenly or too quickly follows a long series of heavy rains, and scorches rather than matures it ... the proper seasons for sowing have not yet been discovered.

A journalist for *The Sydney Gazette* said of the erratic spring conditions in September 1821 that to 'calculate with unerring precision on the seasons of this country appear next to impossibility—the changes are truly astonishing'.

While periods of drought were reported during the 1820s, luckily these dry conditions were broken up by years of moderate and above-average rainfall. Historical accounts of high water levels during the 1820s at Lake George, a rainfall-sensitive basin in New South Wales near where Canberra was later built, also suggest that dry conditions probably occurred against a background of fairly wet conditions. An analysis by HC Russell showed that Lake George contained water between 1817 and 1828, and perhaps achieved its highest level in June 1823. For example, in 1821 the lake was described as a 'magnificent sheet of water', and in 1824 it was reported to be '20 miles [32 kilometres] long and 8 miles [13 kilometres] wide, almost entirely enclosed with thickly wooded, steep hills'.

Although wet conditions probably buffered the colony from the effects of severe drought for a while, in the years 1824–30 they were gripped by a 'fearfully dry' period that once again brought the settlers to their knees. During 1826–28 there were reports from an old-timer suggesting that the rain that fell during this period 'would not have filled his hat'. A newspaper account from 31 October 1827 read: 'such season of drought … was never known in this colony. The beds of rivers which have always had a rapid and deep stream in the driest weather are now quite dry and traversable for miles'. In 1828, there were reports that the waters of Lake George had begun 'to dry up and continued to evaporate steadily for several years, until they entirely disappeared'. In other country areas, the drought was now considered 'truly deplorable' as cattle began 'perishing in numbers'. In response to the severe water shortages, the government ordered 150 men to lay piping along the South Head Road to supply public wells in Sydney, to try to avoid major water shortages.

Figure 10. View of Lake George in 1825, when it had very high water levels.

Source: Lycett, Joseph (1825). *View of Lake George, New South Wales, from the North East.* Reproduced courtesy of the National Library of Australia.

Figure 11. The very low water levels in Lake George following peak drought conditions in 1829.

Source: Hoddle, Robert (1830). *South End of Lake George, New South Wales*. Reproduced courtesy of the Mitchell Library, State Library of New South Wales.

William Stanley Jevons' 1859 compilation contains excerpts from a letter from Sydney dated 2 March 1829 that stated: 'We are all burnt up, it is frightful to go into the garden. Not a drop of water'. HC Russell reported that severe water shortages resulted in people paying 4 pence per gallon in Sydney that year. By October 1829, 'every mind was filled with the dreaded alarm of famine' as barns and granaries emptied throughout New South Wales. In response to the food shortage, the colony called on Van Diemen's Land to boost grain supplies. On 12 November, a public thanksgiving mass was called to pray for relief from the 'long and destructive drought'.

Mercifully, drought-breaking rains began to fall in the summer of 1829–30. There were reports of 'delightful showers' and 'torrents of rain' falling throughout December. In January 1830, there was talk of a 'good deal of rain up country, especially in the neighbourhood of Lake Macquarie', and subsequent flooding in the Sydney and Hunter regions. In April, flooding destroyed some of the colony's infrastructure, leading to requests for an increase in road gangs to repair flood- and rain-damaged bridges around the Sydney, Parramatta and Hawkesbury settlements. The following month, *The Sydney Gazette* reported that 'The late rain has refreshed everything. Nature so long pent up by drought is bursting forth in overflowing fecundity', resulting in a 'super-abundant' harvest in the spring and summer of 1830.

The colony had expanded beyond New South Wales to Tasmania in 1803, Queensland in 1824, Western Australia in 1826, and in 1834 it took in Victoria, followed by South Australia by 1836. Claire Fenby's analysis of historical documents suggested that, from 1837 to 1843, a widespread drought was experienced throughout the south-eastern states. The drought seems to have peaked in the year 1838, when there were increasing reports of intensified dry conditions from many parts of the country. By winter, it was said about the Sydney region that 'the whole country was dried up, and the dust lay on the roads, especially towards Parramatta, at least a foot thick. Whoever attempted to travel, therefore seemed if the wind blew as though he had been passing through a mill'.

In November 1839, the *Asiatic Journal* declared: 'The present year must be looked upon as the most calamitous the colony has ever experienced, occasioned by the long continued drought. Reports from all parts give the most alarming picture of things'. The Murrumbidgee River in western New South Wales was reported to have 'decreased so considerably as to become dry in many places, and fish may be seen lying in a putrid state on the bed of the river'. In the Hunter River region, a correspondent noted that 'The country is in a desponding state for want of rain. There will be no maize. God knows what will become of us all if some change does not take place very soon'.

A day of 'general fast and humiliation' was called on 2 November 1839 in response to the 'alarming continuance of the drought', to be strictly observed throughout the colony. In his sermon on that day, Presbyterian minister John Dunmore Lang identified the sins he believed were responsible for bringing drought to Australia. Fenby noted that along with tendencies to ignore the Sabbath and abuse the working class, Lang believed the long drought was also attributable to the vicious actions of white men against Aboriginal people, whom Lang described as 'bone of our bone and flesh of our flesh—formed originally after the image of God, like ourselves'. Sickened by what he had observed, Lang said in his sermon:

> We despoiled [the Aboriginal people] of their land, and given them in exchange European vice and European disease in every foul and fatal form, but the blood of hundreds, nay of thousands, of their number who have fallen from time to time in their native forests, when waging unequal warfare with their civilized aggressors, still stains the hands of many of the inhabitants of the land.

It's an interesting social comment highlighting that some people believed human behaviour was to blame for the extreme drought faced by the colony. But while the mistreatment of Indigenous Australians was undoubtedly appalling, of course it wasn't the physical cause of the dry spell. It wasn't until decades later, when instrumental weather records were collated from this period, that we would discover the scientific reasons for the extreme conditions experienced by Australia's early colonial settlers.

The wet and dry cycles of the early to mid nineteenth century prompted some members of the colony to think more about climate variability and question what was 'normal' weather in Australia. Dramatic shifts between droughts and floods made people consider a wider range of crops and different ways to manage livestock. Although the settlers were becoming more familiar with the country's climate, the need for quantitative weather records to make sense of what they were experiencing was now obvious. After all, is it really possible to accurately measure rainfall and temperature trends through a person's subjective memory? Until that point, it's pretty much all they had. They struggled on until something new came along that would forever change our understanding of our erratic climate.

PART II
WEATHER WATCHERS

9
WHAT DOES 'ON RECORD' ACTUALLY MEAN?

The schoolchildren huddled under their desks as the electricity failed. Frightened, they watched daylight vanish outside the window. The room descended into panicked darkness—it was 43°C and the trees outside were thrashing around like flags in the wind. An angry orange swirl stifled the horizon as a 320-metre-thick cloud laced with one million kilograms of farming topsoil was dumped on Melbourne. When the children emerged nearly an hour later, the playground was dusted orange and brown.

The severe dust storm that hit Melbourne on 8 February 1983 was part of a series of events following the previous winter's failed rains that left the land baking in one of the worst Australian droughts of the twentieth century. Record high temperatures saw the little summer rain that did fall evaporate before hitting the ground. On 16 February, just one week later, seventy-five people were killed across the country's south-east in the notorious Ash Wednesday fires. The bushfires of the 1982–83 El Niño raged across Victoria and South Australia for nearly a month. In the end, around 5200 square kilometres—an area more than twice as big as the Australian Capital Territory—was incinerated. Nearly half of it burned in a single day. But exactly what type of records do scientists use to place recent climate extremes like these into a historical context?

By the late nineteenth century, weather stations and telegraph networks for the transmission of meteorological data had been set up across the states and territories of Australia. Soon it became clear that instead of a piecemeal organisation run by individual state governments, it would be better to monitor Australia's weather on a national scale. This led to the birth of the Bureau of Meteorology in 1908. Over the 110 years since then, the 'Bureau', as it's affectionately known, has been meticulously collecting, managing and safeguarding Australia's climate records.

While the high-quality instrumental records held by the Bureau are the best we've got, the relatively short century of observations does not give us a complete picture of our natural climate variability. Statistically speaking, the records may not be extensive enough to capture rare or extreme events, leaving important gaps in our knowledge. For example, until very recently, our understanding of drought was confined to the twentieth century, and projections of Australia's future climate calculated by global climate models are mostly just tested against these 110 years of instrumental observations. This is not to make light of the achievement: it is important to remember that these records are attempting to capture one of the most spectacularly erratic climates in the world. But how do events of the past compare to those of today? How do we know if recent extremes are within the 'normal' range of our natural climate variability?

Humans have always been fascinated by the weather. Over time it has become increasingly clear that weather and climate have played a huge role in shaping our societies. In recognition of this, the first meteorological instruments were invented in the early eighteenth century to try to measure daily weather conditions. In 1714, Daniel Gabriel Fahrenheit created the first modern mercury thermometer with a standardised scale. In 1724, he introduced the scale that bears his name to accurately record fluctuations in temperature.

The Age of Reason, a movement that dominated Europe's intellectual life during the eighteenth century, ushered in an era of monumental scientific progress. Rational thought and the means for collecting objective, quantitative scientific observations became highly prized. The study of natural history and astronomy became a globally competitive pursuit. European astronomers, explorers and naturalists were desperate to get their hands on new scientific instruments that could potentially underpin breakthroughs that explained the world around them. Explorer ships were routinely sent off with thermometers and atmospheric pressure barometers to record the weather experienced during their expeditions into uncharted territory.

As people made more use of these newly developed instruments, there was less reliance on descriptive accounts of the weather. During the early years of Australian settlement, only a few scientifically minded people kept meticulous weather records on ships, government buildings or colonial outposts. They included government officials, astronomers, doctors, farmers and trained convicts. Systematic meteorological observations did not begin until the late nineteenth century in many parts of the world. Australia's official 'high quality' temperature record began in 1910 with the introduction as a national standard of the Stevenson screen—a specialised shelter that helps standardise the exposure of the thermometer by protecting the sensor from direct sunlight and rain while allowing air to flow around it. Our rainfall record extends back to 1900 due to the slightly earlier standardisation of rain gauges across the country.

While there is more uncertainty about what we can infer from historical sources in the pre-1900 period, observations from this era still provide us with valuable approximations of what the weather was like in the past. They allow us to reconstruct evidence of past temperature and rainfall variability and how it may have impacted people. Unfortunately for modern-day scientists, there was no common standard for observing equipment during the colonial period. In the worst circumstances, thermometers were sometimes housed in beer crates on outback verandahs or in underground cellars. According to a report published in 1886 by meteorologist Clement Wragge, some thermometers

> are hung under verandahs and over wooden floors; others are placed against stone walls and fences. Such exposures (not to mention the several remarkable instances of thermometers being placed and observed indoors) give results which are not only not intercomparable and so valueless to meteorology, but which are affected by artificial and secondary conditions, giving misleading values.

As a result of these non-standard practices, unadjusted values of temperatures in Australia before the twentieth century are more uncertain unless there has been careful quality control to account for changes in the record, like the use of a new instrument or a shift in a site's location noted in a station's logbooks.

By 1910, the recently formed Bureau of Meteorology had standardised measurement practices in many parts of the country, giving us greater confidence in the data available from then onwards. While some temperature records for individual locations like Sydney stretch back to the mid-nineteenth century, the Bureau's nationwide analysis began in 1910 for temperature and 1900 for rainfall. The consistent observational practices—which include temperature measurements taken at regular times during the day in the shade at a height of 1.5 m above a flat grassed surface—means that readings are comparable over time. Statistical quality control and homogenisation standards are also applied by the Bureau to ensure our data meet the international monitoring standards set by the World Meteorological Organization, a specialised agency of the United Nations.

Following these rigorous practices, our national temperature record is currently calculated from a network of 112 observing stations, and Australia's high-quality rainfall record is calculated from a network of 151 rainfall stations. While there are many more stations offering observations in some areas, this subset has passed the strict quality and homogeneity requirements for accurately monitoring long-term trends and variability in the Australian climate. Temperatures in the upper atmosphere have been monitored from weather balloons since 1963 using standard instruments, and from 1979 onwards, we also have satellite records that measure the temperature of the atmosphere at various altitudes, as well as sea and land surface temperatures. Together, these weather observations make up the lion's share of our understanding of Australian climate variability. This is where climatologists calculate our 'on record' statistics, from as they are based on the most precise and direct measurements that we have.

Climate can be thought of as the accumulation of all the daily weather experienced at a given location, providing a long-term history of the variability recorded at each station around the country. Each observation from every high-quality temperature and rainfall station is then overlain on a digital map of Australia and averaged over time. Obviously, weather observations are not available from every square kilometre of Australia; it's just not feasible to monitor every single location in such a vast country. Instead, we use information from every individual weather station that passes strict quality tests and combine them into a unified geographical grid for climate analysis. These grids are developed using weather records wherever they exist, with conditions for areas without direct observations approximated from neighbouring stations—like the remote deserts of outback Australia. This interpolation method effectively fills in the gaps, allowing us to visualise a complete picture of the rainfall, temperature, pressure, wind and humidity conditions simultaneously across Australia.

Luckily, analysis has shown that there is often very good consistency between the climate conditions experienced in one area and those of distant locations because of the large-scale signature of circulation features like El Niño that influence our mostly flat country simultaneously. Using this understanding of the large-scale drivers of Australian climate and the features of our landscape, we can accurately infer conditions from an incomplete network.

Together, these national climate grids form the observational foundation of Australia's climate record. They are a little bit like the weather maps you see on the news, but instead of all of the simultaneous observations recorded for a single day, gridded climate data are available for every day since the start of the twentieth century. These daily observations are then used to calculate how the climates of past months, seasons and years have fluctuated over the full length of the record. This provides us with an extensive baseline with which to evaluate short-lived climate variability and long-term trends.

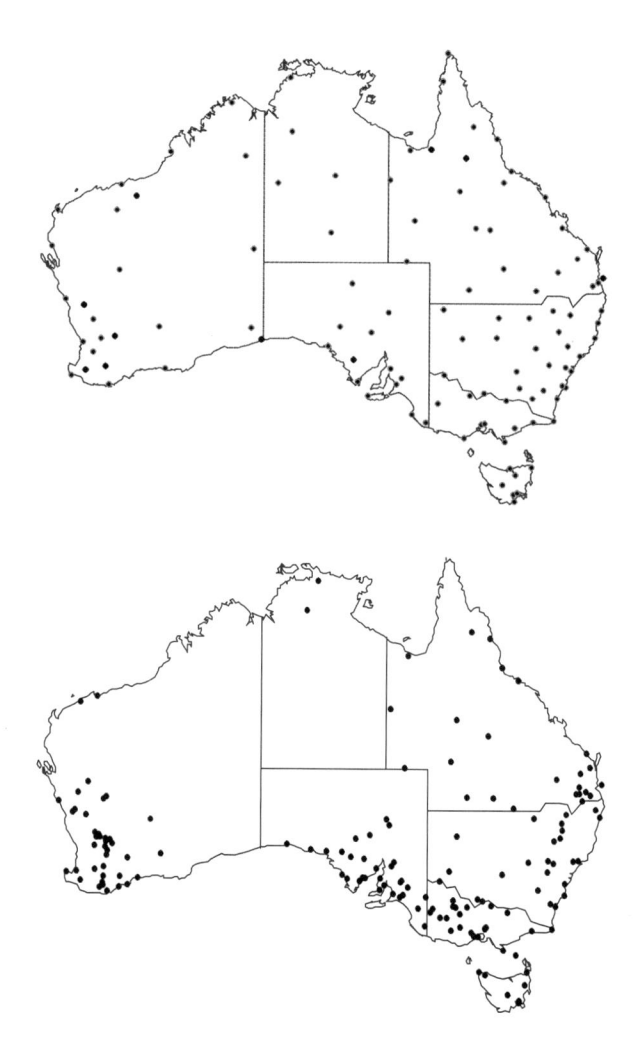

Figure 12. Australia's high-quality daily temperature (top) and rainfall (bottom) observational networks managed by the Bureau of Meteorology. Temperature network adapted from Trewin (2013).

Source: Reproduced courtesy of the Bureau of Meteorology.

But what happened before the year 1900? This is where the SEARCH initiative I discussed in chapter 2 comes in. This was the large project I led that focused on rescuing early Australian weather records to extend our understanding of our region's climate variability before the start of the Bureau of Meteorology's official twentieth-century climate record. We collected thirty-nine different historical sources of weather data from archival collections covering the 1788–1860 period from south-eastern Australia, the region of first European settlement. For the time from 1860, when more instrumental weather stations were available, to the start of the Bureau's records in 1900, we recovered another eighty-seven temperature, rainfall and atmospheric pressure records that were carefully quality controlled to reliably extend the climate record.

We unearthed over 3400 pages of historical weather records covering the 1788–1900 period using early newspapers, ship logs, farm records, government records, explorer accounts and early settler diaries from Sydney, Melbourne, Adelaide and Tasmania. We found handwritten weather observations taken by scientists, convicts, sailors, farmers, doctors and priests, stretching all the way back to the earliest days in Sydney Cove. It was the first time that so many early observations had been drawn together to reconstruct the weather and climate experienced by Australia's colonial settlers. The feat was made possible by a dedicated group of scientists and historians who made the most of huge advances in digital archiving and online databases that past generations could never have imagined.

While discovering new climate records is always exciting for scientists, of course we appreciate that humans have been in Australia long before Europeans arrived. There are many ways of describing nature—weather observations are just one method. While meteorologists base their forecasts on instrumental data and synoptic charts, Aboriginal people look for things like the time when wattle blooms and the arrival of black cockatoos. For them, understanding the weather is about reading the landscape. Intricate observations of these climatic cues have been passed down for thousands of generations in the form of stories. Unlike weather measurements, which can be turned into computer-readable material and analysed by climate scientists, oral history is shared by elders with their children as they grow up experiencing their local 'country'.

While these cultural observations provide amazing information about the environmental indicators that herald a shift in seasons, they can't be turned into the specific numbers needed to contribute to the quantitative weather observations that form the backbone of Australia's climate record. That doesn't mean this knowledge isn't valuable or important; it's just another way of looking at things. In recognition of the vast wealth of information carried by the First Australians, over recent years the Bureau has been working closely with a dozen different Indigenous communities across Australia to record seasonal calendars, from the Tiwi Islands in the north to Victoria in the south. It's the tip of the iceberg but a critically important start. Digitally recording the weather knowledge of the oldest continuous culture on Earth will ensure that these stories will be forever captured for future generations. Who knows what role this information might play in helping people adapt to life in a shifting climate?

So when did the first weather observations actually begin in Australia? Are historical climate records even reliable? And have we always been the land of legendary droughts and floods?

10
THE WEATHERMAN

Australia's first weather records, as measured by meteorological instruments, began with the arrival of the First Fleet. Aboard HMS *Sirius* was Lieutenant William Dawes, a man now recognised as Australia's first non-Aboriginal weatherman. Dawes had brought some astronomical instruments with him to look out for a comet expected in 1788. He was also equipped with meteorological instruments, including a thermometer and barometer, having been ordered by Governor Arthur Phillip to set up an observatory as soon as possible after settlement. Phillip wanted to get an idea of the climate of Sydney Cove to assess the feasibility of growing crops that would be vital to the survival of the isolated colonial outpost.

Dawes set up his observatory near where the south-west pylon of Sydney Harbour Bridge rests today, a location now known as Dawes Point. While participating in local exploration and general life in the colony, he meticulously kept weather records of temperature, pressure and winds from 1788 until he left Sydney in December 1791. These observations are the first formal record of Australian weather. Dawes maintained his observations with great dedication, often taking readings up to six times each day, before he was returned to England prematurely for refusing to follow Governor Phillip's order to carry out punishment raids against local Aboriginal people. Dawes was a compassionate man who had spent time with a young Aboriginal girl, Patyegarang, learning the local Eora language. In her novel *The Lieutenant*, Australian author Kate Grenville fictionalises the pair as Daniel Rooke and Tagaran, offering an imaginative glimpse into the possibility of more harmonious relationships between First Australians and the colonial settlers.

As a climate scientist, I began wondering what Dawes' measurements might have to say about what the weather was like when the First Fleet arrived. I got in touch with contacts at the Bureau of Meteorology and experts in early weather data, to see if they'd ever come across the record. While people had heard of it, they had never actually seen it. And ironically, the two people who seemed to know the most about the Australian records worked in the United Kingdom and United States!

When I called the Australian historical climate expert Rob Allan, who is now based at the Hadley Centre in the UK's Met Office in Exeter, he said the closest anyone had ever come to looking at the data was in 1981 when an American PhD student studying at Sydney's Macquarie University, Robert McAfee, prepared a special report on William Dawes for the Bureau of Meteorology. Rob had a hunch that the observations might be in there. He went on to explain how, all over the world, there are stacks of old weather records in paper format curling with age. In a rapidly changing climate, rescuing these early weather observations is essential for estimating the Earth's pre-industrial climate variability used to test the climate models that predict future climate change. The more data points we have, the better our chances of teasing out the exact influence of increasing greenhouse gas concentrations on natural climate variability.

As soon as I got off the phone to Rob, I decided to try my luck by sending a request to my library to track down McAfee's report. But as the busy weeks slipped past, I forgot about Dawes and his journal. I was in the middle of writing up a large-scale grant proposal—trying to get some formal funding to consolidate our climate history using these old weather records—when one morning an inter-library loans notification popped up in my inbox, announcing the arrival of McAfee's publication. Surprised that the library had actually managed to find it, I dropped everything, jumped straight on my bike and headed to the University of Melbourne's Baillieu Library. As I zipped across campus, I wondered if, despite Dawes' work being the most historically significant weather record in Australia, could it be possible that by 2008—220 years after Dawes first started his weather journal—not a single person anywhere in the world had ever bothered to transcribe and analyse the data?

I felt a little disappointed when I finally held the lean volume in my hand. As I flipped through it, all I could see was a brief history of William Dawes, the man, as well as some information on his observatory and snippets of his weather journal. It was a little more concise than I'd expected. There was no tabulated data in sight. It seemed it had been too good to be true.

As I made my way out through the automatic doors of the library, I noticed a small sleeve pasted to the book's inside back cover. Tucked inside were two black microfilms about the size of an old filing card. I carefully slid one out and held it up to the sky. Miniature pages of centuries-old cursive handwriting appeared in the daylight. I turned around and immediately headed straight for the microfilm readers. Rob was right after all—the observations really did exist!

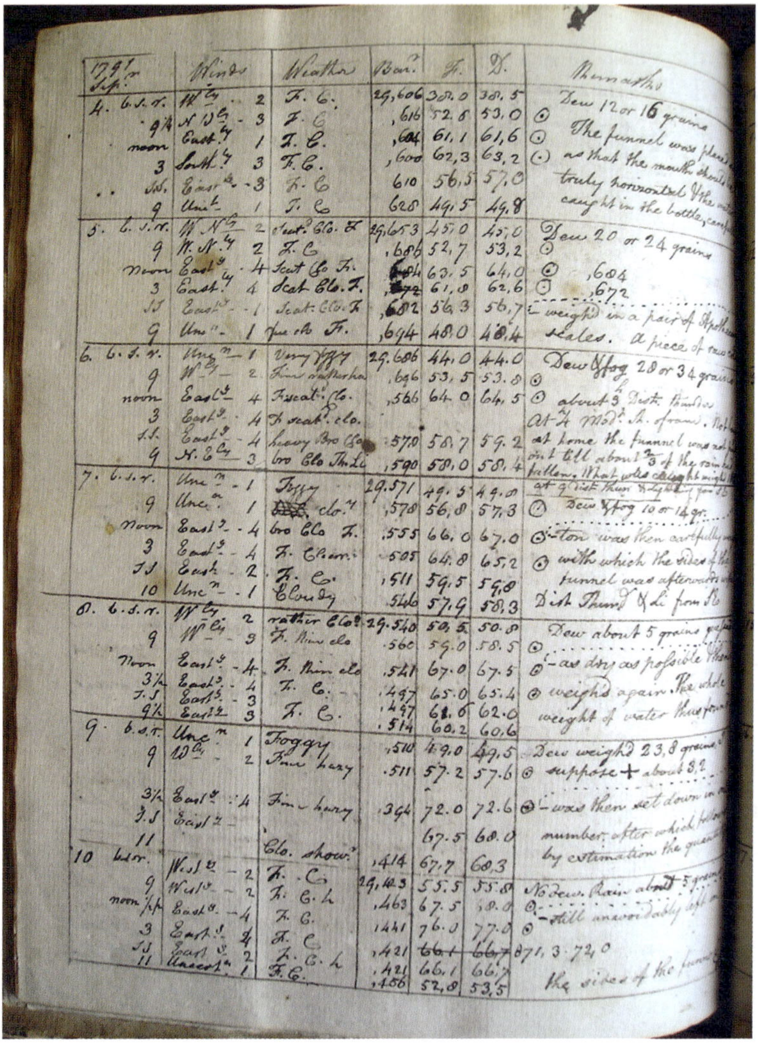

Figure 13. A page from Australia's first meteorological record, kept by William Dawes in Sydney Cove, September 1788 – December 1791, archived at the Royal Society of London.

Source: Joëlle Gergis.

As I spun through the microfilm, I wished that someone were there to share in this rare moment of scientific rediscovery. But when I looked around, all I saw was a young guy blankly scanning old newspaper reels, while nearby another student was flopped across their desk, snoozing as noisy fuzz buzzed from their headphones. It didn't matter. I was just blown away to see every page of William Dawes' weather journal. It was all there, 180 pages from 14 September 1788 to 6 December 1791, in remarkably legible handwriting.

A comment made by one of the founding fathers of Australian meteorology, HC Russell, that 'there seems little doubt that Dawes kept weather records but there are no records of them', must have deterred meteorologists of the day from pursuing William Dawes' invaluable journal. In 2009 I managed to track down the original diary in the archives of the Royal Society of London, along with another collection of very early colonial weather records for New South Wales and Tasmania. Robert McAfee, author of the thin volume I found in Melbourne, wrote that apart from the intrinsic cultural value of the journal, 'it serves as a monumental foundation on which to start a history of climate for the emerging country of Australia'.

During that period of my career, I found another culturally priceless weather record: a ship's logbook containing the weather conditions experienced during the First Fleet's voyage from southern England to Botany Bay in 1787–88. On board the fleet's flagship, the *Sirius*, was a young marine, William Bradley, who recorded daily weather observations, including temperature, barometric pressure and wind. He was also an exceptional artist who produced the finest watercolour paintings of Sydney's early colonial history. I extracted the noon temperature and pressure readings taken from 20 January 1788 until 13 September 1788 while the *Sirius* was anchored in Botany Bay and then Port Jackson, and compared them with observations from Dawes' land observatory.

When I looked at the midday temperature recorded in Sydney from 20 January 1788 to 4 December 1791 using Dawes' and Bradley's records, the first thing I noticed was the steady ebb and flow of the seasonal cycle; that is, the temperatures were highest in summer (December–February) and coolest in winter (June–August). Despite the fact that the temperatures recorded offshore on the *Sirius* were likely to be a couple of degrees cooler than those on land, temperatures were actually quite cold during the first few months of European settlement.

Figure 14. A page from the meteorological record kept by William Bradley aboard HMS *Sirius*.

Source: Bradley, W (1802). *A Voyage to New South Wales, December 1786– May 1792.* Reproduced courtesy of the Mitchell Library, State Library of New South Wales.

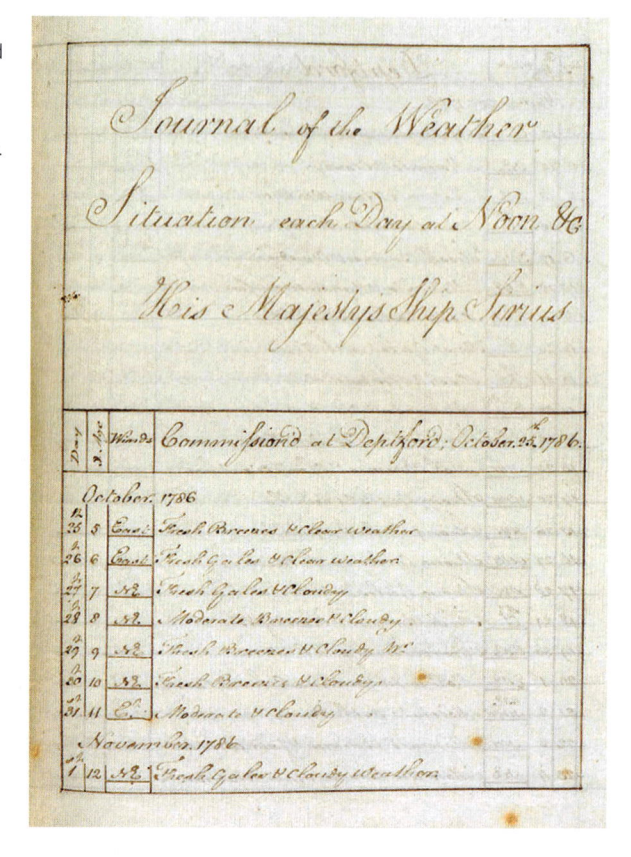

The similarity between the average seasonal cycle present in Dawes' eighteenth-century maximum and minimum temperature observations and the modern-day climate of Sydney's Observatory Hill, located just 500 metres away from Dawes' original site, was really surprising. Remarkably, there was also very good agreement between the two temperature records, with the exception of Dawes' slightly higher readings in the summer months and marginally cooler winter temperatures. This may be due to the way the thermometers were housed; that is, the absence of a Stevenson screen. These screens provide a well-ventilated environment not affected by direct sunlight that better represents the surrounding air temperature, moderating the erroneous temperature spikes that generally explain the differences between twentieth-century and earlier instruments.

The results suggest that Dawes' weather observations are useful for examining relative ups and downs, rather than being treated as absolutely precise weather measurements experienced during the first years of

European settlement in Australia. As you'd expect, the modern observations from Sydney contains more detail as they are calculated using more data points than Dawes' three-year record. Nevertheless, Dawes' readings were clearly able to reproduce Sydney's modern seasonal cycle.

The rediscovery of Dawes' journal provided a rare opportunity to compare the personal accounts written by the first settlers with direct weather measurements. An eighteenth-century weather journal with comparable detail for this period anywhere in the world is a rare find. For the Asia–Pacific region, Dawes' weather journal is only matched by the English East India Company observations made in Madras (Chennai), India, from 1796 onwards—another priceless gem uncovered by Rob Allan.

So how well do the narratives of cool summers and searing heat written in diaries and government records compare with the temperature records kept by William Dawes and William Bradley in the early years of the colony? Although considerable variability can be seen throughout the whole temperature record, there is a noticeable lack of warm temperature extremes recorded in the summer of 1788–89. While there were a handful of above-average hot days, there were substantially more cool extremes noted in the autumn–winter period in 1789 than in later years. These conditions closely match the diary accounts of cool and wet weather that had the early settlers shivering in their boots.

Looking at the noon temperatures provided by Bradley's ship log (before Dawes' observatory had been set up), we see a cool bias in the temperature record. While temperatures over the ocean are always cooler than over land, and maximum temperatures tend to peak close to 3 p.m., noon temperatures don't seem to nudge past a maximum of 26.7°C for the whole 1788 summer. Looking at the maximum temperatures recorded by Dawes, there was even one winter day—12 June 1789—when the temperature only reached a teeth-chattering 6.9°C. According to the long-term climatology recorded at Observatory Hill, the lowest maximum June temperature on record was 9.7°C on 13 June 1899. Even factoring in a cool bias of up to 2°C, as seen in Dawes' record, it's still 0.8°C cooler than the lowest maximum observed at Observatory Hill since 1876.

Aside from a few hot days in the summer of 1789–90, it wasn't until the summer of 1790–91 that a consistent series of temperatures in the thirties and low forties (°C) was experienced in Sydney Cove. A close look at the record shows a clustering of extreme hot temperatures from September 1790 to March 1791. This confirms the settlers' accounts of searing temperatures, like when the birds and bats fell out of the sky on a 38.6°C day in February 1791.

The hottest day recorded by William Dawes was 41.4°C on 25 December 1789. The hottest maximum temperature recorded at modern Sydney's Observatory Hill was 45.8°C on 18 January 2013. It is possible that modern maximum temperatures may be over 4°C warmer than they were in pre-industrial Sydney, but again we can't be sure. Keep in mind that Dawes' temperature record was also found to slightly overestimate maximum temperatures due to inadequate thermometer exposure. But compared with 21st-century observations, is it possible that the maximum temperatures experienced in eighteenth-century Sydney were lower than the extremes recorded during recent decades?

While we can't be confident about the exact temperatures experienced during those early years of settlement, and we can't use non-standard observations from one record in one place to infer widespread conditions, we can draw a couple of interesting conclusions. These First Fleet weather records reproduce the observed modern pattern of seasonal extremes incredibly well. While the record suggests a shift from cooler eighteenth-century conditions to a warmer background climate in post-industrial Sydney, we can't say precisely by how much. But as we'll see, cooler conditions in late eighteenth-century Australia are consistent across a range of scientific records from our region and other areas of the world.

The observations have provided us with a valuable opportunity to cross-check our results against early settlers' accounts, bringing to life the human stories behind the numbers. They show us that climate extremes have long been a quintessential part of Australian life, yet, until now, fascinating early stories about these extremes have remained largely untold or scattered throughout the forgotten pages of our history.

11
AUSTRALIA'S EARLY CLIMATE RECORDS

While historical records like William Dawes' weather journal provide intriguing glimpses into Sydney's past climate, observations made over two centuries ago are not quite the same as those taken today. The problem is that they were recorded in different ways to modern methods. Many of the instruments were not kept in ideal locations using internationally recognised standards. Differences in instrument exposure, observer practices and equipment also mean that it's difficult to use these observations to quantify the exact size of the temperature change in these early records. We can estimate whether a month or a year in a historical record was wetter or hotter relative to other observations within the same record, but we can't be entirely confident about the precise value of how much wetter or hotter it actually was in the past compared with modern climate records without adjusting for known biases that may have influenced a record's baseline.

Historical rainfall observations are generally less prone to the large biases seen in temperature records, because rain gauges are less complex instruments than thermometers or barometers. But rain gauges have their own problems, with issues of under-reporting in strong winds and during very heavy rain events when a gauge may overflow. So before historical observations can be analysed as part of reliable climate research, the quality of the data needs to be assessed and adjusted as necessary. Quality checks and statistical techniques must be used to identify and adjust for what climatologists call 'data inhomogeneities'.

Quality control generally refers to the checking of all original observations for obvious errors or suspicious outliers that might be due to short-term instrument faults, accidental readings or transcription errors from the historical observer or modern person who entered the value into a computer. Once any clear errors have been removed, the process known as 'homogenisation' is run to identify changes in a data series that are caused by non-climatic features associated with the observation practice—like changes in the position of the thermometer or the time the readings were taken—rather than changes in the climate.

This process firstly involves investigating the specific details of an individual station's location, history and observer practices. Following these careful checks, statistical techniques are used to identify significant differences between data from a station of interest and other available observations. This can be established in a few different ways, but it's often done by comparing one location with a reference site developed by combining data from a number of highly correlated neighbouring stations, or lots of individual neighbouring sites, to see where the most common changes occur. After adjustments have been made to remove non-climatic influences, early data are considered officially homogenised and ready for reliable climate analysis.

Some climate change sceptics like to point to historical, unadjusted temperature data as evidence that in the past we have experienced warmer temperature extremes than we have today. Usually, these claims are based on unsubstantiated readings from single locations using non-standard methods, like a thermometer mounted on the side of a tin shed in a back paddock. Some even go as far as to say that when the Bureau of Meteorology adjusts raw temperature data, it's a devious attempt to wipe past extremes from the official record.

As we've already seen, there are very real scientific reasons why raw historical climate data sometimes needs to be adjusted. It is important to remember that all the unadjusted records in Australia are available for investigation by anyone. Rather than trying to be sneaky, scientists are simply confining their conclusions to the period where they have most confidence in the underlying data—a hallmark of rigorous science. Again, it's important to stress that because the measurements weren't recorded using the same methods as today, it's not exactly an apples-to-apples comparison. Still, once they've been appropriately adjusted and disclosures about data uncertainties have been clearly stated, historical observations provide us with incredibly valuable insights into how our climate has varied in the past. Perhaps most importantly, it's a great way to test whether the people who wrote about weather extremes in the past were just spinning us a colourful yarn!

After 1791, when William Dawes' weather journal ends, Australia's instrumental climate record is patchy until about 1820. Some early European settlers logged weather remarks in their journals as they explored the new colony. While these mostly contain narrative accounts of the weather, they included sporadic observations, usually taken during a particularly notable event, especially throughout the 1788–94 period. The First Fleet marine officer Watkin Tench includes several irregular temperature observations in his published journal, and even makes reference to a specific 'meteorological journal' at one stage, although this has never been discovered. (What a find that would be!) For example, on 27 December 1790, Tench comments that a north-westerly wind 'felt like the blast of a heated oven', noting a temperature of as high as 42.7°C. This is higher than the 39.7°C Dawes recorded at Sydney Cove, perhaps suggesting a more inland location or inadequate thermometer exposure.

Similarly, magistrate Richard Atkins took temperature observations from November 1792 to March 1793 in Parramatta. Unverified readings from his diary indicate a three-day heatwave from 6–8 March 1793 of temperatures over 40°C. While we can't be sure of the precise temperatures experienced in these early years of settlement, it's probably safe to say that the colony experienced very hot conditions during those autumn days of 1793.

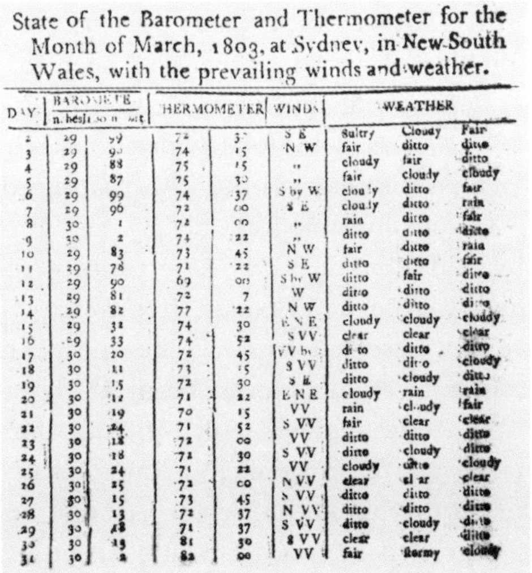

The first continuous set of meteorological observations from Sydney appeared from March 1803 to April 1805, when daily tables of thermometer, barometer, wind and weather remarks were published in Australia's earliest newspapers: *The Sydney Gazette* and *New South Wales Advertiser*.

Figure 15. Australia's earliest weather table, published in March 1803 in *The Sydney Gazette* and *New South Wales Advertiser*.

Source: Reproduced courtesy of the National Library of Australia.

Unfortunately, a paper shortage forced a decrease in the size of newspapers in mid-1805, so tragically the weather tables were dropped. Historical research suggests that the weather observations that appeared in these early newspapers were taken at First Government House—where the Sydney Museum now stands—on the corner of College and William streets in the CBD.

We unearthed these early weather tables in the National Library of Australia's collection of digitised historical material, archived by the Trove online database. This incredible portal contains countless treasures, including digital images of rare manuscripts and pictures, and an assortment of Australian newspapers. With the help of text correctors from the library, Linden Ashcroft collected all of these newspaper weather tables and assessed their quality as part of her groundbreaking PhD research into Australia's early climate records. Her analysis showed that the dry conditions experienced in Sydney during 1803 were associated with an El Niño event inferred from independent palaeoclimate sources like tree-ring and coral records, followed by wetter conditions in 1804–05 as a La Niña event developed. The results agree well with documentary and palaeoclimate sources that also report drought conditions followed by a period of very heavy rainfall. In March 1805, there were reports of 'incessant' rain and 'deluges' submerging low-lying farms in the colony. Sadly, the newspaper weather tables end before these wet conditions culminated in the iconic Great Flood on the Hawkesbury River in March 1806.

Unfortunately, there are still many gaps in Australia's early instrumental climate record. The biggest occurs between 1806 and 1821, but luckily there are many historical documents for the Sydney region available from this time. While it's possible that weather observations do exist for this early period, they are yet to discovered. Perhaps they have been lost or were destroyed in an effort to clear ageing paper records from cluttered government organisations over the years. The hope is that they remain buried in archival collections across Australia and the UK, waiting to be rediscovered by curious historians and climatologists.

As European settlement expanded in the early nineteenth century and the extreme nature of Australia's climate became increasingly clear, the number of instrumental weather observations slowly began to extend beyond Sydney into the surrounding regional areas. From 1821, when the first wave of scientifically minded immigrants settled in Australia, the availability of observations picked up. By November, Thomas Brisbane had arrived in Sydney to take up the post of governor of New South Wales. As he was particularly interested in astronomy and meteorology, he'd also brought along two assistants, James Dunlop and Charles Rumker, to help take scientific observations in the new colony. Brisbane quickly set about building an observatory at the governor's residence in Parramatta. The observations began in May 1822 and continued until 1838, when his successors grew weary of the demanding work.

Brisbane was acutely aware of the need for accurate weather records in a colony highly dependent on agriculture, so he opened weather stations in Newcastle, Sydney, Port Macquarie and Bathurst, and in Macquarie Harbour and Hobart in Van Diemen's Land. When I visited the Royal Society of London on a research trip in 2009, I came across some of the original weather registers kept at Parramatta, Sydney, Port Macquarie and Hobart. Each record contains temperature and atmospheric pressure observations that were made up to six times a day, and all except the Port Macquarie register provide accompanying remarks, allowing the estimation of rainfall by counting the mentions of rain days. Together, these records make up a valuable collection of the earliest weather records available outside of Sydney.

In June 1826, weather tables began to reappear in the Sydney newspapers, probably in response to the severe drought conditions experienced earlier that year. This provided my team with the opportunity to develop a continuous climate record for Sydney that extends from 1826 to the

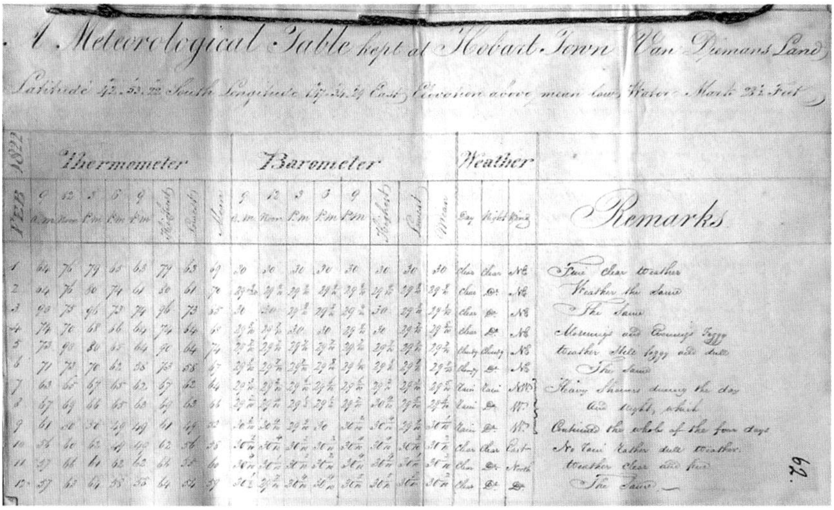

Figure 16. Original meteorological register kept in Hobart in February 1822, archived at the Royal Society of London.

Source: Joëlle Gergis.

present day. As the colony continued to expand, weather readings were not only taken at official government observatories but also by an eclectic array of people from New South Wales, Victoria, South Australia and Tasmania. For example, during the 1840s, then NSW Governor George Gipps ordered a group known as the 'Specials', a gentlemanly class of convicts, to be trained in the taking of meteorological observations at Port Macquarie, Port Phillip and Port Jackson. Edward Peacock, the convict stationed at the Port Jackson Observatory, also happened to be a talented artist. Along with the weather observations he made from April 1840 to December 1855, he contributed many evocative landscape paintings.

Another interesting group of amateur observers was the colony surgeons who believed that human health was influenced by weather conditions—an aspect of modern medicine that holds true to this day. Some of the most valuable observations are the earliest records kept in the colony of South Australia by William Wyatt. He recorded the temperature and weather conditions three times a day in Adelaide from January 1838

Figure 17. In this painting, the South Head lighthouse can be seen below the squall line. Edward Peacock most likely took his weather observations here or at the signal station nearby.

Source: Peacock, GE (1846). *The Heads of Port Jackson, New South Wales from off the North Head–a Squall, 1846.* Reproduced courtesy of the Mitchell Library, State Library of New South Wales.

until the end of 1847, making this one of the earliest continuous weather records in the country. Wyatt was so passionate about the weather that he even brought his own meteorological instruments from England to Australia, and he didn't miss a single observation in close to ten years. Talk about dedication!

One of the largest sources of nineteenth-century weather observations was published as monthly abstracts of the meteorological journals in the New South Wales and Victorian government gazettes. These valuable weather observations were located in historical documents archived by our state and national libraries, highlighting that scientific discoveries aren't always where you would expect them to be. Generally speaking, libraries and archival collections are more widely used by historians, artists and writers interested in recovering our collective memory or tracing back through family history. Unfortunately, scientists don't often make use of these historical records as a valuable data source.

Teaming up with historians, librarians and museums was an important reminder that while scientists are on a relentless mission to find hard data to quantify our environment, there are countless human stories that are invaluable in helping us understand how people were impacted by past weather conditions. By using multiple lines of evidence, we can reconstruct history with more confidence. So after collecting all of these old weather records, what did we learn about our past? What are some of the key events in our recorded history that have shaped Australian society?

12
FROST AND FIRE

The temperature and rainfall records published in Sydney newspapers from June 1826 provide us with an exciting glimpse of what the weather was like during the early years of the colony. But because there is limited information about how or where the observations were taken, only tentative conclusions can be drawn. The good news is that data from the early newspaper records were often published alongside narrative accounts, providing us with an opportunity to cross-check our sources.

The newspaper observations show that 1826–29 was a period of high temperatures and average rainfall conditions, while independent documentary evidence described this period as a 'fearful drought'. For example, the inland explorer Charles Sturt detailed the effects of the 1826–29 drought in New South Wales, stating: 'Culinary herbs were raised with difficulty, and crops failed even in the most favourable situations. The settlers drove their flocks and herds to distant tracts for pasture and water, neither remaining for them in the located districts … Men at length began to despond under so alarming a visitation'. In 1829 he also reported that he saw 'rivers cease to flow and sheets of water disappear' in his expedition north of Sydney. So while the rain days recorded in Sydney were only average, historical records suggest that drought conditions were felt more severely inland of the coastal regions—a pattern seen in modern instrumental records.

The Sydney weather records also suggest that the drought broke spectacularly in 1829. This is inferred from the very high number of rain days recorded for each season from the winter of 1829 to the spring of 1830. Again, this lines up with the historical evidence that reported heavy rainfall, flooding and a dramatic increase in crop yields, as described in Part I.

Between 1832 and 1834, the agreement between the instrumental rainfall observations and historical documents in the Sydney region was amazingly high. With one exception, all wet months were associated with an increase in rainfall or rain-day counts in the corresponding instrumental records. Such striking agreement suggests that documentary records were able to accurately capture month-to-month rainfall variations and so are an invaluable way of verifying the accuracy of historical instrumental data.

It isn't until 1835 that more widespread weather records became available from a number of locations outside of the Sydney region. Along with the records from Thomas Brisbane's weather observatories from New South Wales, observations from Melbourne, Tasmania and South Australia provide us with the first opportunity to sketch a broader picture of climate conditions from 1835 to 1859. The first stand-out event in the record appeared in 1835–36 when very cold conditions were reported, especially in the winter of 1836. In 2011, Gary Cook, a State Library of New South Wales volunteer who helped recover valuable historical weather material as part of our OzDocs citizen science project, discovered an account of a very unusual event in the National Library of Australia's Trove database.

On the bitterly cold morning of 28 June 1836, Sydney was blanketed in snow. *The Sydney Herald* reported: 'About seven o'clock in the morning a drifting fall covered the streets, nearly an inch in depth … a razor-keen wind from the west blew pretty strongly at the time and altogether, it was the most English like winter morning … ever experienced'. The corresponding weather table in the newspaper recorded that on the morning the snow fell, the temperature dropped to a frosty 3°C. According to another newspaper, *The Monitor*, the snow disrupted trading in the colony, with vendors unable to transport their goods to local markets.

METEOROLOGICAL TABLE.

The Weather, and variation of the Thermometer since last day's publication, in Sydney, at 6 in the morning, at noon, and at 6 o'clock in the evening.

	6 a. m.	12 noon.	6 p. m.
Monday	Cloudy 46 S W	Cloudy 50 NW	Cloudy 48 S W
Tuesday ...	Snow 38 S W	Windy 50 S W	Cloudy 47 S W
Wednesday	Clear 42 S W	Fine 54 S W	Clear 49 S W

Mean Temperature 47.

Figure 18. A newspaper weather table reporting snow in Sydney on Tuesday 28 June 1836.

Source: The Sydney Herald (1836). 'Meteorological table.' Reproduced courtesy of the National Library of Australia.

The surprised colony members made light of the unusual occurrence, commenting that 'Some of the "Old hands" express a hope that their old acquaintances, Messrs. Frost and Snow do not intend emigrating to New South Wales'. On 30 June, snow reportedly fell again, but this time in less abundance than two days earlier. Heavy snowfall was also reported in Hobart that same month, suggesting that freezing conditions swept across the south-east of the country that winter.

Linden Ashcroft's analysis of historical climate data shows that along with the bitterly cold temperatures, the year of 1836 was also very wet. The Parramatta Observatory recorded rainfall of 400 millimetres above average historical winter conditions, calculated using the 1910–50 average from the Bureau of Meteorology's modern records. This cold and wet interval coincides with the height of what is referred to as the 'Little Ice Age', a global cold period in recent geologic history that spanned 1300–1850.

In Australia, one of the peaks of this cool interval occurred during the early nineteenth century, as calculated from a network of independent palaeoclimate observations, including tree-ring and coral records from the region. The period had a cluster of volcanic eruptions between 1836 and 1839, which are known to cool temperatures by injecting a veil of ash and sulphate particles into the upper atmosphere, blocking incoming sunlight. These historical weather observations are the first Australian records of their kind to provide us with regional insights into one of the major periods of global climate variability in modern history.

Following the cool and wet start to the 1830s, the documentary records suggest that a prolonged drought spanned the 1837–43 period. For example, Manning Clark's *Selected Documents in Australian History 1788–1850* includes an account by Victorian pioneer T Chirnside of very dry conditions in New South Wales in 1839:

> [O]n my way to the Murrumbidgee [I] did not travel a single mile without seeing dead horses and working bullocks. Hay and corn was not to be had at the inns. I saw upon stations where cattle were eager to get a little water, them crawl to a water hole all but dried up and there get bogged and leave their carcasses where there were hundreds of others. No one but an eye-witness can have an idea of the state of New South Wales at that time.

A closer look at the instrumental observations suggests a more complex picture between eastern and southern Australia. Widespread drought conditions are seen in the observations at sightly different times during 1837–38 and 1840–42, with particularly hot conditions in the southern states in 1840–43. A comparison with independent records of large-scale circulation changes shows that a period of enhanced westerlies over the southern Australia region dominated the climate during that period. This in turn suggests that the early nineteenth-century stretch of the Little Ice Age in Australia may have been characterised by an increase in the dominance of polar influences, and weakening of the typical influence of the tropical Pacific through El Niño and La Niña events during this time.

Aside from looking at the temperature and rainfall fluctuations associated with large-scale climate patterns, there is also huge potential to use historical observations to shed light on past extreme events like the catastrophic Black Thursday bushfires that ravaged the state of Victoria on 6 February 1851. Historical weather observations during the fires show that the year 1850 had been exceptionally dry and hot. Rainfall records from the southern states suggest that the wet conditions of 1848–50 encouraged widespread vegetation growth. When it dried up during the hot spring and summer of 1850–51, dangerously high fuel loads were littered across the landscape, eventuating in the enormous fires of February 1851.

Claire Fenby reports that in the months leading up to the Black Thursday fires there were frequent reports of 'hot winds' (from as early as October 1850), increasing evaporation and reducing soil moisture. The *Geelong Advertiser* reported that a 'brickfielder'—a hot north-west wind—blew through the town on 26 October 1850: 'the dust occasionally rising in impenetrable columns, and totally obscuring the sky; the wind blew hot and strong from the north; the heat in the middle of the day was oppressive, which joined to the thick clouds of dust made it anything but agreeable'. Dust storms occurred again in Geelong the following month, when a strong westerly wind 'brought with it as a treat to Geelong, all the dust it could collect in its passage'. On 21 November, 'the heat, wind, and dust … rendered the weather almost intolerable' before rain brought some relief. The hot winds that scorched Geelong that December were likened to the dry and dusty 'simoom' that blows across the Sahara desert, making the town feel 'like an enlarged baker's oven'. In November 1850, a Melbourne resident had written: 'we are now suffering bleak November's winds, we at this moment are so hot that you would fancy you were frying'.

On Black Thursday, Victorians awoke to the first catastrophic bushfire experienced by European settlers in the state. Eyewitness accounts described the terror, including one from Robert Watchorn in Melbourne: 'The scorching wind, flames, smoke and blazing cinders swept the greater part of the region north of Melbourne and obscured the daylight till men cried out in fear of the Day of Judgment'. Another terrified resident reported: 'Ashes were falling everywhere, the wind was like the blast from a furnace; and candles had to be burned in the houses to see'.

Historical accounts described it as 'a dreadful day, [with] the strong hot wind blowing from the north ... the country took fire in all directions—burning all before it, huts and crops of all descriptions and in some places several parties lost their lives in trying to stop the progress or get away from it'. The fierce heat was likened to 'the same as if you stood before your kitchen fire within a yard, when you are roasting a large joint of meat'. Cross-checking with instrumental observations confirms a maximum temperature of 42°C, and the presence of northerly winds were reported in the *Victoria Government Gazette* meteorological table from February 1851. As is still the case today, strong northerly winds whipped up the fires, causing them to spread and wreak havoc across Victoria.

In the end, twelve people lost their lives and millions of livestock were killed. The fires were estimated to have destroyed approximately 50 000 square kilometres of land, making them close to ten times the size of the 1983 Ash Wednesday fires. Claire Fenby's research also noted that the event occurred the very year that Victoria gained independence from New South Wales, and the same year that the gold rush began, placing immense pressure on the young colony.

Although we don't have extensive local weather data to be certain of the precise weather conditions that prevailed during the fires of 1851, the recently recovered weather records have provided us with fresh insights into one of the most ferocious natural disasters in Australian history.

Figure 19. People attempting to flee Victoria's Black Thursday bushfires of 6 February 1851.
Source: Myers, HG (c. 1900–14). *Black Thursday.* Reproduced courtesy of the State Library Victoria.

13
BURSTING BUBBLES OF OPTIMISM

The period from 1856 to 1900 was one of rapid growth in Australian meteorology. During the 1850s, government observatories were built at Observatory Hill in Sydney and Flagstaff Hill in Melbourne, where official weather observations continue to this day. The colonies' government astronomers and meteorologists were responsible for maintaining local weather records and extending the meteorological networks covering their regions.

William Stanley Jevons published the first detailed study of the Australian climate in 1859. He collated as many documentary and instrumental records as he could find into his pivotal work 'Some Data Concerning the Climate of Australia & New Zealand'. Jevons also developed the first detailed listing of droughts and floods either published in newspaper reports or compiled by eminent writers of the time. His pioneering study was further developed in 1877 by HC Russell.

Russell was the first Australian-born government astronomer to work in the colony of New South Wales. During his prolific career at the Sydney Observatory, he initiated a rapid expansion of the observing networks throughout the state. Under his guidance, the number of weather stations increased from just twelve in 1870 to 1800 by the time of his retirement in 1905. In his epic 1877 publication *Climate of New South Wales: Descriptive, Historical, and Tabular*, he compiled a state-of-the-art summary of all the weather and climate information held by the colony into a single 'convenient reference'. It covers a vast range of topics, including lists of floods, droughts, insect plagues, 'hot winds', theoretical discussions of natural cycles, and a comprehensive appendix containing valuable nineteenth-century weather observations.

The beauty of Russell's publication is that he was interested in both narrative and quantitative accounts of the weather, so his work was particularly insightful. It remains one of the most special and fascinating contributions to Australian meteorology long after his death, which incidentally was just a year before the birth of the Bureau of Meteorology. In his 1885 presidential address to the Royal Society of New South Wales, at the height of his career, Russell said that the lesson to scientists is that they must be 'patient in investigation, accurate in measurement, cautious in accepting results, content to stand one in a long series who, for the good of humanity, are striving to interpret the laws of Nature'. It's a reminder to modern-day scientists that we are playing the long game. All we can do is carefully build on the shoulders of giants like HC Russell, in the hope that our work might help future generations live in a safe and prosperous world.

Linden Ashcroft is an Australian climatologist rising to this challenge. She has worked extensively on recovering, homogenising and carefully analysing diverse pre-twentieth-century weather sources. She spent years recovering valuable temperature, rainfall and atmospheric pressure records and implementing quality-control practices used by the Bureau of Meteorology to reconstruct a reliable record of south-eastern Australia's climate from 1860 to the start of official records in 1900. Her work shows that overall, the mid to late nineteenth century was characterised by a highly variable string of events influenced by large-scale circulation features including the El Niño–Southern Oscillation (ENSO) and Indian Ocean Dipole (IOD) events. Extending the Bureau's records back to 1860 revealed a number of previously unquantified cool and wet spells in the years 1860–64, 1870–75 and 1889–95.

In his book *Droughts, Floods & Cyclones*, environmental historian Don Garden examined the wet period of the 1860s and its role in shaping colonial society. He described how, until the 1850s, the Australian economy was 'riding on the sheep's back'. Exploration, settlement and economic development were based on sheep pastoralism and wool exports. Then gold was discovered in Victoria and New South Wales, prompting an influx of immigrants. As the mining boom eventually declined during the second half of the 1850s, a period of mild economic recession highlighted the need for new employment opportunities in the colonies. A solution was to take land back from pastoralists and make it available for farmers to grow food, increasing the vulnerability of Australian prosperity to the vagaries of the weather, as the settlers were about to find out.

From 1860 to 1864, La Niña conditions brought repeated widespread flooding to settlements across eastern Australia. This succession of natural disasters demoralised rural communities and devastated agricultural start-ups. In December 1860, during the Victorian gold-mining boom, a severe storm hit Melbourne and unleashed a deluge that swamped the CBD. Arriving just two weeks before Christmas, the floodwaters swept through downtown Melbourne, leaving a trail of destruction in their wake. *The Argus* newspaper reported:

> The immense mass and force of the water in various parts may be imagined from the fact, that the streets in many places were completely torn up, the water washing away the whole of the earth, and leaving merely the bluestone metal underneath. At the foot of Elizabeth-street, near the railway station, the metal itself seems to have been torn away, for large holes are left in all directions.

The Argus stated that the downpour started at midnight on Saturday 8 December and that it rained non-stop for nearly twenty-four hours.

Figure 20. Almost exactly two years after the deluge of December 1860, more flooding hit Elizabeth Street in Melbourne.

Source: Photographer unknown (c. 1908). 'The Flood, Elizabeth St, 6 pm, 8 Dec. 1862'. Reproduced courtesy of the State Library Victoria.

This heavy rain created a torrent of water running along Elizabeth Street that swept away a pedestrian trying to cross the road. According to the *Portland Guardian*: 'One old man was carried off his legs by the flood, but was rescued by a cabman, who boldly drove to his rescue and succeeded in snatching him from a watery grave, but lost his horse, and wrecked his cab in the attempt'. The flood struck Melbourne at a time when the burgeoning city was undergoing rapid expansion thanks to the Victorian gold fields. The population had grown from 70 000 to half a million people over the previous ten years, compounding the impact of the floods.

From 1863 to 1864, there were reports of severe flooding in parts of New South Wales, Victoria and South Australia. Once again, Melbourne experienced major floods in the CBD, while floodwaters inundated communities in the New England and Hunter Valley regions of New South Wales. After heavy rain in February 1863, a correspondent from Casino in the Northern Rivers region of New South Wales reported: 'We have been visited by the largest flood ever witnessed by white men ... The water rose at a rapid rate—the last twelve hours two feet an hour ... I believe that is ten or twelve feet higher than the largest ever seen'. Similar stories were reported for Grafton, Armidale and settlements along the Bremer and Brisbane rivers in Queensland.

This spate of wet weather in 1863 put a strain on the newly founded trade route between the Clarence Valley region of northern New South Wales and southern Queensland. According to *The Clarence and Richmond Examiner*:

> The first visit of the "Grafton" [ship] to Brisbane could not have happened at a time more prejudicial to opening a trade between Queensland and the Clarence ... The district was suffering from the ravages of the most extraordinary flood with which we have ever been visited, and unfortunately the floods have been succeeded by such continuous wet weather, that the producers of the district, have been so thoroughly dispirited that they have been unable even to make the best of the circumstances, through which they have been passing.

The following year, the Northern Rivers district once again endured extensive flooding, as did towns further south such as Tamworth and Maitland. *The Sydney Morning Herald* reported: 'This part of the country [Tamworth] has been visited with one of those awful floods, with which the colony is sometimes afflicted, attended with a loss of life and property which will bring utter ruin to many and sadness and sorrow to all'.

With houses completely submerged, Tamworth residents rallied to rescue their stranded neighbours:

> Pattison with the assistance of everyone who could render it, set to work, and made and launched a tolerable boat, with oars complete, in little more than an hour ... The force of the current was, however, too great. The boat was dashed against a stump, upset and sank. Firth swam to the nearest tree where he remained the night. Pattison took shelter on a house-top, and Dalton struck boldly out for the shore which he reached in a very exhausted state, cheered by an assembled multitude.

Like the summer of 1850–51, when a sustained period of heavy rain promoted abundant vegetation growth, the wet conditions of the early 1860s saw bushfires sweep through the Gippsland region of Victoria in February 1863, destroying farmlands and recently formed towns. The fires were so fierce and extensive that observers named it 'Black Monday', comparing the severity of the event to the infamous Black Thursday fires of February 1851. *The Gippsland Times* reported:

> The Backwater, near Sale, reserved for a town commonage, and which was the only refuge of the poor starved, and scorched beasts of the surrounding district, became on Monday one fierce, crackling, raging, burning furnace. Trees of immense size were soon burned to the ground, and the smoke and heat became so oppressive, that it was the nearest approach to 'Black Thursday' which we have experienced in the colony.

The fires were ignited during a heatwave with temperatures reportedly as high as 39°C. *The Gippsland Times* reporter who observed numerous tree stumps spontaneously combusting struggled to explain this phenomenon: 'In fact there is something about bush fires still unexplained, and we are rather inclined to believe that electrical or some other unexplained cause produces effects which we can hardly attribute to a small spark'. The new settlers were still getting used to the land, so hadn't yet grasped how the ferocious heat of bushfire fronts can spark Australia's highly flammable eucalyptus-dominated forests.

The agricultural sector was hit hard by the 1863 fires, which wiped out feed for cattle. Pastoralists rushed to offload their marketable cattle to buyers in Tasmania and New Zealand before they lost too much weight. Financial losses ran into the thousands of pounds, which would be equivalent to over a million dollars by today's standards. Luckily, the bulk of the grain in the region was spared, having been harvested prior to the fires.

Meanwhile, in South Australia, heavy rains during the early 1860s caused local rivers to rise. The winter of 1862 was very wet, prompting the Torrens, Sturt, Para and Gawler rivers to break their banks, damaging homes, crops, bridges and roads. Perhaps the stand-out incident was the major flooding of Port Adelaide on 12 May 1865. Gale-force winds and an extremely high tide caused a major storm surge event that flooded the streets to a depth of 1.2 metres, trapping people in their homes.

However, these floods occurred against a background of dry conditions being severely felt by South Australian farmers further inland from 1864 to 1866. It was at the peak of this drought period, in November 1865, that George Goyder, the then surveyor-general of South Australia, was asked to map the boundary between those areas that received good rainfall and those more prone to drought. After covering an estimated 3200 kilometres on horseback, he submitted his report and map to the state government. The map included a line of demarcation, the areas north of which being

Figure 21. Engraving of the flooding that impacted Port Adelaide on 12 May 1865 due to the combination of an extremely high tide, strong gales and heavy rainfall.

Source: Bruce, Robert (1865). *The Inundations at Port Adelaide*. Image published in *The Illustrated Melbourne Post* on 24 June 1865. Reproduced courtesy of the State Library Victoria.

those Goyder judged 'liable to drought', with mallee scrub–dominated areas to the south deemed arable. His recommendation was to discourage farmers from planting crops north of his line, declaring the area saltbush country, only suitable for light grazing. The infamous Goyder Line of agricultural viability was born, and it remains remarkably accurate to this day. It runs east–west across South Australia, joining places with an average annual rainfall of about 250 millimetres, marking the boundary between semi-arid and arid regions.

A return of good rainfall during the early 1870s prompted farmers to ignore Goyder's report and push north to start farms and plant crops. The deluded idea that 'rain follows the plow', which developed during the westward expansion of cropping in the United States, further encouraged people to follow this questionable logic. Sure enough, in the 1880s, when a long drought hit the region, entire towns and farms were abandoned as the rain eased and there was a return to the drier, long-term average rainfall that characterises Australia's arid zone. As the current warming and drying trend of South Australia continues, it is likely that the Goyder Line will shift further south and become associated with an increase in the proportion of rainfall that falls over the Southern Ocean. The retreat of agriculture from inland South Australia is a striking example of how the brutal reality of the Australian climate has a way of bursting bubbles of optimism, no matter what the political spin of the day might be.

From 1870 to 1875, the colonies experienced one of the wettest periods since European settlement. Once again, it was associated with sustained La Niña conditions, which brought heavy rains. Areas from Queensland to Tasmania flooded, with some of the most devastating impacts felt across much of New South Wales and southern Queensland. In the nineteenth century it was quite common during droughts to hold days of prayer and penance, begging God to deliver rain, but rarely were there prayers to stop rain. A deluge in May 1870 was so severe, however, that a correspondent to *The Sydney Morning Herald* believed it to be divine punishment and called for a special day of fasting:

> The continued rains and floods remind us of the flood of forty days we read of in Genesis, when 'God saw the wickedness of man was great in the earth'. If the wickedness of man then caused that once great flood which covered the whole earth, why should not our wickedness be the

cause of the present and recent floods. Think of our much unnecessary work on Sundays, our general extravagance, particularly in drink and ladies' dress, our propensities for money making, and our self neglect ... if we obtain a public fast-day, general or limited, and humble ourselves, the continued rains will probably cease, and temporal and spiritual prosperity will yet be gained, and that speedily.

By 1872, the Goyder Line had been enshrined in law under the *Waste Lands Alienation Act*, marking the limit of land for agriculture in South Australia. However, following years of abundant rain, pressure to release new land had become too much for the state government to politically withstand. The Act was repealed in 1874, allowing the sale of marginal land under credit agreements outside the Goyder Line. The next few years saw a generally successful northward expansion of agricultural settlement. It wasn't until a run of bad seasons in the 1880s that the northward progression was stopped, forcing many farmers to abandon their homesteads and walk off the land for good. As conditions worsened at the turn of the century, more and more of the remaining farmers gave up the struggle as the last of the climate optimism dried up. The ruins that dot the landscape to this day in outback South Australia are testament to their fate.

As the nineteenth century began to draw to a close, a series of big rains drenched the continent from 1889 to 1895. In particular, eastern Australia bore the brunt of the wet conditions. Several floods were recorded across New South Wales and Queensland as a series of tropical cyclones slammed the coast. Perhaps the most dramatic event of the era was 1893's Black February, when the Brisbane River burst its banks on three occasions, peaking at 7 metres above its usual level. The first tropical cyclone, named Buninyong, saw a phenomenal 907 millimetres of rain fall at Crohamhurst in the Glasshouse Mountains in one 24-hour period on 1 February 1893. A wall of water 15.2 metres high was observed roaring down a Stanley River gorge after the cyclonic weather. This caused the swollen Brisbane River to burst its banks and inundate large parts of the CBD and many of the city's low-lying suburbs. Both of the bridges that crossed the river—the Victoria Bridge and the railway bridge at Indooroopilly—collapsed, killing thirty-five people and injuring another 300. Unprecedented flooding also occurred at Maryborough, around 250 kilometres north of Brisbane, where the Mary River Bridge was washed away and more than 130 families were made homeless.

The second cyclone struck on 11 February, causing relatively minor flooding compared with the first flood. But when the third cyclone hit on 17 February, it proved almost as devastating as the first, leaving 5000 people homeless. Thirty-five residents, including children and rescue workers, drowned as people tried to cross flooded rivers or boats capsized in the treacherous conditions.

It was clear that help was needed to deal with the enormity of the Black February disaster, but the government of the day was not keen to step in. In the Legislative Assembly, former NSW premier Sir Henry Parkes asked if, 'in view of the disastrous floods in Brisbane, the Government had considered the desirableness of assisting by direct relief those suffering from the effects of the appalling disaster'. In reply, the current premier, Sir George Dibbs, said: 'The citizens had initiated such a movement, and no doubt members of the Government and of the House would join in it', but he did not see that it was a matter where 'the Government could offer direct assistance'. Recent advances in photography did mean that many images were taken of the event, so those outside the area were able to get a sense of the scale of the disaster. People from across Australia, and indeed the world, were subsequently moved by the suffering of the locals.

Figure 22. Children playing in the receding Brisbane floodwaters in February 1893.
Source: Murphy, GS (1893). Reproduced courtesy of the State Library of Queensland.

On 11 February 1893, a reader of Melbourne's *The Argus* newspaper wrote in to say:

> The terrible disaster which has befallen Brisbane during the past few days has aroused universal sympathy amongst all classes. The magnitude of the present calamity in Queensland calls for worldwide recognition and should touch the hearts and pockets of everyone whose last coin is not yet spent or pledged. I trust that Victoria, as a colony, will once more respond promptly and generously to the cry of suffering humanity beyond her borders.

In another letter published in *The Argus* two days later, a reader highlighted the plight of the flood victims: 'At the Municipal chambers, women, dirt besmeared and almost naked, trooped into the rooms set apart as supply stores, while their husbands carried on cleansing operations. The mayor, aldermen, town clerk, and other officers of the council have worked with a will to cope with the distress'.

Messages of sympathy were received from all over the world, including condolences from Queen Victoria, the premier of New Zealand and Canada's secretary of state. In the end, £83015 in relief funds—estimated to be worth $11.8 million in 2016 dollars—were received from Australian and international donors. This remarkable outpouring of support may be one of the earliest examples of foreign aid for a natural disaster anywhere in the world.

The Brisbane floods of February 1893 remain the worst on record for the region. During that month, 1026 millimetres of rain fell, nearly seven times Brisbane's average February rainfall of 158 millimetres. According to a study of historical Brisbane floods by Robin van den Honert and John McAneney from Macquarie University's Risk Frontiers group, river flood heights of over 8.35 metres were recorded during the 1893 event, representing a depth of around 6.5 metres above the high-tide level. By comparison, the largest flood of the twentieth century occurred in January 1974, when a height of 5.45 metres was recorded at the Brisbane City Gauge. During the more recent floods of January 2011, the Brisbane River at the City Gauge peaked at 4.46 metres—more than 15000 properties were inundated in the metropolitan area; some 3600 homes evacuated.

It's confronting to imagine what an event of a similar magnitude to the 1893 floods would do to a city that housed close to 2.4 million people in 2016, compared with an estimated 28000 people who lived in the area in 1893. In recent years, the Wivenhoe and Somerset dams have been built to help regulate river flows and minimise the risk of densely populated urban areas being inundated by floodwaters. However, where and when the rain falls in the catchment, and how much of it there is, continue to determine the dams' effectiveness as flood mitigation measures.

It's also worth remembering that the Brisbane floods of February 1893 took place in the era before widespread warning systems were in place to help lessen the blow of natural disasters. It was up to people to keep themselves informed by word of mouth or telegraph notices. At the time of the floods, Henry Somerset was a landowner in the area at the junction of the Stanley and Upper Brisbane rivers. After the heavy rains caused by tropical cyclone Buninyong, he reported seeing the great wall of water raging down the Stanley River from his porch. Realising that people downriver were in danger, he ordered one of his workers to send a telegraph to the Brisbane General Post Office to warn that Brisbane, Ipswich and other areas were in great danger of flooding. As the weather had momentarily fined up, people didn't seem to be too fussed, so the post office only posted the warning on a single noticeboard. Unsurprisingly, the warning went unnoticed.

As the third cyclone crossed the Queensland coast near Bundaberg on 17 February, the already saturated Brisbane River catchment received another drenching. A panicked Somerset sent a worker out in treacherous conditions on his only surviving horse to deliver a warning message to North Pine (now Petrie), as the telegraph lines were down between Esk and Brisbane. While the warning once again went unheeded, Caboonbah station, Somerset's homestead on the elevated southern bank of the Brisbane River, was eventually set up as an official flood warning station with a telegraph line to the Esk region near Wivenhoe Dam, north-west of Brisbane. Somerset, who initially operated the station, used Morse code for twelve years before the introduction of the telephone.

It's hard to imagine what life in nineteenth-century Australia would have been like before emergency weather warnings were possible. Unlike past generations, thankfully we now have the Bureau of Meteorology to provide us with severe weather warnings. We can only hope that future generations will continue to build on what we now understand about our inbuilt vulnerability to climate extremes.

While the mid to late 1800s were predominantly characterised by wet and cool conditions, there were a handful of notable droughts that impacted

Australian society as the nation approached the turn of the century. The short but sharp drought of 1876–78 was associated with a very strong El Niño event of 1877. While instrumental records show that the period was dominated by warm and dry conditions, Don Garden has suggested that there were no severe agricultural or economic impacts in south-eastern Australia. But although the impacts of the El Niño were not as great in Australia as they were elsewhere, there was now an increasing awareness that droughts could have significant impacts in other regions of the world. Throughout 1877, newspapers carried reports and commentary on the droughts that were taking place in countries such as India and China, causing devastating famines that killed millions of people. One response was the establishment of Indian Famine Relief and the widespread collection of foreign aid from Australian communities. The late nineteenth century in Australia also saw rapid expansion of the network of weather stations in an attempt to better understand our climate. New weather observatories became possible as agriculture spread, urban centres developed and the network of telegraph lines grew.

Garden suggests that while short and intense periods of dry weather can cause localised hardship, the most serious Australian droughts that have major impacts on society are the ones that accumulate after years of below-average rainfall. According to Linden Ashcroft's instrumental analysis of historical climate data from this period, a moderate but prolonged drought influenced south-eastern Australia from 1880 to 1885 but was associated with generally average temperatures. It's true that it was dry: the southern states did not experience a year of significantly above-average rainfall for over a decade from 1876, while the eastern states experienced rainfall deficits for five out of seven years between 1880 and 1886. But perhaps because of the buffering of years of heavy rainfall, there is limited evidence of major drought impacts in historical documents until 1895. From this year on, the nation experienced one of the most iconic droughts in Australian history. It was to span the turn of the century and, in the end, irreversibly shape the way we respond to one of the most defining aspects of life in our country.

14
DUST AND DESOLATION

Australia's climate record will always have a geographical bias towards the earliest colonial centre of Sydney the further back in time you go. There will also always be gaps in the record in some of the most remote desert regions of the country. But given the profound influence of weather conditions on the development of human society, meticulous British bureaucrats left a legacy of a remarkably long and high-quality climate record. While colonial outposts in places like South America and South Africa have long weather records in paper format, most instrumental observations are only available in digital form from the mid-twentieth century onwards. By comparison, Australia's modern temperature and rainfall observation networks are some of the best in the world. In 2011, the Bureau of Meteorology had 774 temperature sites and nearly 6000 rain gauges operating across Australia. Of these, a subset of 151 rainfall stations and 112 temperature stations with daily observations meet the strict quality and homogeneity requirements needed to accurately monitor national trends in Australian climate. So what do our highest-quality climate records tell us about our recent climate history?

A number of notable twentieth-century droughts in eastern Australia have been captured by the high-quality instrumental climate record. The three longest are the Federation (1895–1902), World War II (1937–45) and Millennium (1997–2009) droughts. Aside from these long dry spells, a number of shorter, intense droughts were also recorded. For example, major droughts occurred in 1914–15, 1965–68 and 1982–83, mostly coinciding with El Niño events that brought dry and hot conditions to eastern Australia, as they do today.

The Federation Drought is recognised by climatologists and historians as being one of the worst droughts in Australian history. The five years leading up to the federation of the colonies saw intermittent dry spells over the majority of the eastern two-thirds of Australia, especially during the years 1897 and 1899. The Federation Drought was concentrated in eastern Australia and parts of south-western Western Australia, but it was most severe in New South Wales and Queensland. By February 1902, there were grave concerns about Sydney's water supply, with the state government declaring 26 February a day of 'humility and prayer'. Not long after, Queensland and Victoria followed suit with public days of prayer as the drought tightened its grip.

Prolonged rainfall deficits and the accompanying heatwaves, dust storms and bushfires had disastrous impacts in cities and regional communities. The event reached its peak in 1902 when the eastern half of the country experienced rainfall totals in the lowest 10 per cent of rainfall records, making that year one of the driest in modern Australian history. For example, St Lawrence in Queensland recorded only 90 millimetres of rainfall from December 1901 to November 1902, a staggering 91 per cent below its annual average of 1019 millimetres. The country was so dry

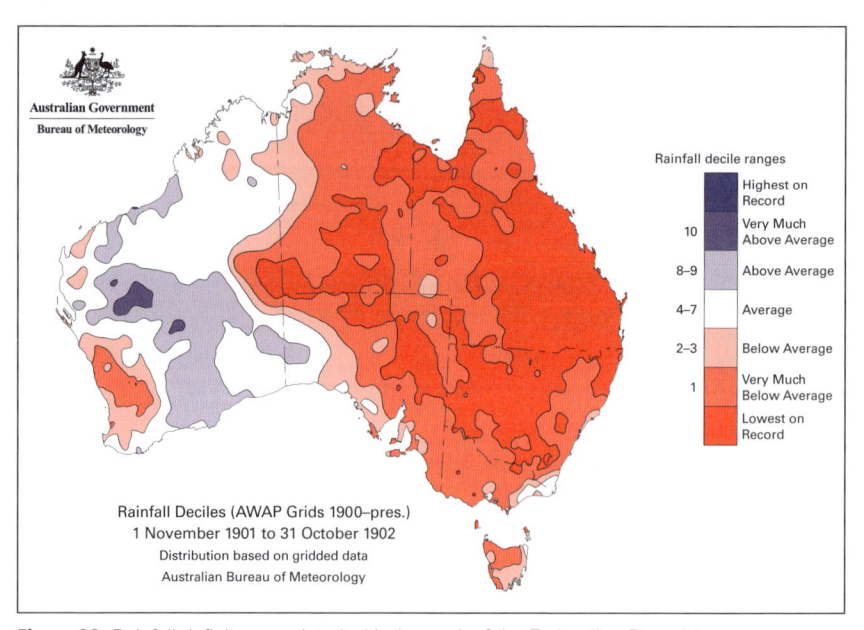

Figure 23. Rainfall deficits associated with the peak of the Federation Drought.

Source: Reproduced courtesy of the Bureau of Meteorology.

that whenever strong winds blew, soil was whipped up into great dust clouds. One of the worst days was 12 November 1902, when a north-westerly gale caused extensive dust storms across South Australia, Victoria and New South Wales. Ferocious winds tore roofs off buildings, uprooted trees and downed telegraph poles across western Victoria. In the Riverina region of Victoria, a sand layer 30 centimetres deep had to be shovelled off the railway line between Kerang and Swan Hill before train services could resume.

Don Garden reported that by the end of the Federation Drought, the number of sheep in Australia had halved and the cattle population had been reduced by 40 per cent. In 1902 the wheat crop was all but lost, with close to the lowest yields of the twentieth century. An article published in the *Sydney Bulletin* in June of that year provides an evocative account of conditions in western Queensland:

A stifling day. The sky a great, flaming oven. Grass withered; water gone; famine-stricken, blear-eyed bullocks, staggering pathetically. Grotesque caricatures of sheep—mere bones holding up the pelt. Plain after plain of parched wilderness. Not a tree nor a shrub for miles; nothing but dust and desolation. Skeletons and bones everywhere.

Figure 24. Scene depicting the devastating loss of sheep in 1897, during the Federation Drought.
Source: Commins, JA (1897). 'In drought time, 1897.' Reproduced courtesy of the National Library of Australia.

After years of punishingly dry conditions, in December 1902 the long drought finally began to break as heavy rain began to soak land that had been baked dry over seven years.

Climatologist Danielle Verdon-Kidd from the University of Newcastle led an analysis on the factors influencing Australian rainfall during the Federation Drought. She concluded that the drought was predominantly due to reductions in spring–summer rainfall, primarily caused by a decrease in the overall number of rain days rather than changes in rainfall intensity. She identified that the long drought occurred during a period of sustained El Niño activity, with only 1898 reaching the La Niña thresholds that traditionally bring heavy rains to eastern Australia. The impacts of this lone La Niña might have been suppressed since it occurred during a positive phase of the Inter-decadal Pacific Oscillation (IPO), when sea surface conditions in our region are cooler than usual, promoting drought.

The Federation Drought shone a spotlight on the need to regulate water use in the Murray–Darling system, Australia's largest river network and agricultural basin. From the 1860s, when water levels were high enough, paddle-steamers and wool barges made their way up the rivers, carrying supplies to outback sheep stations and towns, and bringing bales of wool back to the two main inland ports of Echuca in Victoria and Morgan in South Australia. By the 1890s, water levels dropped due to the Federation Drought, bringing most steamers to a standstill. This undermined the agricultural prosperity and livelihoods of many people in the region, highlighting the need for management of Australia's precious water resources. Yet, despite these severe societal impacts, it wasn't until 1917 that the River Murray Commission—now the Murray–Darling Basin Authority—was established to begin managing water rights and environmental flows in the river system, an issue that remains unresolved and highly contentious to this day.

The World War II Drought that spanned the years 1937–45 was the next severe and persistent drought to shape Australian society. It had a huge impact on communities still recovering from World War I (1914–18) and the Great Depression of the 1930s, the deepest and longest economic downturn in the history of the Western world. The first major rainfall deficits occurred in 1937 over New South Wales, Queensland and parts of Western Australia. Despite 1938 being a La Niña year, conditions deteriorated substantially, and the Australian wheat yield fell to its lowest levels since 1914, a very strong El Niño drought year. By the summer of 1938–39, the topsoil over much of Victoria and New South Wales was so dry that it didn't take much for gusty conditions to create billowing dust storms that were frequent until well into the 1940s when good rains returned.

In Victoria, a run of extremely dry years caused usually wet temperate forests to drastically dry out, leading to the catastrophic Black Friday bushfires of January 1939. As bushfires royal commissioner Leonard Stretton observed in the report he submitted later that year:

> The rich plains, denied their beneficent rains, lay bare and baking; and the forests, from the foothills to the alpine heights, were tinder. The soft carpet of the forest floor was gone; the bone-dry litter crackled underfoot; dry heat and hot dry winds worked upon a land already dry, to suck from it the last, least drop of moisture.

Figure 25. Animal carcasses prevent a paddle-steamer from navigating the Darling River in New South Wales following a drought in 1876.

Source: Artist unknown. 'Troubles of navigation on the River Darling, NSW, after a drought.' Image published by Ebenezer and David Syme in *Illustrated Australian News*. Reproduced courtesy of the State Library Victoria.

Strong winds fanned several fires into a massive front which swept over the alpine country in north-eastern Victoria and along the coast in the south-west. Large areas of state forest, including precious stands of giant mountain ash, were killed. The fires burned two million hectares of land, with three-quarters of Victoria estimated to have been directly or indirectly affected by the disaster.

The Bushfires Royal Commission noted that on Friday 13 January 1939, 'it appeared the whole State was alight'. Several towns, including Narbethong in central Victoria and Hill End in East Gippsland, were completely destroyed. Seventy-one people died, and over 1300 homes, sixty-nine sawmills and 3700 other buildings were destroyed. The environmental effects of the fires continued for many years, including the loss of vast tracts of native forests and the resident wildlife. Large tree hollows and other important habitats for mammals and birds, such as the Leadbeater's possum and powerful owl, were destroyed when the mature mountain ash forests burned. The intensity of the fire also produced huge amounts of smoke and ash, with reports of ash falling as far away as New Zealand. Local soils took decades to recover from the damage, and in some areas water supplies were contaminated for years afterwards due to ash and debris washing into catchment areas.

Figure 26. Blackened trees line Black's Spur Road between Healesville and Marysville following the Black Friday bushfire of January 1939.

Source: Photographer unknown (1939). Reproduced courtesy of the Victorian Department of Environment, Land, Water and Planning.

Importantly, the Black Friday bushfires led to major changes in forest management. The resulting royal commission concluded that 'these fires were lit by the hand of man' as a result of careless land clearing and campfire practices. It made a number of recommendations to improve forest management and safety, including the construction of a network of access trails, towers for early detection of fires, the implementation of controlled burns during spring and autumn to reduce fuel loads, and improved fire prevention education. The fires contributed directly to the passing of the *Forests Act*, which gave the Forests Commission responsibility for forest fire protection on public land. The other main recommendation of the royal commission was the establishment of a state fire authority, laying the foundation for the Country Fire Authority (CFA) in 1945. The CFA is a dedicated group of highly trained, largely volunteer firefighters from Victorian rural and urban areas that works closely with the other emergency services to fight fires that threaten their communities.

The weather conditions experienced during the great heatwave of 5–15 January 1939 were some of the most extreme ever recorded in Australia. Many temperature records were set that month, some of which still stand today. The heatwave of the second week of January 1939 is regarded as the most severe to have affected south-eastern Australia during the twentieth century. The worst of the heat took hold from 8 January, with temperatures soaring into the forties (°C) throughout inland Victoria and New South Wales. The towns of Mildura and Wagga Wagga reached 47.2°C, while Wilcannia recorded a staggering 50°C on 11 January. Two days earlier, the temperature at Kyancutta in South Australia reached 49.3°C, the highest temperature ever recorded in South Australia at that time. On 10 January, Menindee in western New South Wales reached 49.7°C, a temperature that remains a record for the state.

On 12 January, a northerly wind gusting ahead of an approaching front pushed temperatures in Adelaide to a record high of 46.1°C. When the change hit Melbourne, temperatures soared to 45.6°C, a January record that remains unchallenged to this day. On 14 January, Sydney reached 45.3°C, a record that stood until 18 January 2013. In the end, at least 420 people died in New South Wales, Victoria and South Australia due to heat during this event, in addition to the seventy-one people killed during the Black Friday fires. While the January 1939 heatwave remains one of the most severe in Australia's recorded history, the frequency of extreme heatwaves in this country has increased since the 1970s. That is, the conditions experienced during years like 1939 used to be very rare events, but they are now turning up more often in our modern climate.

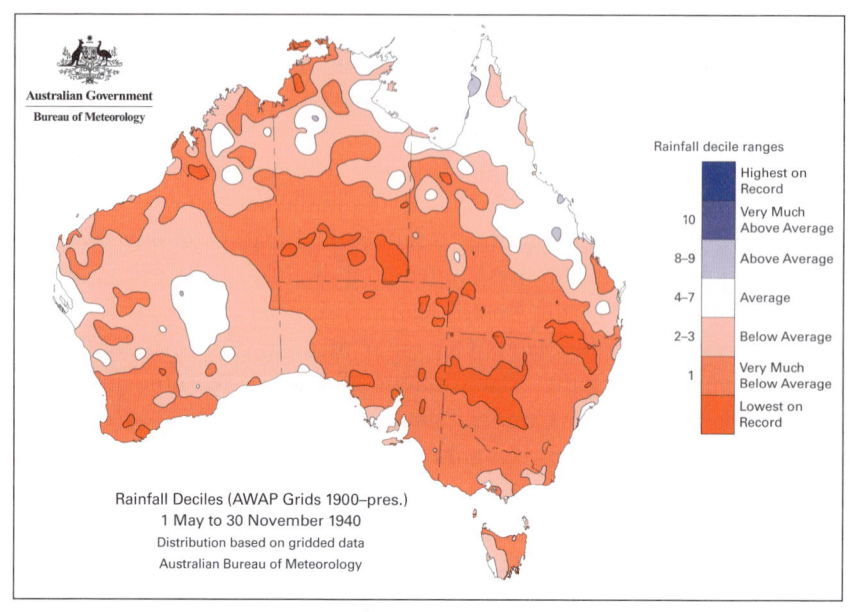

Figure 27. Rainfall deficits associated with the peak of the World War II Drought.
Source: Reproduced courtesy of the Bureau of Meteorology.

In late February 1939, heavy rain finally began falling over eastern and central Australia, providing much-needed respite from the drought for the remainder of the year. Unfortunately, the relief didn't last long. By early 1940, a strong El Niño event had kicked in, resulting in one of the driest years of the twentieth century over much of southern Australia. By winter, Sydney's Nepean Dam was empty, and water restrictions were enforced in Brisbane to avoid water shortages. In Western Australia, Perth experienced its driest year on record (until 2006, and then 2010).

The country was truly in slow-bake mode, until more heavy rains arrived in December 1940. January 1941 was an exceptionally wet month over eastern Australia. However, by winter 1941 dry conditions had returned to the eastern seaboard. Aside from a weak La Niña easing rainfall deficits for a while during 1942, the drought regrouped, and by 1944 northern Victorians were carting water into the region as the failure of the winter–spring rains led to a collapse of the wheat crop. It's estimated that around 40 million sheep died during the extreme conditions.

As the soil dried up and vegetation died, major dust storms blew across much of eastern Australia during the summer of 1944–45. In October 1944, a widespread dust storm tore across western New South Wales, billowing brown clouds that extended as far east as Sydney and required lights to be turned on during the day. A few weeks later, thick dust blanketed Mildura for eight hours and the railway lines in the region were buried in sand—in some places up to a metre of it. As the summer continued, choking dust repeatedly smothered vast areas of the country from South Australia to Queensland. The devastating impact on the landscape of that summer raised serious concerns about soil erosion and the need for preventative measures, as farmers watched their livelihoods blow away in the wind.

As the long drought continued, low rainfall and high evaporation saw large rivers dry up. By December 1944, the Hunter River in the Newcastle region of New South Wales had stopped flowing along most of its course, and the Hawkesbury River in Sydney was dry at North Richmond. By 1945, most Victorian water storages were empty, the Murray River had dried up at Echuca, and Adelaide also faced serious water scarcity. There were even water shortages as far north as the tropical town of Townsville in far north Queensland. It wasn't until the winter of 1945 that the drought broke in the southern states, but good rains didn't fall in Queensland until 1946, which was the worst year of all in some regions. By 1947 the drought had finally broken in all areas of the country, bringing to an end one of the most punishing periods in Australian history.

Figure 28. Dust storm smothering the town of Mildura in north-western Victoria, November 1940.

Source: 'Dust storm, Mildura' (c. 1940). Reproduced courtesy of the State Library Victoria.

While the World War II Drought saw rainfall declines across all seasons, they occurred in different parts of the country at different times. The impact was greatest in the Murray–Darling Basin, resulting in significant water shortages and agricultural losses. Research conducted by scientists from the Bureau of Meteorology and CSIRO has shown that the drought was caused by cool tropical sea surface conditions associated with El Niño conditions and the strengthening of the subtropical ridge—the area of high pressure that forms above Australia as warm, moist air flows south from the equator. Recent research suggests that the tropics are expanding, which is associated with an increase in the intensity of the subtropical ridge and is responsible for pushing mid-latitude storm tracks further south, a feature observed during the World War II Drought.

The Millennium Drought, also referred to as the 'Big Dry', was the last major drought of the twentieth century. The bone-dry conditions experienced from 1997 through 2009 across much of southern and eastern Australia represent the driest thirteen-year rainfall period in the instrumental record. The average annual rainfall for south-eastern Australia during the drought was 512 millimetres, or 12 per cent below the long-term (1900–2010) average. Interestingly, the Millennium Drought happened at a time when Australia as a whole was experiencing above-average rainfall, which was primarily due to high summer rainfall over the north-western regions of the continent. In contrast to historical events, previous droughts across south-eastern Australia tended to occur when the entire continent was also experiencing dry conditions, suggesting different influences were at play.

Unlike previous dry spells, the Millennium Drought had a different seasonal pattern of rainfall decline. Autumn rains, usually relied upon to deliver drought-breaking rains, consistently failed in large parts of southern Australia from 1997 until 2010. In 2007, the Murray–Darling Basin, which accounts for 41 per cent of the nation's gross value of agricultural production and for 70 per cent of all water used for irrigation, experienced its hottest year and lowest water inflows on record. Although modern streamflow regulation has made it less likely today that rivers will dry up as they did during the early twentieth century, during the Millennium Drought the mighty Murray River shrivelled into brown trickles snaking through cracked land. With paddocks reduced to dust bowls, farmers were forced to sell stock for a pittance, or buy feed to keep emaciated stock alive.

In September 2007, the plight of drought-ravaged farmers became so dire that the federal government offered the most severely affected $150 000 to walk off their land. Some gave up, abandoning properties that had been in their families for generations. Research has found that between 1988 and 1997, one farmer committed suicide every four days under the stress of failing crops, dying livestock, mounting debt and the decay of rural towns. Between 2005 and 2007, male suicide rates in rural Queensland were twice as high as in city areas, and tended to occur in clusters around stress triggers like prolonged drought.

Another defining feature of the Millennium Drought was the stark absence of recovery wet months and years. The rainfall deficits recorded in that period were 45 per cent larger than those of the previous driest thirteen-year period of 1933–45. Although shorter low-rainfall periods had been observed during the Federation and World War II droughts, the duration of the Millennium Drought was unprecedented in the instrumental record. The affected region experienced 180 consecutive months without a very wet month. The likelihood of observing such a long sequence of dry years by chance is less than 0.5 per cent. And even as the drought was broken in 2010–12, only one very wet month was recorded during the traditional cool season in southern Australia. The other wet months were associated with tropical influences during the warm season, suggesting a significant decline in southern Australian rainfall over this period.

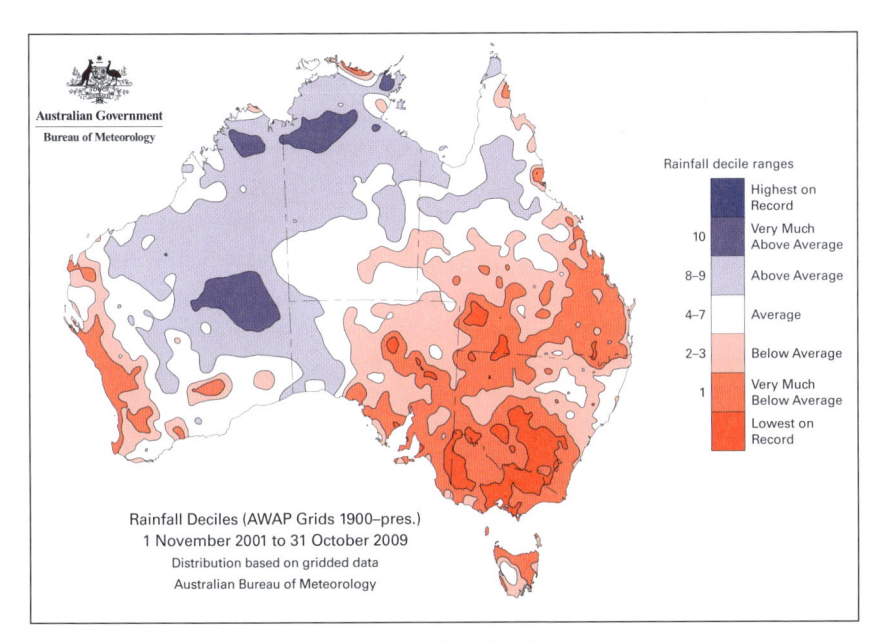

Figure 29. Rainfall deficits at the peak of the Millennium Drought.

Source: Reproduced courtesy of the Bureau of Meteorology.

So what's been happening to Australian rainfall since the late 1990s? The biggest difference between historical droughts and the Millennium Drought is that south-eastern Australia has experienced significant warming over the last fifty years, consistent with the overall warming of the rest of the planet. Trend analysis confirms a 1.1°C increase in maximum temperature and a 0.9°C increase in minimum temperature since 1960.

Like the World War II Drought, the Millennium Drought was characterised by changes in the intensity and position of the subtropical ridge (the belt of high pressure that sits over the middle of Australia). While these factors account for up to 34 per cent of the rainfall deficits from 1935 to 1945, the intensity of the subtropical ridge during the Millennium Drought is estimated to account for a huge 80 per cent of the observed rainfall decline in the south-western part of eastern Australia. Experiments using climate model simulations have shown that this expansion of the tropics can only be reproduced when human influences—in the form of greenhouse gases, aerosols and stratospheric ozone depletion—are included in the model runs, especially in autumn across south-eastern Australia.

While work in this area is still ongoing, the latest research suggests that the Millennium Drought was linked to global warming. A 2013 study by the Bureau of Meteorology's Bertrand Timbal and Wasyl Drosdowsky suggested that the World War II Drought could be seen as the first dry decade of the twentieth century in south-eastern Australia that could be partially due to global warming through the intensification of the subtropical ridge. While we are very confident that the sustained warming experienced during the second half of the twentieth century is extremely likely to have been influenced by human factors, the short-lived warm periods of the first half of the century were predominantly caused by natural factors like El Niño events. It is in the middle of the twentieth century that the human fingerprint emerges above natural variability and can be clearly detected through climate models that compare worlds with and without greenhouse gases.

Could it be that the nature of Australian droughts is changing as we continue to warm the planet? Are our droughts getting hotter? It's a question we need to start taking seriously before the next heavy rains arrive and wash away our concerns.

15
GUMBOOT WEATHER

Australia is a nation defined by its spectacular rainfall variability. While droughts have historically tended to grab most of the attention, there have been times when phenomenal swings back to wet conditions have resulted in devastating deluges across the country. Floods in Australia range from localised flash flooding as a result of thunderstorms, to more widespread inundations following heavy rain over water-catchment areas. During these periods, rivers break their banks and spill into surrounding areas, causing extensive damage to homes, infrastructure, agricultural crops and livestock.

In fact, floods are Australia's most expensive natural disasters, with each event causing hundreds of millions of dollars of damage. During some of the most extreme events, the impact on our economy has been substantially higher. For example, the severe floods that inundated Queensland over the summer of 2010–11 saw three-quarters of the state declared a disaster zone, with over 2.5 million people affected. According to the Australian Business Roundtable for Disaster Resilience and Safer Communities' 2016 report, the 2010–11 Queensland floods had a colossal price tag of $14.1 billion (in 2015 dollars), with $6.7 billion in tangible damages and $7.4 billion in social impacts.

Like many of the wettest periods in Australian history, the mammoth floods of 2010–11 were associated with La Niña conditions. But aside from the influence of the Pacific Ocean, significant flooding can also be caused by cyclone activity, monsoonal storms, east-coast lows, warmer than average sea temperatures in the Indian Ocean, or enhanced storm fronts embedded in the westerly winds that sweep across the Southern Ocean. It all hangs on the large-scale climate conditions that shift from season to season. Our vulnerability to flooding depends on our proximity to low-lying river floodplains, whether the soils in an area are able to soak up excessive rain, and the degree to which natural land has been converted into human surfaces like roads, or from native vegetation into agricultural crops and pasture.

There are two key wet periods that stand out above all others in the Bureau of Meteorology's high-quality rainfall network: the 1950s and 1970s, both recognised as being the wettest periods of the twentieth century across large parts of the country. The 1950s were interesting because they contained a string of strong La Niña events that resulted in remarkable flooding in eastern Australia. From December 1949 until February 1951, much of eastern and northern Australia recorded very high rainfall during one of the strongest La Niña events of the twentieth century. Around 95 per cent of Queensland and 76 per cent of New South Wales (especially in the east) received well above average or record-breaking rain. The year 1950 was the wettest since 1900 averaged over Queensland and New South Wales, mainly due to several cyclones hitting the north-eastern coast early that year.

The wet conditions saw forty-eight cases of Murray Valley encephalitis appear in 1951. Although the virus is endemic to northern Australia, it can be spread by infected mosquitoes to the southern states during times of heavy rainfall in the summer monsoon season by seasonal flooding of the Murray–Darling river system. While most people with this infection only develop a mild illness with fever, a small proportion develop a severe brain infection known as encephalitis, which sometimes results in death.

In the autumn of 1952, abundant rain fell on already saturated soils across much of Victoria and New South Wales. On 14 June, an east-coast low system developed in Bass Strait, unleashing torrential rain over south-eastern Australia. Tanybryn in Victoria's Otway Ranges received 587 millimetres of rain over three days—huge totals for an area outside of the subtropics. The deluge resulted in parts of the Great Ocean Road being washed away, cutting off the coastal town of Apollo Bay. In the Barwon River region near Geelong, 600 people were left homeless because of the flooding. In the town of Walhalla, an old goldmining town set in a narrow valley in the Gippsland region, heavy rainfall caused a dangerous avalanche of water, rocks and logs that covered the town in up to 2 metres of debris. Meanwhile, in New South Wales, the Lachlan and Murrumbidgee rivers flooded nearby towns like Wagga Wagga, many highways were cut, and landslides in the Illawarra region south of Sydney rendered railways impassable for two months. The remainder of 1952 was also very wet, with further severe flooding impacting south-eastern Australia in October and November.

After some relief during 1953, La Niña conditions re-formed from early 1954 until the start of 1957, ushering in a highly active tropical cyclone season. While most of the damage from tropical cyclones affects Australia's eastern seaboard in northern and central Queensland, occasionally cyclonic systems can extend as far south as south-eastern Queensland and north-eastern New South Wales. So it was in February 1954, when a severe cyclone slammed into the Gold Coast region, making landfall at Coolangatta near the New South Wales–Queensland border. Huge seas, torrential rain and an intense storm surge pounded the coast, causing devastating flooding and widespread erosion of beaches and infrastructure. Rooftops were blown away, dunes swept out to sea and boats washed ashore. Just south of the border, the Byron Bay jetty was washed away, taking with it virtually the entire town's fishing fleet.

In the Gold Cost hinterland, humid air masses raced up the mountainous terrain, amplifying the ferocity of the rains. In the area of Springbrook, on the headwaters of the Nerang River, 900 millimetres of rain fell in just twenty-four hours. Further south, the town of Dorrigo near the Bellinger River received 809 millimetres on 21 February, setting the New South Wales state record for the highest 24-hour rainfall total. As the cyclone moved inland and passed west of the town of Lismore in the Northern Rivers region, a literal wall of water with whitewater rapids raged down the Richmond River. After peaking at 13.4 metres, the river flooded so quickly that many people were trapped in their homes and had to be rescued from their rooftops. Twenty-six people lost their lives, and the region's infrastructure and agriculture suffered serious blows during the ordeal.

It's interesting to consider that the population of the Gold Coast area in 1954 was just under 20 000. It's hard to imagine the damage a similar cyclone would do to a region that in 2016 housed approximately 625 000 residents, and one of the highest densities of tourist accommodation in the country. It's a reminder that our coastal populations are vulnerable to increased exposure to extreme weather events that have had enormous impacts on Australian society in the past.

By April 1954, another La Niña event had formed in the Pacific. More than 70 per cent of Queensland, New South Wales and Victoria received rainfall totals in the wettest 10 per cent of observations, with some areas resetting their rainfall records. In February 1955 extensive flooding occurred in New South Wales, affecting nearly all of the state's river catchments. Around 15 000 people were evacuated, fifty people died, 100 000 livestock perished, and there were large agricultural losses. Some of the worst flooding occurred in the Hunter River region just north of Newcastle, where floodwaters up to 5 metres deep inundated towns such as Maitland. Images of the event have come to symbolise iconic Australian flooding, perhaps also reflecting advances in technology at the time that made film footage more readily available. More than 5000 homes were submerged in metres of water, with around 15 000 people evacuated from rooftops by boat or helicopter. Along with major damage to homes, fourteen lives were lost, including five people who were electrocuted during rescue operations.

The following year, from March until December, the regions surrounding the Murray–Darling system flooded extensively, resulting in the year 1956 being classified the wettest on record for the basin, and the highest flood level of the twentieth century in the lower Murray. During this time there was a Ross River virus outbreak, with over 2000 cases reported throughout South Australia, Victoria and New South Wales near the river system in April 1956.

The La Niña event spanned thirty-six months until finally decaying in January 1957, rounding off one of the wettest decades in Australian history. We now know that the events that took place during the 1950s were associated with a strongly negative phase of the Inter-decadal Pacific Oscillation (IPO). During the twentieth century, there were positive IPO phases from 1925 to 1946 and from 1978 to 1998, punctuated by a negative phase occurred from 1947 to 1976. Just like the El Niño–Southern Oscillation (ENSO), the IPO is a natural climate pattern providing ocean conditions that influence whether decades have more wet or dry years

Figure 30. February 1955 flooding of Maitland, in the Hunter River region of New South Wales.

Source: Photographer unknown (1955). Reproduced courtesy of the Picture Maitland Collection, Maitland City Library.

than others. These decade-long cycles are slowly churning away in the deep ocean, gradually setting up the background conditions that enhance or supress Australian rainfall.

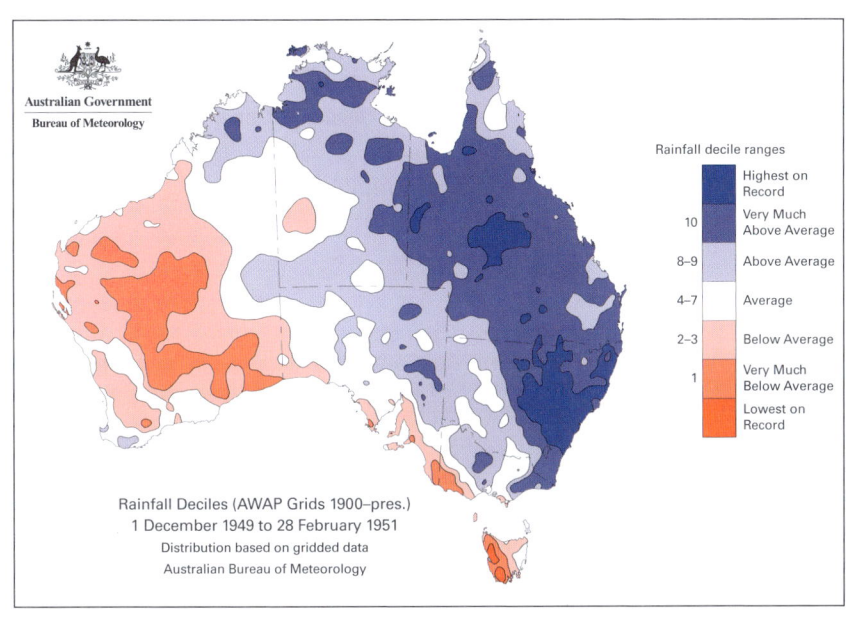

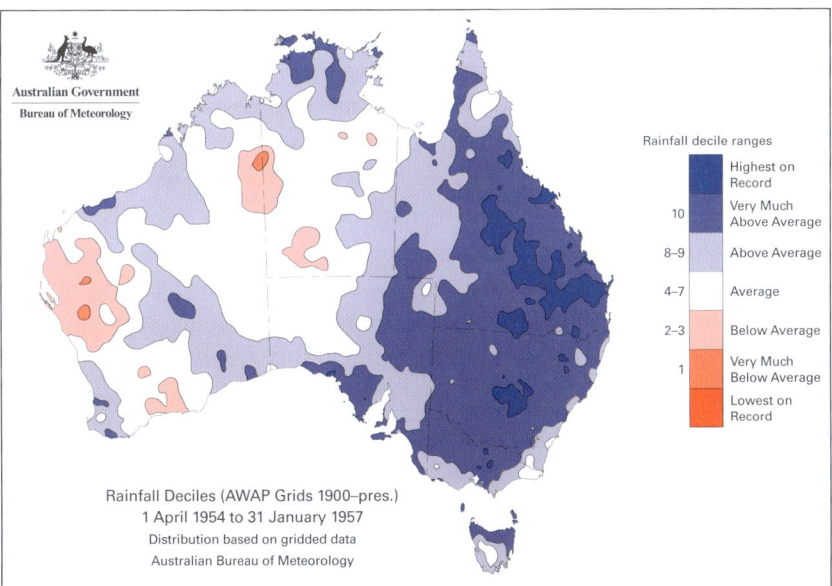

Figure 31. Rainfall patterns associated with the 1949–51 (top) and 1954–57 (bottom) La Niña events that brought record-breaking rainfall to eastern Australia.

Source: Reproduced courtesy of the Bureau of Meteorology.

Research led by Scott Power from the Bureau of Meteorology has shown that the link between the negative phase of the IPO and Australian rainfall is stronger than during its positive phase. This means that when we are in a negative IPO phase, we tend to receive higher than average rainfall. But positive IPO conditions aren't always linked to drought conditions in Australia. This is likely to reflect the fact that rainfall is a limiting factor in a country like Australia, which is mostly classified as arid or semi-arid. We are predisposed to dry conditions because of our physical location in one of the vast subtropical desert belts of the world. So when it finally does rain, the signal clearly pops out from the background of our otherwise dry climate.

The next major wet phase in Australian history was the 1970s. Like the 1950s, this period was real gumboot weather. The decade also fell within the negative IPO phase that stretched from 1947 to 1976. Things kicked off with a moderate La Niña event spanning June 1970 to March 1972. Rainfall was above average in many parts of Queensland, New South Wales, Victoria, Tasmania and south-eastern Southern Australia. Tasmania was particularly wet, with most of the state having totals in the wettest 10 per cent of its historical records, and the towns of Deloraine and La Trobe in the north experiencing major flooding.

Several tropical cyclones also contributed to the drenching of 1971. Tropical cyclone Dora, which hit the Queensland coast just north of Brisbane in February, caused widespread structural damage. Another tropical cyclone, Althea, crossed the coast at Townsville on Christmas Eve 1971, causing $50 million damage. The cyclone generated a 3.7-metre storm surge whose pounding surf destroyed roads and seawalls. Beaches receded by as much as 15.8 metres due to coastal erosion. In Townsville itself, thousands of homes were damaged or destroyed, and 90 per cent of the houses on Magnetic Island were obliterated. There were also two outbreaks of Ross River virus during this La Niña event, with thirty-three reported cases in December 1970 in the western New South Wales town of Coleambally, and another 109 cases reported in February 1971 in the Murray River region.

From March 1972 until May 1973, the climate shifted into El Niño conditions, which saw large parts of southern and eastern Australia bake through a strong but short-lived drought. In 1972 the Indian Ocean was cooler than average, or in its positive Indian Ocean Dipole (IOD) phase, further supressing rainfall conditions in the region. Following this break from the rain, Australia experienced the longest period of sustained La Niña conditions in the instrumental record, which unleashed phenomenal deluges across virtually the entire country. By the end of 1973, many catchment areas were already saturated as the wet season started early, culminating in the wettest January in Australia's rainfall records. During January 1974, Australia as a whole, the Northern Territory and Queensland recorded their wettest month on record, while South Australia and New South Wales recorded their second-wettest January on record. Torrential monsoon rains in the gulf country of Queensland transformed the normally dry interior into vast inland seas, flooding all the way to Lake Eyre in the arid interior of South Australia.

To make matters worse, on 24 January, tropical cyclone Wanda drifted south and crossed the coast near Brisbane. Although not as severe as in 1893, the wet conditions resulted in one of Brisbane's worst floods on record and a period of major beach erosion on the Gold Coast. The system generated enormous quantities of rain over the Australia Day weekend, with Brisbane receiving over 300 millimetres within twenty-four hours. Over a three-day period, the city was pelted by 580 millimetres of rain, causing swollen rivers to burst their banks and submerge nearby homes. By 29 January the Brisbane area had recorded in excess of 1 metre of rain. The Bremer and Brisbane rivers peaked at their highest levels since the catastrophic floods of 1893.

The 1974 flood was a defining event for a generation of Brisbane residents and remains the most severe example of urban flooding in Australia. Although the flood was smaller in magnitude than the 1893 event, the damage was greater because the city's population had grown in that time from an estimated 28 000 to about one million, and because of the increased exposure of more buildings and infrastructure. At least 8500 homes flooded in Brisbane and Ipswich, 6000 of which could not be recovered from an inland sea created by the floodwaters. The floods killed sixteen people and injured 300 more.

According to a study by Robin van den Honert and John McAneney from Macquarie University's Risk Frontiers group, the insured losses from the 1974 event were estimated to be almost $3.3 billion (adjusted to 2011 exposure). A decade after the events of that year, Wivenhoe Dam was built on the Brisbane River 80 kilometres from the city to regulate water flow and reduce the flood risk of the region. Even so, many people bought up land in the floodplain area not long after the waters receded, the risks of which were to be made clear in the destructive flooding of December 2010 and January 2011.

Figure 32. Flood damage at St Lucia, Brisbane, caused by the 1974 flood.
Source: Photographer unknown (1974). Reproduced courtesy of the State Library of Queensland.

By the end of January 1974, much of the country was underwater. Torrential rain swept down the east coast, inundating large parts of New South Wales and Tasmania. Extensive areas of inland Australia remained submerged in floodwaters for weeks, and in some cases months. The extensive rain produced abundant vegetation growth in central Australia, but when it dried out in late spring it provided rich fuel for igniting fires, which subsequently blazed across the region. The wet conditions during this La Niña event caused yet another major outbreak of Murray Valley encephalitis, with fifty-eight cases reported throughout south-eastern Australia. An estimated 400 to 500 cases of Ross River virus were also reported from South Australia's Murray Valley region to Queensland.

At the end of that year came a disaster on a scale unparalleled in Australian history. On Christmas Day 1974, Cyclone Tracy struck Darwin. The storm destroyed more than 70 per cent of the city's buildings, including 80 per cent of its houses, and caused $837 million in damage (in 1974 dollars). Seventy-one people were killed and many thousands injured. It was soon determined that Darwin was only capable of supporting less than a quarter of its population of 45 000, so the decision was made to start

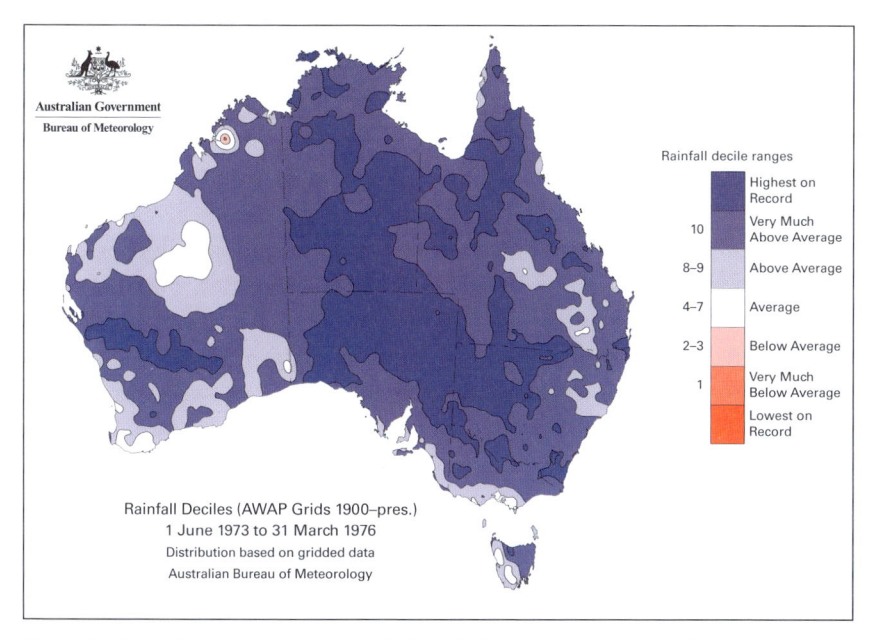

Figure 33. Rainfall patterns associated with the 1973–76 La Niña events that brought record-breaking rainfall to virtually all of Australia.

Source: Reproduced courtesy of the Bureau of Meteorology.

evacuating people, both by road and by airlifts involving civilian and military aircraft. Within weeks, 30 000 residents had fled to Adelaide, Whyalla, Alice Springs and Sydney; many never returned. Those who remained in Darwin faced the threat of disease due to much of the city being without water, electricity or basic sanitation.

After receiving news of the damage, community groups like the Red Cross began fundraising and relief efforts to help the survivors of the cyclone. Volunteers poured into Darwin from across the country to help the emergency relief efforts. Trench latrines were dug, water supplies delivered by tankers, and mass immunisation programs targeting typhoid and cholera begun. The army was given the task of searching houses for the bodies of people and animal carcasses. It was also tasked with cleaning out the rotting contents of fridges and freezers across the city to minimise public health risks, and the city was sprayed with pesticide to prevent mosquitoes from spreading tropical diseases.

It was a disaster of monumental proportions, a brutal reminder of our vulnerability to extreme weather conditions. It's chilling to think how natural disasters of a similar scale in the future might trigger a wave of displacement, not just in distant low-lying Pacific islands or other vulnerable coastal nations of the world, but here at home in Australia.

Although the Northern Territory was still a Commonwealth territory in 1974, the event exposed inadequacies in the national response to disasters of such magnitude. Disaster response management has traditionally been the responsibility of local and state governments. But as Cyclone Tracy demonstrated, it is possible for natural disasters to completely overwhelm the local capacity to respond, highlighting the need for Commonwealth support. When this happened in 1974, there was unclear and fragmented legal support for the actions taken by the federal government. The Natural Disasters Organisation, a Commonwealth body whose powers were poorly defined at the time of the cyclone, oversaw the mass evacuation from the city. This was a support organisation only able to provide a coordination and training role. It did not control the state organisations, manage the response, or own the resources required to respond effectively to a crisis.

In 1993, the Natural Disasters Organisation was relaunched as Emergency Management Australia and transferred from the Department of Defence to the Attorney-General's Department. The umbrella body

Figure 34. The devastating impact of Cyclone Tracy, which made landfall in Darwin on Christmas Day 1974. The suburb of Casuarina was flattened.

Source: Photographer unknown (1974). Reproduced courtesy of the National Library of Australia.

now coordinates federal government support for emergency management with the states and territories, which have their own disaster acts. To this day, there is no federal emergency management legislation, which results in significant confusion about the Commonwealth's role in disaster relief. However, since Cyclone Tracy devastated Darwin in 1974, the power of the Commonwealth to intervene has been increased during national emergencies and it is now better placed to provide funds for large-scale reconstruction. In Darwin's case, it was rebuilt using cyclone-proof building codes and other aspects of disaster planning.

In 2015, the Australian Government established the Australian Institute for Disaster Resilience to support the implementation of the National Strategy for Disaster Resilience. This body acts as an information hub that coordinates the development, sharing and use of information for anyone working with or affected by disasters. But while Australia is closer to having a defined Commonwealth response to natural disasters than it was in 1974, there is still much uncertainty as to what exactly could be done if an event similar to Cyclone Tracy were to happen again. Disaster relief still remains the responsibility of state governments and local communities while our population continues to grow, increasing our exposure and vulnerability to future climate extremes.

While policymakers continue to wrestle with the huge task of responding to nationally significant natural disasters, scientists have been working hard to understand the climate conditions that caused the continent-wide drenching Australia received during the 1970s. In hindsight, we now recognise that the period was influenced by a range of climate factors. Like the 1950s, the 1970s were characterised by a negative IPO phase, when we tend to receive higher than average rainfall because of warmer than average seas around Australia. Two strong La Niña events in the Pacific, and a warmer than average Indian Ocean in the year 1974, added to the potential for wet weather. When negative IOD events coincide with La Niña conditions, the warm sea surface temperatures reinforce each other. This double whammy resulted in the exceptionally wet conditions experienced across the country during the 1970s.

A major topic of interest to farmers, insurance companies and scientists is how a warming planet might change the frequency and intensity of the flood and drought years we've experienced throughout our history. Australia's land and oceans have warmed by 1°C since 1910, with much of this warming occurring since 1970. Importantly, warmer ocean temperatures recorded since the late twentieth century influence the background conditions that both extremes of the rainfall cycle will operate under every year the planet continues to warm. This has major implications for the Australian monsoon and the wet season experienced in tropical and subtropical regions of the country.

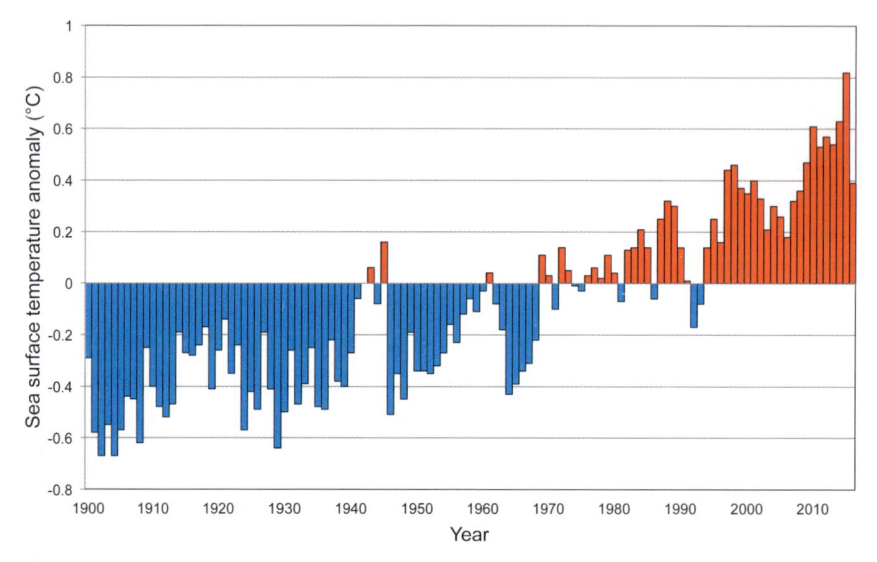

Figure 35. Australian sea surface temperatures for the northern wet season (October–April), 1900–2016. Anomalies are relative to the 1961–90 average.

Source: Reproduced courtesy of the Bureau of Meteorology.

It's fascinating to look back and recognise that past generations of Australians were as exposed to climate extremes as we are today. They saw their crops wilt in searing heat as the rains failed, and watched the resurrection of the land as the drought-breaking rains soaked in. Over time we have learned how to adapt to life in our hugely variable climate. But while the 'She'll be right' mentality is invaluable in times of crisis and recovery, it's important that we plan for our future with our eyes wide open, with all the tough realities in plain sight. History has shown us, time and time again, that as Australians we are vulnerable to severe weather extremes like droughts, floods, cyclones and bushfires. The question is, will we see this vulnerability as an invitation to plan for a future that minimises our exposure to some of the harshest aspects of our climate?

Centuries before we began grappling with these curly questions, there were already people in the landscape who had been coming to terms with the nature of the Australian climate. Long before the First Fleet sailed into Sydney Cove in 1788, thousands of generations of Aboriginal and Torres Strait Islander peoples had already survived through at least 40 000 years of life in this country. So exactly how did the First Australians know when the seasons were beginning to turn? How did they learn to live in such an erratic climate?

16
WISDOM OF THE ELDERS

In the steamy Top End, clouds are building. It is Gunumeleng, the transition between the dry and wet seasons in Kakadu. Thunder grumbles across the flashing night sky as everything waits for the rain. The orange and blue Leichhardt's grasshoppers, Aljurr, call out to their father, the Lightning Man, to leave his cave. They want him to line up all the clouds in the sky to bring storms to the thirsty country. During the build-up, the westerly winds begin to blow until, finally, the heavy clouds burst like giant water bombs on the dry land below. As the monsoonal rains begin to wash away dusty roads, life re-emerges. The tall paperbark trees become covered with white flowers. Their thick scent fills the night air, drawing flying foxes that feast noisily on their nectar.

The First Australians have followed intricate seasonal cycles of plant and animal cues for over 40 000 years, passing them down from generation to generation through stories like these. The ability to adapt to extremely harsh weather conditions has allowed countless generations of Aboriginal people to survive. An intimate knowledge of the environment was literally a matter of life and death: it was used for practical purposes like tracking hunting grounds or identifying safe travelling routes as the seasons began to change.

Over millennia, Australia's Indigenous people have witnessed immense shifts in the climate of the continent. For example, the Willandra Lakes, which sit on a tributary of the Lachlan River in western New South Wales, have been dry for the past 15 000 years. But long ago, a series of interconnected basins there once had a surface area of more than 1000 square kilometres of fresh water—that's eighteen times the surface area of Sydney Harbour. According to renowned landscape evolution specialist and University of Melbourne professor Jim Bowler, around 50 000 years ago the Willandra Lakes were full of fresh water, teeming with large fish and mussels. The now dry bed of Lake Mungo would have been 20 kilometres long, 10 kilometres wide and 15 metres deep. On its eastern side, sand dunes would have provided sheltered campsites by the lakeshore.

It is here at Lake Mungo that one of the oldest ritualistic burials in the world was discovered in 1969. Careful analysis of the 25 000-year-old evidence at the site revealed that after cremation, the remains—especially the face—were thoroughly smashed and then placed in a small depression near the funeral pyre. According to archaeologists, this method was still used in historic times by Aboriginal people in eastern Australia and Tasmania. In 1974, the team found a complete male skeleton lying with its hands clasped, surrounded by pink ochre. The two front teeth were missing: a clear sign that the male had been initiated. Dated to around 30 000 years old, it was more evidence that a complex spiritual system existed on the banks of the once-thriving lakes.

During the peak of the last ice age, around 20 000 years ago, the Willandra Lakes began to dry up as global temperatures took a dive. That ice age lasted for around 5000 years, and global average temperatures fell by around 3–8°C. The sea level dropped by around 120 metres as the world's water drained out of rivers and oceans, becoming locked up in frozen ice sheets. This turned the 2.5 million square kilometres of continental shelf fringing Australia into dry land, adding an area the size of the Indian subcontinent to South-East Asia. As the sea retreated and the deep freeze took hold, much of the water between northern Australia and Papua New Guinea drained away, to be replaced by savannah woodland and swamps. It would have been possible to walk from Port Moresby to Port Douglas, or from Geelong in Victoria to George Town in Tasmania.

The last ice age made much of Australia a desolate and inhospitable place, where rainfall decreased as cold, dry winds blew across the land. This threatened the survival of Indigenous people who, where possible, took refuge from the wind chill and icy conditions deep within limestone caves. Research suggests a decline of up to 80 per cent of the entire Aboriginal population during this cold and dry period. But despite the fierce conditions, pockets of people survived by sheltering in parts of the Pilbara and Kimberley regions in Western Australia, Kakadu and Arnhem Land in the Northern Territory, and in some parts of New South Wales, Victoria and Tasmania.

Some research suggests that the Bibbulmun people of south-western Western Australia recall the time of the last ice age in their stories. If true, anthropologists would consider the age of this folk memory extraordinary. The following excerpt tells the story of the bringing of fire to Aboriginal people. The Moon possesses this source of warmth but is reluctant to share it:

> In Nyitting time, the cold, cold time of long ago, no one had fire but Meeka the Moon. All the inhabitants of the Earth had to eat their meat and vegetable food raw, because they had no cooking fires; they shivered and shivered because they had no fire to warm them. Meeka kept the fire for himself and would not give it to anyone else. He kept it hidden in his tail.

This story was recorded by anthropologist Daisy Bates, who was nicknamed Kabbarli or 'wise woman' by the Aboriginal people she lived with from 1899 to 1945. She was known as a *kallower*, or magic woman, and so was allowed to join the men around their campfires during storytelling time that followed dinner. In her numerous publications, she graphically described the atmosphere as she listened to the old men telling their tales and watched the narrators act out the behaviour of the creatures in each story. Her work is a trove of priceless cultural information that sheds new light on how the First Australians experienced climate cycles deep in the past.

Indigenous people have long recognised that subtle changes to plants and animals provide clues about the weather. They've used the responses of plants and animals to gauge changes in the environment for many thousands of years. For example, in the Simpson Desert of central Australia, the arrival of wading birds called plovers is linked to the onset of seasonal rains. In the humid Top End, an influx of the brolga crane was traditionally seen as heralding the beginning of the monsoon season. The flowering of rough-barked gum trees in the Kakadu region means that winds will blow from the south-east, ushering in the dry season.

The seasonal cycles described by different Aboriginal groups are as varied as the land itself. The Northern Hemisphere pattern sits uncomfortably with the reality of Australia's climate that covers tropical monsoon, desert, savannah, alpine and temperate zones. This sheer diversity seems to defy the concept of a rigid European seasonal calendar—spring, summer, autumn and winter—applied to the entire continent.

In contrast, Aboriginal people can recognise up to six distinct seasons. For instance, in the Sydney region, September–October is known by the Tharawal (formerly D'harawal) people as Ngoonungi, the time when the flying foxes gather and the red waratah flower blooms. In Kakadu, this period marks the transition between Gurrung, the hot dry season, and Gunumeleng, when the Lightning Man's storms return. Further south in Walabunnba country (300 kilometres north of Alice Springs), October–March ushers in Watangka, a time of hot summer rains and bushfires. When the local people hear the rainbird (Mirrlarr) call out, they know a lot of rain is on the way and will fill up the waterholes.

In the remote north-western corner of the Northern Territory, the people in the Yarralin region believe that the transition from the wet to the dry is caused by two spiritual beings: the sun and the rain. In the time of creation, the sun travelled across the world in human form and then became the source of light and heat. Rain is characterised as the Rainbow Serpent, a snake of extraordinary power that inhabits permanent waterholes and the sea. Yarralin people are particularly interested in the behaviour of the rain, or *yipu*, which takes many forms: the cold weather rain, the hot weather rain, the first rain after the really hot time of the year, and the smell of the first rain.

Normally, rain comes because the Rainbow Serpent has brought together a series of interlinked messages. During the cold time, flying foxes are said to live in the bush, eating nectar from eucalyptus flowers. As the flowers dry up, they move to the rivers and roost in the pandanus palms. Their presence tells the Rainbow Serpent that the earth is getting hot, the trees are drying out and land-based food is becoming scarce. The Rainbow Serpent then rises up and releases lightning, thunder and rain. The first rains alert other species like tadpoles to start hatching. The frogs call out, asking for more rain. Yarralin people say that the Rainbow Serpent walks the sky during the wet season, feeding rain to the clouds on which it walks. In an abnormal year, people believe that someone, somewhere, has done something to interfere with the set of messages that bring the rains. Since the wet season rains are usually carried by westerly winds, Aboriginal people living in that region are thought to have a particular influence over the rain, believing that they can withhold it.

If the Yarralin people decide that the causes of unusual rain behaviour are social, they believe they can respond by taking actions into their own hands to bring on the rains. In many regions, people use crystals called 'rain stones' in an effort to manage rain, flood and drought. Perhaps unsurprisingly, rain Dreamings (divine creation stories) are especially prominent in the desert, and rainmaking is a highly valued art throughout the arid regions. Like the dangerous power of some Dreamings, their belief in the power to bring floods or withhold rain could be used in warfare. Accordingly, these practices are usually secret business, although recognition that such knowledge exists is not. However, Yarralin people are generally reluctant to interfere with the system, as they believe that nature behaves according to laws that benefit all species, not just their own self-interest.

More than two centuries after the first British settlement, there is increasing recognition that over 40 000 years of Aboriginal knowledge may help us understand the complex cycles of Australia's erratic climate and how to care for country. It's good to know that knowledge about the weather is not secret business—it can be shared with anyone—but we should respectfully acknowledge local people. As we continue to learn more about the Australian climate, it's clear that we have so much to learn from the First Australians about the natural cycles of our ancient land.

PART III
TIME TRAVELLERS

17
SENTINELS OF DEEP TIME

So far we've looked back through our history from when official weather records began in 1900, to colonial accounts of our climate, and Indigenous people's understanding of the weather. But how do scientists know what our climate was like before people began writing or telling stories? Is it possible to tell if recent climate change is unusual or if it's just part of our region's longstanding natural climate cycles?

Long before humans were keeping track of the weather, the natural world was busy tattooing the passing of time—year after year, for centuries. Cycles of good and poor seasons influence the size of a tree's annual growth ring, while river run-off and changes in sea temperature influence the chemical composition of corals growing in tropical waters. The signatures of wet and dry years are also encoded in lake sediments, as heavy rains sweep across the landscape depositing gritty bands as floodwaters settle. Ice cores taken from the poles also contain bands of accumulated snow that respond to changes in moisture availability as the seasonal winds shift. By studying these natural climate records, we are teleported back in time, gaining an unparalleled perspective on the past. This field of science is known as palaeoclimatology: 'palaeo' means old or ancient, and 'climatology' is the study of accumulated weather over past seasons and years. Analysing these seasonally layered records is like reading every page of nature's handwritten memoirs.

The science of tree rings, or dendrochronology, is the most extensively used tool for precisely reconstructing the Earth's most recent climatic past. It builds off the simple idea that a tree's annual growth ring reflects the climate conditions that it grew in. The sequence of narrow and wide rings tells the story of the good and poor growing seasons experienced by the tree throughout its life in the forest. Tree-ring records form the basis of most year-to-year climate reconstructions around the world, with the majority of climate-sensitive species found in the high-latitude regions of Europe, Asia and North America. The vast, ocean-dominated Southern Hemisphere contains relatively fewer long-lived tree species, but it is home to the majority of the world's coral reef systems. These massive corals are a time capsule of past ocean temperatures and salinity changes that have influenced the reef as it has grown over past centuries. At the ends of the Earth, ice cores drilled from the polar ice caps in Antarctica and the Arctic have been used to reconstruct the planet's past atmospheric composition from air bubbles trapped in the ice.

When these natural records form a seasonal or annual band, they can be accurately dated by using multiple samples or precise radiometric dating. Each layer of a natural record can then be directly compared with the overlapping time period covered by instrumental weather records. The process of comparing palaeoclimate variables like tree-ring widths or snow-accumulation layers against direct instrumental climate observations is called calibration. The basic aim is to establish and define any statistical relationship between a geologic or biological climate 'proxy' and direct observations of variables like temperature or rainfall. This allows scientists to convert a climate proxy measurement into an instrumental climate estimate.

If you're lucky, a climate proxy might capture over 50 per cent of the local year-to-year climate signal that is present in the instrumental climate record. That means that while half of the variations in the palaeoclimate record are tracking real climate variations, the other half is being influenced by factors other than climate. This might include things like biological competition in a forest canopy or a coral reef, storms that disturb snowfall layers, or bugs burrowing into a sediment core, smearing individual bands.

While a natural climate record might be a good substitute for the instrumental climate record, it is never going to be as good as having direct weather records from a given location. To further complicate things, the available instrumental data are often from a different but nearby location, meaning that the palaeoclimate record can never precisely represent observed climate conditions. The problem is, the oldest instrumental climate records only stretch back about 300 years in just one or two places in the world. In most places, reliable data only became available from the early to mid twentieth century. This means that palaeoclimate records, however imperfect, are still our only way of reconstructing what climate conditions were like centuries before weather instruments were even invented.

Scientists try and overcome this issue by using as many records as possible from a given location to check if the patterns observed from one site match other records from nearby. This idea of replication, or reproducibility, is one of the fundamental hallmarks of science. It demands that scientists check that their results are not a one-off fluke specific to a single location. Instead, our results need to be substantiated using multiple lines of evidence. When reconstructing past climates, this becomes even more important the further back in time you go, when fewer old records are available to cross-check against each other.

Establishing a reliably dated record from a given climate proxy can take decades, but once you've dialled in your chronology, that's where the fun starts. You can then begin comparing the patterns seen in other records close by and in other locations around the globe. It's like piecing together a giant jigsaw puzzle: you have snippets from the land, ocean and polar areas of the planet, and it's often a mystery how they fit together. But the more records you have—especially from critically under-represented regions of the Southern Hemisphere—the clearer is the picture of how the Earth's climate system has worked over past centuries. The results are often hard to figure out, but when reconstructing our planet's climate history for the first time from one site or 100, the discoveries are guaranteed to be amazing.

18
OLD-GROWTH RECORDS

We bow our heads in silence. The old chief is chanting a *karakia* prayer to protect our work here in this relic of the Earth's early rainforests. After months of liaison with local Māori *kaumatua* (elders), they finally grant us access to some of the oldest kauri trees in remote northern New Zealand. On cue, an ethereal mist shrouds the isolated, moss-drenched plateau. Prehistoric-looking ferns the size of trees tower overhead. It seems as if someone has sprinkled pixie dust all through this breathtaking forest: it's glowing shades of green I never knew existed.

Kauri (*Agathis australis*) is a primitive conifer pine that belongs to the ancient Araucariaceae family of trees that were prolific before the Gondwanan super-continent broke up more than 180 million years ago. Since dinosaurs roamed the Earth, these forest giants have been recording the relentless passage of time. They include some of the longest-living trees in Australasia, some more than 2000 years old and with girths greater than 10 metres. They are the Southern Hemisphere's answer to the giant sequoias (redwoods) of California, the largest trees in the world.

The kauri is the biological cousin of the celebrated Wollemi pine: the 'living fossil' discovered in the Blue Mountains World Heritage Area in 1994. But where only a handful of Wollemi pines have survived, Northland—the most northerly region of New Zealand—still contains tracts of magnificent kauri forest. They've escaped the ravages of logging, resin bleeding and fire that have claimed so many mighty kauris. These forests are a reminder of what our Earth was like when it was young, a time when pterodactyls ruled the roost.

Since only a handful of records are available for unravelling the history of the planet's vast oceanic south, every single one is priceless. Subjected to the eternal tug of war between Antarctica's icy grip and the lazy warmth of the tropical Pacific, the kauri record is a unique time capsule of the climate cycles experienced in the Southern Hemisphere. Data from this remote part of the world are essential for climate models to realistically reproduce a picture of the Earth's climate history, sharpening predictions of our greenhouse future.

The planet's largest year-to-year natural climate cycle, the El Niño–Southern Oscillation (ENSO), creates many of Australia's iconic droughts and floods. Changes in ocean temperature and atmospheric pressure across the tropical Pacific cause massive dislocations of global weather patterns. This ramps up extremes like droughts, floods, bushfires and cyclones, affecting around 60 per cent of the Earth. In Australia, El Niño coincides with most of the extreme droughts on record. During the 2006–07

Figure 36. The author measuring the girth of one of the largest Kauri trees in New Zealand in 2003. The Yakkas tree in Waipoua Forest has a diameter of 4.65 metres.

Source: Reproduced courtesy of the Tree Ring Laboratory, University of Auckland, New Zealand.

event, the Murray–Darling River basin, which provides over one-third of Australia's annual agricultural production, ran dry for the first time since the Federation drought. Yet despite ENSO affecting the livelihoods of millions, our long-term understanding of it is surprisingly patchy.

Over twenty-five years, ten researchers built up what has become the world's longest record of El Niño activity from tree rings. Made up of hundreds of individual trees, the kauri record now spans 3721 continuous years. Dendrochronology provides us with a portal to the past, centuries before meteorological recordings began. In 2000, Dr Anthony Fowler from the University of Auckland discovered that the kauri has an ENSO signal recorded in its growth rings. By examining patterns in growth rings over time, he was able to get a precise idea of what climate conditions were like—year by year—back through time. A detailed study of the tree-ring record was published in *Nature Climate Change* in 2012. It revealed that the twentieth century was the most 'ENSO-active' period of the past 500 years. It also showed that there were extreme years during medieval times that exceeded anything recorded in the twentieth century. This means that modern societies may not have experienced the full range of natural climate variability that occurred in the past, suggesting that we could be in for some nasty climate surprises in the future.

Blessings complete, we were led further into the remote pocket of old-growth forest. To reach the kauris, we crashed through a thick tangle of undergrowth, unable to see a metre in front of us. But the moment I encountered one of the giant trees, I stopped dead in my tracks. It's like turning a corner to be confronted by a wall of wood. I was overwhelmed by the immensity of the tree's size and spirit. These sacred trees are so charged with an awe-inspiring presence, known as *mana* by the Māori, that visiting a kauri grove is a mystical experience for many.

The Waipoua Forest in Northland is home to two of the largest living kauri trees left in New Zealand: Tāne Mahuta (Lord of the Forest) and Te Matua Ngahere (Father of the Forest). Tāne Mahuta is the biggest kauri left standing today. It is 51 metres tall and has a staggering girth of 13.8 metres (or 4.4 metres in diameter). Although the tree's age is unknown, it is estimated to be around 2500 years old. Te Matua Ngahere, which is estimated to be over 2000 years old, is Tāne's shorter, stockier neighbour. With a girth of just over 16.5 metres (5.3 metres in diameter), we're talking about a tree as wide as a twelve-seat minibus is long.

There was a swarm of activity as the team swung into action: each tree was sampled, measured and photographed, and its location accurately mapped. I scribed each detail on special waterproof paper designed to withstand the cool, damp conditions of the misty forest. We collected samples by using an increment borer—an oversized corkscrew fitted with a tiny shaft—to hand-drill into the trees. Although the tiny hole left from the extraction quickly filled with natural gums and resins, to be on the safe side, we also injected a small amount of insecticide into the opening to make sure the trees weren't harmed.

I carefully extracted the thin wooden cores and slipped them gently into drinking straws for safe transport back to the lab. With the help of Peter Crossley, the lab's technician, I sanded the samples to a fine polish until hundreds of growth bands sprung up under the microscope. I was amazed at how each of these tiny rings was etched by baking El Niño–driven droughts and drenching La Niña rains that fell centuries ago.

Around 1840, when the European settlement of New Zealand began, kauri forest may have covered 16 000 square kilometres of the North Island. Rampant destruction caused by logging, fire, and land clearing has left a mere 70 square kilometres standing today. Even so, Northland's kauri forests are very biodiverse, containing over 620 plant species, including sixty found nowhere else on Earth. Rare bird species such as the kiwi, kākā and kōkako are often found rustling through the forest. Today, the New Zealand Department of Conservation protects the kauri forests on Crown land. Given their cultural and ecological significance, it's no wonder that local communities and conservationists are protective of their sacred forests. Local people feel a strong custodial stewardship that ensures trees like the iconic specimens of Waipoua will be around for future generations.

While it was my role to analyse cores from living trees in the lab, others in the team analysed samples from colossal trees entombed centuries ago in humid swamps. In many parts of the Northern Hemisphere, the advance of ice sheets and glaciers during the last ice age bulldozed away the top layers of the landscape, forever erasing millennia of environmental history. Closer to home, New Zealand's North Island remained relatively ice-free. The result? Ancient underground kauri rainforests are scattered beneath the unassuming paddocks of the island. Landowners often pull out buried logs weighing 30–60 tonnes. Some are so big they need an excavator pulling in tandem with a bulldozer to unearth them. The material is useful for looking at climate before the peak of the last ice age (20 000 years Before Present, or BP—the year 1950 in radiocarbon dating terms) and even out beyond the limits of radiocarbon dating (around 55 000 years BP).

It gives scientists an opportunity to see the Southern Hemisphere's climate history with a resolution that is unparalleled. Some of the wood is a quarter of a million years old, around thirty times the age of the oldest pyramids in Egypt.

Back across the Tasman, another long tree-ring record has been developed from ancient Tasmanian forests. Since the early 1990s, a team led by tree-ring guru Dr Ed Cook from the University of Columbia has collected wood samples from Huon pine to reconstruct summer temperatures over 3600 years. This seminal record shows that since 1965, Huon pine growth has been unusually rapid for trees that are in many cases over 700 years old. The growth increase corresponds to warming recorded over Tasmania since the 1960s. The reconstruction shows that the most recent 100 years of climate has been highly unusual: the coldest period was recorded in Tasmania from 1890 to 1914 and the warmest was from 1965 to 1989 (the end of the record at the time the study was first published). That is, the tree-ring temperature reconstruction showed a high degree of climate variability—including its highest and lowest extremes—during the twentieth century.

In subsequent studies, the researchers concluded that warming over Tasmania roughly began in 1965 and was largely sustained up to the end of the record in 2001 (when the last tree-ring samples were collected). The late twentieth century is the warmest period of the past 2000 years, and is highly unusual when viewed in the context of the past 3602 years. This finding places the current warming in a much longer historical perspective, adding new support for the existence of anomalous late-twentieth-century warming from a remote corner of the Southern Hemisphere. Interestingly, when compared with many records of the Northern Hemisphere, the variability of low and high temperature extremes contained in the Huon pine record are not as pronounced. This suggests that the vast Southern Ocean may have acted as a buffer, staving off the most extreme temperature swings in Tasmania.

For decades, scientists have been trying to crack the code to use eucalyptus tree rings to develop climate reconstructions from mainland Australia. Eucalypts are a classic Australian tree genus that includes more than 700 species, spanning diverse ecosystems from the monsoonal tropics to the temperate and sub-alpine forests and woodlands of south-eastern Australia. Because of the diversity of ecosystems and environmental conditions in which the genus is found, progress in developing eucalypt tree-ring chronologies would significantly improve the current understanding of Australia's long-term climate. Unfortunately, the most dominant genus on the continent is notoriously difficult to accurately date. Cross-dating, or cross-matching tree-ring sequences against other samples or established tree-ring chronologies, provides the dating control and critical replication needed for the precise science of dendrochronology. The lack of clearly defined annual rings, extensive insect attack and the relatively short life span of eucalyptus species are the main reasons there has been great difficulty in using these trees for climate reconstruction work.

Recently, Matthew Brookhouse, a tenacious dendrochronologist from the Australian National University, has made some exciting progress working with this difficult material. The most promising is his research in the Mount Baw Baw alpine region of Victoria that demonstrates that *Eucalyptus pauciflora*, or the snow gum, has real climate reconstruction potential. Brookhouse has demonstrated that the snow gum's ring width correlates significantly with precipitation (rain and snowfall) and temperature during the winter and spring leading up to the growing season. If enough samples can be collected to improve the replication of the climate signal, the possibility of understanding climate variations in the high country of Victoria would provide us with the first opportunity to make a long-term assessment of the rapid decline in snowfall recorded in Australia's alpine areas in recent decades. Since these trees don't live as long as the Huon pine and kauris, we will never get the long chronologies possible from those ancient forests. But still, these records would go a long way to helping us understand climate variability on the Australian mainland over the past few centuries.

Given that tree rings are just one way to measure past climates, how confident can we be in the conclusion that global warming is moving us out beyond the range of natural climate variability? Fringing the tropical coastlines of northern Australia, coral reefs have also been busy recording the passing of time. So what does the ocean have to say about the possibility of a warming planet?

19
TALES FROM THE TROPICS

The phrase 'It never rains, it pours' rings true in tropical north Queensland. The area receives an average of just over 2 metres of rain per year: that's more than three times the rain that soaks Melbourne in a whole year, and nearly twice that of Sydney. Generally speaking, northern Australia has two distinct seasons: the cooler dry season that spans April through September, and 'the wet' that lasts from October to March. Eighty per cent of the region's rain falls during the tropical downpours of the wet season, when dramatic electrical storms light up the night sky. After the long, hot dry, the warm monsoonal rains resuscitate stagnant tropical river systems. The highly seasonal rainfall of north-eastern Australia results in incredibly variable stream flows, making these rivers some of the most spectacularly erratic in the world.

The Great Barrier Reef snakes along 2300 kilometres of the Queensland coast and contains nearly 3000 separate coral reefs, from just off the coast to 200 kilometres offshore. The staggering scale of this massive reef ecosystem makes it the largest living organism on the face of the planet, one that can even be seen from space. The growth of band-forming coral reef communities varies with how far north they grow and how close they are to the rivers that drain into the surrounding coastal waters. The pulse of fresh river water creates sediment-laden flood plumes that smother the near-shore reefs, and occasionally the reefs further offshore during big rains.

During typical El Niño events, Australia's summer monsoon is weaker than normal, resulting in reduced rainfall, river flow and the number of tropical cyclones that batter the coast. During La Niña events, the summer monsoon is more active than normal, leading to more flooding due to increased tropical cyclone and storm activity. An understanding of how the climate influences present-day corals allows scientists to use these relationships to reconstruct a history of wet and dry years beyond the period covered by weather observations. That is, we use observable, modern conditions to infer changes that are likely to have taken place in the past by looking at wide and narrow sediment or growth layers contained in the coral.

Using X-ray technology, scientists can measure distinct bands in the coral cores that are like the yearly growth rings of trees. The areas where the X-rays strike the image will produce photographic density that turns black when developed, indicating the boundary of annual growth bands. This allows the coral's age to be determined by counting individual bands. To investigate the chemical changes associated with each year, slices from a coral skeleton are placed under ultraviolet (UV) light, revealing bright luminescent bands. We can see alternations between thin and thick layers, peppered with materials washed by flooding rivers into the reef ecosystem. Researchers first identified these seasonal layers in near-shore corals of the Great Barrier Reef in the early 1980s, and were able to link them to the occurrence and intensity of river floods. These bands can be used as a surrogate—or proxy—for annual river flow and seawater salinity back in time. The intensity of the luminescence is related to the distance of the

Figure 37. A slice of Great Barrier Reef coral under ultraviolet light shows annual luminescent banding that provides a history of freshwater river floods.

Source: Reproduced courtesy of Eric Matson, Australian Institute of Marine Studies.

reef away from the coast along the underwater continental shelf, and the average water depth between a reef and the mainland.

In 2015, Dr Janice Lough of the Australian Institute of Marine Studies (AIMS), our region's leading coral expert, compiled a history of floods and droughts going back to 1648 using multiple, accurately dated coral samples collected from the Great Barrier Reef over the past twenty years. The reconstruction highlighted that the frequency of major flood events has increased in far north Queensland's Burdekin River catchment from one in every twenty years before European settlement, to one in every six years since the late twentieth century. Three of the most extreme events in the past 364 years have occurred since 1974, including the extremely wet La Niña year of 2011.

Changes in Burdekin River flow characteristics appears to be associated with a shift towards greater El Niño–Southern Oscillation (ENSO) variability, and rapid ocean warming in the south-western Pacific confirmed by independent palaeoclimatic records throughout the region. This trend in increased tropical rainfall is consistent with the region's future climate change predictions. This groundbreaking work provides evidence that altering the chemical composition of our atmosphere and oceans through increased greenhouse gas concentrations is starting to change tropical rainfall extremes in one of our country's top tourist destinations and biological hotspots.

It's not widely known that more than 90 per cent of the total heat accumulated in the climate system since 1970 has been soaked up by the world's oceans. The greatest warming has taken place close to the surface, with the upper 75 metres of the ocean warming by an average of 0.11°C each decade between 1971 and 2010. The waters surrounding Australia have warmed significantly since 1950, with the greatest surface warming recorded around the west and south-east of the continent. Just like heatwaves on land, long periods of high temperatures can also cause heatwaves in the ocean. Favourable conditions for marine heatwaves can occur due to natural variability, such as the warmer Pacific and Indian ocean waters brought to our region during La Niña conditions. However, research has shown that background warming of the global ocean has led to increased frequency of underwater heatwaves in our region, with the Tasman Sea in particular experiencing surface warming three to four times the global rate. Since 1998, major marine heatwave events have occurred off the coast of Western Australia and Tasmania and in the Coral Sea, greatly affecting the diversity and abundance of fragile coral reef and massive kelp forest ecosystems.

Over the last fifty years, as well as absorbing much of the excess heat held in the atmosphere, the ocean has taken up about 25 per cent of the world's total carbon dioxide (CO_2) emissions. The uptake of CO_2 in seawater causes an increase in acidity, which changes the availability of the carbonate ions that are needed by marine organisms. Acidic conditions dissolve carbonate minerals like calcite and aragonite which are building blocks in the process of calcification. Marine plants and animals use these minerals to make their shells and skeletons. Shell-forming animals, including corals, oysters, shrimp, lobster, many planktonic organisms, and even some fish species, are starting to be affected. This process, known as ocean acidification, is estimated to have increased by around 30 per cent (registered as a decline of 0.1 pH units in the surface ocean) in the 250 years since the beginning of the industrial age.

In a study led by Glenn De'ath from the AIMS in 2009, scientists investigated 328 colonies of massive *Porites* corals from sixty-nine individual reefs of the Great Barrier Reef. Their skeletal records showed that calcification has declined by 14.2 per cent since 1990 and the surrounding waters have acidified. They concluded that such a severe and sudden decline in calcification is unprecedented in the context of at least the past 400 years. It tells us that increases in ocean acidity have the power to decrease the capacity of corals to build skeletons, which in turn decreases their capacity to create a habitat for entire reef ecosystems. The compounding effects of ocean warming and acidification pose a very serious threat to the future diversity and viability of Australia's marine ecosystems. The signs of a warming planet are now being more deeply imprinted on our natural world with every passing year.

To understand how ocean temperatures have varied over past centuries, coral records have also been used to reconstruct past temperatures of the tropical oceans around Australia. Sea surface temperature reconstructions from coral records typically rely on fluctuations in geochemical tracers recorded in coral skeletons. These are mostly based on measurements of stable oxygen isotopes or strontium/calcium ratios that vary primarily as a function of water temperature. Coral records provide rich information about tropical climate dynamics like the variability associated with ENSO events, and longer-term changes related to the phenomenon known as the Inter-decadal Pacific Oscillation (IPO). The IPO can be thought of as the deep memory of all the accumulated El Niño and La Niña events that have been experienced from decade to decade.

In Australia, the negative phase of the IPO is associated with more La Niña events that bring widespread rainfall as warmer than average sea surface temperatures collect in the waters around Indonesia, known as the Western Pacific warm pool. This body of water, which spans the western waters of the equatorial Pacific to the eastern Indian Ocean, holds the warmest seawaters in the world. Understanding the long-term behaviour of the tropical Indo–Pacific waters and their associated influence on regional rainfall is one of the key challenges facing the climate science community today. The area is the heat engine of the Asian and Australian monsoon systems that impacts the livelihoods of millions of people.

Coral records collected from the tropical Indo-Pacific region show the unusual nature of the late-twentieth-century warming of the tropical oceans. In 2006, using a network of fourteen coral cores to reconstruct the whole of the tropics that fall between 30 degrees north and 30 degrees south for the first time, British palaeoclimatologist Rob Wilson and his colleagues showed that the 1990s were the warmest period in the tropics for the last 250 years. They estimated that there has been a 0.5–1°C warming of tropical sea surface temperatures from the coolest period of the early nineteenth century (before the onset of the Industrial Revolution) to the present. They compared their results to climate model simulations and concluded that only models that included greenhouse gases can explain the recent warming seen in the coral record. Subsequent studies have confirmed and expanded these original results.

In 2002, palaeoclimatologist Erica Hendy reconstructed a detailed temperature and ocean water history of the Great Barrier Reef going back to 1565 using eight coral cores. Her results showed a dramatic freshening of waters in the Coral Sea after 1870, coinciding with warming tropical ocean temperatures following the start of the Industrial Revolution until the 1980s, when the coral cores were collected. This trend is also seen simultaneously throughout the south-western Pacific in areas including New Caledonia and Vanuatu. A 2012 study by marine scientist Kristine DeLong reconstructed regional sea surface temperature variability from New Caledonia back to 1649. It also reported a significant regional warming trend of 0.73°C from 1890 to 1999, in line with the observed modern warming of the global ocean.

In the summer of 2010–11, a La Niña event led to unprecedented warming of the waters surrounding Western Australia. A severe underwater heatwave resulted in the first-ever reports of large-scale coral bleaching and fish kills in the region. The long-term warming trend in the western Pacific and eastern Indian Ocean exacerbated the so-called 'Ningaloo Niño' event. An analysis of coral reef records by marine scientist Jens Zinke reconstructed past sea surface temperatures from the Houtman

Abrolhos islands, around 50 kilometres off the coast of Western Australia, to determine whether the 2010–11 Ningaloo Niño was unusual in a longer-term context. The study showed a significant warming trend of around 1.16°C from 1795 to 2010, with 0.58°C of the warming occurring after 1950. It concluded that ocean warming in the region is at its highest level since 1795, when the coral records begin.

The coral analysis suggests that the warming trend recently observed in the tropical waters of the Indo-Pacific region has significantly altered the severity of ocean temperature extremes. Using long-term coral estimates, the research team calculated that the waters off Western Australia were 0.64°C warmer after 1980 than they were between 1795 and 1979. They concluded that recently recorded marine heatwaves are unprecedented in severity, and are likely to become more frequent as ocean warming accelerates as the planet continues to warm. This threatens the current diversity of coral reef ecosystems and associated fishing and tourism industries. Our rapidly warming planet is now prompting profound changes in Australia's oceans. Scientists can barely keep up with reporting the changes as records continue to be broken with every passing year.

20
FROZEN IN TIME

Far from the warmth of the tropical oceans, ice sheets and mountain glaciers are also busy entombing past seasons in the snows that fall in remote wilderness regions of the world. Ice-core records allow scientists to reconstruct snow accumulation, temperature and air chemistry to generate detailed records of past climate going back 800 000 years. By looking at air bubbles trapped in ice core layers, we can calculate how modern amounts of carbon dioxide and other greenhouse gases like methane compare with those of the past. It also allows us to see how past concentrations of greenhouse gases have fluctuated with temperature, providing an insight into the interconnectedness of the Earth's climate system.

Aside from Australia, Antarctica is the only other continent in the world that lies entirely within the Southern Hemisphere. Our southern neighbour is the coldest, windiest and driest continent on Earth. The average annual temperature ranges from about −10°C on the coast to −60°C in the vast interior of the east Antarctic ice sheet. The lowest temperature ever reliably measured on Earth was a mind-blowing −89.2°C registered at Vostok Station on 21 July 1983, at the heart of east Antarctica.

Over 3800 kilometres south of Perth lies Casey Station, the Australian Antarctic Division's research outpost on the icy coast of eastern Antarctica. For years now, a group of dedicated scientists led by Tas van Ommen have been studying ice cores drilled from Law Dome, a very high snow accumulation site that has been studied intensively to decipher the isolated region's climate history. Each year, approximately 70 centimetres of snow falls in the study area, providing an unparalleled, seasonally resolved record of the climate of the east coast of Antarctica.

Australian scientists are especially interested in ice cores collected from Law Dome because it provides a long-term history of the climate variability influencing the vast Southern Ocean. Australia being a giant island that spans the latitudes of 9–44 degrees south, it is surrounded by the huge expanses of the Indian, Pacific and Southern oceans, which exert their dominance at different times during the year. The weather experienced during each season is driven by differences between the heating of the land and the sea as the Earth rotates around the sun. These contrasting temperature and pressure gradients set the scene for the complex atmospheric and ocean cycles that drive Australia's climate.

As the south-western corner of Western Australia doesn't have tropical sources influencing its rainfall, the region is more reliant on winter rains from the Southern Ocean westerlies. A recent analysis of snow accumulation from Law Dome ice cores going back to 1250 shows a significant increase in the precipitation falling in eastern Antarctica since the 1970s. This corresponds with a simultaneous decrease in winter rainfall observed in the south-western corner of Western Australia, of approximately 15–20 per cent. Since 1996, this decline from the long-term average has increased to around 25 per cent. Although there are complex seasonal factors at play, the results are consistent with observed and modelled circulation changes that suggest a positive phase of the Southern Annular Mode (SAM)—the north–south migration of the westerly wind belt that circles Antarctica—experienced since the mid-1970s has been driven by the cooling of Antarctica's lower stratosphere, mainly through human-caused ozone depletion.

Using a reconstruction developed using ice cores and tree rings from across the Southern Hemisphere, palaeoclimatologist Nerilie Abram from the Australian National University demonstrated that the SAM may currently be in the most extreme positive phase recorded over the last 1000 years. She also compared her palaeoclimate estimates to climate model simulations and found that the positive trend in the SAM, seen as early as the 1940s in the palaeoclimate record, is associated with not only stratospheric ozone depletion but also increasing greenhouse gas levels which have altered the north–south temperature difference that fuels westerlies in the Southern Ocean. Continued increases in atmospheric greenhouse gases are predicted to force the SAM further towards its positive phase over the coming century even as the ozone hole repairs, with serious implications for the future of southern Australian rainfall.

Despite Law Dome's importance in understanding past changes in regional rainfall, the record is perhaps better known for its globally significant 2000-year carbon dioxide history. As snow transforms into ice each year, it traps air bubbles that provide a sample of the composition of our ancient atmosphere. The ratio of stable isotopes of either oxygen or hydrogen in the water molecules is related to the temperature at the time when the snow fell. Scientists from the CSIRO have reconstructed changes in the greenhouse gases of carbon dioxide, methane and nitrous oxide in meticulous detail, year by year for the past two millennia.

Data from Law Dome show us that carbon dioxide concentrations were stable over the last millennium until the early nineteenth century, when concentrations started to rise sharply. The ice-core record allows us to contextualise the dramatic rise in carbon dioxide levels from about 280 ppm (parts per million) at around the start of the industrial era in the year 1800, to 409 ppm in May 2017. That's an increase of 46 per cent in just over 200 years, primarily a result of the burning of fossil fuels and land clearing to support human activity around the world. Unfortunately, carbon dioxide levels are increasing by around 3 ppm with every passing year, baking in even more warming of the planet.

Measurements from the longest ice cores drilled on Earth show that even slight changes in temperature can influence other climate variables, like the concentration of greenhouse gases in the atmosphere, amplifying

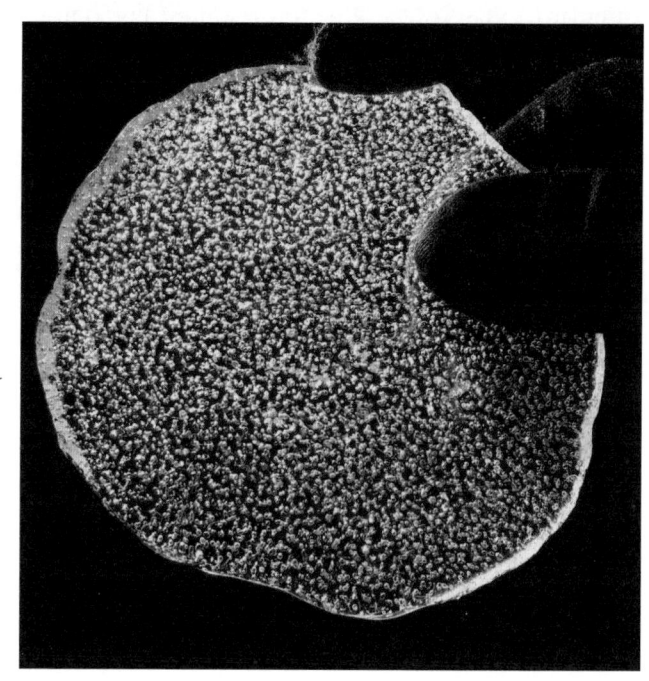

Figure 38. Ancient air bubbles trapped in a slice of an Antarctic ice core reveal information about the Earth's pre-industrial climate.

Source: Reproduced courtesy of Tas van Ommen, Australian Antarctic Division.

initial disturbances. This process is known as a positive feedback loop; that is, a nudge to one factor leads to a change in another, which in turn causes the first factor to change more, shifting everything in the same direction. For example, some palaeoclimate records suggest that during warm periods there was a lagged but corresponding increase in greenhouse gas concentrations. Melting ice sheets in the Northern Hemisphere flooded the ocean with fresh water, disrupting ocean circulation and shifting the energy balance between the hemispheres.

The loss of ice sheets also means less sunlight was reflected back into space, so the land surface surrounding the oceans absorbed more of the incoming solar radiation. Permafrost areas that previously buried frozen forests under thick ice sheets began to thaw, releasing vast quantities of carbon dioxide and methane into the atmosphere. As ocean temperatures increased, sea water began releasing stored carbon dioxide into the atmosphere. All these factors amplified the warming trend that led to even more carbon dioxide being released, a vicious cycle of sorts.

Sometimes climate change sceptics seize on this apparent lag in greenhouse gas concentrations to say that carbon dioxide is not the cause of the recent warming. It's an erroneous 'chicken or the egg' argument. Regardless of which came first, increasing levels of carbon dioxide become both the cause and effect of further warming. However, in a more recent 2013 analysis of Antarctic ice cores over the past 800 000 years, Frederic Parrenin found no evidence of a significant lag, indicating that temperatures did not begin to rise hundreds of years before the concentration of atmospheric carbon dioxide, as was suggested by earlier studies which may have suffered from dating uncertainties that may have obscured these fine-scale features of the climate record.

The real takeaway message here is that the long-term relationship between warm temperatures and high greenhouse gas levels seen in ice cores confirm that these aspects of the climate system are intricately linked. The balance of the Earth's climate is in fact very sensitive to small disturbances that, once in play, can be reinforced by complex feedback processes that will continue indefinitely until a new equilibrium is found. This is why scientists are nervously monitoring the planet's receding ice sheets in Greenland and the west Antarctic, wondering if yet another record-breaking summer will trigger instability in the Earth's thermostat and cause abrupt and dramatic changes to the climatic stability we've enjoyed for thousands of years.

While climatic destabilisation might sound like science fiction, the observable laws of physics playing out in real time tell us that this day will surely come. The real question is not if this will happen, but when. As the planet continues to warm because of increased industrial activity, we'll see further increases in greenhouse gas concentrations. It really is as simple as that. The evidence observed each year continues to reinforce our fundamental understanding of the theoretical thermodynamics of the climate system.

On 10 May 2016, the symbolic carbon dioxide level of 400 ppm was recorded at the Bureau of Meteorology's Cape Grim atmospheric monitoring station. Cape Grim, on the remote north-western tip of Tasmania, is one of the only stations analysing baseline carbon levels in the Southern Hemisphere. Because most greenhouse gas emissions come from the more densely populated and industrialised Northern Hemisphere, it takes a few years for the atmosphere to mix enough to be registered in Southern Hemisphere readings. However, not long after Cape Grim crossed the symbolic threshold, on 14 May 2016, Casey Station in eastern Antarctica also recorded 400 ppm. These measurements indicate that the atmospheric carbon dioxide concentration of the entire Southern Hemisphere is now at or above 400 ppm, and it is unlikely to drop back below this level for many decades or even centuries to come.

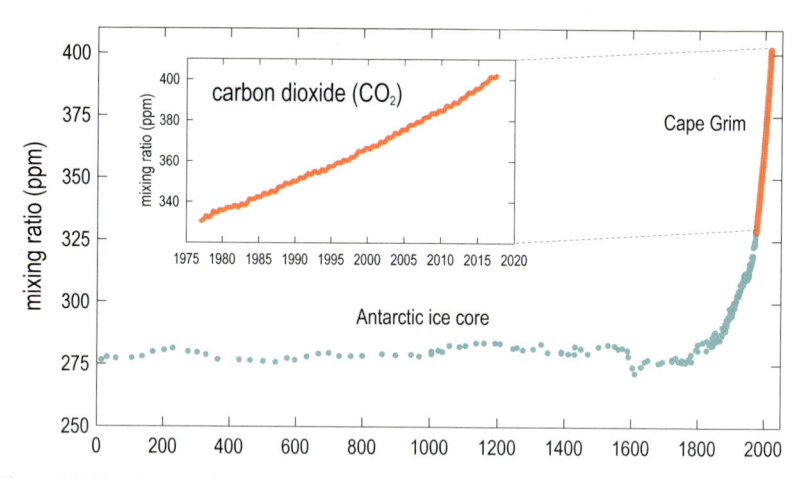

Figure 39. Two thousand-year ice-core measurements from Law Dome, east Antarctica, combined with instrumental observations from Cape Grim from 1976 to 2016. Together they show the rapid increase of carbon dioxide since around 1800 as global industrialisation accelerated the burning of fossil fuels to support human activities.

Source: Reproduced courtesy of Paul Krummel and David Etheridge, CSIRO Oceans & Atmosphere Climate Science Centre. Data courtesy of the Cape Grim Baseline Air Pollution Station/Australian Bureau of Meteorology and the Australian Antarctic Division.

The record high levels of carbon dioxide concentrations recently measured in the Southern Hemisphere are well outside the natural variability recorded in the longest ice cores drilled from the iconic Dome C record in eastern Antarctica that spans 800 000 years. The last time carbon dioxide levels were at 400 ppm was during the mid-Pliocene geologic period, around three million years ago. Humans did not yet exist and the planet was some 2–3°C warmer than it is today. Ice sheets had melted to the point where the sea level was higher by between 10 and 40 metres, with a best estimate of 25 metres often adopted in climate modelling studies. A repeat of this now would be unthinkable. It would reconfigure the world map and human societies in ways we couldn't even imagine. The acceleration of carbon dioxide levels is pushing global temperatures beyond any point human civilisation has ever experienced before. Sea level rise is currently underway, and in places like western Antarctica it is now considered unstoppable by some experts. Although it will take some time for melting ice from the land to reach the ocean, at least a 1-metre rise in the global sea level is considered likely by 2100.

When other heat-trapping greenhouse gases, such as methane and nitrous oxide, are considered in the calculations, the situation becomes even more alarming. The so-called 'carbon dioxide-equivalent' level, which takes the full suite of greenhouse gases into account, reached 489 ppm in 2016. If emissions continue unchecked for another two decades, we are on track to pass a carbon dioxide concentration of 450 ppm. Once that is reached, the levels of all greenhouse gases put together (carbon dioxide, methane, nitrous oxide and synthetic greenhouse gases) would add up to the equivalent of about 550 ppm of carbon dioxide. At that point, average global temperatures would likely reach 2°C above pre-industrial levels and continue rising for decades as the Earth tries to adjust to the incredibly rapid changes being forced upon it. A 2°C warming would see the disappearance of virtually all of the world's coral reef ecosystems, devastating losses affecting the Earth's biodiversity, and increased vulnerability of human populations to sea level rise, cyclones, floods and droughts. It's an apocalyptic future that we must do everything humanly possible to avoid.

21
EBBS AND FLOWS

As humans, we have been drawn to water for millennia. Being by the ocean, a lake or a river always has a way of reconnecting us with our most primitive essence. It reacquaints us with the wisdom found in the ebb and flow of all things, and the insights that arise from being a silent witness to the beauty of our natural world. Our early ancestors also gathered around water bodies to feed from their abundance, access the fresh water needed to sustain life, or simply to play and be refreshed in the way only water can do.

Many of the lakes and wetlands found on mainland Australia are ephemeral. They swell and shrink in response to the erratic rains that characterise our country. When good rains fall, sediments are washed into low-lying areas of the landscape, leaving behind gritty layers that settle at the bottom of water bodies. In drier times, silty particles that hang suspended in the water finally start to settle during calmer conditions. Just like tree rings, sequences of sedimentary layers are a good proxy for understanding how climate has varied in a local area.

But unlike trees, sediment bands are not often annually layered in Australian waters. As we swing from baking droughts to torrential rains, lake levels rise and fall. In many parts of Australia, rainfall is influenced by large-scale fluctuations in the Pacific, Indian and Southern oceans, as well as more localised rains associated with intense storms or cyclones. The lion's share of Australian rainfall is influenced by La Niña events that generally occur every 3–7 years. Since heavy rainfall is so erratic, Australian lakes rarely record year-to-year conditions. Instead, they offer excellent long-term records that span thousands of years, well beyond what is available from tree-ring and coral records, providing invaluable insights into our climatic history.

In the early years of European settlement, explorers expected to find a vast sea in the middle of Australia. Many went searching for it, and died in the process. In 1840, Edward John Eyre became the first European to lay eyes on the prize, but the immense salt pan was a far cry from the shimmering sea he'd dreamed of. As its catchment lies completely within the arid and semi-arid deserts of central Australia, Lake Eyre usually contains little or no water. In fact, located in the most arid part of Australia, the region receives an average annual rainfall of less than 125 millimetres and has a staggering evaporation rate of 2.5 metres per year. At 1.2 million square kilometres, the Lake Eyre Basin covers almost one-sixth of Australia and is one of the world's largest internally draining river systems. On the rare occasions when it is full, it is the largest lake in Australia, covering approximately 9700 square kilometres. The basin lies approximately 15 metres below sea level, the lowest elevation on the Australian mainland.

Since 2012, the lake has been known by the joint name of Kati Thanda–Lake Eyre. The local name Kati Thanda means 'wetland in the desert'. It is probably the most spectacular example of an outback lake that fills in response to La Niña rains. Rainfall associated with warmer than average conditions in the Indian Ocean around Indonesia, known as a negative Indian Ocean Dipole (IOD) event, has also been associated with the significant flooding and incredible greening of the driest deserts of Australia.

Even though the Kati Thanda–Lake Eyre Basin contains some of the world's last unregulated wild river systems, the arid climate means that these are not typical rivers. All of the creeks and rivers only run for short periods following rain. The sporadic rainfall that flows down the Coopers Creek and Diamantina River systems are the most variable in Australia, and even more erratic than those in other arid parts of the world like Africa and South America. In modern times, the lake filled in 1950, 1955, 1974, 1976, and most recently in 2010–11 forming a stunning ephemeral wetland. The filling of 1974, when the lake rose by 6 metres during the nationwide drenching of that year, is considered the most famous in the region's history.

When the floodwaters pulse down the inland river systems of Queensland and the Northern Territory, the usually dry lakebed covered by a thick salty crust is dramatically transformed into a shallow lake. Enormous flocks of birds arrive to feast on the bounty of fish life and aquatic invertebrates now teeming in the extraordinary oasis. The air is filled with the sound of thousands of birds, including pelicans, swans, sandpipers and terns, migrating to breed on the shores and newly formed sandbar islands. As the lake dries up and the water evaporates, its salinity increases and it often turns pink as gypsum salt crystals form. The filling of the lake is such a big occasion that there is even a Lake Eyre Yacht Club—a group of dedicated sailors who come from all over Australia to navigate the fleeting waters of one of the most ethereal landscapes in the world.

Because of the highly erratic nature of flooding in the lake and its remote location, a recent sedimentary history of Kati Thanda–Lake Eyre remains elusive. We know that the rainfall is the lifeblood of the lake system and the wildlife it supports. Future changes to this delicately balanced ecosystem have the potential to endanger the diversity of the rare and unique plants and animals that call this remarkable part of Australia home. Continued warming of Australia is projected to hit the arid zone the hardest. Under our current high-greenhouse-emissions path, the rangeland regions of central Australia are estimated to warm a further 2.9–5.3°C by 2090. In areas that already have summer temperatures well into the forties, it's very likely that 50°C summer temperatures will soon become the new normal.

While rainfall is more difficult to predict, the latest CSIRO climate change projections have medium–high confidence that the area will experience substantial declines in winter and spring rainfall of up to 50 per cent of the 1986–2005 average by the end of the century. While changes to rainfall during the summer monsoon and cyclone season remain uncertain, the clear increase in temperature and evaporation rates is very likely to see an overall drying out of the region. As these projections come to pass, it may see the collapse of some of the most unique desert ecosystems on the planet. An already precariously balanced environment where rainfall is too low or erratic for agricultural cropping is likely to become even more hostile. Conditions that are currently only suitable for livestock grazing may become unviable as extreme heat and limited water availability transform our arid zone into a truly uninhabitable region.

It's hard to imagine a future where large parts of our country may be too hot and too dry to support life as we know it today. But as extreme as this might sound, these are the conservative projections that state-of-the-art science is telling us are a very real probability.

Forty kilometres north of Canberra, just over the New South Wales border, lies another iconic Australian lake that has been the subject of local legends for decades. Shrouded in mystery, Lake George has captured the imagination of locals who have marvelled at the 'disappearing lake' for generations. The lake's notoriety was entrenched long before Europeans arrived. Local Ngunnawal people say that Lake George, or Weereewa, was known for its bad spirits, including Birik who tormented people, and a bunyip—a mythical creature of Aboriginal legend which haunted swamps and billabongs. More recent local myths suggest that the lake level has the ability to predict the outcome of Australia's federal elections.

For scientists, there is no great mystery about the lake's changing water levels. Far less exotically, Lake George is just a rainfall-sensitive basin with no known outlet, so lake levels rise and fall in direct response to changes in rainfall and evaporation. The lake has long been recognised as having highly variable levels due to its location west of the Great Dividing Range, a mountain chain that provides a barrier to coastal rain-bearing systems heading for inland Australia. Lake level measurements began in 1816 and were first published by HC Russell in 1877. The historical record shows big swings in water levels, from a very wet period in the 1820s when the lake was described as a 'magnificent sheet of water'. In 1824 Lake George was reported to be '20 miles long and 8 miles wide, almost entirely enclosed with thickly wooded, steep hills'. Not long after, in the 1840s, the region experienced a severe drought that saw the lake evaporate into thin air.

Figure 40. Artist's impression of the national capital of Canberra built around Lake George.
Source: Coulter, C (1901). Reproduced courtesy of the National Library of Australia.

The late nineteenth century was also very wet from around 1875, up to the early twentieth century. Water levels were so high that in 1901 bureaucrats considered placing Lake George at the centre of a planned 'Federal City'. An artistic sketch held by the National Library of Australia shows a Venice-like scene of buildings on the shores of Lake George. It's a good thing they didn't actually place the nation's capital on the banks of a lake that comes and goes with the rain!

Although there were reports of locals fishing, swimming and boating on the lake during the 1950s and 1970s, the lake has slowly dried up again following the marked rainfall decline experienced in south-eastern Australia since the 1990s. During the height of the Big Dry in 2009, the lake dried up completely, but it refilled after the heavy rains of June 2016. This dance of boom and bust has played out so many times it is now firmly entrenched in the Australian psyche. The difference is that now scientists are asking us to consider a collective future where there is a longer wait between drought-breaking rains. And when they do finally arrive, they may have the power to unleash extreme deluges that will wreak havoc on our communities.

22
PIECING TOGETHER THE CLIMATE JIGSAW

As the availability of individual palaeoclimate records began to increase, efforts to reconstruct the Earth's temperature history began to emerge. It's a little known fact that the first quantitative reconstruction of Northern Hemisphere temperatures was actually published in 1979 in the journal *Geophysical Research Letters*. The obscure paper was prepared by PhD student Brian Groveman and his advisor Helmut Landsberg from the University of Maryland. The authors compiled twenty instrumental records and two tree-ring chronologies from Alaska and Finland to reconstruct annual Northern Hemisphere temperatures back to 1579. The paper, which mostly emphasised the feasibility of the method rather than the results, unsurprisingly didn't receive too much attention at the time.

The potential of the idea lay dormant until 1989 when two leading American dendrochronologists, Gordon Jacoby and Rosanne D'Arrigo from Columbia University, used eleven tree-ring chronologies from Canada and Alaska to estimate Northern Hemisphere temperatures back to 1671. By using key regions that were identified in instrumental records as being highly representative indicators of hemisphere-wide conditions, the pair reported that twentieth-century warmth was anomalous in the context of at least three centuries. It was the first time a conclusion about an entire hemisphere's temperature history had been published.

During the early 1990s, renowned American palaeoclimatologist Raymond Bradley and British climatologist Phil Jones expanded these ideas by drawing together the first rudimentary 'global' survey of twenty-two palaeoclimate records. As they could only find four records from the whole Southern Hemisphere, again the study focused on the Northern

Hemisphere. They reported hemispheric temperature variations over the past 500 years using a basic averaging technique that still gets used today.

The first statistically sophisticated analysis, involving 112 palaeoclimate records, was published in a seminal 1998 *Nature* paper by Michael Mann, Raymond Bradley and Malcolm Hughes. Their study used tree rings, corals, ice cores, lake sediments, historical documents and long instrumental records to reconstruct temperature over the last 600 years in the Northern Hemisphere. They reported that greenhouse gases emerged as the dominant influence on temperature variability during the twentieth century. The analysis was extended in 1999 to cover the last 1000 years, and the results incorporated into the third United Nations global climate report coordinated by the Intergovernmental Panel on Climate Change (IPCC) in 2001. In 2003, Mike Mann and Phil Jones extended the reconstruction again to cover the last 1800 years, providing the most comprehensive estimates of Northern Hemisphere and global temperatures ever attempted.

On the basis of these Northern Hemisphere and global temperature reconstructions, it was concluded that temperatures gradually dropped from relative highs at around 1000 CE during a period known as the Medieval Climate Anomaly, to a minimum at around 1850 during an epoch known as the Little Ice Age. The most striking feature of the reconstruction that received the most attention was the sharp rise in temperatures that began emerging during the twentieth century. The graph that illustrated the trend was nicknamed the 'hockey stick' curve, as it showed slowly declining temperatures over about 900 years followed by an abrupt warming in the late twentieth century, akin to the shape of the upturned blade of a hockey stick.

The hockey stick received widespread attention as it was showcased in the IPCC's *Third Assessment Report* released in 2001 because the precision of the work represented a major leap forward in the science. For the first time, researchers were able to accurately trace global temperatures back, year by year, for 1000 years, when the lion's share of Earth's annually banded records are available. From this vantage point, scientists were able to confidently place twentieth-century temperature trends into a context that was no longer limited to that century's instrumental record. The strength of the results was reinforced by the multiple lines of evidence collected from tropical coral reefs, ancient forests, deep-sea sediments and remote polar ice caps. By using temperature estimates from the natural world, it became clear that the warming of the planet experienced since the 1990s was exceptional. The groundbreaking work was widely viewed as definitive evidence of human-induced global warming. It became an iconic graph, a symbol of the clear imprint of human activity on the Earth's climate system.

Perhaps unsurprisingly, the hockey stick immediately became a target for climate change sceptics. A number of vocal critics began debating the data and methods used in the reconstruction, as well as the professional integrity of Mann, Bradley and Hughes. They argued that the scientists had engaged in data manipulation to reverse-engineer politically driven evidence for a warming planet. The furore received a lot of political attention, including a lengthy 'Civil Investigative Demand' by the attorney-general of Virginia, Mann's home state at the time. Under the accusation of academic misconduct, the University of Virginia was instructed to produce documents dating from 1999 to 2005, including all emailed or written correspondence from, to or relating to lead author Michael Mann and thirty-nine named climate scientists, research assistants and administrative staff at the university. Anything connected with Mann's research, including six years' worth of emails, thousands of lines of computer code, and records of all financial transactions associated with his research grants, were demanded and then picked over by hostile lawyers.

Several years later, after ongoing attempts to derail the work of some of the world's leading climate scientists, the arguments against both the studies and the integrity of the scientists involved were dismissed by no less than eight independent investigations. The rock-solid integrity of science had held up against the battering it received. But it was a Pyrrhic victory. Scientists had been subjected to hate mail and even death threats, and the harassment had taken an enormous personal toll. Some of the brightest climate scientists of our time began contemplating suicide and developed a need for medication to cope with the anxiety of the vicious scrutiny. When my team published Australasia's first 1000-year temperature reconstruction, my life would also become a total nightmare. Personal and legal harassment is intended to bully scientists into silence, to have us question ourselves more than we already do under the rigorous code of professional scientific practice.

The real issue has never been the hockey stick's data or methods but rather its implied threat to the status quo of those who oppose government regulation to reduce global greenhouse gas emissions. It really isn't any more complex than that. The burning of fossil fuels to support human activities is rapidly warming the planet to the point where we are drastically changing the equilibrium needed to sustain life on Earth. Meanwhile, a mountain of scientific evidence tells us that we must price pollution and stop treating the atmosphere as an unregulated industrial sewer.

Since the original 1998 hockey stick graph, more than two dozen reconstructions, using various statistical methods and combinations of palaeoclimate records, have supported the broad consensus shown in the results of the seminal studies by Mike Mann and his colleagues. The IPCC's *Fifth Assessment Report*, released in 2013, strengthened the conclusion that it was 'likely'—a 66–100 per cent probability in IPCC language—that the period 1983–2012 was the warmest thirty-year period of the last 1400 years in the Northern Hemisphere.

The most concerted effort to reconstruct regional temperatures over the past 2000 years was coordinated by the international Past Global Change (PAGES) 'Regional 2k' network. The PAGES International Project Office in Switzerland serves as an international headquarters to facilitate collaborative research on the Earth's past climates. The 2k network is a group of self-organised volunteer scientists working on reconstructing climate histories from each of the continents of the world as well as the oceans. The network was formed in 2008 as a response to the gaps highlighted in the IPCC's *Fourth Assessment Report*. Mike Mann's hockey stick had given us a clearer understanding of Northern Hemisphere temperature variations, but what happened in different regions of the world? Was the climate history of Europe or the Arctic the same as that of South America or Australasia?

From the insights gained from the Northern Hemisphere temperature reconstructions, broadly speaking the last 1000 years, which is the period of the Earth's history that has the greatest availability of annually banded palaeoclimate records, can be divided into three distinct epochs. The first is known as the Medieval Climate Anomaly, a period of relative warmth that broadly spans the 900–1300 period. Until the late 1990s, the period was referred to as the Medieval Warm Period, but the name change acknowledges that there were also significant swings in precipitation in some areas during that time. The warm period was first described from Northern Hemisphere regions around the North Atlantic. The most famous example comes from Greenland when the retreat of sea ice influenced the exploration of the Arctic by the Vikings. Historical records reveal that the coast of Iceland was relatively ice-free, so people were able to settle in formerly inhospitable parts of the country. There is evidence to suggest that Nordic people settled south-western Greenland along the fringes of the ice sheet, where they even managed to grow barley in the usually brutal cold of the high Arctic.

Following this warm period, the pronounced cooling known as the Little Ice Age occurred, from around 1300–1850 CE. This period contains a lot of evidence of explosive volcanic activity, including the massive tropical eruption of Tambora, Indonesia, in 1816, known as the 'year without a summer' in the Northern Hemisphere. There is evidence of the expansion of glaciers in the European Alps and the Southern Alps of New Zealand from the mid-seventeenth to the mid-nineteenth centuries. Very cold conditions resulted in historical reports of frost fairs and ice skating on the River Thames in England and the Pompenburg canal in The Netherlands. Our team's work with historical records from south-eastern Australia also provides fascinating accounts of snow falling in the coastal, low-elevation cities of Sydney and Melbourne during the 1830s.

The Little Ice Age ended with the start of the Industrial Revolution. The period from approximately 1750 to the present is referred to as the Industrial Period, or more recently, the Anthropocene. This period saw the rapid introduction of greenhouse gases and aerosols into the atmosphere from human activities. For the first time, natural variability was not the only show in town. Our climate now contained the imprint of human activity on the Earth's natural systems. Since 1850, global temperatures have risen by approximately 0.87°C relative to 1961–90 levels, or around 1°C above pre-industrial levels (1850–1900 average). During this period there has been an exponential increase in the size of the human population, and consequentially vast modifications to the Earth's surface to support human activities.

The most pronounced feature of the Anthropocene is known as the 'great acceleration': a period from the 1950s when unprecedented rates of environmental change altered the face of the planet. These changes are so profound that they will be permanently engraved in the Earth's geologic records in ways that will be clear millions of years from today. It is now evident that the Earth is changing faster than the adaptation and resilience thresholds of many natural ecosystems that support human activity. Scientists fear that human societies may not be able to adapt to the rate or nature of these changes as the planet attempts to restore its equilibrium. For example, currently productive agricultural areas like the Murray–Darling Basin may transition into unusable arid land, or the desert regions of Australia will become uninhabitable. If left unchecked, climate change will trigger a cascade of irreversible change to our landscapes and the way we live in our country.

Of these three periods of the last 1000 years, the most controversial is probably the Medieval Climate Anomaly. Debate has raged as to whether medieval times were warmer than twentieth-century extremes, and if this warmth was recorded globally. Climate change sceptics often argue that this event is evidence that the globe has been through other warm periods that were equally as warm or warmer than today's climate. Although the Northern Hemisphere temperature reconstructions showed the late twentieth century was the warmest period of the last 1400 years, some climate change sceptics remain adamant that the recent warming is being blown out of proportion. They reason that we've been through warm periods before, so why is the current warming any different?

From the perspective of a professional climate scientist, the logic of that argument is flawed. The real interest lies in being able to study how the climate varied during pre-industrial times, when the Earth was only operating under natural conditions, before the introduction of human-generated greenhouse gases tainted the climate records. If there are dramatic climate extremes that occur naturally, then what happens when you add greenhouse gases to the system? Do historical climate extremes pale in comparison?

A handful of studies have shown that epic periods of drought spanning decades, known as 'mega-droughts', occurred in the south-western United States and monsoon Asia over the past 1000 years. The thought of the world's global monsoon systems, which help support over half the human population, collapsing for decades on end would be catastrophic today. But if such dramatic events have happened naturally in the past, is it possible that such extreme shifts in our climate could happen again? The societal implications were so great that they warranted further attention. Armed with these curly questions, the global army of the PAGES Regional 2k network scientists got to work.

From 2009 until 2013, palaeoclimatologists from all over the globe held workshops to bring together and archive all of the annually banded palaeo-climate records that existed from each region of the world that spanned as much of the past 2000 years as possible. The goal was to use the expertise of local scientists who best understood their regional climate to develop 'best estimate' temperature reconstructions for Europe, North America, the Arctic, Antarctic, Asia, Australasia and South America. An African region was also defined but unfortunately records from this part of the world are not yet able to support this type of analysis. As I was the leader of the Australasian working group, my team at the University of Melbourne was responsible for developing the temperature curve for Australia, New Zealand and the surrounding oceans. It was a challenging job, but one that needed to be done to make sure our region didn't get left behind.

In 2013, seventy-eight scientists from twenty-eight countries developed the most comprehensive study of regional temperatures over the last 2000 years ever compiled. The results as published in the journal *Nature Geoscience* painted a complex picture, one of diversity and difference. But the most consistent feature across all the regions was a long-term cooling trend that lasted until the mid to late 1800s. From then on, after just a century of industrial activity, the Earth reversed a 1400-year cooling trend. Temperatures during the period 1971–2000 were higher than at any other time in those 1400 years. The warming was seen across all regions of the world, suggesting a common influence. The study also showed that regional warm periods like the Medieval Climate Anomaly did not occur everywhere, like the late-twentieth-century warming. In Europe, the Arctic and Antarctica, medieval temperatures were equally as warm as the late twentieth century. There was no clear signal of the medieval warming in Australasia. Instead, temperatures recorded during 1971–2000 were warmer than any other thirty-year period over the past 1000 years in our region.

It turned out the Medieval Climate Anomaly wasn't a global event after all. It was a big leap forward in the science, but many questions still remained unanswered.

23
TAKING THE TEMPERATURE OF THE SOUTHERN HEMISPHERE

As regional temperature reconstruction efforts began to take shape, my long-held feeling that more could be done to better understand the climate history of the Southern Hemisphere started to stir once more. At the first meeting of the PAGES Regional 2k network in Oregon in July 2009, I gave a presentation on the availability of palaeoclimate records from Australasia. I also presented some preliminary results of a rainfall reconstruction I was working on for south-eastern Australia with my colleagues in Melbourne as we remained in the tight grip of the Big Dry, then entering its thirteenth year. During a coffee break, I met Swiss palaeoclimatologist Raphael (Raphi) Neukom, who was in the process of wrapping up his PhD work on pulling together South America's palaeoclimate records, and had just finished developing temperature and rainfall reconstructions for that region. We talked excitedly about possibilities that finally felt within reach: Did we now have enough records to develop a reliable temperature history of the Southern Hemisphere?

Of over twenty-five hemispheric-scale temperature reconstructions published in recent decades, only three covered the ocean-dominated Southern Hemisphere. The reconstructions that did exist only included seven or fewer records for the entire hemisphere. They were always provided as peripheral components of Northern Hemisphere and global reconstruction efforts, with the caveat that 'more confident statements about long-term temperature variations in the Southern Hemisphere and globe on the whole must await additional proxy data collection'. At the time, I was the only person in Australia trying to collate all the annually resolved records, and here was Raphi with his amazing collection from

South America. It was clear what needed to be done, so we wasted no time in getting started.

In September 2009, I visited Raphi at the Oeschger Centre for Climate Change at the University of Bern in Switzerland, the first of many trips to one of the international climate research hotspots of the world. Before attempting a major climate reconstruction, you need to make sure all the underlying records are in order. So Raphi and I discussed the holes in our collective database and ways of trying to fill the gaps. We decided the first step was to write a review paper cataloguing and assessing all of the palaeoclimate records that existed for the Southern Hemisphere at the time. In 2010, Raphael received a Swiss National Science Foundation fellowship grant to work on the Southern Hemisphere temperature reconstruction with our group. During two research visits to the University of Melbourne over 2010 and 2011, we both worked tirelessly on the database and statistical code needed to develop the reconstruction.

Weeks were spent in my office reading phone book–sized stacks of literature on every coral, tree-ring, lake, cave, ice-core or historical documentary record ever developed from the Southern Hemisphere. We began individually emailing all the researchers we knew who had worked in sites in South America, Antarctica, Australia, Africa, New Zealand and the tropical Pacific and Indian oceans, asking them to contribute their data to our effort. Used to the collaborative nature of scientific research, colleagues from all over the world responded positively, and slowly more records started filling our inboxes. There was a sense of a race against the clock, as my time together with Raphi was limited and there was so much to be done. But more importantly than that, we both felt the excitement that goes with the breaking of new scientific ground. Bringing together all of the climate records from the Southern Hemisphere had never been done on this scale before. Who knew what global climate secrets would be revealed once the data snapped into sharp focus?

In September 2011, our mammoth review paper was accepted for publication in the UK palaeoclimate journal *The Holocene*. It presented the first comprehensive collection of every monthly to annually banded palaeoclimate record available from the Southern Hemisphere. We provided a complete reassessment of close to 200 records, including reviewing all of the original data, extensive quality assessment and climate sensitivity analyses.

In the years that followed, we painstakingly developed the first extensive temperature reconstruction for the Southern Hemisphere, and finally published our work in the prestigious journal *Nature Climate*

Change in March 2014. The approach we took was new. Instead of just developing one reconstruction, we developed 3000 versions to test the influence that different statistical permutations had on the results. We used an unprecedented network of 111 temperature records from over 300 individual sites across the region, doing our best to calculate the uncertainty of our results by using different combinations of records, statistical methods and inputs into our computer code. We also compared our results to a suite of independent Northern Hemisphere temperature reconstructions to see if we could identify the differences and similarities between the two halves of the globe.

Our results were fascinating. Over the past 1000 years, there have only been two periods when the hemispheres' temperature curves have lined up for decades at a time. The first was during the Little Ice Age period where they overlapped from 1594 to 1677. The second similarity was the current warming. Our analysis revealed that the post-1974 warming is the only period of the past millennium when both hemispheres displayed simultaneous warm extremes. Our results showed that 99.7 per cent of our Southern Hemisphere temperature reconstructions indicated that the late twentieth century contained the warmest decade of the past millennium. It was a strong result that showed up no matter which way you wanted to dice up the data.

Just like Mike Mann's original Northern Hemisphere hockey stick and the PAGES 2k network's regional work, our new results showed that the Southern Hemisphere was also experiencing unprecedented late-twentieth-century warming. That is, for the first time we were able to definitively conclude that, just like our northern counterpart, the Southern Hemisphere was now experiencing temperatures that lay outside the bounds of natural variability experienced since medieval times. It was the first time climate science could confidently confirm that the entire globe is warmer now than it has been at any other time over the past 1000 years. It was a truly groundbreaking result.

Our study also confirmed that the Medieval Climate Anomaly was not a global event. While both hemispheres did experience a relative warming, they occurred at different times. The Northern Hemisphere was warm from around 1050 to 1250, while the Southern Hemisphere temperatures peaked from 1280 to 1350. This suggested that the Medieval Climate Anomaly is a distinctively Northern Hemisphere event with regional triggers. It was an important reminder of the dangers of extrapolating Northern Hemisphere trends to the oceanic south. We have our own unique climate history that scientists are only just beginning to figure out.

The other major component of our study involved an extensive comparison with state-of-the-art climate models. The analysis showed that the models that have been used to simulate the climate of the last millennium tended to overemphasise synchronous decade-to-decade temperature variations in both hemispheres, as they underestimated the role of deep ocean circulation. That is, the south is not a mirror image of the north, and the Northern Hemisphere alone is not an accurate representation of the complete global climate system.

The practical implications of this finding were profound. The climate models that have been used to simulate past climate may be missing important components, like a realistic representation of Southern Hemisphere ocean circulation that heavily influences the Australian climate. This means that our estimates of natural climate variability in future climate change projections might be oversimplified. Representing the full complexity of our climate system is a phenomenally difficult goal that is still out of our grasp, and may always be the case.

This doesn't mean that we have to fall into the trap of black-and-white thinking and throw away everything climate models have to tell us. Independent palaeoclimate records clearly show that we are now leaving the bounds of natural variability experienced by the majority of all humans that have ever lived on Earth. We understand the fundamental physics of the climate system enough to know that global warming now gravely threatens the stability and quality of future life on the planet. Scientists are not trying to be alarmist when we say things like this. We are just the unfortunate messengers of alarming information. At this critical crossroads, the biggest mistake would be to shoot the bearers of bad news.

24
THE SAGA OF THE MILLENNIUM

Bringing together the palaeoclimate records in the Australian region was a big job. It took two international workshops, careful negotiation with many research groups to access precious data, then endless hours spent reprocessing and finally analysing each group's records to test their suitability for reconstructing past temperature over the land and sea areas of Australasia (Australia, New Zealand and the surrounding oceans). By the end of 2011, we'd finally developed the first 1000-year temperature reconstruction for the region and submitted our work for peer review.

In May 2012, our Australasian temperature reconstruction paper was accepted for publication in the *Journal of Climate* with minor corrections. The study showed that temperatures recorded in our region since 1950 were warmer than at any time in the past 1000 years, and that the warming was associated with the increasing greenhouse gases seen in climate models. It was a strong result, made even stronger by the unprecedented number of palaeoclimate records we had been able to consider for the study. We now had multiple lines of evidence, from corals growing in the Great Barrier Reef and the south-western Pacific, to tree rings collected from the ancient forests of Tasmania and New Zealand. The natural world was clearly telling us that our region was warming.

For the first time, we were able to demonstrate the unusual nature of late-twentieth-century warming in our region in the extended context of the past millennium, and its link to human activity. Because the results had relevance for the climate change policies that were being fiercely debated in Canberra at the time, the paper received more attention than I could have ever imagined. The Labor government led by Julia Gillard had just introduced a carbon pricing scheme in Australia, known as the *Clean Energy Act 2011*, which was due to come into effect on 1 July 2012. Talk about timing. The media were quick to seize on our results as evidence for the need to address climate change, and soon I found myself doing interviews for television, radio, newspapers and online media. I was sucked into a raging political storm that my training as a scientist had never prepared me for.

Following the early online release of the paper, as the manuscript was being typeset for proofing before appearing in a print edition, one of our team spotted a typo in the methods section of the manuscript. While the paper said the study had used 'detrended' data—temperature data from which the longer-term trends have been removed—the study had in fact used raw data. When we checked the computer code, the DETREND command said 'FALSE' when it should have said 'TRUE'. Both raw and detrended data have been used in similar studies, and both are scientifically justifiable approaches. The issue for our team was the fact that what was written in the paper did not match what was actually done in the final version of the analysis—an innocent mistake, but a mistake nonetheless.

Given the meticulous care we had applied to every other aspect of the paper, of course we were horrified to have found this minor error in the description of our method. Like every good scientific team, we are our own harshest critics. So instead of taking the easy way out and just correcting the single word at proof stage, we asked the publisher to put our paper on hold and remove the online version while we compared the influence that the different method had on the results.

As this was unfolding, it turned out that someone online had spotted the typo too. Two days after we identified the issue, a commenter on the sceptical Climate Audit blog also pointed it out. The Canadian website's author, Stephen McIntyre, proceeded to incorrectly claim that there were 'fundamental issues' with the study. It marked the start of a concerted campaign aimed at discrediting our science, and my reputation. As well as being discussed by bloggers, sometimes with a deeply offensive and openly sexist tone, the 'flaw' was seized upon by sections of the mainstream Australian media known for their conservative and sometimes outrageously flawed views on climate change.

Meanwhile, I received a flurry of hate mail and was subjected to an onslaught of time-consuming Freedom of Information requests for access to our data and years of our emails, in search of ammunition to undermine and discredit our team and results. This is part of a range of tactics used in Australia and overseas in an attempt to intimidate scientists and derail our efforts to do our job. I knew of Mike Mann's experience with the hockey stick, but I'd never considered the possibility I'd have to go through the same thing in Australia. Wouldn't the strength of the science speak for itself? Wasn't the debate already over?

As the days passed, critics began to accuse us of conspiring to reverse-engineer our results to dramatise the warming in our region. Former geologist and prominent climate change sceptic Bob Carter published an opinion piece in *The Australian* newspaper claiming that the peer-review process is faulty and climate science cannot be trusted. This was all ahead of the release of the *Fifth Assessment Report* of the Intergovernmental Panel on Climate Change (IPCC), which was in the final stages of being compiled for its release in 2013.

The IPCC is the most authoritative international body on climate science. Its assessment reports provide a comprehensive summary of global climate change, including the physical sciences, the societal impacts, and how to potentially address these monumental challenges. The reports inform our understanding of climate change and its implications for nations around the world, including Australia. The *Fifth Assessment Report* was the most comprehensive assessment of climate change ever undertaken. It involved thousands of contributing experts, including over 800 lead authors from more than eighty countries. As such, efforts to undermine the science that the report was to contain were in full swing in Australia and abroad in the months leading up to its release, in the hope that it would confuse the public about the need for urgent policy action on climate change.

Against the backdrop of this highly politically charged period for climate scientists all over the world, our team set about rigorously checking and rechecking every step of our region's study, in a bid to dispel any doubts about its accuracy. The results were critically important for Australia, so we had to be 100 per cent sure that we had got things right. Our reassessment included extensive reprocessing of the data using independently generated computer code, three additional reconstruction methods, detrended and non-detrended statistical approaches, and new climate model data to further verify the results.

An independent team from the PAGES Regional 2k network had already reproduced our results using three different methods that appeared alongside our original version of the reconstruction published in the global paper in *Nature Geoscience* in 2013. They concluded that 1971–2000 temperatures in Australia were warmer than in any other thirty-year period over the past 1000 years, confirming our original conclusions.

As important as this was, the Australian part of the analysis was only a small component of the global study. We had to make sure all of the regional detail we had worked so hard to discover was not left on the cutting room floor, so the team pushed on despite the immense pressure and hostility.

The colossal process involved three extra rounds of peer review and four new expert reviewers. From the original submission on 3 November 2011 to the paper's reacceptance on 26 April 2016, the manuscript was checked by seven reviewers and two editors, underwent nine rounds of revisions, and was assessed a total of twenty-one times—not to mention the countless rounds of internal revisions made by our research team and data contributors. We had also become embroiled in some stubborn technical and theoretical debates as the paper's symbolism took on heightened meaning within the scientific community as the public looked on. The harshest critics of Mike Mann's work had teamed up with their Australian counterparts and declared war on the new 'Australian hockey stick'. They seemed hell-bent on trying to destroy the power of an iconic scientific study in the critical months leading up to the release of the IPCC's new report.

In a field of climate science that is barely twenty years old, there are still no universal guidelines on how best to use palaeoclimate records to reconstruct the Earth's past climate. At times it felt like we had been charged with the impossible task of trying to resolve all of our field's unanswered problems. We patiently responded to detailed reviewer comments requesting incredibly specific clarifications related to their own disciplinary expertise that spanned multivariate palaeoclimate analysis, tree-ring science, meteorology, and theoretical statistics. Consequently, the revisions made were substantial and lengthy to satisfy the diversity of the disciplinary rigour requested by each assessor. Towards the end, one reviewer even commented that we had done 'a commendable, perhaps bordering on an insane, amount of work'. One of the long-suffering reviewers went so far as to say that any remaining quibbles were just downright 'petty'.

So after an exceptionally gruelling four and a half years, on 11 July 2016 our results were published again with virtually the same conclusion: the recent temperatures experienced from 1985 to 2014 in Australia, New Zealand and the surrounding oceans were warmer than in any other thirty-year period over the past 1000 years. The upside was that our updated analysis provided extra confidence in our original results. For example, we calculated that there were some thirty-year periods in our palaeoclimate reconstructions during the twelfth century that may have been fractionally (0.03–0.04°C) warmer than the 1961–90 average.

But these results are more uncertain as they are based on a sparse network of only two records. And in any event, they are still about 0.3°C cooler than the most recent 1985–2014 average recorded by the most accurate instrumental climate network available for the region.

Overall, we are confident that observed temperatures in Australasia have been warmer in the past thirty years than in every other thirty-year period over the entire previous millennium—90 per cent confident, based on 12 000 reconstructions, developed using four independent statistical methods and three different data subsets. Importantly, the climate modelling component of our study also showed that only human-caused greenhouse emissions can explain the recent warming recorded in our region.

At long last, our study once again rejoined the by-now vast body of evidence showing that our region, in line with the rest of the planet, warmed rapidly during the late twentieth century, with all the impacts that climate change brings. Releasing the paper in 2016, the results felt more important than ever as a mammoth El Niño event seared the planet. We saw bushfires ravage Tasmania's usually cool World Heritage rainforests, while 93 per cent of the northern Great Barrier Reef bleached amid Australia's hottest ever sea temperatures—an event made 175 times more likely by climate change. Worldwide, it had never been hotter in recorded history.

There were a handful of people in my life that kept me in the game during this ordeal. One of the most important was my mentor, professor David Karoly, one of the great climate scientists of our time. He is one of the few people in Australia who has been subjected to similar attacks, so he always had rock-solid scientific, legal and personal advice I could count on. The depth of his understanding of the science and his relentless dedication to communicate the urgency of climate change threats have been a great inspiration not only to me but others lucky enough to be in his orbit. When others would have retreated, he stepped forward to shield me from the onslaught. Despite the relentless demands on his time from so many people, he did everything he could to prevent my career and life from being completely derailed.

I remember talking to a friend during that time who said, 'Hang in there and just remember you are on the right side of history'. Even though life had become a living hell, there was a tiny ember of hope that was fanned by the wisdom of their words.

Despite the smears and bluster, a rummage through hundreds of our emails revealed nothing but a group of colleagues doing their best to resolve an honest mistake under duress. It wasn't the guilty retreat from a flawed study produced by radical climate activists that the bloggers would have people believe. Instead, it showed the self-correcting nature of science and the steadfast dedication of researchers to work painstakingly around the clock to produce the best science humanly possible. In the end, this saga will be remembered as a footnote in climate science, a storm in a teacup, all played out against the backdrop of a planet that has never been hotter in human history.

25
WELCOME TO THE ANTHROPOCENE

The global cool period known as the Little Ice Age was brought to an abrupt end by the start of the Industrial Revolution. This marked the time when human activities started to have a noticeable impact on the Earth's climate and ecosystems. Fuelled by coal, then oil, the inventions of railways and cars began connecting people across the globe. Medical discoveries saved millions of people from dying of infectious diseases, and soon the world's population exploded. New artificial fertilisers meant that we could feed more people, and more of the Earth's natural landscapes were cleared to support mass agriculture and livestock grazing.

By the 1950s, the great acceleration had begun. In a single lifetime, humans had grown into a force of nature. Globalisation, marketing, international tourism and financial investment helped fuel enormous economic growth. We now move more sediment and rock each year than all the natural processes like erosion and rivers. Greenhouse gas concentrations this high have not been seen in more than three million years, and have caused global temperatures to rise by nearly 1°C. We created a hole in our ozone layer by using a group of synthetic chemicals known as chlorofluorocarbons (CFCs), which were once used widely in refrigerants and aerosol propellants. Even though the use of CFCs has now been banned or is heavily regulated, the impact of their historical use remains with us.

We have altered the Earth's natural cycles to the point that we have now entered a new geologic epoch dominated by humanity. The Anthropocene formally recognises that humans are now considered a geologic agent along with great forces of nature like erosion, volcanism and plate tectonics. We have modified the Earth's surface and altered the chemistry of the atmosphere to the point where we have upset the equilibrium of a climate that has remained relatively stable for thousands of years. This relentless pressure on the planet now finds us on the unprecedented threshold of destabilising the conditions that allow life to exist on Earth. We are the first generation of people to realise the gravitas of bearing responsibility for maintaining a safe operating environment for humanity and the diverse life forms we share the planet with.

Recently I was involved in a study, led by Australian palaeoclimatologist Nerilie Abram, that showed that the Industrial Revolution kickstarted global warming earlier than we'd realised. To our surprise, our results showed that human-caused global warming began as early as the 1830s in the Northern Hemisphere. This redefined our understanding of when human activity began to influence the global climate. These findings were assembled from marine and land-based palaeoclimate records that extended back 500 years—well before the Industrial Revolution—to provide a critical baseline for the planet's past climate, one that is impossible to obtain otherwise.

According to our evidence, all regions except for Antarctica are now showing clear signs of global warming. We know this because the only climate models that can reproduce the results seen in our palaeoclimate records are those that factor in the effect of the carbon dioxide released into the atmosphere by humans. By pinpointing the date when human-induced climate change started, we can then begin to work out when the warming trend broke through the boundaries of the Earth's natural limits, because it takes decades for the global warming signal to emerge above natural climate variability.

Our landmark study, published in the scientific journal *Nature* in 2016, showed that warming did not develop at the same time across the planet. The tropical oceans and the Arctic were the first regions to show signs of warming as early as the 1830s. Europe, North America and Asia followed roughly two decades later. Southern Hemisphere temperatures increased much later, with Australasia and South America starting to warm from the early twentieth century. According to our evidence, all regions except for Antarctica show distinct and widespread warming.

While some parts of Antarctica have clearly begun to warm, a distinct warming signal over the entire continent is still not detectable. This is because the westerly winds that circulate through the Southern Ocean keep warm air masses from tropical regions at bay. Ozone depletion and rising greenhouse gas concentrations during the twentieth century have also caused this wind barrier to get stronger. The Southern Ocean currents that flow around Antarctica also tend to move warmer surface waters away from the continent, as colder deep water that hasn't yet been penetrated by surface greenhouse warming upwells. But even though these ancient waters have not been exposed to the atmosphere for centuries, they are now warm enough to melt the underbelly of some west Antarctic ice shelves. According to Eric Rignot from the University of California, this process of 'basal melting' is now considered 'unstoppable' and will result in the irreversible retreat of a large sector of the west Antarctic ice sheet, as reflected by the imminent collapse of the Larsen C ice shelf reported in June 2017.

The delay in warming observed in the rest of the Southern Hemisphere is something we do not yet fully understand. But like Antarctica, the Southern Hemisphere's oceans could be holding back warming—partly through winds and ocean currents, but perhaps also because of a process known as 'thermal inertia'. This means that the ocean can absorb far more heat than the atmosphere or the land before it starts to warm. Essentially, the coolness of the Southern Hemisphere's vast oceans acts to insulate Australasia and South America from the impact of surface warming. The question is, for how long?

If our evidence for delayed warming in the Southern Hemisphere holds true, it could mean that we are in for more climate surprises as global warming begins to overcome the natural buffering capacity of our surrounding oceans. Could the recent record warming of Australian waters, and the widespread damage to the Great Barrier Reef in 2016 and 2017, be an early sign that this is already occurring?

Global climate change policy set out in the United Nation's Paris Agreement has the ambitious goal of limiting average global warming to 1.5°C above pre-industrial levels by the end of the century. In 2015, global temperatures crossed the 1°C threshold, and 2016 was 1.1°C above pre-industrial conditions. But there's one major hitch. The baseline is relative to 1850–1900, when most of our thermometer-based temperature records begin. What our study shows is that for many parts of the world, that baseline may be an imperfect estimate of pre-industrial climate because human activities had already tainted the temperature record as early as the 1830s. As a result, the real baseline for a safe climate would actually need to be cooler than the most ambitious 1.5°C target currently on the table at international climate talks.

The small increases in greenhouse gases during the nineteenth century had a small effect on Earth's temperatures, but with the longer perspective we gain from palaeoclimate records, we can see that big changes are possible. These fractions of a degree of extra warming might seem insignificant at first, maybe even trivial. But as we nudge ever closer to the 1.5°C guardrail thought to keep the Earth's climate stable, the past tells us that even very small changes really do make a difference.

PART IV
HISTORY REPEATING?

26
WHAT ABOUT THE ICE AGES?

We all know that the Earth has been through natural climate cycles like ice ages in the past. Does that mean that we don't need to worry about the climate change we are experiencing today? Haven't humans been through this all before?

The planet's climate varies naturally for reasons that are well understood by scientists. As early as the 1920s, Serbian geophysicist and astronomer Milutin Milanković was the first scientist to theorise that variations in the Earth's orbit strongly influence the geographic distribution of sunlight, which influences surface climate. He proposed that there have been shifts in the orbit of the planet around the sun, variation in its tilt, and changes in the wobble of the Earth on its rotational axis.

The path of the Earth's orbit around the sun is not a perfect circle but actually an ellipse. This can vary from nearly circular to a more elongated shape due to the gravitational fields of large neighbouring planets like Jupiter and Saturn. The measure of deviation of the Earth's orbit from being circular is called its 'eccentricity'. That is, the larger the eccentricity, the greater the deviation from a circle. The Earth's orbit undergoes a cyclical change from less eccentric to more eccentric and back. One complete cycle of this kind of orbital variation lasts around 100 000 years.

We know the Earth is spinning around its own axis, which is the reason why we have night and day. However, this axis is not upright. Instead, it tilts at angles of between 22.1 degrees and 24.5 degrees and back. It's the tilt of the Earth that creates the seasons, as the distribution of sunlight received at the equator and poles shifts throughout the 365 days it takes to orbit the sun. Greater tilt results in more sunlight hitting the polar areas in summer and less in tropical locations. During times of increased tilt, the hemisphere closest to the sun—that is, the one experiencing summer—will expose more surface area to incoming solar energy than during times when the tilt is more upright. During a period of maximum tilt, polar locations will experience the hotter summers and colder winters. A complete cycle for the axial tilt lasts for about 41 000 years.

Aside from our planet's eccentricity and tilt, the Earth's axis also wobbles like a spinning top, changing the direction of its axis. This phenomenon, known as 'precession', is caused by the tidal forces exerted by the sun and moon. This changes where Earth's North Pole points to in the sky. Currently it is pointing at Polaris, the North Star, but it's drifted off in the past, pointing towards other stars like Vega. Precession causes the poles to trace out circles in the sky approximately once every 26 000 years, governing the timing of the seasons. This changes the timing of summer and winter solstices that mark the longest and shortest days of the year, and equinoxes, when the lengths of day and night are equal.

Collectively, these orbital parameters are referred to as 'Milankovitch cycles'. This recognises that at the most fundamental level, we are a planet floating in space, being pulled around by other bodies in the solar system as we circle the sun. These changes influence the amount of solar energy reaching the Earth, where it lands and for how long. These cycles take place over thousands of years—ranging from 26 000 years to 100 000 years.

The astronomical variations combine to influence the seasonal intensity of the solar radiation reaching the poles. This causes the great ice sheets of the world to grow and shrink, influencing the energy balance of the Earth as snow reflects more solar radiation back into space. Cooling the ocean surface changes ocean circulation and the atmospheric winds that flow over them. Large continental ice sheets in the Northern Hemisphere have expanded and retreated many times in the past, drifting in and out of natural ice age cycles. Times with large ice sheets are known as 'glacial' periods and times without large ice sheets are called 'interglacial' periods. During warm interglacials like the one we are currently experiencing, ice caps recede, sea levels rise, and forests return to areas that were once covered by ice. Over the best-documented past 430 000 years of the Earth's history, we have spent around 20 per cent of each glacial–interglacial cycle in warm interglacial periods and around 80 per cent in ice ages. The geologic record tells us that warm conditions are more the exception than the rule.

The thing about ice age cycles is that they happen really slowly on geologic timescales that are imperceptible to humans. We are more used to thinking in terms of days, weeks, months and years, not thousands or millions of years. Those timescales are pretty irrelevant when you are talking about living in modern, industrialised societies. The peak of the last ice age was around 20 000 years ago, long before modern human civilisations existed. Vast ice sheets covered 25 per cent of the Earth's surface, engulfing many continents and some of the seas around North America, northern Europe and Asia (compared with ice sheets that now only cover around 10 per cent of the planet). These massive sheets of ice locked away water, lowering the sea level by around 120 metres. As the sea drained away, formerly submerged continental shelves fringing the coast became land bridges, connecting the Australian mainland with Tasmania and Papua New Guinea.

Sometimes, climate change sceptics seize on the concept of long-term natural climate variability as evidence that current conditions are no cause for concern. According to them, the Earth's current warming is just part of a series of cyclical events that take thousands of years to complete, and therefore can't be stopped or influenced by us. They believe that human activities have little or nothing to do with the planet's climatic conditions. They quote evidence from Greenland ice cores that show that temperatures increased by between 4°C and 7°C coming out of the last ice age. The planet survived that, so what's all the fuss about?

The thing they might not tell you is that when this natural global warming happened at various times in the past two million years, it took the planet about 5000 years to warm around 5°C. That's about 1°C warming every thousand years, or 0.1°C per century. Since 1880, average global temperatures have climbed 0.85°C, around 8.5 times faster than the average rate of ice age recovery warming. Currently, we are on track to warm by around 4°C over the next eighty years, which is lightning-fast in the context of deep geologic time. Carbon dioxide (CO_2) concentrations measured from ice-core records drilled from Antarctica show that the closest we get to finding CO_2 levels somewhat similar to those in the present day is around three million years ago, during a geologic period known as the Pliocene.

The other major difference regarding past ice ages is the fact that we now have people living on the planet in increasingly complex societies finely tuned to current climate conditions. As of October 2017, the world's population stands at 7.6 billion people, with over 80 million people added every year. During the peak of the last ice age, around 18 000 years ago, about 4–5 million people are thought to have inhabited the Earth in low-tech, nomadic tribal groups. That's the equivalent of a population smaller than Sydney's spread all over the globe. Going back 800 000 years, primitive

Homo erectus were still roaming the Earth—modern-day *Homo sapiens* were still 600 000 years away.

According to Antarctic ice-core records, atmospheric carbon dioxide concentrations varied between a low of 180 ppm (parts per million) during ice ages and a high of 300 ppm during warm interglacial periods. Coming out of the last ice age, carbon dioxide levels increased by around 80 ppm over 5000 years. Since then, carbon dioxide levels have shot up from pre-industrial values of about 280 ppm to approximately 409 ppm in 2016. That's a rise of around 130 ppm in just over 260 years—or thirty times faster than pre-industrial rates of change. It's staggering to think that human activities have increased carbon dioxide levels so dramatically in just a handful of centuries.

Before British settlement in 1788, Indigenous Australians had existed in dynamic equilibrium with the landscape for thousands of generations. As detailed by historian Bill Gammage in *The Biggest Estate on Earth*, Aboriginal people managed the land in complex ways, living by the seasonal cues written into the landscape, plants and animals that characterised their country for at least 40 000 years. They respected the limits of the land, and developed ways of managing its health and productivity. They used practices like firestick farming to encourage trees to seed and prevent fuel loads building up to the dangerous levels capable of producing ferocious wildfires that could annihilate their country and people. In the 230 years since then, we have cleared much of the land's native vegetation and developed large-scale agricultural and mining practices that have taken a heavy toll on our soil and waters. The balance we once had with our country has been drastically altered; our connection with nature has been severed as we've crammed ourselves into crowded cities and traded sunsets for screens.

Over about two centuries, the Earth has transitioned into what scientists now term a 'non-analogue' state. That is, the pace of global environmental change we are witnessing today has no historical counterpart at any time in our geologic past. That's why scientists felt compelled to introduce the new geologic epoch we now know as the Anthropocene. It recognises that humans have actually become a new force of nature on the planet. There are now unprecedented numbers of people altering the landscape and using record-high levels of fossil fuels at a faster rate than any other time in human history. So what does it mean to be in a geological age dominated by humanity? Do human activities really have the power to alter natural cycles that have been with us for millennia?

27
NATURAL VARIABILITY VERSUS HUMAN INFLUENCE

Before the Industrial Revolution kicked off around 1750, the Earth's climate was almost purely operating under natural conditions. Because the human population was still pretty small, our impact on the planet was limited and localised. Aside from the deep-time fluctuations in the Earth's orbit, there were other influences taking place on shorter, more human timescales of years, decades and centuries. The main natural factors that influence our climate are solar activity, volcanic eruptions and ocean–atmosphere cycles like the El Niño–Southern Oscillation (ENSO). Palaeoclimate records have been used to build up a record of estimates of all these factors over past centuries to help us get a sense of how these influences have waxed and waned over time.

Changes in the surface of the sun have fascinated people for centuries. Naked-eye observations of sunspots—dark regions on the sun caused by concentrated magnetic fields—date back to ancient times. But it was only after the invention of the telescope in 1607 that it became possible to monitor the number, size and position of these 'stains' on the surface of the sun. The longest reliable estimate of the sun's activity is provided by variations of sunspots recorded by humans dating back to 1610.

Total solar irradiance is much higher during 'solar maximum', when sunspot numbers and general solar activity are high. During 'solar minimum', the sun is inactive and there are fewer sunspots. In 1844, Heinrich Schwabe published his discovery of an eleven-year cycle of sunspot activity, ranging from periods of stormy flare-ups to quiet inactivity. These changes in the sun's output cause fluctuations that impact Earth's global temperature by about 0.1°C, making it slightly hotter during solar maximum and cooler during solar minimum.

There have been some notable highs and lows in the sun's activity over past centuries. Perhaps the most striking example is when almost no sunspots were observed on the sun's surface from 1650 to 1715. This extended period of low solar activity, now known as the Maunder Minimum, may have been partly responsible for the Little Ice Age. During this period, winters in Europe were longer and colder by about 1°C than they are today. Similarly, high sunspot activity from 1100 to 1250, estimated from Beryllium (^{10}Be) isotopes in ice cores, has been associated with the medieval warming experienced in the Northern Hemisphere at this time.

Since around 1820, there has been a slow increase in solar activity. Even so, it is estimated that the sun has only contributed about 10 per cent or less of the surface warming over the last century. Unless we find a way to reduce the amount of greenhouse gases we put into the atmosphere, solar activity is not expected to emerge as the dominant cause of future climate change. Instead, solar variations are expected to continue to modulate both warming and cooling trends by one-tenth or two-tenths of a degree. With such a minor influence, it's clear there are other factors at play.

Perhaps the most spectacular source of natural climate variability is the dramatic changes to the Earth's atmosphere caused by explosive volcanic eruptions. The gases, ash and dust ejected from volcanoes cool the planet by blocking incoming sunlight, an effect that can last from a few months up to several years depending on the characteristics of the eruption. Because of atmospheric circulation patterns, eruptions in the tropics can have a greater impact on the climate in both hemispheres, while eruptions at mid or high latitudes typically only impact the hemisphere they are located in.

Past volcanic activity has been reconstructed from ash layers and chemical compounds recorded in ice cores drilled from Antarctica and Greenland. Sulphur dioxide is the main volcanic index measured from snow samples. As it is finer than ash particles, tiny sulphur dioxide molecules readily travel high into the stratosphere—around 10–50 kilometres above the Earth's surface—where they combine with water to form sulphuric acid aerosols. This creates a haze of tiny droplets in the upper atmosphere that reflects incoming solar radiation, causing a cooling of the Earth's surface climate.

Aerosols can stay in the stratosphere for up to three years, moved around by wind currents, causing significant cooling worldwide. Eventually, the droplets grow large enough to fall back down to Earth, and the surface climate starts to restabilise. During massive eruptions, volcanoes also release large amounts of greenhouse gases such as carbon dioxide and water vapour. There have been times during the Earth's deep history when intense volcanism increased the amount of carbon dioxide in the atmosphere and caused global warming. But keep in mind that volcanoes in more recent times have emitted insignificant amounts of carbon dioxide compared with recent industrial emissions. The major impact of volcanoes on the Earth's climate is actually caused by sulphur dioxide.

In recent times, there have been some huge tropical volcanic eruptions that have had major impacts on society. One of the most powerful eruptions in human history was the 1815 Tambora eruption in Indonesia which blasted an enormous crater 7 kilometres wide and 1.2 kilometres deep. During the eruption, approximately 60–80 megatons of sulphur dioxide was injected into the stratosphere. That's three or four times more than during the 1991 eruption of Mount Pinatubo in the Philippines, the biggest eruption of the twentieth century. After Tambora, global temperatures dropped by approximately 1°C, causing the collapse of the Indian and Asian monsoons. The cold weather and lack of sunshine made it difficult to grow crops, leading to harvest failures in many parts of the world. In Europe and North America, 1816 became known as the 'Year without a Summer'. Over 100 000 people died worldwide from famine, disease and drinking water poisoned by contaminants like highly corrosive sulphuric acid.

For the population of Central Europe, the endless rainfall was more problematic than cold temperatures. Johann Peter Hoffmann, a farmer and magistrate from Alsace in eastern France wrote in his diary in July 1816: 'The rain continues, there is no day without rain. The misery is indescribable. This is the worst time in my memory'. It is estimated that precipitation in Central Europe was 20–80 per cent above normal in the summer of 1816. Cold and rainy summers led to poor harvests, which was one of the factors that caused famine and the last major food crisis experienced in the Western world. Loaves of bread became smaller and barely edible as meagre ingredients were mixed into the flour. Even so, these 'hunger breads' were sold at extremely high prices to people struggling with malnutrition and diseases. The high death toll saw mass migration, riots due to inflation, and other major political and social disruptions.

Some experts have suggested that the 1815 Tambora eruption also affected European art and culture. It is believed that gothic literature like Mary Shelley's *Frankenstein*, Lord Byron's poem 'Darkness' and John William Polidori's *The Vampyre* were influenced by the grimness of the time. While the volcanic ash settled after a few days, the sulphate aerosol particles ejected from Tambora continued to affect the global atmosphere for two to three years. They led to spectacular sunsets around the world that inspired the romantic painters in Europe, such as JMW (William) Turner, to paint colourful sunsets in 1817–18.

The final natural factor that influences the Earth's climate is the colossal interaction of the world's atmosphere and oceans. Because this takes place within the climate system, these processes are referred to as 'internal' variability, as opposed to 'external' influences like the sun. In the Australian region, the seasonal heating and cooling of the waters of the Pacific, Indian and Southern oceans impacts the way in which the air above them behaves. Surface winds are generated from temperature differences: air rises over warmer land and ocean surfaces and drifts towards cooler areas, where it sinks in great convection loops. As oceans are warmed by the sun, water evaporates and condenses into huge cumulus cloud bands. As the humidity rises, excess moisture in the atmosphere eventually falls as rain, or snow at high elevations or more southerly locations. The presence of clouds, in turn, impacts surface temperatures by trapping heat from the land surface. This means that in most parts of Australia, when it is hot it is generally dry, and when it is cool it is usually wet. The exception is the tropics, which receives constantly high solar radiation throughout the year. In these regions of tropical Australia, it is mostly just warm and dry or warm and wet!

The endless interaction of the atmosphere and ocean is caused by essentially random fluctuations in the climate system. While some of the great natural cycles have some regularity in their timing, generally they are hard to predict because the exact physical conditions never repeat in entirely the same way. Water is constantly flowing across huge ocean basins around continents and throughout the globe, upwelling cooler waters from the depths to mix with the warmer surface waters. The chemical composition of the atmosphere is being altered with every passing year as the planet continues to warm from a build-up of excessive greenhouse gases. Everything is in dynamic motion, making it hard to know precisely what the future will bring.

Sometimes people like to beat up on weather forecasters, saying they never get things right. But when you consider how hard it is to measure things as vast and complex as the planet's ocean or atmosphere, it's incredible how much we can actually predict from the incomplete observations we have to represent the whole system. The monitoring of ENSO events, the largest source of natural global climate variability aside from the seasons, is a good example of this. These events are made up of two components: ocean warming in the equatorial Pacific, and large-scale changes to the atmospheric trade winds generated across the largest expanse of ocean on Earth. The trigger for these events is still one of these scientific 'chicken and egg' debates: Does the ocean warm first, then cause changes to the atmosphere, or vice versa? Again, it's not overly important. The main things are that the two systems are intricately linked by incredibly complex thermodynamics, and both aspects of the phenomenon need to be simultaneously monitored for accurate seasonal forecasts.

As described in Part I, normally strong trade winds blow from east to west across the Pacific Ocean around the equator. During an El Niño year, the trade winds weaken or break down. The warm water that is normally pushed towards the western Pacific flows back across the Pacific, piling up on the eastern Pacific coastline from California to Chile, increasing rain and stormy weather. Although El Niño's strongest impacts are felt around the equatorial Pacific, they can affect weather around the world by influencing high and low pressure systems, winds and precipitation patterns. As warmer ocean waters release excess heat into the atmosphere, global temperatures rise.

One of the biggest challenges facing climate science is how natural variability caused by large-scale climate cycles like ENSO will change as the planet continues to warm. El Niño years tend to increase global temperatures, as changing wind patterns in the Pacific mean the giant ocean absorbs less heat from the atmosphere. La Niña events reverse the process, soaking up more heat from the air into the ocean, suppressing global temperatures.

Oceans play a critical role in the climate system—the world's oceans absorb more than 90 per cent of the energy generated by the burning of fossil fuels, resulting in increases in ocean heat content. The increasing heat content of the upper ocean has a very important influence on the global climate. A 2016 paper by US scientist Peter Gleckler studying the amount of heat the ocean has absorbed since 1865 found that nearly 50 per cent of the ocean warming occurred in the past twenty years, with over a third of that heat accumulated below 700 metres.

Twenty years ago, the deep ocean contained just 20 per cent of the extra heat from greenhouse gas emissions. This finding is linked to La Niña conditions when stronger trade winds cool the sea surface, drawing more energy (heat) out of the atmosphere. As the warm water accumulates in the western Pacific, it pushes large amounts of warm upper-ocean water down deeper than usual, where the heat is stored. There are now also concerns that significant warming of the adjacent Southern Ocean will occur when the warm deep water formed during the twentieth century reaches the surface in coming decades. While it is accepted that there is a variable but steady increase in ocean heat content, no-one yet knows exactly how that might influence the ENSO cycle in the future.

We are already starting to get clues about what might happen to the ENSO cycle as the planet continues to warm. In 2016, the world experienced a major El Niño event on top of the background global warming trend. The result? Exceptionally warm temperatures drove dramatic and unprecedented climate impacts, including the worst coral bleaching events in the Great Barrier Reef's history, an unparalleled large-scale dieback of tropical mangrove forests on the Gulf of Carpentaria, and a major algae bloom in up to 1700 kilometres of the Murray River. Even so, experts have estimated that the El Niño is likely to have only contributed around 0.2°C of the new global hottest year on record set in 2016. The El Niño just provided a little extra kick to an already warm system.

It's clear that natural variability isn't the only factor at play, so what is going on with our climate now that is different to the past? In short, human activity. The concentration of greenhouse gas in the atmosphere and land-use patterns have radically changed since the dawn of the industrial era. We've cleared the world's forests to make way for agriculture and cities with their paved streets and vast highways. In the past, natural surfaces were able to regulate the absorption of carbon dioxide by plant uptake and filter water through soils, keeping the great water and carbon cycles circulating. Excess carbon from the burning of fossil fuels has now flooded the atmosphere to the degree where it can no longer be mopped up by the great natural cycle of photosynthesis that has regulated our climate since the dawn of life on Earth. Altering the carbon cycle through industrial emissions and the balance between natural and synthetic surfaces is causing the Earth's lungs to fail. Our natural equilibrium has been disturbed.

Fifty-four per cent of the world's population now lives in urban areas, with a huge 90 per cent of Australians calling cities home. These regions are so different to the surrounding natural landscapes that they actually generate their own climate. This urban heat island effect arises from the heavy modification of the land surfaces we live on. For example, dark surfaces absorb significantly more solar radiation, which causes urban concentrations of roads and buildings to heat more than rural areas during the day. Materials commonly used in urban areas for pavement and roofs, such as concrete and asphalt, have significantly different thermal characteristics like heat capacity, conductivity and reflectance. This causes a change in the energy balance of urban areas, often leading to higher temperatures than in surrounding rural areas. The lack of vegetation in urban areas also compounds the issue by decreasing the cooling effect of tree shading. A 2017 *Nature Climate Change* study by Francisco Estrada estimated that under the combined influence of global warming and localised urban heating, temperatures could become a staggering 7°C warmer by 2100 in around

25 per cent of the 1692 largest cities in the world, under the business as usual emissions scenario.

Current research on heatwaves, Australia's deadliest natural disasters, has shown that their impacts are amplified in urban areas where the built environment traps heat, preventing cities from cooling down as fast as rural areas. A recent example was the 2009 Black Saturday bushfires in Victoria that had a death toll of 374 from the preceding heatwave compared with the 173 killed in the actual fires. The temperature in Melbourne was above 43°C for three consecutive days for the first time since records had been kept. Even though the effect of urbanisation might seem small, these temperatures were extreme enough to have a big impact on human health in one of the most densely populated urban regions of Australia.

With more people on the planet, there is increased demand for electricity, transport and manufacturing to support our increasingly high-tech societies. Over the past century, the burning of fossil fuels to power these activities has accelerated the release of greenhouse gases like carbon dioxide, methane and other industrial pollutants into the atmosphere. Ice-core and instrumental measurements show that carbon dioxide levels are now at 409 ppm, the highest they've been in at least three million years. As the Anthropocene continues to unfold, we will see more and more modifications to the Earth's surface, ocean and atmosphere. This, in turn, will influence the range of natural climate variability already present in the system.

Sometimes people dismiss the changes they are seeing as simply the natural variability Australians have always had to live with. But as our monitoring and analysis of the climate system has dramatically improved in recent decades, scientists can now quantify the influence that natural factors have on our climate. On very long timescales, changes to the Earth's astronomical orbit have been the main influence on our climate. But on timescales of the past one to two thousand years, changes in solar variability, explosive volcanism and ocean–atmosphere circulation have played a bigger role. Since the Industrial Revolution, human activities have introduced land-use changes and greenhouse gas concentrations that our ancestors never had to contend with.

So unfortunately it's not a simple case of natural climate variability versus human-caused climate change. It's a combination of both now interacting with each other in ways that scientists are just beginning to understand. But knowing what we know about the fundamental physics of the climate system, we can begin to get a sense of what will happen to the Australian climate as the planet continues to warm. So what does climate change in our own backyard actually look like?

28
LIFE IN A SHIFTING CLIMATE

When trying to understand climate change, people sometimes find it hard to imagine what life in a shifting climate might be like. The easiest way of thinking about it is to consider changes in extreme events. When average temperatures increase as the planet warms, temperatures at the hot and cold ends of the range also change. Although these trends can be either amplified or offset by things like soil moisture, generally speaking, everything gets a little nudge in a warmer direction, meaning we experience fewer cold extremes and more hot extremes. Conditions that were once considered rare in our past climate start to become more common in our new climate. That is, there are shifts in the frequency or probability of cold and warm extremes. Australian temperatures, for instance, are projected to continue increasing, with more extremely hot days and fewer extremely cool days.

The most obvious example of Australia's changing climate is seen through changes in hot extremes. Greenhouse gases continue to accumulate as we relentlessly burn fossil fuels, trapping more heat in the lower atmosphere. This increases the likelihood that hot weather will occur and that heatwaves will become longer and more intense. Weather observations over the past fifty years are consistent with scientific understanding of the theoretical physics of a warming climate, first formally proposed in the 1890s by Swedish scientist Svante Arrhenius.

In Australia, eight of the ten warmest years on record have occurred since 1998. Over the past fifteen years, the frequency of very warm months has increased five-fold and the frequency of very cool months has declined by around a third, compared with a 1951–80 reference period.

Our hottest year on record so far is 2013, which was 1.2°C above the 1961–90 average. During that year, the nation experienced the hottest summer, hottest January and hottest day on record for Australia as a whole, and the extreme heat saw bushfires ignite in every state and territory. The duration, frequency and intensity of heatwaves have also increased across large parts of Australia since 1950. Days where extreme heat (warmest 1 per cent of records) is widespread across the continent have become more common in the past twenty years.

Since the 1970s, there has been an increase in extreme fire weather, and a longer fire season, across large parts of the country. As our climate becomes warmer and more extreme than historical conditions, scientists are starting to redefine what's 'normal'. A 2016 study by Sophie Lewis from the Australian National University estimated that the record-breaking global temperature set in 2015, which was 0.75°C higher than the World Meteorological Organization's 1961–90 reference period, will become the 'new normal' by 2040 under all greenhouse gas emissions scenarios. In 2016, the global temperature record was broken for the third year running, highlighting just how fast things are changing.

Across Australia, one of the clearest signs of a warming climate is an increase in average maximum and minimum temperatures. Since 1950, there has been a shift in both tails of the temperature distribution.

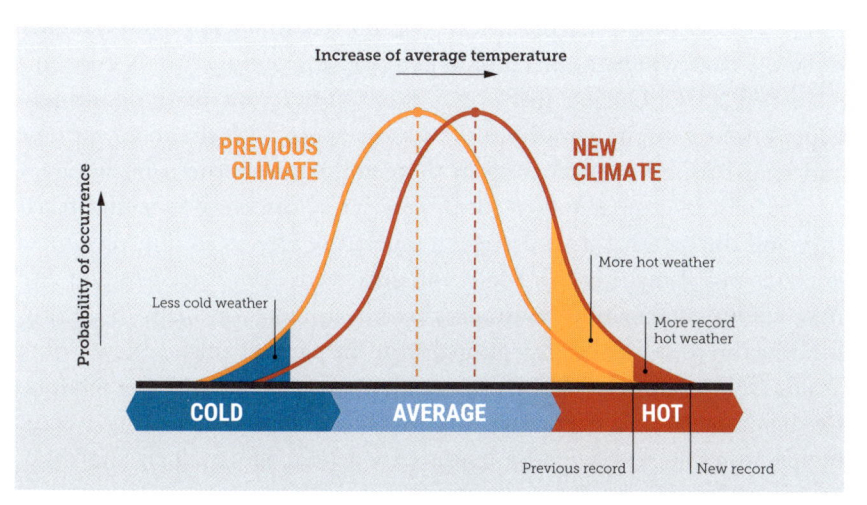

Figure 41. Relationship between an increase in average temperature and the shift in the proportion and likelihood of extreme events. Under a global warming climate, we experience fewer cold extremes and more frequent hot extremes.

Source: Reproduced courtesy of the Climate Council (2017). *Cranking up the Intensity: Climate Change and Extreme Weather Events.*

According to the Bureau of Meteorology's 2016 *State of the Climate* report, the very warm monthly maximum temperatures that were observed just 2 per cent of the time during the 1951–80 period, occurred around 10 per cent of the time during the 1999–2013 period.

Since 2001, the number of extreme heat records in Australia has outnumbered extreme cool records by almost three to one for daytime maximum temperatures, and by almost five to one for night-time minimum temperatures. Very warm months (those with an average temperature above two standard deviations) were five times more likely to occur in 2001–15 than in 1951–80. The frequency of very cool months has declined by around a third over the same period. Consequently, heatwaves have also increased in duration, frequency and intensity in many parts of the country.

Many heat-related records were broken in the exceptionally hot 'Angry Summer' of 2012–13. The year 2013 included Australia's hottest day, week, month and year averaged across the country, despite occurring in the absence of an El Niño event. Surface air temperatures and regional sea surface temperatures for the December–February period were the highest ever recorded in Australia. Averaged nationally, the January maximum temperature was 36.9°C, a huge 2.28°C above the 1961–90 average, and 0.1°C above the previous record set in January 1932.

That summer also included the longest and most widespread national heatwave on record, which lasted from 25 December 2012 until 18 January 2013. It was also the warmest heatwave on record, including a sequence of seven days when the maximum temperature averaged over Australia exceeded 39°C. During this event, over 70 per cent of the continent experienced extreme temperatures at some stage, with the most extreme and long-lasting heat occurring in the central and southern inland areas. A total of 123 temperature records were set across every state and territory, and the national daily average temperature rose to an unprecedented 40.3°C on 7 January 2013. Meteorologists were even forced to add two new colour categories to Australia's weather prediction maps to accommodate the scale of the exceptional heat. In parts of inland New South Wales, South Australia and Queensland, average maximum temperatures for the month were a staggering 5°C to 6°C above normal. Usually, average temperatures are exceeded by tenths of a degree, not by such enormous margins. These observations triggered alarm bells in the minds of scientists across the country, an unmistakable sign of future summers in Australia.

A major feature of the 2012–13 heatwave was its abnormal duration, particularly in inland areas, where some stations experienced well above average temperatures on every, or almost every, day over a period of three weeks or more. A number of stations set records for the longest continuous run of extremely hot days. For example, Alice Springs sweltered through seventeen consecutive days of 40°C or above, easily breaking its previous record of twelve days set in 2006. Above 40°C, people are at serious risk of experiencing heat stroke, a potentially life-threatening condition caused by the body's inability to regulate its core temperature and central nervous system under prolonged exposure to high temperatures, especially in regions of high humidity. The condition can cause brain damage, organ failure, seizures, unconsciousness, coma and even death. As these events become the 'new normal', it's hard to imagine towns like Alice Springs remaining liveable in the future.

While the summer of 2012–13 was truly off the charts, there is further evidence that Australia's capital cities are already experiencing longer, hotter and more frequent heatwaves. The average intensity of heatwaves in Melbourne is now 1.5°C hotter and they occur on average seventeen days earlier than they did between 1950 and 1980. In Sydney, heatwaves now start nineteen days earlier and the number of heatwave days has increased by 50 per cent. In Adelaide, the number of heatwave days has nearly doubled, while the average intensity of heatwaves is 2.5°C hotter.

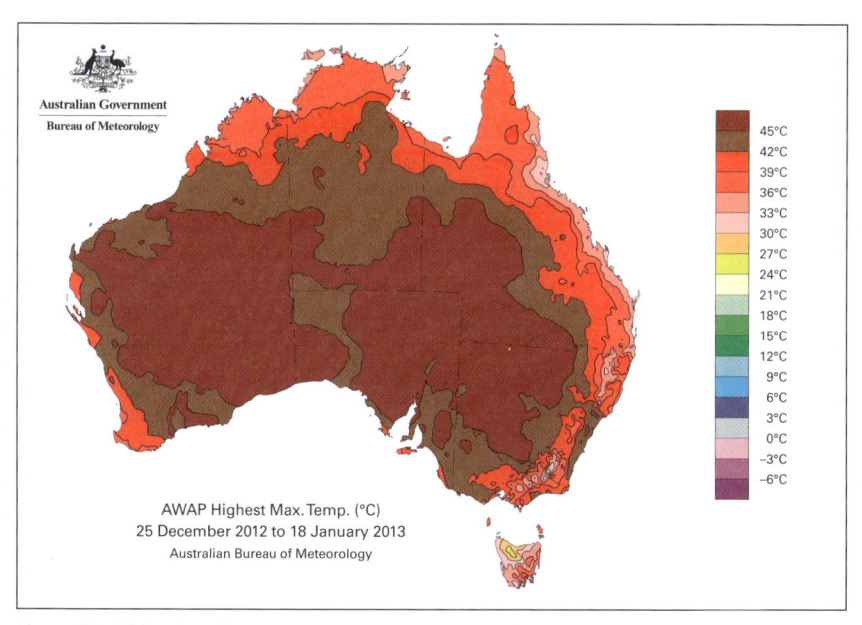

Figure 42. Highest maximum temperatures recorded during the abnormally long and widespread national heatwave experienced from 25 December 2012 to 18 January 2013.

Source: Reproduced courtesy of the Bureau of Meteorology.

The CSIRO and the Bureau of Meteorology have estimated that the annual average number of days over 35°C may increase from 11 at present in Melbourne to 16–24 by 2090 (depending on the intermediate or high greenhouse gas emissions scenarios). Perhaps most shockingly, Darwin's average of 11 days is predicted to increase to 265 days of the year above 35°C under business as usual. If we continue down the high greenhouse gas emissions track we're currently on, it is possible that extreme heat will combine with high humidity to make Australia's largest tropical population centre unliveable within our children's lifetime.

As Australia continues to warm, we will experience an increasingly extreme climate. All weather events, including heat events, are now occurring in an atmosphere that is significantly hotter than it was fifty years ago. This means that all weather is now influenced by climate change. The additional heat in the atmosphere and ocean from human emissions of greenhouse gases drives up the risk of more intense and frequent extreme heat events.

The shift towards more frequent and severe heatwaves in Australia is part of a larger global trend. As even more greenhouse gases accumulate in the atmosphere over the coming decades, the fundamental physics of the climate system will escalate the risk of extreme heat. Across Australia, a one-in-twenty-years extreme hot day is expected to occur every 2–5 years by the middle of the century; that is, extreme hot days are expected to occur four to ten times more often. Towards the end of the century, the frequency and intensity of extreme heat will depend strongly on our success, or not, in reducing greenhouse gas emissions. Without effective action on climate change, what is classified as extreme heat today will become average summer conditions in our new climate.

As anyone living in Australia knows, extremes are already a characteristic of our climate; they are a defining feature of our national identity. The issue is that climate change exacerbated by human activity is now stacking the odds when it comes to record heat, pushing us into dangerous climate change territory. As the planet continues to warm, climate change will amplify Australia's already erratic variability. We will begin to notice an even more extreme version of our current climate. It will play out like an amplified version of our natural variability, with records smashed with every season and year that passes. But how can we tell exactly how much of an influence humans are having on naturally occurring extremes? How can the past help us understand future climate change risks?

29
HUMAN FINGERPRINTS ON OUR CLIMATE

Scientists can quantify how the probability of an observed extreme weather event has changed due to human influences or natural factors using global climate models. The most common approach to assess potential links between individual events and climate change is to mathematically calculate the likelihood of events occurring with and without additional greenhouse gases from human activities. This area of climate science is known as 'detection and attribution'.

'Detection' refers to the emergence of a signal from background noise, demonstrating that climate has changed more than possible due to natural variability alone, in some defined statistical sense. 'Attribution' is the process of establishing the most likely physical causes for a detected change. State-of-the-art climate models that incorporate natural forces like solar, volcanic and ocean–atmosphere variability are compared with simulations that also include anthropogenic factors including greenhouse gases, ozone and land-use changes. The two experiments are run separately, a world with and without greenhouse gases, to help quantify the effect that natural variability and human activities are potentially having on extremes recorded in instrumental climate records.

Detection and attribution studies using instrumental temperature records from all over the world show that recently observed warming can only be reproduced by models that include human influences. When compared with models run only using natural variability, the two curves diverge. When greenhouse gases are added to the mix, modelled and observed temperatures fit hand-in-glove. When the results were first featured in the *Third Assessment Report* of the Intergovernmental Panel on Climate Change (IPCC) in 2001, the implications were powerful as they definitively showed that the global climate is no longer only being influenced by natural variability. Direct temperature observations matched the fundamental thermodynamics represented in independent climate models.

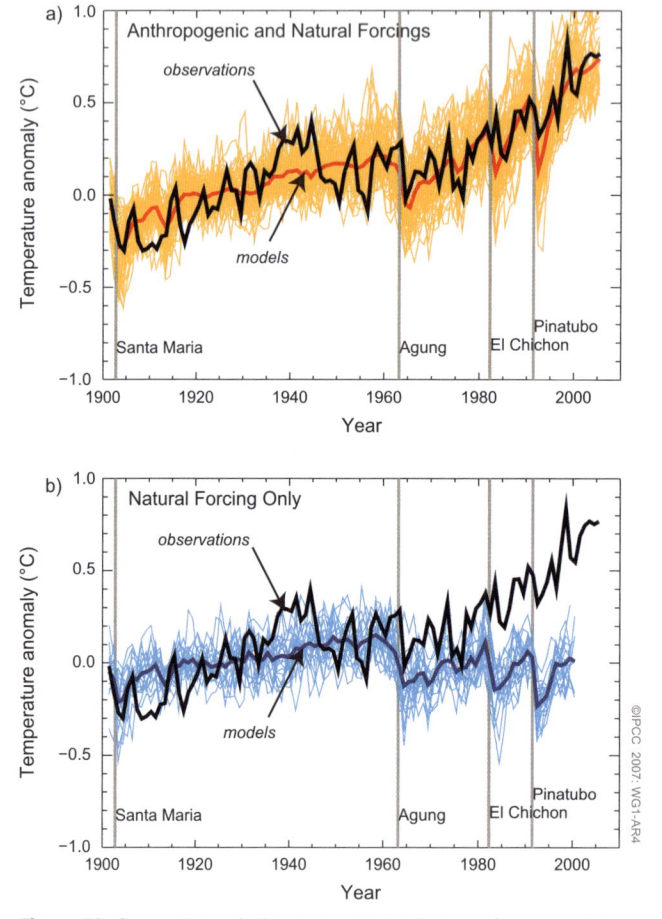

Figure 43. Comparison of climate model simulations of average global temperature run only with natural factors like volcanoes, solar, volcanic and ocean–atmosphere variability (blue line) and natural and anthropogenic factors including greenhouse gases, ozone and land-use changes (red). Instrumental global average temperature observations (black) are also shown. Vertical grey lines denote years containing large volcanic eruptions.

Source: Reproduced courtesy of the IPCC. Solomon, S, Qin, D, Manning, M, Chen, Z, Marquis, M, Averyt, KB, Tignor, M and Miller, HL (eds) 2007. *Climate Change 2007: the Physical Science Basis. Contribution of Working Group I to the Fourth Assessment Report of the Intergovernmental Panel on Climate Change.* Figure TS.23.

In 2013, the *Fifth Assessment Report* of the IPCC concluded that it is 'extremely likely' (more than a 95 per cent chance) that human activities are 'the dominant cause of the observed warming since the 1950s'. Climate change sceptics can squabble all they like, but the evidence is clear: our tinkering with the globe's thermostat—not natural climate variability alone—is responsible for the recently observed rapid warming of our world. The more important question for Australia is: How will human activity continue to influence natural climate variability in our country?

So far, limited research has looked at statistically comparing the increase in greenhouse gas concentrations with observed changes in temperature and rainfall in Australia. Renowned climate scientist professor David Karoly and Bureau of Meteorology scientist Dr Karl Braganza published the first such study in the *Journal of Climate* in 2005. They showed that increases in mean and maximum temperatures in Australia were linked to anthropogenic climate change, and reported their results in the IPCC *Fourth Assessment Report* in 2007. Their best estimate of the anthropogenic contribution to average maximum temperature increases was about 0.6°C from 1950 to 1999; that is, up to 60 per cent of the warming experienced over Australia since the 1950s.

One method for attributing extreme event likelihood is called Fraction of Attributable Risk (FAR), which calculates the risk of exceeding a particular climatic threshold that can be attributed to climate change. Using this method, climate model simulations run with and without increases in greenhouse gas concentrations are compared. The risk of a particular extreme climatic event occurring in each of these two worlds is quantified, with the FAR indicating the change in risk under climate change.

Based on the Australian network of long-term, high-quality temperature stations, no event before the summer of 2012–13 had ever resulted in so many extreme heat records. In 2013, climate scientists Sophie Lewis and David Karoly used a FAR analysis to test whether the extreme summer temperatures of 2012–13 were likely to have been caused by natural variability alone. Comparing climate models with and without greenhouse gases showed that the presence of greenhouse gases led to a five-fold increase in the odds of Australia recording the temperatures experienced in January 2013. Using this method, it was found to be virtually impossible to achieve the 2013 calendar year's temperatures without the presence of human influences on the climate. The study showed that without human influences, the record temperatures Australia experienced in 2013 would occur only once in 12 300 years. The results were important as they showed that greenhouse gases resulting from human activities are significantly increasing the risk of extreme temperatures in Australia—not some time off in a distant future, but here at home, right now.

Other studies have explored several factors that could have influenced the record-breaking 2013 heat in Australia. One led by Monash University's Julie Arblaster used both long-term observations and simulations by a seasonal forecasting model to examine the relative effects of natural variability, the unusually dry conditions that were being experienced in inland eastern Australia in September 2013, and the background warming trend due to climate change. It found that all three factors played significant roles, and concluded that human activity had a discernible influence on the record high September temperatures of 2013.

Further research by Andrew King from the University of Melbourne explored the role of severe drought along with human influences in driving the extreme heat of 2013. They found this heat was made much more likely by important contributions from both climate change and the very dry conditions over the eastern inland regions of the continent. Their results showed that the risk of the record 2013 heat exceeding a high temperature threshold is twenty-three times greater now than it was in the late nineteenth century due to climate change. They also showed that the risk of extreme heat was twenty-five times greater in dry years than wet years, highlighting the tight link between temperature and rainfall in much of Australia.

To extend the length of the observations that may be compared to climate model simulations, in recent years, detection and attribution studies have also been conducted using palaeoclimate records around the world. Using the climate reconstructions developed with precise, annually resolved data, we are able to extend the possible perspective using just a century of instrumental observations alone. As described in Part III, I led the publication of a study that presented a 1000-year reconstruction of Australasian land and sea temperatures, which showed that the warmest thirty-year period in the last 1000 years occurred between 1985 and 2014. We then compared our suite of palaeoclimate results to climate model simulations run over the past millennium to assess the long-term role of natural and human factors on temperature variations in our region.

Our results showed that natural atmosphere–ocean circulation and anthropogenic greenhouse gases had the greatest influence on reconstructed Australasian temperatures, rather than natural solar and volcanic variations. Significantly, anthropogenic greenhouse gases were required to reproduce the rate and magnitude of post-1950 warming recorded in the Australasian temperature reconstruction. We then calculated the differences in temperature between consecutive multiple decades to assess the historical rates of change in temperatures over the past 1000 years.

Under natural pre-industrial conditions, the difference in average temperature between consecutive fifty-year periods never exceeded 0.12°C in magnitude. This contrasts with the observed (0.33°C) and reconstructed (between 0.31°C and 0.34°C) mean temperature change noted between the 1901–50 and 1951–2000 periods. This suggests that even when longer estimates of natural variability are included through the use of palaeoclimate reconstructions, the observed post-1950 warming does not arise solely as a result of natural variability. The increase is nearly three times what you'd expect from natural variability alone. Our results were consistent with independent instrumental studies that clearly link the post-1950 temperature increase seen in instrumental global and Australian temperature records to increases in greenhouse gas concentrations. Yet another sign that climate change is already with us.

30
UP IN FLAMES

While Australia has a long history of bushfires, since the 1970s, more and more large and uncontrollable fires have wreaked havoc in many areas of our most densely populated region of south-eastern Australia. The bushfires that devastated parts of Victoria on 7 February 2009 became Australia's deadliest natural disaster. It's a grisly hall of fame: the blazes killed 173 people and razed over 2000 homes. Kangaroo corpses lay scattered by the roadsides, while wombats that survived the wildfires' onslaught emerged from their underground burrows to find blackened earth and nothing to eat. It is estimated that millions of plants and animals were incinerated across the state during the fires.

Entire towns—like Marysville, just 100 kilometres north-east of Melbourne—were effectively wiped off the map. Haunting images from the area show ghost towns that look more like a bombsite than the remains of a bushfire. The heat was so ferocious that cars were liquefied into eerie metallic pools. Images of the grime-streaked faces and glistening red eyes of residents and emergency workers were harrowing. The trauma of the Black Saturday fires is now carved into our national psyche. It's a brutal reminder of the 'beauty' and the 'terror' of life in Australia that poet Dorothea Mackellar wrote about over a century ago.

Along with the southern regions of California and France, southern Australia is one of the three most fire-prone areas in the world. Strong northerly winds, extreme heat and low humidity can combine to create disastrous bushfire conditions like the ones that tore through Victoria on 7 February 2009. So how do the Black Saturday fires compare to past fires, like the Black Friday fires of 13 January 1939, or the Ash Wednesday fires of 16 February 1983? How do scientists measure the intensity of firestorms?

The McArthur Forest Fire Danger Index (FFDI) was developed in the 1960s to measure the weather conditions associated with fire danger and the difficulty of fire suppression. The FFDI takes into account the effects of air temperature, relative humidity, wind speed and drought. The larger the FFDI number, the greater the danger, with classifications of low–moderate (0–11), high (12–24), very high (25–49), severe (50–74) and extreme (75–99). The FFDI scale was developed by setting the disastrous Black Friday fires, which killed seventy-one people, to a value of 100. The Ash Wednesday fires, which killed forty-seven people, reached an FFDI of over 100, though lower in some areas within the Melbourne region.

On Black Saturday, many areas of Victoria recorded an FFDI of 100–130, with half-a-dozen sites recording 170–190. A terrifying FFDI record of 191 was recorded at Kilmore, highlighting that the extreme fires were well outside the range of historical experience. Indeed, the weather conditions of Black Saturday were so extreme that they actually changed the way in which severe bushfire conditions were rated. A new six-tiered fire danger warning scheme was introduced to accommodate the new 'catastrophic' fire level (FFDI values of >100, known as 'code red' in Victoria) set during the horrific event.

It is now well known that southern Australia has become hotter and drier since the 1950s. Higher temperatures are baking the land for longer, sucking the landscape dry. After over a decade of drought in south-eastern Australia, much of Victoria was a tinderbox waiting to ignite. Research on bushfire weather trends has shown a rapid increase in the FFDI since the 1970s. We have seen an increase in extreme fire weather, and a longer fire season, especially in southern and eastern Australia. In the 1973–2010 period, twenty-four of the thirty-eight reference stations showed a significant increase in the highest 10 per cent of FFDI values, indicating a marked jump in extreme fire weather days.

Whether bushfires occur at a given place depends on four 'switches': ignition, either human-caused or because of natural sources like lightning; fuel load; fuel dryness; and suitable weather for fire spread, generally hot, dry and windy conditions. The settings of these switches depend on weather conditions across a variety of timescales, particularly fuel availability, which can build up over years in some regions, especially after heavy rains (as we saw in the Victorian 1851 Black Thursday fires). Given this strong dependency on the weather, experts predict that climate change will have a significant impact on future fire weather.

CSIRO climate change projections released in 2015 warn that warming and drying in southern and eastern Australia will lead to fuels that are drier and more ready to burn, with increases in the average FFDI and a greater number of days with severe fire danger. Across both regions, the number of severe fire days increases by up to 160–190 per cent in the driest model in the high-emissions-scenario experiments. That's nearly a three-fold increase from present conditions. Increases of 30–35 per cent in annual total FFDI are also projected by 2090 in the worst case, indicating an increase in the intensity of fire conditions.

Climate change projections associated with low- and high-emissions scenarios across all or parts of Australia typically show increases of around 10–30 per cent in FFDI, although increases of up to 50 per cent by 2100 are reported for northern Tasmania. The number of days when FFDI is above 40, when there is a very high chance of bushfires resulting in house destruction in southern Australia, could increase from 30 to 200 per cent by the end of the century in eastern Australia during months of highest fire danger. Research shows that a longer fire season expanding into spring and autumn is also likely. This narrows the window for fuel-control burns and increases the threat to water catchment areas as more fires dump soot and ash into our water supplies.

The question on everyone's mind is: What role, if any, did climate change play in the 2009 Black Saturday bushfires? The first thing to keep in mind is that it is very difficult to attribute a single event to climate change, as who's to say it isn't just a freak peak in extreme weather? Climate variability is a fact of life. Each day the temperature goes up and down with the rising sun; the seasons cycle from summer to winter as the Earth orbits our sun. Large-scale changes in ocean currents and atmospheric weather patterns shift in response to the seasons, as things like sea ice expand and shrink or the oceans are topped up with warm spring run-off from the land.

This is all known as natural, year-to-year climate variability. It is distinct from human-caused climate change that has altered the chemical composition of the air and the oceans by introducing industrial pollution associated with the burning of fossil fuels. It's important that we understand the 'natural baseline' of our climate before we can tell how it is being influenced by human-generated influxes of industrial pollution or the removal of global forests that are important regulators of carbon dioxide and oxygen in the atmosphere. So when looking at events like the Black Saturday fires, scientists look to long-term trends and the factors that might be causing consistent, rather than one-off, changes in the underlying climate.

The seminal 2005 temperature study by David Karoly and Karl Braganza showed that up to 60 per cent of the warming experienced over Australia since the 1950s was caused by human activities. Although formal attribution studies quantifying the influence of climate change on the increased likelihood of extreme fire danger in south-eastern Australia are currently underway, it is very likely that anthropogenic climate change contributed to the unprecedented temperature extremes witnessed on 7 February 2009. In the two weeks leading up to Black Saturday, southern Australia experienced an exceptional heatwave. Between 28 and 30 January, extreme heat blasted the southern states: Adelaide experienced nine consecutive days above 35°C, with six consecutive days above 40°C. From 27 to 30 January, the temperature was over 43°C four days in a row—a doubling of the previous record. Melbourne had three consecutive days over 43°C, with the highest temperature of 45.1°C—the second-highest on record behind 45.6°C on 13 January 1939—occurring on 30 January. The sequence is unprecedented in 154 years of Melbourne weather observations.

It wasn't until the second phase of the heatwave, between 6 and 8 February, that records really got obliterated. After a slight drop in temperatures during the first few days of that month, extreme heat returned to the south-east on 6 February. Temperatures rose sharply in South Australia and western Victoria then, but it was the next day which saw the most exceptional heat of the whole event. The hot air passed over Adelaide overnight on 6 February, allowing it to escape the scorching inflicted on Victoria the following morning. On Saturday 7 February, daily anomalies for most of the southern Victoria coastline were at least 18°C above normal. Some individual stations were up to 20–22°C above normal, representing colossal departures from the historical climate record.

Victoria set a state record of 48.8°C at Hopetoun, following thirty-five days of virtually no rain. Seventy per cent of all Victorian weather stations with forty years or more of weather records set all-time records. Melbourne broke its all-time record with 46.4°C, which was 0.8°C hotter than the previous record-holder, Black Friday 1939, based on 154 years of observations. The city's previous February record was broken by an incredible 3°C, replacing what had been set on the day of a dramatic dust storm in Melbourne on 8 February during the strong El Niño year of 1983. Keep in mind that temperature records are more commonly broken by a fraction of a degree rather than the terrifying margins recorded on Black Saturday.

Very recently, climatologist Mitchell Black from the Bureau of Meteorology undertook the first attribution study of fire events in Australia. He assessed how the likelihood of catastrophic and extreme fire events changed in climate models run with and without greenhouse gases. He found that there was a 17 per cent increase of catastrophic fire conditions like Black Saturday, and an 11 per cent increase in extreme fire conditions in a world with greenhouse gases. The study is important for two reasons. It shows that the climate is changing so fast that new areas of science are being developed as we attempt to understand the events that are currently unfolding. It also reconfirms the increased risk of disastrous events we face in our local communities as we continue to warm the planet to dangerous levels. What is happening now is a fundamental shift in the way we are already experiencing the Australian climate. What we expect in our future climate is playing out right now, not decades in the future. As we begin to drift away from the safe shores of historical variability, the only certainty is that life in the 'new normal' will be outside the range of human experience.

31
VANISHING SNOW

On 28 June 1836, the first report of snow falling in Sydney appears in the historical record. Although *The Sydney Herald* published meteorological tables from 1831 until 1838, it was the only time that the word 'snow' appeared in the descriptive remarks. It's hard to imagine a flake of snow falling in downtown 21st-century Sydney. Even during the nineteenth century, snow at such low elevations would have been rare, but in 2016 Sydney recorded its hottest year in records going back to 1859. Most months in Sydney were about 1°C above average temperatures, and Australia's biggest city recorded more days above 25°C than in any other year. This all occurred on a national mean temperature that was 0.87°C above the historical 1961–90 average, and the surrounding oceans also set a record high of 0.73°C. As our climate continues to warm, we have seen a decrease in the number of cold extremes. Night-time temperatures have risen and there have been significant changes to snow falling in our high-country areas.

The alpine regions of Australia extend over 500 kilometres between Sydney and Melbourne in south-eastern Australia, occupying just 0.3 per cent of the country. Eleven national parks and conservation reserves extend across the Australian Alps region. There are ten ski resorts in or adjacent to the protected areas, with winter visits worth $906 million in 2005. The ski season in the alpine zone typically lasts from early June to early October, although the season is shorter and more erratic at low elevations. The region also houses population centres that largely depend on jobs generated from tourism. Agricultural productivity downstream from the Australian Alps is partially dependent on snow meltwaters from the mountains for some of its irrigation needs. In fact, much of south-eastern Australia depends on the Australian Alps for its water resources and hydroelectric power.

Our high country is also home to unique landscapes and highly alpine sensitive species. This environment is unique as a result of the old age of the landscape, and the lack of mountain building that results from its location in the middle of a tectonic plate. Only minor glacial activity occurred between 10 000 and 30 000 years ago, creating very ancient and weathered landscapes. The total area of the true alpine environment (above the tree line) is small, approximately 770 square kilometres, which is found as a series of 'islands' on top of mountains within a sub-alpine 'sea'. Only around 6500 square kilometres of the alpine and sub-alpine areas see snow fall every year.

The CSIRO has reported declines in average snow depth and duration of snow cover since the 1950s. One study showed that over the past forty years, south-eastern Australian snow depths at the start of October have dropped by 40 per cent. There is very high confidence that as warming progresses, there will be ongoing decreases in snowfall and an increase in snowmelt, leading to an overall reduction of snow cover. Larger changes are expected at lower elevations, especially at the start and end of the snow season.

Climate change projections clearly show a continued reduction in snowfall during the twenty-first century. The magnitude of the decrease depends on the altitude of the region and the emissions scenario. At the low-elevation regions (about 1400 metres above sea level), years without snowfall start to be observed as early as 2030 in some models. By 2090, these years become common under the worst-case scenario. This highlights the fact that even under a low-emissions scenario, years without snowfall will become possible. Years with normal snowfall (by today's standard) will still occur at the end of the twenty-first century but less frequently. At high-elevation locations (around 1900 metres above sea level), snowfall declines by 50–80 per cent.

The CSIRO's climate change modelling predicts that the Australian ski season could shrink by up to eighty days a year by 2050 under the worst-case predictions for climate change. Under a low-emissions scenario, the average snow season across Victoria and some of New South Wales will become twenty to fifty-five days shorter, and under a worst-case scenario, thirty to eighty days shorter—all but obliterating the 112-day ski season. Bigger changes are expected at lower elevations, such as Mount Baw Baw and Lake Mountain in Victoria. Some people working in the tourism industry have suggested that ski resorts in high-elevation sites in New South Wales won't have enough snow for the viable commercial operation of snow resorts in the future. While snow making can operate during dry winters, it can't handle warm and rainy ones. As artificial snow is the primary climate-change adaptation response by the ski tourism industry, it may not be economically, physically or socially viable in the future.

Typically, a minimum operational depth for alpine skiing in Australia is approximately 30 centimetres, although this varies considerably depending on the terrain, and is lower for cross-country ski resorts. By 2050 at the Falls Creek ski resort in Victoria, the average maximum depth is predicted to be 50–105 centimetres for the low-emissions scenario and between 20 and 80 centimetres for the high-emissions scenario. Depending on which emissions path we take, it's possible that the natural snow base of this popular ski field may be too thin to be sustainable in coming decades.

Australia has the highest level of biological endemism of any continent in the world. That is, we have more native plants and animals that are only found here and nowhere else in the world. The uniqueness of Australia's biodiversity is due to our continent being separated from other landmasses for millions of years. The range and diversity of environmental conditions in Australia are also different from most other countries due to characteristics such as nutrient-poor soils, high fire frequencies and generally flat landscapes. Many of Australia's species, and even whole groups of species that comprise taxonomic families, are unique to this continent. As a result, Australia is identified as one of the world's 'megadiverse' countries, along with places like Brazil, the Congo, Madagascar and Papua New Guinea.

These factors combine to make the alpine areas of a country mostly made up of arid land extremely rare and unique. Alpine species have largely evolved in isolation from other continents or in the isolated mountaintops of remote rugged ranges. Species such as the mountain pygmy-possum and broad-toothed rat, and vegetation communities like the short alpine herbfields, alpine bogs and peatlands, have very narrow environmental tolerances. As temperatures continue to warm, our alpine communities are in real danger of quite literally being pushed off mountaintops, having nowhere to migrate to and no way of moving from or between these alpine 'islands'.

As Australia continues to warm, corresponding declines in the duration and depth of snow cover will dramatically alter alpine communities and landscapes. The risk of more fires in alpine peatlands becomes more likely as these ancient swamps begin to dry out. In the early months of 2016, savage bushfires ravaged western Tasmania's precious World Heritage rainforests, burning alpine areas that have not experienced fire for over 8000 years. More than 72 000 hectares of land were incinerated. Tragically, the fire-sensitive cushion plants and 1000-year-old pine trees are unlikely to ever recover from the devastation. The state of our alpine areas may be one of the clearest signs that despite the incredible resilience of our natural heritage over millennia, Australia's most precious landscapes will vanish within our lifetime, an eventual death by a thousand cuts.

32
FLOODING RAINS

A rapidly warming climate means that storms are now occurring in a supercharged atmosphere. As temperatures increase, the water-holding capacity and water vapour content of the lower atmosphere rises. The oceans are also warming, especially at the surface, and this is driving higher evaporation rates that, in turn, further increase the amount of water vapour in the atmosphere. The globe's average surface temperature has already risen by over 1°C above pre-industrial levels, leading to an increase of about 7 per cent in the amount of water vapour in the atmosphere.

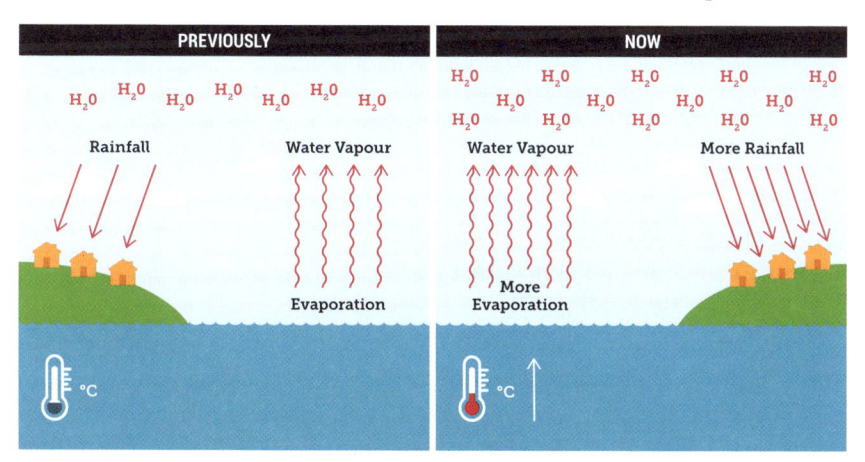

Figure 44. The influence of climate change on the water cycle: the pre-climate change water cycle (left) compared with the water cycle operating under higher surface ocean and air temperatures (right). The symbol H_2O represents water vapour.

Source: Reproduced courtesy of the Climate Council (2017). *Cranking up the Intensity: Climate Change and Extreme Weather Events.*

While that might not sound like much, a warmer and wetter atmosphere is starting to cause more frequent and heavy rainfall in many parts of the world, including Australia. A 2017 study by University of New South Wales researcher Jiawei Bao estimated that a 2°C rise in average global temperatures would lead to an 11–30 per cent increase in extreme downpours across Australia as a result of higher humidity driven by increased temperatures. The findings suggest that if we continue along a high greenhouse gas emissions path and warm by 4°C, we could experience a 23–60 per cent increase in the most extreme (wettest 0.1 per cent) of rainfall events.

The CSIRO's 2015 climate change projections also show that in a hotter climate we will experience an increase in extreme rainfall, even in areas where average rainfall declines. This means more-intense dry spells interspersed with periods of increased extreme downpours over much of Australia. In turn, that means longer and more-severe droughts followed by torrential deluges capable of washing away houses, roads and agricultural crops. Whether Australians can adapt to a more extreme version of our already erratic climate remains to be seen.

While climate models and dynamical theory show that extreme rainfall increases in a warmer climate due to increased atmospheric humidity, it can be difficult to determine the exact impact of climate change on individual rainfall events. Unlike the widespread signature of temperature patterns, rainfall extremes are harder to attribute because of the higher degree of natural variability of rainfall. This is especially the case in Australia, where modes of natural variability such as the El Niño–Southern Oscillation (ENSO), the Indian Ocean Dipole (IOD), monsoonal storms and tropical cyclones play an important role in influencing regional rainfall. Events can also be quite localised, as nearby mountain ranges and surrounding oceans influence the behaviour of cloud development. The combination of circulation changes and the effects of a wetter atmosphere due to climate change make understanding rainfall changes difficult. Consequently, there are more competing influences that obscure the clarity of a climate change signal in rainfall variability.

The attribution of extreme rainfall events in a changing climate is an emerging area of international research. A clear example of climate change potentially exacerbating the intensity of a naturally occurring event was the 2010–11 period of record-breaking rainfall across much of Australia. The nation experienced its wettest spring on record in 2010, leading to extensive flooding in eastern Australia in the summer of 2010–11. These exceptionally wet periods coincided with two consecutive La Niña phases of the ENSO and a negative IOD event, which are typically associated with cool, wet summers in eastern Australia. During these events, warmer ocean conditions in the Indo–Pacific region increases atmospheric convection, driving moisture from the oceans into the atmosphere. As global warming continued to warm surface ocean waters around the world, it is very likely to have pushed up the already high La Niña sea surface temperatures around northern Australia during this event.

One of the strongest naturally occurring La Niña events in history, coupled with very warm sea surface temperatures to the north of Australia and in the eastern Indian Ocean, contributed to making 2010–11 Australia's wettest two-year period on record. Averaged across Australia, back-to-back La Niña events resulted in a two-year rainfall total of 1409 millimetres for 2010–11, surpassing the old record set during the great floods of 1973–74. The heavy rainfall in 2010–11 was remarkable in terms of its spatial extent, covering every region of Australia except south-western Western Australia and parts of Tasmania.

Heavy rainfall in Queensland resulted in extensive flooding, impacting more than 78 per cent of the state and over 2.5 million people, and leading to the loss of thirty-three lives. Around 29 000 homes and businesses suffered some form of inundation, with costs in excess of $14.1 billion. To make matters worse, tropical cyclone Yasi made landfall on Mission Beach in Queensland on 3 February 2011. It was one of the most powerful cyclones to be recorded since 1918—it was rated a category 5, with wind speeds of up to 205 kilometres per hour, gusts of up to 285 kilometres per hour, and a 5-metre tidal surge. Talk about a hell of a year.

All of this came on the back of a record-breaking drought that had baked south-eastern Australia from 1997 to 2009. The region had recorded its lowest thirteen-year rainfall period in the entire historical record. The rainfall deficit during the Big Dry or Millennium Drought was 45 per cent larger than the previous driest thirteen-year recorded during the World War II drought of 1933–45. While shorter low-rainfall periods were observed at the time of Australian Federation and during World War II, the duration of the drought was unprecedented in the instrumental record.

When I joined the climate research group in the School of Earth Sciences at the University of Melbourne in 2008, the drought was in full swing. David Karoly had employed me to follow my idea of gathering up the region's annually resolved palaeoclimate records to see if we could place the drought in a longer-term context. Despite being one of the countries most affected by ENSO events, our knowledge of Australian drought at the time was still largely confined to the twentieth century. Hard to believe, but true.

I teamed up with a very bright meteorologist in the team, Ailie Gallant, to see if we could develop the region's first consolidated rainfall reconstruction. We used Tasmanian and New Zealand tree rings, coral records from the Great Barrier Reef and south-western Pacific, and the Law Dome ice core from eastern Antarctica to develop a 'proof of concept' rainfall reconstruction back to the year 1783. To our amazement, we found that just twelve palaeoclimate records could capture 72 per cent of decade-to-decade variations in instrumental rainfall observations for the region. We had selected records from locations we knew were sensitive to large-scale climate variability associated with the Pacific, Indian and Southern oceans known to influence south-eastern Australia's rainfall.

Satisfied we had a strong rainfall signal in our records, we went ahead and developed the first rainfall reconstruction for the region to extend back past first European settlement. Instead of developing the traditional single version of the reconstruction, we took a new approach and calculated 10 000 different versions of the reconstruction, using a similar 'ensemble' approach to that used to reconstruct Australasian temperatures. We did this to get a good estimate of the uncertainty of the reconstruction when we mixed and matched different combinations of the calibration and verification period. That is, we wanted to see how the results changed if we used different initial conditions to develop the reconstruction. Most importantly, we wanted a large dataset with which to run our probability calculations to assess how unusual the Big Dry really was.

The rainfall reconstruction showed distinct wet and dry cycles, revealing the high degree of natural variability throughout the record. The palaeoclimate record was able to faithfully reproduce the big wets of the 1970s and 1950s. As we continued back beyond the start of the official rainfall record in 1900, we saw very wet conditions during the 1890s, 1860s, and the wettest period of the entire record—the 1820s. It was exciting to see these lesser-known events appear from the data. In terms of droughts, again the palaeoclimate record was able to track the Big Dry, World War II and Federation droughts we explored in Part II. We then saw the 1840s and 1810s emerge as other periods of severe drought we knew next to nothing about.

When we later compared our palaeoclimate reconstruction with early rainfall records and historical documents, we found the strongest agreement after 1860, and some differences that reflected real climatic differences. Because the palaeoclimate records came from areas like Tasmania that are well outside the coastal New South Wales region where the historical records were from, we wouldn't expect them to line up perfectly—the climate of Sydney is quite different to a place like Hobart. The documentary records also tended to report long-lasting droughts more often than normal or less-extreme rainfall conditions. Nevertheless, the comparison of the combination of these records gave us an opportunity to try to reconstruct south-eastern Australia's rainfall history as best we could for the first time, hoping others would build on our results in the future.

One noticeable feature of the palaeoclimate reconstruction was the duration of wet conditions experienced during the late eighteenth to early nineteenth centuries. For example, there was a thirteen-year wet period from 1797 to 1809, and a whopping sixteen-year wet spell from 1818 to 1833. This compares with the longest twelve-year wet period of 1949–60 seen in the twentieth-century instrumental record. In comparison to the markedly wetter late eighteenth to early nineteenth century stretch containing 75 per cent of sustained wet periods, 70 per cent of all reconstructed long droughts in south-eastern Australia occurred during the twentieth century.

Since the 1970s, there had been very few wet 'recovery' years in the reconstruction or instrumental observations. Based on our suite of 10 000 rainfall reconstructions, we then calculated that there was a 97.1 per cent probability that the rainfall deficits recorded during the 1998–2008 Big Dry were the worst experienced since the first European settlement of Australia. Our results showed that the region had been much wetter in

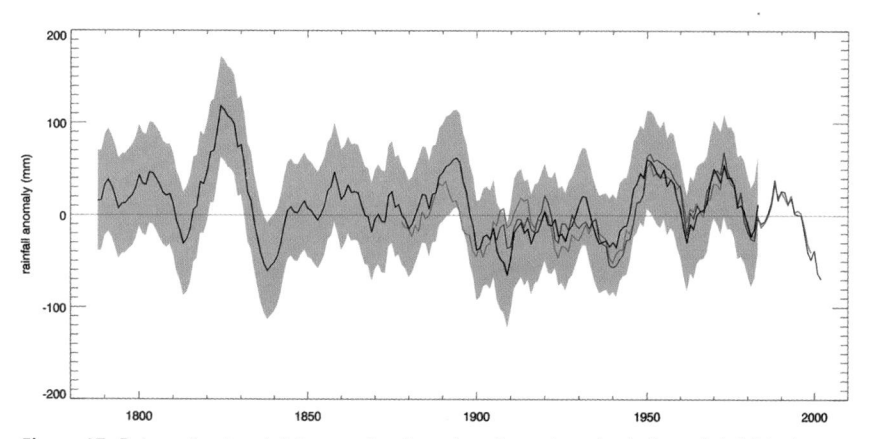

Figure 45. Palaeoclimate rainfall reconstruction of south-eastern Australian rainfall (black line), 1783–1988; regionally averaged instrumental rainfall record for south-eastern Australia (red) for 1900–2009 period; and independent historical rainfall observations (green), 1873–2009. Grey shading denotes uncertainty estimates based on the 10 000 calibration/verification intervals.

Source: Ailie Gallant and Joëlle Gergis.

the past, and was at the time in a very dry period unprecedented in the nation's recorded history.

As we had begun working with water managers from Melbourne Water, the Murray–Darling Basin Authority and the Victorian State Government Office of Water on a large collaborative project reconstructing south-eastern Australia's climate history, we were also interested to see how these rainfall deficits were affecting the Murray–Darling Basin. To check, we used the same method, this time reconstructing River Murray streamflow. Our analysis showed that the 1998–2008 streamflow deficit experienced during the Big Dry was a one-in-1500-year event. It was a startling result, telling us that something very unusual was happening to rainfall in our region.

Subsequent research led by dendrochronologist Jonathan Palmer from the University of New South Wales saw the development of a rainfall reconstruction for the broader region of eastern Australia, and extended the length of rainfall reconstructions back over the past five centuries. Using a much larger region than our south-eastern Australia study, different statistical methods and an expanded network of palaeoclimate records, the researchers estimated that the five worst droughts in their reconstruction occurred before 1900, especially during the 1700s. By contrast, some of the wettest years identified in the study took place after 1950, with 2011 the wettest year. From the vantage point of a longer record, they were able to see that droughts possibly even more severe than the Big Dry have occurred naturally over the past 513 years. That's a frightening prospect, given the severity of the rainfall deficits we experienced from 1997 to 2009. They also saw a pattern of more wet extremes appearing in the record since the mid-twentieth century.

The team compared the rainfall reconstruction with an instrumental index of sea surface temperatures across the Pacific Ocean called the Inter-decadal Pacific Oscillation (IPO), and found remarkable consistency between the two. The relationship is well known: when the IPO is positive, eastern Australia generally experiences drought conditions for several decades, but when the IPO is negative, the region experiences pervasive wet conditions. From 1999 to 2012 the Pacific was in a negative phase of the IPO. Instrumental observations now show that we have entered a positive phase of the cycle, which could mean that background climate conditions may be priming Australia for a prolonged period of increased drought.

An interesting finding was that the Big Dry happened during a negative IPO phase, which is usually associated with wet conditions in our region. The study suggested that there was a strong relationship between the phases of the IPO and drought until around 1976. After that, the relationship weakened. While it is still unknown exactly how the nature of Australian drought will change as the planet continues to warm, the latest palaeoclimate, observational and modelling studies suggest that some of the relationships that have historically held true may be starting to break down. Our climate is changing in ways that future generations of scientists may one day identify as the point of no return.

33
GIRT BY RISING SEAS

In 2016, the world experienced its hottest year on record. Global carbon dioxide levels reached 409 ppm (parts per million), the highest recorded in at least three million years. The record warmth of 2016 was part of this long-term trend which has seen all of the world's ten warmest years in the instrumental record occur since 1997. Human activities, such as the burning of coal, oil and gas for electricity, are driving up greenhouse gas emissions and fuelling global warming. The year 2016 was the fortieth consecutive year with above-average global temperatures, meaning no-one born after 1976 has lived in a year when global average temperatures have been at or below the global twentieth-century average.

In 2016, Australia sweltered through its warmest autumn on record. Much of eastern and northern Australia, including Queensland, New South Wales, Victoria and the Northern Territory, broke temperature records. During that year's summer, the sea surface temperatures in the Coral Sea over the northern, most pristine part of the Great Barrier Reef were around 0.8°C above average. The warm waters of 2016 caused devastating bleaching and resulted in the death of 30 per cent of the coral on the reef. Western Australian and other reefs throughout the world were also badly affected by this mass global bleaching event, the worst in recorded history, driven by climate change and the strong El Niño event. These events are all among the observable signs that the Australian region is experiencing climate change right now.

As the global climate system has warmed, changes have occurred in the frequency and severity of extreme weather. In Australia, the most obvious change has been an increase in the occurrence of record-breaking heat.

Australia's top five warmest years on record occurred in 2005, 2013, 2014, 2015 and 2016, with 2013 our warmest year on record. This warming trend has occurred against a background of year-to-year climate variability, mostly associated with El Niño and La Niña in the tropical Pacific Ocean. Sea surface temperatures in the Australian region have also warmed by nearly 1°C since 1900. The years between 2013 and 2016 were our region's warmest years on record.

When water heats up, it expands. About half of the recent rise in the sea level is due to warmer oceans simply occupying more space from this process of thermal expansion. Over the past century, the oceans have absorbed more than 90 per cent of the increased atmospheric heat associated with greenhouse gas emissions from human activity. The other major cause of sea level rise is the increased melting of land-based ice, such as glaciers and ice sheets, which flows into the sea. Since the early 1970s, ocean thermal expansion and glacier mass loss from warming together explain about 75 per cent of the observed 21-centimetre rise in global mean sea level since 1880. Since 1993, the sea level has been rising faster still, at about 3 millimetres per year, or 30 centimetres per century. Research published in May 2017 estimated that before 1990, oceans were rising at about 1.1 millimetres per year. From 1993 through 2012 sea level rose at 3.1 millimetres per year. This suggests that the world's oceans are rising nearly three times as rapidly as they were throughout most of the twentieth century, one of the strongest indications yet that accelerated sea level rise is now underway.

Average sea levels in Australian waters have been rising at rates similar to the global average. Since 1993, Australian tide gauges have shown an average rise of 2.1–3.1 millimetres per year, with regional impacts determined by the shape and depth of the sea floor. While this rate might not sound like much, any rise in the sea level amplifies the threats posed by high tides and storm surges associated with intense low-pressure systems (like tropical cyclones or severe east-coast lows) to communities and infrastructure close to the coast.

Over 85 per cent of the Australian population lives in the coastal zone, with population growth in regional areas expanding significantly in recent years. Approximately 90 per cent of us live within 30 kilometres of the coast. In 2006, it was estimated that over 6 per cent of Australian addresses—some 1.5 million properties—were located within 3 kilometres of the coast and less than 5 metres above sea level. Of these, more than 30 per cent were located in Queensland and New South Wales. Around 39 000 properties are within 110 metres of soft, erodible shorelines.

Australia's shipping ports and harbours, along with many airports and tourism assets, are located on the coast. Aside from human activity, many nationally and internationally significant environmental and cultural heritage sites are also found in the coastal zone. Sea level rise combined with changes in weather patterns, ocean currents, ocean temperature and storm surges will increase the threats to our coastal communities. Beach erosion, inundation of low-lying coastal regions, and saltwater intrusion into freshwater aquifers, deltas and estuaries are all major threats to our vast coastline.

During a series of east-coast lows in June 2016, a storm surge caused extensive flooding and damage to coastal infrastructure from Queensland to Tasmania. The systems produced heavy rainfall, strong winds and large sea swells, resulting in massive coastal erosion along much of the eastern Australian seaboard. People living along Sydney's northern beaches saw first-hand the damage the ocean can wreak on coastal properties hit by such a severe event during a king tide. Huge waves eroded about 50 metres of the Narrabeen and Collaroy beaches, where a number of badly damaged waterfront properties were at serious risk of toppling into the sea. Dramatic footage of the event showed the foundations of houses being severely undercut, as large chunks of the beach were gouged out by huge 8-metre waves. Some residents of Collaroy reported having 20 metres of their backyards washed away in the storm, while further south, enormous waves lashed multimillion-dollar cliff-top properties in the suburb of Vaucluse.

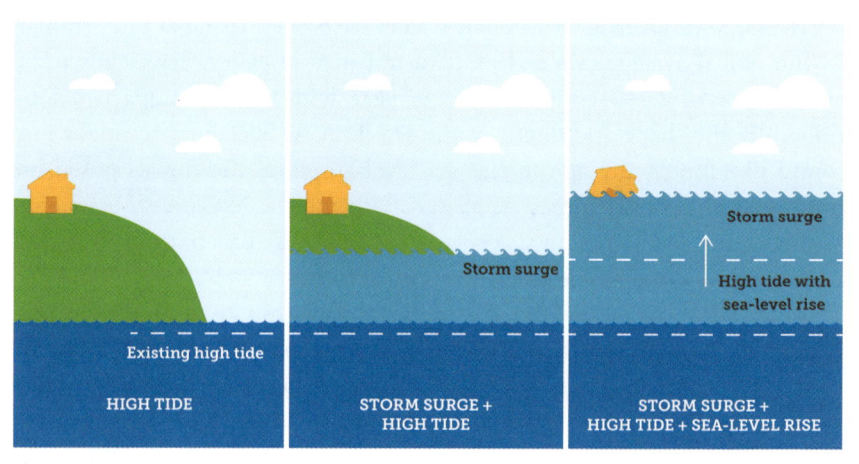

Figure 46. Sea level rise exacerbates the impacts of a storm surge and high tides on coastal communities.

Source: Reproduced courtesy of the Climate Council (2017). *Cranking up the Intensity: Climate Change and Extreme Weather Events.*

While east-coast lows are not uncommon, this event stood out because of the exceptionally widespread extent of the heavy rainfall. These systems are typically smaller-scale, with major impacts confined to a few hundred kilometres of the coastline, not enormous tracts of the Australian seaboard. But during the June 2016 event, severe conditions were experienced all the way from southern Queensland to Tasmania. Many locations in south-eastern Queensland and eastern New South Wales recorded their highest June rainfall record. Averaged across eastern New South Wales, 5 June was the wettest day on record with a regional average of 73.11 millimetres, surpassing the previous record of 68.89 millimetres set on 19 January 1950. Heavy rainfall brought major flooding to Tasmania's northern river basins. Twenty-four-hour totals to 9 a.m. on 6 June saw northern Tasmanian locations receive over 200 millimetres of rainfall, with several reporting their wettest day for any month on record.

While no formal attribution study has been conducted on the event, it is likely that record warm ocean temperatures in the Tasman and Coral seas experienced during a major El Niño year contributed to the formation of these conditions. In May 2016, the sea surface temperature anomaly for the Coral Sea was +0.99°C (0.21°C warmer than the previous highest set in 2006), while for the Tasman Sea it was +1.33°C (0.6°C warmer than the previous equal highest set in May 1998, after the end of the huge 1997–98 El Niño).

Although the system was only associated with a relatively moderate storm surge of around 30 centimetres in Sydney, it combined with high tide, generating damaging waves that resulted in local inundation of low-lying areas and widespread erosion along the New South Wales coast. This event also occurred against a background of an increasing sea level trend. At Fort Denison in Sydney Harbour, the sea level trend over the period 1966–2010 was 1.33 millimetres per year, representing an overall rise in the sea level of more than 5 centimetres over that period. While this might not sound like much, it means the difference between your home being safe and dry, or flooded by high tides and storm surges.

Watching the television news reports unfold during the event, I remember commenting to my partner: 'This is what climate change looks like in Australia'. A few months later, I was teaching second-year university students about natural and human-caused climate variability, and their influence on Australia's future climate. I showed them slides of the event, walked them through the evidence, and began connecting the dots. The class was unusually silent; even the back row, usually glued to their screens, looked up and listened.

To me, the events that unfolded in June 2016 along the eastern seaboard are one of the clearest and most concerning examples of the threats facing Australians as our climate continues to warm. When there is more heat in the system, everything compounds to amplify normal seasonal storms into monster events, as we graphically saw even more recently when Cyclone Debbie caused immense flooding and destruction along the Queensland and New South Wales coasts in March 2017.

A recent study of twenty-nine locations around Australia found that for a mid-range sea level rise of 50 centimetres, extreme sea level events that used to happen every ten years are likely to occur every ten days by 2100. On average, Australia will experience a roughly 300-fold increase in inundation. This means that areas that are currently impacted once every century will be flooded several times each year with a sea level rise of 50 centimetres, with the greatest risks in the Sydney region. A sea level rise of 1.1 metres (a high-end scenario for 2100) would expose more than $226 billion worth of coastal assets, including infrastructure and homes, to inundation and erosion hazards. According to the Climate Council's 2014 coastal risk assessment report, if the threat of sea level rise is ignored, by 2050 the combined global losses from coastal flooding and land subsidence are projected to rise to US$1 trillion per year, around the size of the entire Australian economy. This future would reconfigure our magnificent coastlines and seriously undermine our ability to enjoy this incredibly blessed aspect of Australian life. A fundamental part of our national identity is washing away, as we look on from an ever-eroding shoreline.

PART V
THE AGE OF CONSEQUENCES

34
THE 'NEW NORMAL'

As the old saying goes, those who fail to learn from history are destined to repeat it. In November 1936, British Prime Minister Winston Churchill delivered a speech to the House of Commons warning of the threat of Hitler invading Poland. He warned: 'The era of procrastination, of half-measures, of soothing and baffling expedience of delays, is coming to its close. In its place we are entering a period of consequences'. Of course this came to pass with World War II, one of the most devastating periods of global instability in human history.

Churchill's quote is a chillingly accurate description of the climate change crisis we face today. The disruption of our planet's climatic equilibrium is now threating the stability and safety of our civilisation—we have entered the age of consequences. If we continue along our current high-emissions path, global average temperatures are projected to increase by between 2.6°C and 4.8°C (above 1986–2005 levels) by the end of the century. An increase of at least 3°C is considered extremely likely, as elevated carbon dioxide concentrations can persist for thousands of years. Only after many millennia will it return in rock form, for example, through the formation of calcium carbonate (limestone) from skeletal fragments of marine organisms settling to the bottom of the ocean, or the formation of new coal beds from decaying plant material. The removal of carbon from our atmosphere through these natural processes is known as carbon sequestration, the general term used for the capture and long-term storage of carbon dioxide.

But on timescales more relevant to society, once released, carbon dioxide is essentially in our environment forever. According to University of Chicago oceanographer David Archer, the climatic impacts of releasing fossil fuel carbon dioxide into the atmosphere will last longer than those of nuclear waste or the entire period of human civilisation so far. We are at the point where excess carbon in our atmosphere will not go away naturally unless we remove it ourselves.

As the planet continues to warm because of the burning of ancient fossil fuels, scientists have discovered that temperature increases aren't uniform across the globe. For example, the Arctic region of the Northern Hemisphere is warming more rapidly than the global average, and warming over land is greater than over the ocean. So what does this mean for Australia? As we've seen, our climate has always varied from year to year and from decade to decade, and always will. The issue is that we have added more and more greenhouse gases to the climate system, so this alters the way natural variability behaves. That is, the global warming trend combines with natural variability to create new climate conditions. In many ways, our naturally high climate variability can lull us into a false sense of security that what we experience is the same as what we've experienced in the past. And because our variability is so high, it can sometimes take a little while for the climate change signal to statistically emerge from the background ups and downs of an already highly variable climate.

But with every passing year we are breaking record after record, redefining what Australia's new climate will be like as the planet continues to warm. In 2015, the CSIRO and Bureau of Meteorology released its most comprehensive climate change projections ever compiled by incorporating simulations from up to forty-eight state-of-the-art climate models used in the Intergovernmental Panel on Climate Change's *Fifth Assessment Report*. The projections used the latest climate science to provide a detailed picture of what climate change might be like in all regions of Australia under different greenhouse gas emissions scenarios. The three main factors that determine the future climate we will experience are a region's underlying natural variability, global greenhouse gas emissions, and the response of the climate based on the level of emissions.

The CSIRO projections show that Australia will warm substantially during the twenty-first century. The question is: How much will this affect our daily lives? Researchers investigated the possible climate conditions we could experience using low-, medium- and high-emissions trajectories, referred to as Representative Concentration Pathways (RCPs). Projections for RCP2.6 (low emissions), RCP4.5 (intermediate emissions) and RCP8.5 (high emissions) scenarios were reported over twenty-year periods centred on 2030 and 2090 relative to present climate conditions represented by the 1986–2005 average. The RCP numbers refer to the amount of extra energy in the atmosphere due to heat-trapping greenhouse gas emissions by the end of the century, relative to pre-industrial levels (measured in watts per square metre). Another way of thinking about this process, known as radiative forcing, is the amount by which the Earth's energy budget is out of balance: the higher the number, the more greenhouse gases there are to trap heat in the atmosphere instead of it being reflected back into space, causing the planet to warm.

In the low-emissions RCP2.6 scenario, we see the environmental benefit of ambitious global action to reduce greenhouse gas emissions. On a RCP8.5 pathway, little global action is taken to reduce greenhouse gas emissions, leaving us in the 'business as usual' position we're currently in. According to the CSIRO, warming will be large compared with natural variability in the near future (up until around 2030), and very large compared with natural variability late in the century under RCP8.5. By 2030, Australia's annual average temperature is projected to increase by 0.6–1.3°C above the climate of 1986–2005 in the middle-of-the-road RCP4.5 scenario, with little difference in warming between the different emission pathways. But after 2030, projected temperature increases vary drastically between the scenarios. Australia's average temperature is projected to rise by 0.6°C to 1.7°C in the low-emissions scenario, 1.4°C to 2.7°C for the intermediate emissions pathway, and 2.8°C to 5.1°C for the high end by the end of the century.

Although global emissions appear to have slowed since 2014, it's very uncertain whether this is temporary or signifies a real start in the decline of global emissions. As some of the climate models used to estimate future climate change do not include carbon cycle feedbacks, which are expected to amplify warming, the projections underestimate the likelihood of high global and regional warming outcomes. As a result, unfortunately, many climate scientists would agree that focusing on the low-emissions scenario is overly optimistic and unlikely to happen. Even if all countries achieve their Paris Agreement pledges, we would still be tracking above the low-emissions scenario needed to stave off dangerous climate change.

So while all figures for each scenario are given in the CSIRO's and Bureau of Meteorology's 222-page technical report, the vast majority of the summaries focus on the more likely intermediate and high-emission pathways to help decision makers realistically plan for the future. Some scientists believe that the low-emissions scenario might be helpful when we inevitably overshoot the aspirational target of a 1.5–2°C increase in global average temperature set out by the United Nations Framework

Convention on Climate Change, and attempt to come back down by implementing strong policies to significantly reduce greenhouse gas emissions to cool the climate in the future. But the problem with overshooting is that it poses substantial threats to the Earth's ecosystems, which may not be able to bounce back after breaching the limits of their natural resilience. And once ice sheets have melted and raised the world's sea level, there will be major devastation to human societies around the globe that will be difficult, if not impossible, to recover from.

A recent study led by climate scientist Sophie Lewis from the Australian National University showed that after setting the recording-breaking global temperatures of 2015 as a reference year, conditions that were considered extreme during the early years of the twenty-first century emerged as the 'new normal' by 2040 under all emissions scenarios. The analysis showed that global average temperatures greater than those observed in 2015 will occur at least every second year by 2040. The researchers concluded that in regions like Australia, negative impacts associated with this new normal could be delayed by major greenhouse gas emissions reductions. But in the absence of strong climate policy, it's hard to imagine that we will be able to put the brakes on in time to avoid a future seared by heat considered exceptional by today's standards.

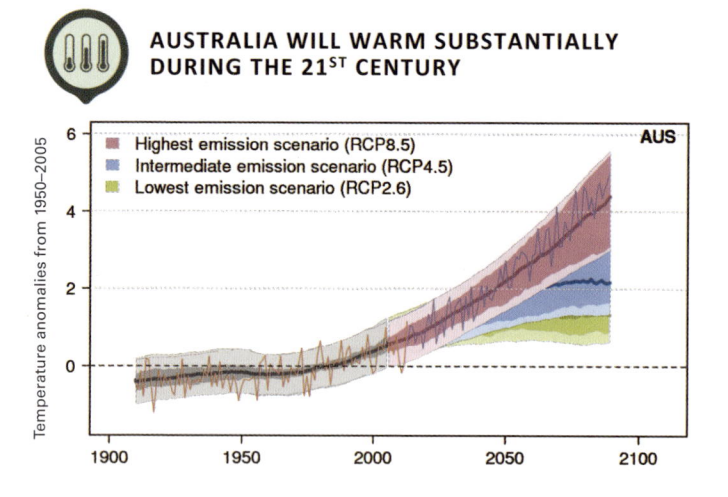

Figure 47. Climate model projections of increases in average temperature across Australia based on low (light green), intermediate (blue) and high (pink) greenhouse gas emissions scenarios, with Bureau of Meteorology ACORN-SAT instrumental temperature observations (brown).

Source: Reproduced courtesy of the CSIRO and Bureau of Meteorology, Climate Change in Australia website (http://www.climatechangeinaustralia.gov.au).

In his comprehensive reviews of climate change and the Australian economy in 2008 and 2011, renowned Australian economist Ross Garnaut clearly pointed out that Australia is the most vulnerable country of the developed world when it comes to climate change. Our dramatic natural climate variability means that climate events are becoming even more extreme as the planet continues to warm. Australia is also a nation heavily reliant on its large agricultural sector, which in turn is highly sensitive to weather and climate extremes. As we've seen, major droughts, cyclones, bushfires and floods have had enormous impacts on the economy and our communities throughout our history, and always will. The question is: How much risk do we want to expose ourselves to?

Compounding our inherent vulnerability to extremes in climate variability is the fact that we are also a country that sits in the heart of the Asia–Pacific region: our direct neighbours are largely developing countries that are not well equipped to deal with the threats posed by climate change, as they already struggle to make basic ends meet. As climate change worsens and exposes already impoverished people to heightened risk of drought, flooding, sea level rise and bushfires, life in some regions will become increasingly unstable, potentially unleashing a flow of refugees. Our region's vulnerability to humanitarian crises resulting from climate change is so high that Asia–Pacific, which includes Australia, has recently been dubbed 'Disaster Alley' by experts in the field. To complicate matters, Australia's economy relies heavily on trade with Asia, meaning that our prosperity is further tied to a region that has high exposure risks associated with climate change. Being a globalised world, all of this means that our neighbours' problems will fast become ours.

35
REDRAWING OUR MAPS

So what will life in 21st-century Australia be like if we continue on, business as usual, and do too little too late to reduce global greenhouse gas emissions? Simply speaking, you can think of climate change in Australia as natural climate variability on steroids, with warmer temperatures artificially enhancing nature's more extreme performances. Increasing amounts of greenhouse gases are making our climate more unpredictable as historically relied-upon weather patterns break down. Forecasting rules that held true in the past are already starting to fail meteorologists, and new colour scales are being added to graphs to accommodate extremes unseen in modern weather records. We're transitioning into a new era where the past may not be a reliable guide to the future as we rapidly accelerate beyond the boundaries of our natural variability.

While there are differences in the climate change projections for each Australian region, the average temperature increase across the country typically will be 4°C by the end of the century. The biggest changes will affect inland Australia, where up to 5.3°C of warming is projected under high-emissions scenarios. In a town like Alice Springs, this means the number of days over 40°C will rise from seventeen per year to an average of eighty-three per year, close to a five-fold increase. It's very likely that parts of the outback will record summer temperatures of over 50°C, making much of inland Australia increasingly unliveable. In a future like this, it is possible that we will see towns in the arid zone abandoned by the mid to late twenty-first century—a much larger and more permanent version of what happened with the Goyder Line in northern South Australia during the late nineteenth century.

Extreme heat will also pose a serious threat to the tourism industry in central Australia, including iconic desert regions like Uluru–Kata Tjuta National Park. Desert tourism is worth tens of billions of dollars each year to the Australian economy, contributing an estimated $94.8 million a day. The huge number of tourists visiting the outback each year creates thousands of jobs for local communities. If these regions become unbearably hot due to climate change, the tourism industry, particularly in the summer months, could become unviable and eventually collapse.

The eastern regions of Queensland and New South Wales, which take in the capital cities of Brisbane and Sydney, will also be hit hard. Mean temperatures are predicted to increase by an average of 3.9°C but by as much as 5°C by 2090 under high emissions. In this scenario, Brisbane will see the number of days over 35°C jump from the current twelve days each year to fifty-five days, making the heat and humidity of the summer wet season excruciating. These conditions are predicted to increase the intensity of heatwaves and extreme rainfall, posing major issues for electricity

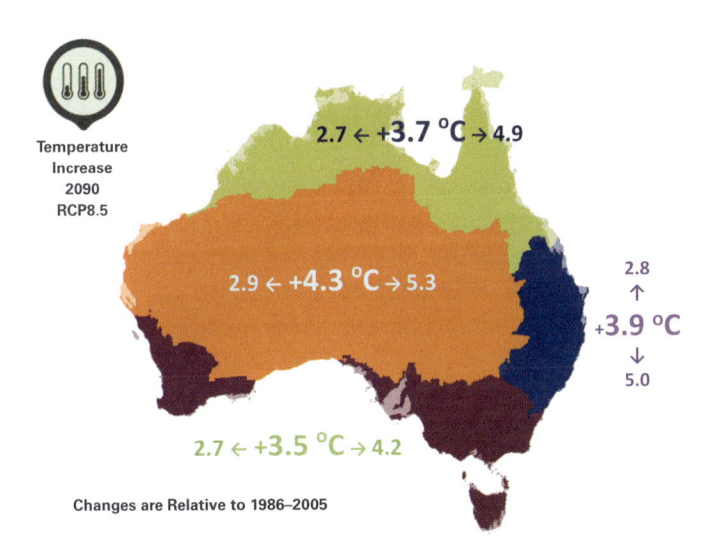

Figure 48. Projected temperature changes relative to 1986–2005 by the year 2090 under high-emissions scenario RCP8.5. Temperature ranges are given for eastern Australia (blue), southern Australia (purple), rangelands (orange) and northern Australia (light green). Central figure gives median temperature projection; that is, half the values fall above and half below this value. Minimum and maximum range based on the warmest and coolest 10 per cent of results calculated from up to forty-eight different climate models.

Source: Reproduced courtesy of the CSIRO and Bureau of Meteorology, Climate Change in Australia website (http://www.climatechangeinaustralia.gov.au).

demand for air-conditioning and the protection of infrastructure from more frequent flood extremes. Changes in temperatures are also projected to affect the spread of agricultural pests and diseases. For example, Queensland's fruit fly is expected to spread southwards in response to future higher temperatures, which threatens to decrease crop yields and increase operational costs in Australia's agricultural sector.

In Sydney, average temperatures will continue to increase across all seasons, resulting in more hot days and heatwaves like the exceptional conditions experienced in the summer of 2016–17. According to the Bureau of Meteorology, January 2017 was the warmest month on record for Sydney (and Brisbane). Every station in the Sydney metropolitan area recorded its highest January mean temperature on record, and most New South Wales sites, including Observatory Hill, broke records for the monthly mean maximum and minimum temperatures. For example, on 11 February, Richmond in the western suburbs recorded a maximum temperature of 47°C, the highest February temperature ever recorded in the Sydney basin. Based on recent observations, it's very possible that future summers in Australia's most densely populated city will soar past the 50°C mark in years to come.

To make matters worse, extreme heat will threaten over 100 000 households in and around Sydney classified as having a high risk of bushfire. In suburbs like Hornsby, where close to 20 000 addresses are located within 100 metres of bushland, homes may become uninsurable as a result of the elevated risk. To the south in Melbourne, the number of days above 35°C will double, leading to harsher bushfire weather conditions in areas like Warrandyte and the Dandenongs in Melbourne's east.

Aside from extreme temperatures and fire weather conditions, rainfall patterns are also projected to change in the coming decades. As Australia has continued to warm, atmospheric circulation has changed, particularly at the boundary of the tropics and the southern part of the country. Simply speaking, the tropics are expanding and bumping our southern storm tracks off the edge of the continent. This is seen through the declines in annual rainfall in many regions of eastern and southern Australia since the 1950s, while rainfall has increased over much of northern Australia over the same period. In fact, increases in heavy daily rainfall account for much of the rise in yearly rainfall recorded over northern Australia since the 1970s, as tropical conditions have intensified.

In southern Australia, an area taking in the cities of Melbourne, Hobart, Adelaide and Perth, there has been an observed drying trend characterised by a 10–20 per cent reduction in cool-season (April–September) rainfall.

Major rainfall declines began around 1970 in south-western Western Australia and in the mid-1990s in the south-east of the country. It has now been established that these rainfall declines have been associated with fewer rain-bearing systems, and less rainfall from the systems that manage to form across the region. Less winter and spring rain means less water for cities, agriculture and natural ecosystems. The CSIRO's and Bureau of Meteorology's projections show that the region will spend more time in drought over the course of this century.

The abrupt decline in rainfall experienced in Perth since the 1970s has now been definitively linked to increasing greenhouse gases and the hole in the ozone layer above Antarctica. The south-west has typically received the bulk of its annual rainfall in winter, which is associated with the passage of cold fronts that bring moist air over the Southern Ocean. In recent decades, climate change has shifted this pattern, as the zone of high pressure has expanded over the continent. In addition, reductions in ozone levels over Antarctica have led to the cooling of the upper atmosphere over the South Pole. This in turn has strengthened the westerly winds that blow around the Southern Ocean, shifting them poleward towards Antarctica. Together, these influences have resulted in the rain-bearing systems that have historically brought relief to southern Australia now tracking further south, dumping precious rain over the ocean instead of the land. As the ozone hole starts to repair itself, its influence has been declining, leaving human-caused atmospheric circulation changes as the main culprit of rainfall declines in the region. If climate change continues unchecked and this pattern establishes itself as the new climate regime, it will compromise the already erratic arrival of the drought-breaking rains that precariously sustain life in 21st-century Australia.

As a result of the water supply crisis during the height of the Millennium Drought (1997–2009), state governments around Australia began building desalination plants that purify seawater into drinking water using reverse osmosis technology. Australia's first desalination facility was the Kwinana plant in Perth, which was completed in November 2006. A second plant opened at Binningup in September 2011, with the capacity to produce nearly a third of Perth's water supply. According to Western Australia's Water Corporation, the two desalinisation plants currently supply 47 per cent of Perth's water needs, and a third facility might be needed if declines in winter rainfall continue.

Elsewhere around the country, other regions followed Western Australia's lead as water stress peaked during the Millennium Drought. A desalinisation plant on the Gold Coast began operation in February 2009, followed by the Kurnell plant in Sydney in January 2010. The Wonthaggi plant in Melbourne was opened in December 2012, after Melbourne's water storages fell to their equal lowest level of 28.7 per cent of capacity in 2007. Ironically, Melbourne's reservoirs were at 81 per cent of capacity when the facility was completed in December 2012 following the heavy La Niña rains of 2010–11, so the plant was put into stand-by mode until March 2017 when the first water for public use was released. In March 2013, the Port Stanvac desalination plant in Adelaide was opened, with the capacity to supply around 50 per cent of Adelaide's domestic water supply.

Although the discharge of concentrated brine needs to be sufficiently diluted to minimise negative environmental impacts on marine environments, many of these plants use accredited renewable energy sources such as wind farms to power their operations. While some environmentalists might argue that these plants are not as good as water-saving measures that don't use any energy and make us rethink our behaviour, they are still an important climate change adaptation measure that will improve future water security in Australia's capital cities.

In the monsoonal north, there is less confidence in projected rainfall trends due to the complexity of mathematically representing tropical processes in climate models. Even so, there is high confidence that the intensity of heavy rainfall events will increase, based on a solid understanding of the fundamental physical dynamics and high model agreement. The number of tropical cyclones is projected to decrease, but there will be a greater proportion of intense cyclones. This has implications for the construction of cyclone-proof buildings and other engineered structures that are currently only designed to cover the latitudes north of 25 degrees south in Queensland and 27 degrees south in Western Australia. Imagine if building codes in places south of Bundaberg on the east coast and Shark Bay in Western Australia needed to be redesigned to resist a category 5 cyclone with sustained wind speeds of over 200 kilometres per hour, and gusts of over 280 kilometres per hour? It's unsettling to recall the immense destruction in Darwin caused by Cyclone Tracy in 1974, when the category 4 system flattened an area with building standards that were inadequate for the climate risks associated with the region.

To avoid wind damage from cyclones, quality design and construction using materials tested in accordance with the Building Code of Australia and other relevant standards might need to be implemented in places like Brisbane. Immense destruction and flooding was caused by the category 3 tropical cyclone that crossed the coast at Coolangatta on 20 February 1954. And as Cyclone Debbie showed us in March 2017, there is a very real possibility of the destruction reaching further south as a rapidly warming climate continues to supercharge our atmosphere, unleashing torrential storms that will be capable of rewriting Australian history. A combination of higher rainfall intensity and sea levels will amplify the distressing impacts of storm surges, resulting in coastal inundation and beach erosion on a scale never before witnessed by modern Australian society.

Temperature projections in the monsoonal north show a substantial increase in the temperatures reached on the hottest days and the frequency and intensity of warm spells. For example, the number of days above 35°C in Broome may increase from fifty-six days to 231 days—a fourfold increase—by the end of the century using high-emissions trajectories (RCP8.5). More alarmingly, the number of days over 40°C increases from just four days per year to thirty, highlighting the extreme temperatures that will compound the humidity of the tropics.

One of the most powerful features of the CSIRO's and Bureau of Meteorology's climate change projections was their use of 'climate analogues' to help explain what future climate change might be like relative to other places in Australia. Using an online tool, you can ask a question like 'What will the future climate of Melbourne be like?' and the database will statistically identify locations where the current climate is similar to the projected future climate of a place of interest. So in this case, under high emissions, Melbourne's future climate will match the current climate of Dubbo in western New South Wales, or that of Gawler, 40 kilometres north of Adelaide, by the end of the century. Sydney will take on the subtropical climate of Brisbane, and Hobart will transition to the aridity of today's Adelaide. By the end of the century, Darwin will not resemble any part of modern-day Australia; entirely new climate conditions will have formed.

In May 2017, the US National Oceanic and Atmospheric Administration (NOAA) released a report revising its physically plausible global sea level rise estimate to as much as 2–2.7 metres by the end of the century based on the high-emissions scenario. The revision takes into account recently observed Antarctic ice-sheet instability, suggesting that sea level rises at the higher end of the scale are more likely than previously thought. A 2015 study by Germany's Potsdam Institute for Climate Impact Research suggested that the west Antarctic ice sheet has likely already been destabilised, committing the world to a minimum 3-metre rise in the global sea level in coming centuries. Even the NOAA's more conservative 2-metre estimate indicates that some of Australia's most densely populated suburbs, major cities and crucial pieces of infrastructure could be underwater by the end of this century, according to new mapping by Coastal Risk Australia that combines the estimates with national high-tide data and the shape of our coastline.

The resulting maps show that airports in Sydney, Brisbane and Hobart will be largely underwater by 2100 if the projected 2-metre rise happens. Many of Australia's most densely populated areas will be at risk of becoming uninhabitable, or subject to an increased risk of destructive storm surges as the sea level rises. For example, in Sydney, Circular Quay, Wentworth Park, the Royal Botanic Gardens, Woolloomooloo and Rose Bay will be inundated. Further north, low-lying parts of Newcastle, Port Macquarie, Ballina and Byron Bay will be among the most heavily hit as the sea gouges away our shorelines. In Victoria, Melbourne's southern suburbs of Port Melbourne, St Kilda and Docklands, as well as the CBD, will be the worst affected. Vast areas of the Gold Coast and Port Douglas in Queensland, and the WACA ground and Cottesloe Beach in Perth, will also be submerged. In this future, maps of the world—not just Australia—will have to be redrawn as the sea level rises, and new rainfall and temperature patterns sculpt new landscapes and coastlines in response to a drastically altered climate.

The kids of today will inherit a world like this if we don't put the brakes on industrial emissions immediately. Maybe future Australians will look back at our government's inadequate action on climate change as an intergenerational crime against humanity. Only time will tell if we will rise to the ethical challenge of safeguarding the world for future generations.

36
SILENT KILLERS

As climate change continues, Australians will experience even more days of extreme heat and related health impacts. Researchers have found that it's the deadly combination of searing temperatures and oppressive humidity that causes dangerous heat stress. Sometimes referred to as the 'silent killer', heat stress occurs when the body absorbs more heat than it can tolerate. High humidity limits the body's ability to cool itself by sweating, causing the body to overheat and develop heat stroke, which can rapidly deteriorate into a life-threatening condition. The severity of recent heatwaves provides alarming examples of how dangerous heat results in increased hospital admissions and deaths in the tropical and more temperate regions of our country.

For example, in late January 2009, during the severe heatwaves in south-eastern Australia preceding the Black Saturday bushfires, Melbourne sweltered through three consecutive days at or above 43°C. Throughout the heatwave, an estimated 2000 people, many of them elderly, were treated by ambulance officers and placed in hospitals for heat-related illnesses in Victoria and South Australia. There were 980 deaths during this period, with 374 of them considered 'excess deaths', representing a 62 per cent increase over what would normally be expected for that time of year. The Victorian coroner announced that at the height of the heatwave, the state morgue took in fifty bodies a day, a tripling of the dead bodies usually received by the mortuary. Conditions were so bad that hospitals and funeral homes were called on to provide temporary storage facilities for corpses. These deaths filled the morgue to capacity before the Black Saturday bushfires added an extra 173 deaths to a system already buckling under the pressure of an exceptional summer. In South Australia, previous heatwaves have also been associated with a 7.3 per cent increase in mental health admissions, and an increase in deaths attributed to psychological and behavioural disorders.

During the 2009 heatwave, on 29 and 30 January, several outdoor tennis matches of that year's Australian Open were cancelled due to the scorching temperatures. A record number of players withdrew from the high-stakes matches in the first round, unable to cope with the fierce heat. According to The Climate Institute's 2015 report on climate change and sport, players hallucinated, collapsed and vomited. Conditions were labelled 'inhumane', as matches as long as six hours were played in sizzling conditions. Players' shoes and water bottles even started to melt in the furnace of the arena. American tennis superstar Serena Williams was quoted as saying it was so hot on court, she felt like she was having an 'out-of-body experience'. She was probably describing the symptoms that occur when a core body temperature of above 39°C causes the body to hover dangerously close to unconsciousness. If the core body temperature goes above 42°C, even for just a short period of time, death is a very real possibility. Placing some of the world's elite athletes and thousands of spectators in danger is something that organisers of summer sporting events will have to factor into future life in Australia.

Sport is a fundamental part of Australian society, contributing over 95 000 jobs and $12.8 billion to the Australian economy in 2011–12. Around 80 per cent of Australians aged over fifteen enjoy sporting activities ranging from bushwalking to competitive team sports at least once a year. Almost two-thirds of Australian children participate in organised sport outside of school. So imagine the impact of extreme events such as the Millennium Drought when ovals and playing grounds across the country dried up and cracked, placing sportsgrounds under immense stress. While elite professional venues may be able to afford expensive upgrades like retractable roofs and improved ventilation, local sportsgrounds struggle to cope with the impacts of longer and hotter droughts. For example, in 2007, 75 per cent of the metropolitan and rural Australian Rules football leagues surveyed in Victoria delayed or cut short their seasons due to temporary or permanent ground closures. Over 100 community cricket clubs in Geelong were forced to end their seasons three months early, and football pre-seasons were affected by the lack of available training ovals. In the Dandenong region east of Melbourne, seventy-four sportsgrounds were damaged by drought conditions and needed rehabilitation at a cost of $1.3 million. Insurance premiums rose, and nine cricket grounds in the

City of Moonee Valley, in Melbourne's north-western suburbs, lost their ability to be insured at all due to dangerous ground surfaces.

Ground closures and restricted access to sports fields results in loss of amenity to local communities, including schools that often rely on such access for competitions and sports carnivals. In response to the sustained hard and dry playing conditions experienced during the Millennium Drought, the governing bodies of all major Australian football codes and Cricket Australia collaborated with a sports insurance company, JLT Trustees (the insurer to both the AFL and Cricket Australia), to develop a new synthetic turf for sports fields. This turf replicates the playing characteristics of natural grass and is one of the first climate change adaptation measures in Australian sporting history—it certainly won't be the last.

In its comprehensive report on the impact of climate change on human health, the Australian Government's former climate change advisory group, the Climate Commission, which was axed by the Abbott government and replaced by the publicly funded Climate Council, outlined the risk that extreme heat exposure posed to outdoor workers. The report discussed how people in the construction, maintenance, landscaping, emergency services, mining and agricultural industries will all be subjected to an increased risk of heat stress. This is sometimes compounded by the use of protective clothing often required in these industries, slowing down the cooling effect of sweating and further increasing the risk of heat exposure.

Although people who live in hot climates across Australia have developed a certain level of resilience to heat, there are upper limits to human thermal tolerance. In a warming world, these limits may be exceeded on dangerous days when sweating is insufficient to regulate a person's temperature and when body temperatures increase by 2.5°C in less than two hours. On these days, heat stroke is a real risk after only a few hours. It has been estimated that in Perth, the number of dangerous days for people acclimatised to doing physical labour in hot conditions will increase from one day per year to twenty-one days per year by 2070. For those not acclimatised to the climate, the number of dangerous days will increase from seventeen days per year to sixty-seven, threatening the sector of the workforce that labours outdoors.

An increase in the number of dangerously hot days could also have major economic impacts. For example, at the Port of Melbourne, workers are allowed to stop working when temperatures reach 38°C. A heatwave slows down or even stops the loading and unloading of ships at the port, significantly delaying global shipments and delivery schedules.

For tradespeople running their own businesses that involve working outdoors, the financial pressure to work during dangerous heat will put thousands of hardworking Australians at increased risk of heat stress and even death in the future.

As Australia's climate continues to change, the spread of infectious tropical diseases will also become a major threat to public health. Frequent travel within and outside Australia, together with the recent spread of exotic mosquito species like the Asian Tiger Mosquito (*Aedes albopictus*) into the country, has the potential to expand the distribution and abundance of tropical viruses. As seasonal rain and floodwaters pond under warmer conditions, they become a breeding ground for disease-carrying mosquitoes. Disease outbreaks may increase because wetter conditions favour mosquito breeding and warmer temperatures speed up the maturation of viruses carried by mosquitoes. The tropical diseases will spread further south as climate change allows mosquitoes to travel to parts of the world that were previously too cold for them to survive.

In Australia, mosquito-borne infectious diseases such as dengue fever, Murray Valley encephalitis, Ross River virus and Barmah Forest virus are likely to extend their range and activity with continued climate change. For example, the main carrier of dengue fever is the mosquito *Aedes aegypti*, whose habitat, geographic range and behaviour are very sensitive to temperature, humidity and the presence of surface water. While hotter and drier conditions reduce the numbers and survival rates of mosquito larvae in inland areas, substantial warming in the monsoonal north of Australia and an increase in the intensity of rainfall projected for the region will significantly increase the threat of tropical diseases. To make matters worse, *Aedes aegypti* are very well adapted to human settlements, with water tanks, neglected swimming pools, garden pots and clogged gutters providing suitable breeding habitats, posing a risk to densely populated urban areas.

Dengue causes symptoms including fever, headache, joint pain, skin rash, haemorrhage, dangerously low blood pressure and long-term post-infectious fatigue. There is no vaccine, but precautions like wearing mosquito repellent and long-sleeved clothing can be taken to prevent infection. Dengue is currently confined to northern Queensland, where outbreaks already occur annually. In 2008–09 there was a spike in dengue fever, with 1003 locally acquired cases reported in the Cairns region. There is already evidence that the geographic range of the disease within Queensland may have expanded in recent years. Research suggests that if no global action is taken to reduce greenhouse gas emissions, the geographic region suitable for dengue transmission may spread southwards, increasing the population at risk of exposure from 430 000 to between five and eight million Australians by the end of the century. Modelling studies show that as the climate becomes hotter and wetter in coming decades, dengue fever could spread as far south as northern New South Wales or even Sydney by the end of the century.

The arrival of the Asian Tiger Mosquito in our region also poses a major public heath threat. The species was first discovered in Torres Strait in 2005, where it was thought to have hitched a ride on Indonesian fishing boats. Disease experts fear that its arrival will further the spread of dengue fever and the lesser-known chikungunya virus, a close relative of Ross River virus which affects around 4000 Australians each year and causes similar symptoms of joint pain, fever, headache, conjunctivitis and rashes. The name chikungunya comes from a Tanzanian word meaning 'to bend up', referring to the stooped posture inflicted on sufferers. Although a full recovery can be expected after a week or two, some cases can be chronic and debilitating. In large epidemics, some cases have resulted in death.

Until recently, the chikungunya virus was unknown in the Americas, but within a year of it being introduced into the Caribbean in late 2013 it had spread to both North America and South America and is suspected of having infected over 1.7 million people. Now that the Asian Tiger Mosquito is on our doorstep, it's only a matter of time before it colonises the Australian mainland from the springboard of the Torres Strait Islands, exacerbating the spread of tropical diseases in Australia. Genetic evidence and historical records suggest that this invasive species may have migrated from East Timor and Papua New Guinea. As it's an aggressive biter and can tolerate much cooler conditions, *Aedes albopictus* could work its way south into the major coastal cities of Australia if it becomes locally established.

In recent years, the east coast of Australia has experienced some of its worst outbreaks of mosquito-borne diseases on record. In 2015, a record 9554 cases of Ross River virus were reported in more southern areas like Brisbane and the Gold Coast after heavy rains associated with tropical cyclones and high tides provided the perfect environment for the proliferation of mosquitoes across areas like south-eastern Queensland. Alarmingly, the number of dengue fever cases has been rising over the past two decades, peaking at 2219 notifications in 2016. The chikungunya virus has only been reported in Australia since 2008, with 113 cases, the highest number yet reported in 2013, the same year that Barmah Forest virus cases peaked at 4237. While the spread of infectious disease is influenced by a range of factors, like international travel, non-human vectors and under-reporting, most experts would agree that warmer and wetter conditions in tropical locations favour the proliferation of mosquito numbers and the conditions necessary for the outbreak of these infectious diseases.

Australia has had outbreaks of malaria over the course of its history, but the disease was considered eradicated by 1981. Although malaria is not currently prevalent in Australia, around 700–800 cases occur here each year through travellers who have been infected elsewhere, mostly in Papua New Guinea. Some cases have also been reported in the malaria transmission zone of tropical Australia north of 19 degrees south, the latitude of Townsville and Broome. Locally acquired cases were reported in the Torres Strait Islands and Cape York Peninsula in 1996 and 2002, but the expansion of the tropics expected with climate change could see the spread of the life-threatening disease into northern Australia in the future.

While there is an urgent need to develop health-related indicators for climate change to help inform policy development and planning decisions, to date no environmental health indicators have been developed for Australia. Recent research from the Australian National University suggests that notifications of climate-sensitive infectious diseases and heat-related hospital admissions and deaths might be a good place to start.

Aside from its effect on physical health, our changing climate is also taking its toll on the mental health of countless Australians, undermining the social fabric of our society. Extreme weather events like droughts, floods, cyclones, heatwaves and bushfires can have traumatic impacts on people and their communities, especially when they happen in close succession or over a long period of time. These events can cause psychological distress due to the loss of loved ones, destruction of property and other major damage to local communities. The displacement of people from their homes causes significant anxiety and uncertainty about what the future holds. People in affected areas also fear unemployment and the risk of further natural disasters. Depression, anxiety and post-traumatic stress disorders may occur as a result, with major long-term effects on individuals, families and communities.

The impacts are greatest in rural and regional areas, where catastrophic weather events can take a huge toll on local communities, including the economic viability of smaller towns. Witnessing the widespread destruction of people's homes and livelihoods similarly has profound psychological effects. Aside from sudden extremes like bushfires and floods, long-term events such as prolonged drought also have a negative effect on mental health. This is particularly the case in farming communities where limited access to mental health services and a stoic 'harden up' culture may stop people seeking the help they really need.

A report on climate change and mental health developed by The Climate Institute in 2011 described how the extent to which each person copes with trauma because of natural disasters depends on many factors, including how well an individual has coped with disasters in the past, the availability of support networks, and whether a person has pre-existing mental health problems such as clinical depression or anxiety. Studies have demonstrated the potential effects of sudden natural disasters on mental health. For example, more than one in ten primary school children were reported to have suffered from post-traumatic stress disorder in the three months following Cyclone Larry, a massive tropical cyclone that devastated far north Queensland in March 2006 and caused over $1 billion in damages, including the decimation of the state's banana crop. Common symptoms in kids from cyclone-impacted regions included flashbacks, nightmares and a general state of distress, all of which can negatively impact a child's education and their sense of security about the future. After Cyclone Yasi impacted the region around Innisfail in February 2011, researchers found an increase in the prescription of antidepressant drugs between Cairns and Townsville, suggesting an increase in psychological distress in those communities.

In a world where extreme events are becoming more frequent and our local environments are noticeably beginning to change, the unpredictability of weather and climate conditions may create a chronic state of anxiety as people become hyper-vigilant when it comes to danger. A loss of sense of place, whether through forced relocation or radical transformation of the place itself, can disturb our sense of belonging and significantly undermine our mental health. Many survivors of natural disasters say that the recovery is as hard and heartbreaking as the disaster itself. It often takes years to bounce back, and some communities never recover fully, lacking the financial resources and emotional energy to rebuild.

For some communities, a one-off major disaster can be a death knell for towns where basic social support breaks down in the chaotic aftermath of the disaster, and there aren't enough people around and back on their feet to rebuild. During the catastrophic flooding of the northern New South Wales town of Lismore caused by Cyclone Debbie in March 2017, there were newspaper reports quoting the sense of urgency small businesses felt about reopening after the floods. Local business owners said this was not only for the sake of their own livelihoods but also to speed up the renewal of Lismore's CBD, so the community could regain a sense of normality and function.

Australian farmers living on the land are an iconic part of our culture and our national story. They are admired for their incredible work ethic and resilience in the face of tough times. But even when things are going well, farming is a hard, stressful job that has always been at the mercy of the elements. In recent years, many farming families and communities have been placed under enormous strain by a long run of drought years, followed by pest outbreaks or extensive flooding. Psychological research has shown that six people take their own lives each day in Australia, with country communities more than twice as likely to lose someone to suicide than metropolitan areas.

While the reasons why a person chooses to end their life are very complex, there is increasing evidence linking drought and suicide. One study by renowned Australian meteorologist Neville Nicholls demonstrated an 8 per cent rise in the suicide rate in New South Wales at a time when the rainfall was 300 millimetres below average due to a drought. A similar study that updated these results reported a 15 per cent increase in the suicide risk of rural males aged 30–49 years from 1970 to 2007. Financial strain, land degradation and declining rural populations were all factors that increased the risk of suicide among older male farmers.

The most consistent finding between these studies is that rural suicides in New South Wales tend to peak during spring. Recent research has suggested that this spring peak reflects a 'broken promise'. The theory is that suicide is triggered in distressed people when the expectation of drought-breaking rains falling during winter isn't met. The CSIRO's and Bureau of Meteorology's climate change projections show that the winter and spring rainfall in southern Australia is expected to continue to decrease in agriculturally intensive areas like the Murray–Darling Basin over the coming century, which will have a huge impact on rural communities. Under high emissions, temperatures across the basin are expected to increase by 2.7–4.5°C by 2090, further exacerbating drought conditions. As droughts become longer and hotter, many farmers may find themselves in enormously stressful conditions that will radically transform rural economies and potentially end in personal tragedy.

It's clear that a future characterised by unmitigated climate change will irreversibly transform life as we know it in Australia. It's hard to know exactly when the Earth will reach these complex, scientifically unpredictable tipping points, but we know we are on track to see them happen. The problem is that these invisible thresholds only become visible—and statistically distinguishable from natural variability—when extreme events keep happening with increasingly more destructive and widespread impacts. We start seeing cyclones tracking further south of their normal range, torrential deluges, record-smashing heat and large-scale ecosystem collapse.

But by the time we start witnessing these changes, it's too late to reverse the destruction we've triggered. The damage will have been done.

The destabilisation of our planet's climate will set off a terrible chain reaction that will leave vast areas of the country inhospitable to modern Australian life. What if Melbourne is regularly ravaged by extreme bushfires like 2009's Black Saturday? What if we risk contracting dengue fever in Sydney? What if the city of Darwin becomes so unbearably hot that it becomes uninhabitable, unleashing a wave of climate refugees? It is unthinkable that we could stand back and gamble on the future liveability of our country. The economic prosperity and physical and mental health of our communities depends on doing everything within our power to protect ourselves from this apocalyptic future.

37
THE LIVING DEAD

The feature of Earth that distinguishes us from other planets is our incredible biodiversity. Recent ecological research has estimated that humans share the planet with around 8.7 million species, with up to 86 per cent of creatures on land and 91 per cent of ocean species still undescribed. Biodiversity is made up of a combination of animals, plants and micro-organisms, their genetic variation, and their organisation into populations that function collectively as ecosystems. Aside from their intrinsic value, living organisms provide the foundation of the ecosystem services that make up the Earth's life-support system that humans depend on. An ecosystem functions by continually cycling energy and materials through living organisms that grow, reproduce and then decay. This cycling of resources has evolved in response to a mix of disturbances like fires, droughts, diseases and ecological processes of competition or predation over millions of years. Together, these processes generate well-functioning ecosystems that are essential to a range of key services such as clean water and air, storage of carbon, and the production of topsoil.

For example, the rivers, wetlands and floodplains of the Murray–Darling system are estimated to provide $187 billion worth of ecosystem services each year. Similarly, Australian terrestrial ecosystems are worth $325 billion annually. Biodiversity-related industries also contribute significantly and directly to the Australian economy. It has been estimated that Australia's commercial fisheries contribute $2.2 billion, kangaroo harvesting $245 million, bushfood production $100 million, and wildflower exports another $30 million to our economy each year.

Australia's national parks and protected areas form the foundation of nature-based tourism experiences that underpin our tourism industry. The sector is heavily dependent on our spectacular natural environments and unique biodiversity. For example, in the year up until March 2017, the tourism dollars spent by local and international travellers in Australia reached a record high of $100 billion. Australians spent $61.7 billion on domestic travel, while 8.4 million foreign visitors chipped in an additional $39.8 billion.

One in every twelve Australians is employed in the tourism sector, further bolstering our economy. For example, more than 2.8 million people visited the Great Barrier Reef in 2016, generating over 64 000 jobs and contributing $6.4 billion to the national economy in 2015–16. According to Queensland's tourism board, around 80 per cent of the state's tourism activity occurs within only 7 per cent of the Great Barrier Reef region. A 2017 report by Deloitte Access Economics estimates the Great Barrier Reef has a staggering economic, social and icon asset value of $56 billion. In 2009–10, the national economic value generated by fifteen of Australia's other World Heritage Areas was around $7.25 billion annually, along with approximately 83 000 jobs. Many individual species also have a measurable monetary value. The koala alone was estimated to be worth over $3.2 billion to the Australian tourism industry in 2014, generating around 30 000 jobs.

The richness of Australia's unique natural heritage and the multibillion-dollar industries that rely on them means we have a lot to lose with climate change. Australia is considered one of the most megadiverse countries on the planet. We are a unique country with a dramatically variable climate that has given rise to the highest level of biological endemism (number of unique species) of any continent on Earth. This means that we have more native plants and animals only found here and nowhere else on the planet. We house more than 50 per cent of the world's marsupial species, 17 per cent of the world's parrots and 57 per cent of the Earth's mangrove species. We are also home to the highest number of unique plant families in the world. About 87 per cent of terrestrial mammals, 92 per cent of flowering plants, 90 per cent of fish, 93 per cent of reptiles and 94 per cent of frogs are found nowhere else. Many of the ecological niches occupied by placental mammals on other continents are filled by a huge diversity of marsupials, birds, reptiles and insects in Australia.

Aridity, high temperatures and frequent burning have shaped the habitats that have supported our unique biodiversity. The scarcity of fresh water has driven many Australian species to evolve ways to reduce water use and loss, and to survive long periods of drought. But despite their evolutionary resilience and adaptive capacity, many Australian plants, animals and microorganisms are already being affected by accelerating rates of environmental change. As our current ecosystems are more used to operating on evolutionary timescales that creep along over millions of years, rapid rates of change may simply overwhelm their capacity to adapt, leading to escalating extinctions and the widespread transformation of ecosystems and habitats.

The loss of biodiversity directly influences the capacity of an ecosystem to produce and supply essential ecosystem services, and can affect the ability of ecological, economic and social systems to adapt and respond to global pressures like climate change. Rates of extinction of species are likely to increase as the global average temperature rises by 1.5°C above pre-industrial levels, and will almost surely accelerate sharply as the temperature rises beyond 2°C, placing many of our most species-rich areas at risk.

Australia's most vulnerable ecosystems include alpine areas, tropical rainforests, coastal zones, bushfire-prone areas and places with limited freshwater availability. Species that could become endangered or extinct include those living near the upper limit of their temperature range, species with restricted climatic niches, those that cannot migrate to new habitats due to habitat fragmentation, areas with high fire risks, or those living in freshwater wetlands inundated by rising sea levels. This means many of Australia's most valued and iconic natural areas, such as the Great Barrier Reef, Western Australia's biodiversity hotspot in the south-west, the Australian Alps, the Gondwana Rainforests of Australia, the Queensland tropics and the Kakadu wetlands.

On a high-emissions path, Australia will warm by around 4°C, which would wipe out alpine areas as we know them today. Average snow depth and cover in Australia have already declined since the 1950s as temperatures have risen rapidly. In high greenhouse gas emissions scenarios, climate models show severe reductions, with snow becoming rare by late this century except on the country's highest peaks. The Australian ski season could shorten by up to eighty days a year by 2050 under business-as-usual conditions. As temperatures continue to rise, our alpine plants and animal communities are in real danger of being pushed to extinction, their habitats vanishing in a rapidly warming world.

Outside of alpine zones, many other Australian ecosystems are also restricted in their geographic and climatic range, and so may be vulnerable to early extinction or displacement because of rapid climate change.

Although rainforests cover only about 0.3 per cent of Australia, they contain about half of all our plant families and about a third of our mammal and bird species. Rainforest tourism in Australia attracts around eight million visitors per year, generating over $3 billion annually for our economy. The Gondwana Rainforests of Australia, located in south-eastern Queensland and northern New South Wales, is a World Heritage Area containing exceptional biodiversity, with outstanding examples of the Earth's evolutionary history and processes. Together with south-western Western Australia, the area is one of Australia's two 'biodiversity hotspots'; that is, globally recognised regions of the world that contain exceptional concentrations of unique plants, but which are also experiencing losses greater than 70 per cent of the original native habitat.

This region of eastern Australia contains the largest remaining stands of subtropical rainforest in the world, and the most significant areas of warm temperate rainforest in the country. It also houses nearly all of the remnant Antarctic beech (*Nothofagus Moorei*) cool temperate rainforests on the planet, which is remarkable for a location so far north. Some of the oldest elements of the world's ferns from the Carboniferous period (around 360–300 million years ago) and conifers from the Jurassic era (around 200–145 million years ago) are also found here. Together, the area has an incredible concentration of primitive plant families that have direct links to the origin and spread of flowering plants (angiosperms) some 100 million years ago across the Earth.

Understandably, these Gondwana Rainforests have exceptional global conservation value. They provide the largest and best stands of subtropical rainforest habitat in Australia, home to more than 200 rare or threatened plant and animal species. Many of these species are rainforest specialists that are vulnerable to extinction from a variety of factors, including the rarity of their rainforest habitat. The region also protects large areas of other vegetation, including a diverse range of heaths, rocky outcrops, forests and woodlands. The complex dynamics between rainforests and adjacent wet eucalyptus forest demonstrates the close evolutionary and ecological links between these communities.

The Border Ranges National Park in northern New South Wales is a particularly rich tract of the Gondwana Rainforests network, containing the highest concentration of frog, snake, bird and marsupial species in Australia. Few places on Earth contain so many plants and animals that remain relatively unchanged from their ancestors in the fossil record. Many of the plants and animals found in the World Heritage region are locally restricted to a few sites or occur in widely separated populations. Climate change will especially impact relict species in restricted habitats at higher altitudes, where particular microclimatic conditions have allowed them to survive. Although these remarkable rainforests have clung on since the age of the dinosaurs, searing heat and lower rainfall is starting to see these wet areas dry out for longer periods of the year, increasing bushfire risk in these precious ecosystems. The UNESCO World Heritage Center describes the rainforest as 'an archipelago of refugia, a series of distinctive habitats that characterise a temporary endpoint in climatic and geomorphological [landscape] evolution'. If rapid climate change destabilises the conditions needed for these ancient rainforests to survive, they may be lost to humanity forever.

Research by renowned Australian ecologist Lesley Hughes has found that 53 per cent of the 800 species of Australian eucalypts have climatic ranges that can tolerate less than 3°C shifts in average temperatures, while only 25 per cent of species survive within 1°C of their current range. Although factors other than climate are likely to play a role in limiting the range of most species, the restricted availability of suitable habitat increases a species' vulnerability to rapid environmental change. The current rate of extinction in Australia is estimated to be 100–1000 times higher than the background rate seen in the fossil record. Australia already has one of the highest extinction rates in the world. Nearly 50 per cent of global mammal extinctions have occurred in Australia over the past 200 years. The extinction of a further fifty species of birds, frogs and plants in our country have also been reported in the scientific literature.

So what are the implications of future climate change for Australia's biodiversity? Even under the most modest emissions scenario, impacts on the natural world will worsen through most of this century. A shift in climate conditions will see the development of new ecosystems, and abrupt changes in ecosystem structure and functioning. If the high-emissions trajectory continues, we are headed for a mass extinction event equivalent to that which wiped out the dinosaurs, along with 80 per cent of all other life on Earth, around 66 million years ago.

Elizabeth Kolbert's book *The Sixth Extinction: an Unnatural History* suggests that we are already in the sixth great extinction event in the Earth's history, which may destroy between 20 and 50 per cent of all living species on Earth by the end of the twenty-first century. Vast and rapid changes to the climate system and ecosystem functioning during the Anthropocene means that many species are unable to migrate ahead of current ecological changes. They encounter artificial barriers like highways and suburban encroachment into their environments that have fragmented the links between viable habitats across the world. It took millions of years for biodiversity to recover from past massive extinction events, a process that modern human civilisation probably won't be around to witness.

In May 2017, the dire extent of the Earth's situation prompted eminent theoretical physicist Stephen Hawking to warn that humans need to colonise another planet within 100 years or face extinction. As crazy as it sounds, multiple efforts are actually already underway to create a human colony on Mars, with plans to try to establish a settlement in coming decades. In 2015, NASA revealed that one of its long-term goals is to 'take steps toward establishing a sustainable human presence beyond Earth, not just to visit but to stay'. Is this really the best solution? Leaving our planet for dead when the technology to address the climate crisis is already with us and just needs to be backed up by political will?

Back here on Earth, nowhere is the impact of global warming in Australia clearer than in the Great Barrier Reef, another one of our World Heritage Areas of exceptional biodiversity. In 2012, Glenn De'ath from the Australian Institute of Marine Science published a study based on the world's most extensive coral reef dataset (2258 surveys of 214 reefs from 1985 to 2012). It was reported that 50.7 per cent of corals in the central and southern regions of the Great Barrier Reef have been killed since 1985. Importantly, the study concluded that in 2012, the most pristine northern region showed no overall decline.

Disastrously, this was to change in 2015–16 when record high sea temperatures during an El Niño event triggered mass coral bleaching across the tropics, the third such global-scale event since mass bleaching was first documented in the 1980s. Based on aerial surveys conducted by Terry Hughes, director of the Australian Research Council's (ARC) Centre of Excellence for Coral Reef Studies at James Cook University in Townsville, during the 2016 event the northern third of the Great Barrier Reef, extending from Port Douglas to Papua New Guinea, experienced the most severe bleaching and subsequent loss of corals. Two-thirds of the corals died along a 700-kilometre northern section of the reef—the single greatest loss of corals ever recorded on the reef. Experts from the centre say that when the mortality rate is this high, it affects even the toughest species that normally survive bleaching events. It is believed that it generally takes at least a decade for a full recovery of even the fastest-growing corals, but mass bleaching events only twelve months apart offer no chance of recovery for reefs that were damaged in 2016.

The proportion of reefs experiencing extreme bleaching in 2016 was over four times higher compared with the 1998 or 2002 events.

Only 8.9 per cent of the 1156 surveyed reefs escaped bleaching, compared with 42.4 per cent of 631 reefs in 2002 and 44.7 per cent of 638 reefs in 1998. The combined footprint of the three major bleaching events now covers almost the entire Great Barrier Reef Marine Park, with the exception of southern offshore reefs.

And then, tragically, the corals on the Great Barrier Reef bleached again in March 2017 after yet another prolonged period of exceptional heat. It was second in severity only to the 2016 episode, and surprised scientists by occurring in the absence of the El Niño event that usually warms the region. It holds the disturbing record of being the only back-to-back coral bleaching event in recorded history. While the 2016 bleaching was most severe in the northern section of the reef, from Torres Strait to Port Douglas, in 2017 the most intense bleaching occurred further south, between Cooktown and Townsville. The footprint of this unprecedented coral bleaching now stretches 1500 kilometres along two-thirds of the Great Barrier Reef.

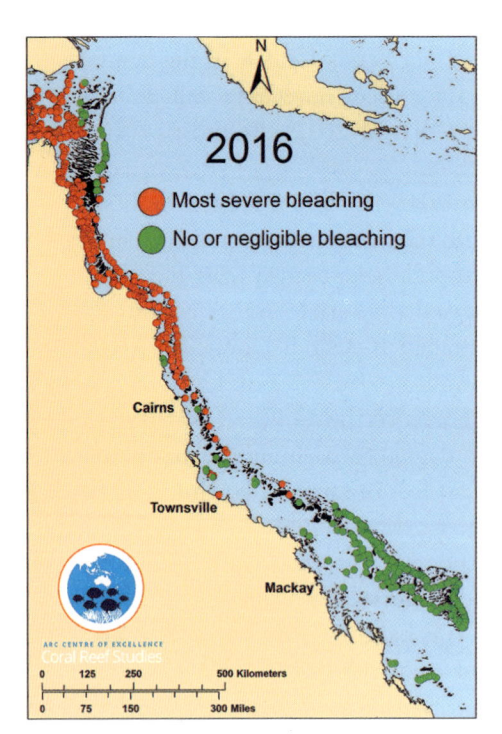

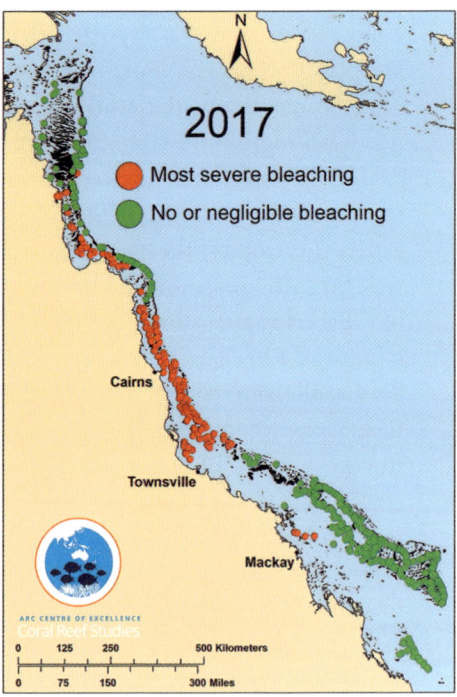

Figure 49. Coral bleaching of the Great Barrier Reef in 2016 (left) and 2017 (right) has now killed 50 per cent of the reef's corals.

Source: Reproduced courtesy of the ARC Centre of Excellence for Coral Reef Studies.

Given there was only a twelve-month gap between the two coral bleaching events, there hasn't been enough time for any significant recovery of reefs that were affected in 2016. It will be a while before the death toll from these combined events can be accurately measured, as it takes several months for severely damaged corals to regain their colour or to die following bleaching. As of September 2017, surveys of the damage suggested that 30 per cent of the shallow water corals died following bleaching in 2016, followed by a further 19 per cent die-off in 2017. That is, half of the coral of the Great Barrier Reef is now dead. It's a global-scale ecological catastrophe that will have serious ramifications in the years ahead for countless marine species and over 64 000 people who rely on the reef for their livelihoods.

Along with severe bleaching, large parts of the reef were also impacted by the destructive ocean swells and crashing waves caused when severe tropical Cyclone Debbie crossed the Queensland coast at Airlie Beach on 28 March 2017. The Great Barrier Reef Marine Park Authority estimated that approximately 28 per cent of the total reef area in the park was within the 'catastrophic damage zone' of the cyclone's path. Surveys conducted by the authority and the Queensland Parks and Wildlife Service have revealed that some sites suffered up to 97 per cent coral loss and are now down to very low coral cover following the summer of 2016–17.

While some critics might say that global warming isn't the only threat to the Great Barrier Reef, Terry Hughes' 2017 study published in *Nature* showed that water quality and fishing pressure had minimal effect on the unprecedented bleaching in 2016, suggesting that local protection of reefs affords little or no resistance to extreme heat. Similarly, past exposure to bleaching in 1998 and 2002 did not lessen the severity of bleaching in 2016.

Once again, scientists are calling for urgent and immediate action to secure the future of coral reefs around the world. While corals can recover from a single bleaching event, persistently high temperatures can kill off entire reefs for good. Further research has shown that global warming of 2°C above pre-industrial levels would put 98 per cent of the world's reefs at risk of coral bleaching from 2050 onwards, compared with 90 per cent for the more ambitious temperature limit of 1.5°C. Even if emissions reductions exceed the pledges made by countries to date under the Paris Agreement, more than 75 per cent of the world's coral reefs will bleach every year from intolerable heat before 2070. Under business-as-usual emissions, 99 per cent of the world's coral reefs are predicted to bleach every year by 2043—a mere twenty-five years away.

Following the catastrophic back-to-back bleaching event on the Great Barrier Reef, water quality expert Jon Brodie, from the ARC Centre of Excellence for Coral Reef Studies, told *The Guardian* newspaper that the reef, one of the seven great natural wonders of the world, was now in a 'terminal stage'. In his book *Atmosphere of Hope*, Tim Flannery wrote:

> It fills me with despair to admit it, but my beloved Great Barrier Reef is doomed. My head tells me what my heart won't. If we exert ourselves to the utmost to reduce CO_2 pollution, the reef may still be able to slowly grow, and even remain beautiful in patches. But, as an extensive ecosystem, it must be counted among the living dead.

It's a profound loss that future generations of Australians will never get to experience the place that the world's greatest naturalist, Sir David Attenborough, has described as the most beautiful thing he ever experienced during his sixty-five years of documenting the natural world. I can barely comprehend that I lived to see this happen in my lifetime. This tragic loss signals that the dreaded climate change genie is now well and truly out of the bottle.

38
A SYMBOLIC START

The world of international climate change politics is as extraordinarily slow-moving as it is complex. While others have written about the history of international climate change politics in great detail, I'm just going to provide highlights of recent efforts to reduce greenhouse gas emissions.

Political recognition that greenhouse gases generated by human activity have the potential to dangerously interfere with the Earth's climate can be traced back to the United Nations Conference on Environment and Development held in Rio de Janeiro in 1992. The landmark summit resulted in a number of significant environmental outcomes, including the first international climate treaty, known as the United Nations Framework Convention on Climate Change (UNFCCC), which came into force in 1994. After decades of diplomatic discussion and failures, a monumentally difficult global climate agreement was finally agreed under the UNFCCC at the 21st Conference of the Parties (COP21) held in Paris from 30 November to 12 December 2015. Former US president Barack Obama famously described the achievement as 'the moment we finally decided to save the planet'.

The historic Paris Agreement aims to deal with greenhouse gases emission mitigation, adaptation and finance starting in the year 2020. The scientific goals are to keep global warming well below 2°C and as close as possible to 1.5°C above pre-industrial levels; for global emissions to peak as soon as possible; and to reach zero net global emissions in the second half of this century. All countries are obliged to commit to publicly disclosed mitigation targets from 2020 and to review the targets every five years to ensure global reductions in greenhouse gas emissions. While all countries need to do their bit, developed countries with more resources at their disposal are expected to take the lead. The Paris Agreement officially took effect on 4 November 2016, with global pledges currently representing around 88 per cent of global emissions.

Unfortunately, on 2 June 2017, Donald Trump, President of the United States, withdrew US support for the global agreement. This saw the world's second-biggest emitter of greenhouse gases, responsible for around 18 per cent of global emissions, snubbing international diplomatic efforts designed to safeguard the planet's climate stability. The United States is currently the only country refusing to take part in the Paris Agreement. The US withdrawal sent the very negative signal to other signatory nations that they also didn't need to honour their pledges. As the world's richest nation, the United States was also expected to provide a considerable portion of the US$100 billion in aid to developing nations by 2020 to help them cut emissions and adapt to the changing climate. With less chance of those funds being found elsewhere, many poorer nations struggling with issues of poverty may be unable to afford to reduce their emissions.

In the wake of this decision, the US Conference of Mayors quickly stepped in to state their strong opposition to Trump's action and vowed that American mayors would continue efforts to reduce greenhouse gas emissions. As of November 2017, a total of 384 'Climate Mayors' representing 68 million Americans in the largest cities in the country, including New York, Los Angeles and Washington DC, had reconfirmed their commitment to intensify efforts to meet each of their cities' current climate goals and push for even further action to meet the goals enshrined in the Paris Agreement. Council CEO Tom Cochran said: 'The nation's mayors have never waited on Washington to act, and have been strong proponents of action on climate for decades. Mayors will continue to harness their collective power to continue to lead the nation on this critical issue, regardless of what happens at the national level'.

Representatives of US cities, states and companies have also signed a statement of support for the Paris Agreement that they plan to submit to the United Nations. Their parallel pledges aim to meet the US greenhouse gas emissions targets despite President Trump's decision to withdraw from the agreement. In the wake of Trump's announcement that his administration will also terminate all support for UN climate change efforts, Michael Bloomberg, former mayor of New York and UN Secretary-General António Guterres' current Special Envoy for Cities and Climate Change, announced a commitment of up to US$15 million to support the operations of the UNFCCC executive secretariat, including its work to help countries implement their commitments under the Paris Agreement.

On 1 June 2017, Bloomberg stated: 'Americans are not walking away from the Paris Climate Agreement ... Americans will honour and fulfil the Paris Agreement by leading from the bottom up—and there isn't anything Washington can do to stop us'. The group has expressed confidence that cities, states, businesses and individuals can collectively achieve the 2025 goal without Trump's support. It's incredibly heartening to see that even in the absence of national political leadership, millions of US citizens are determined to surge ahead with the rest of the world's leaders to support a global clean energy revolution.

As of November 2017, 170 of the 197 parties to the convention, including Australia, had ratified the Paris Agreement in good faith. The federal government has agreed to reduce emissions by 26–28 per cent below 2005 levels by 2030. Experts believe that our domestic emission targets and policies are more aligned to global warming of 3–4°C. Our 2030 targets would still leave us as the highest greenhouse gas emitter per person in the developed world. While it was an enormous political achievement, unlike an international treaty, the Paris Agreement does not legally bind nations to achieve their emission reduction plans, referred to as Nationally Determined Contributions (NDCs). The same non-binding status holds for specific commitments to provide financial support to developing countries to reduce their greenhouse gas emissions.

In 2016, the United Nations Environment Programme (UNEP) released a report assessing the emissions gap between national pledges and the Paris Agreement's target of keeping global temperatures at 1.5–2°C above pre-industrial levels by the end of this century. The report found that, even with full implementation of all national pledges, average global temperatures have a greater than 66 per cent probability of rising between 2.9°C and 3.4°C above pre-industrial levels by 2100. These pledges are only enough to reduce emissions by a third of the levels required by 2030 to avert disaster. The report also goes on to say that global greenhouse gas emissions need to peak before 2020 to keep global warming to 1.5°C by 2100, which is not going to happen. According to UNEP, there is a 50 per cent probability that the 1.5°C warming threshold will be exceeded by around 2030 based on currently pledged emissions reductions.

More recent 2017 estimates published in *Nature Climate Change* by Adrian Raftery showed that there is only a 5 per cent chance of limiting warming to less than 2°C, according to a forecast drawn from a statistical analysis of population, carbon emission and gross domestic product data from 152 countries that account for 98.7 per cent of the world's population as of 2015. Alarmingly, it was estimated that there is a mere 1 per cent chance that warming will stay at or below 1.5°C. Instead, there is a 90 per cent chance that warming this century will increase between 2°C and 4.9°C, with a middle-of-the-road estimate of 3.2°C. This suggests that the Paris Agreement's upper end of 2°C warming—the benchmark recognised as the threshold for 'dangerous' climate change—is a best-case scenario.

Stabilising global warming below 2°C will require drastic emissions reductions and 'negative emissions' to fill the gap left by collectively insufficient targets. Negative emissions see carbon dioxide drawn out of the atmosphere permanently through a process known as 'carbon sequestration'. There are number of ways in which carbon can be drawn out of the air to reverse global warming. Examples include capture at the point of emission from existing power stations or industrial plants, and storage through natural processes which remove carbon dioxide from the Earth's atmosphere. This can be done by increasing the storage of carbon in soil, vegetation, geological formations, deep ocean trenches or in mineral form through processes that mimic natural weathering.

One of the forms of carbon capture and storage currently favoured by the Australian Government to facilitate 'clean coal' is called geosequestration: a process that attempts to store carbon dioxide in the Earth's crust by injecting it into underground rocks as a gas or in the form of insoluble carbonate salts. As intriguing as this might sound, unfortunately, long-term carbon-capture technology remains unproven and is yet to be commercially demonstrated. The benefits of these kinds of technologies could also be quickly undermined by earthquakes or mining activities disrupting underground structures, rapidly releasing large amounts of carbon into the atmosphere. It's a very expensive way to try to sweep our problems under the rug, without addressing the root cause of the issue: humans need to stop burning fossil fuels and polluting the Earth and causing dangerous climate change. It's also a very blatant attempt to keep the dying fossil fuel industry on life support, instead of investing in the clean renewable energy revolution that's already underway.

Given the collectively weak global emissions targets, negative greenhouse gas emissions are needed to meet the more realistic upper end of the Paris targets. However, the feasibility of negative emissions mainly depends on technologies not yet developed. Reliance on future technological breakthroughs could very well prove unfounded and provide excuses for continued carbon emissions that will have severe repercussions for the planet. While the initial pledges are an important symbolic start, experts are calling for immediate amendments that will lead to stronger emission-reduction targets and stronger adaptation measures. The global community needs to urgently redouble its efforts to reduce carbon emissions if we are to stay within cooee of our goal to avoid dangerous and irreversible climate change.

39
OUR POLITICAL HOT POTATO

Despite Australia's alarming vulnerability to climate change, some people argue that because we are only responsible for 1.3 per cent of total global greenhouse gas emissions, what we do doesn't matter. But if you count up all of the countries that have emissions under 2 per cent, pretty quickly it adds up to around 40 per cent of total international emissions. And when you look at emissions per person, we are the most emissions-intensive Western society in the world. Aside from those reasons, most people would agree that because we all live on this planet together, it's our ethical responsibility to do our bit to be good global citizens. But given Australia's heavy reliance on fossil fuels and their exportation, climate change policy has proved to be political poison in Australian politics. It brought to an end the leadership of Kevin Rudd in 2010 and Julia Gillard in 2013. Similarly, Malcolm Turnbull's run as Liberal Opposition leader ended in 2009 when he lost a leadership ballot centred on the government's Emissions Trading Scheme. Following the 2013 federal election, vocal climate change sceptic Tony Abbott took office as prime minister, before being replaced by Turnbull in 2015. Although Prime Minister Turnbull previously took a stand on strong climate policy, he currently appears to be hamstrung by very conservative members of his party.

As outlined in Clive Hamilton's 2007 analysis of Australian climate change politics, *Scorcher: The Dirty Politics of Climate Change*, there is a powerful group of fossil fuel lobbyists doing everything they can to protect their coal export interests and block international efforts to address climate change. But far from Canberra, numerous public polls over the past decade have shown that between 70 and 90 per cent of Australians accept the reality of our changing climate. Results released by The Climate Institute in June 2017 put the figure at 71 per cent, with the majority of Australians wanting our government to address climate change because they see strong economic, environmental and social benefits and opportunities in the transition to a clean energy economy.

The science tells us that if Australia is to meet its international obligations and contribute its fair share to efforts to keep global warming below 2°C, as set out in the Paris Agreement, then there has to be an upper limit to the amount of greenhouse gases we can emit into the atmosphere over the coming decades. This is known as a carbon budget. As with all budgets, if we blow it all now, there will be less to spend in the future. Australia's current target is to reduce its emissions by 26–28 per cent by 2030 (below 2000 levels). In September 2016, climate scientist professor David Karoly and policy expert Clive Hamilton, both members (at the time) of the Climate Change Authority which is charged with making science-based policy recommendations to the Australian Government, said the target lacked technical credibility and would not meet Australia's obligation to meet the internationally agreed 2°C goal. By adapting such a target, Australia would have used up 90 per cent of its total carbon budget by 2030. To meet our international obligations, this would mean we'd have to reduce our emissions to zero by 2035, which would be impossible.

Karoly and Hamilton argued that the target was so weak, and likely to lead to a future policy crisis, that the experts could not in good conscience put their names to the authority's review. Instead of letting politics get in the way of sound science, the pair released a 'minority report' calling for the development of policies that are capable of being scaled up to meet more-ambitious net zero emissions goals in the decades ahead to play our part in decarbonising the global economy. They recommended that the Australian Government formally adopt a budget approach with climate change policy, which involves setting a minimum 40–60 per cent cut in emissions by 2030.

After hearing government ministers, led by Prime Minister Malcolm Turnbull, promoting the contradiction of clean coal, Hamilton quit the Climate Change Authority in March 2017. Speaking of the government's renewed advocacy for coal, he told *The Guardian* newspaper: 'I wasn't disappointed, or upset, I was disgusted'. It's easy to understand why the government is caving under the pressure of the coal industry: Australia is the world's largest coal exporter, accounting for 35 per cent of global exports. The problem is that global demand for coal is now declining, a trend that organisations like the International Energy Agency say is likely to be irreversible as the world shifts towards generating power from clean energy sources. Karoly's term on the Climate Change Authority ended on 30 June 2017, leaving no climate scientists in the climate change advisory group.

It often feels like Australia seems hell-bent on holding on to the past while the rest of the world races forward to lead the twenty-first century's clean energy revolution. On 9 June 2017, the Chief Scientist of Australia, Alan Finkel, released his review of the Australian electricity market. It called for a Clean Energy Target that requires electricity retailers and industrial users to use a set percentage of power generated from low-emission technologies like renewables or efficient gas. It recommended that 26–28 per cent of our electricity be generated by low-emissions technologies by 2030.

Effectively, this would force retailers to buy cleaner energy, promoting renewables into the market while slowly pricing highly polluting coal power plants out of the market. However, coal generation would continue to provide over 50 per cent of Australia's electricity in 2030 and 24 per cent in 2050, prompting experts to criticise the proposed target as being far too weak. Even so, many hailed it as a step in the right direction.

To encourage a further reduction of carbon emissions in the electricity sector, gas and coal-fired power stations that are fitted with carbon capture and storage technology would receive a subsidy in the form of tradeable clean energy certificates. The Turnbull government had hopes that the proposed Clean Energy Target would attract bipartisan support and give business the chance to make long-term investment decisions.

But the pressure from conservative members of the party, spearheaded by Tony Abbott, proved too much. Coalition conservatives fiercely opposed Finkel's Clean Energy Target, fearing that it would provide ongoing subsidies to renewable energy, disadvantaging coal generators. So on 17 October 2017, the federal government scrapped the Clean Energy Target, effectively slamming the brakes on renewable energy investment in Australia. Instead they replaced it with the 'National Energy Guarantee' that favours the use of 'reliable' fossil fuel sources of coal and gas.

The plan will require electricity retailers to make available a certain amount of 'dispatchable' electricity from sources that can be readily switched on—essentially favouring anything except solar and wind power. It also includes an emissions guarantee that sets an upper limit for the emissions intensity of electricity provided by retailers. This limit for emissions intensity would reduce over time to help meet Australia's international commitments.

Based on the limited detail available so far, there are serious concerns about whether the proposal can deliver scientifically credible emission reductions, and the unfair burden being placed on the electricity sector that is only responsible for 28 per cent of our total greenhouse gas emissions. While it is still too early to tell whether this controversial policy will be accepted by the state governments, it's a sign that strong pressure to reduce global greenhouse gas emissions is now being felt at all levels of Australian politics.

By contrast, the scientific urgency is startlingly simple. We know that as emissions continue to rise, the world is projected to warm rapidly over the twenty-first century, exceeding 2°C within the next few decades, and 4°C or more by the end of the century. How quickly we reduce carbon emissions will have dramatic consequences for future life in Australia. The more the planet warms, the more likely we are to experience severe, widespread and irreversible climate change impacts. Even at warming of 1°C or 2°C above pre-industrial levels, the risks arising from more frequent extreme weather events, changes in rainfall patterns and major impacts on Australia's ecosystems are considerable.

A recent study by Andrew King from the University of Melbourne compared the impact the 1.5°C and 2°C warming thresholds set in the Paris Agreement would have on Australian climate. He found that in a world with 2°C of global warming, the exceptional heat experienced during the 'Angry Summer' of 2012–13—our hottest on record—would become the average by the end of the century. He also reported that we can expect similarly hot summer conditions to occur even during La Niña periods, breaking the classic relationship between La Niña and cooler temperatures that has held true throughout our history. Sadly, the 2016 mass bleaching event on the Great Barrier Reef, which was virtually impossible to reproduce in models without the influence of climate change, will become the norm in either scenario, signifying another nail in the coffin for the struggling region.

Triggering several highly disruptive climate feedbacks could amplify the initial warming caused by greenhouse gases and increase the severity of climate change impacts. These impacts would impose a heavy financial burden, and, in many cases, prove to be beyond Australia's capacity to adapt to. There would be large-scale inundation of low-lying coastal areas, the climate change–induced migration of millions of people, growing risks to human health, and the collapse of many vulnerable ecosystems, including our coral reefs, alpine areas and iconic wetland areas like Kakadu.

Although global average warming of 2°C has been identified as the threshold for dangerous climate change, it is likely that we are going to miss this target, probably by a long shot. In a recent book, *Four Degrees of Global Warming: Australia in a Hot World*, Peter Christoff and his colleagues explored the risks to Australia if high emissions continue, estimating that 4°C of warming would be reached around the 2070s. He noted that 'what emerges [under 4°C projections] is a disturbing and bleak vision of a continent under assault ... our everyday lives will change profoundly even if adaptation succeeds'.

Jean Palutikof, one of Australia's pioneers in climate change adaptation research, has discussed how, in a 4°C warmer world, many Australians will be subjected to life-threatening heat in urban areas during summer and the need for the mass relocation of populations from flood- or fire-prone areas, as well as issues of food security. She also warned that in some cases, the risks and vulnerabilities will be so major that they will require enormous transformation rather than incremental adaptations. The message is clear: we are already committed to dangerous levels of climate change, and Australia is the most vulnerable nation in the developed world.

40
THE CLEAN ENERGY REVOLUTION

So can we actually avoid catastrophic climate change, or is it time to start packing our bags for Mars? Although global emissions appear to have stalled since 2014, it's very uncertain whether this trend will continue. Only if we have a strong political commitment to reduce global greenhouse gas emissions from all sources, as quickly as possible, can we avoid the more apocalyptic aspects of climate change. Where we will end up depends on decisive political action and how well we plan our climate change adaptation strategies. The good news is that humanity already possesses the fundamental scientific and technological know-how to solve the climate change crisis. First, we must accept that the age of dirty fossil fuels has come to an end. Simply speaking, the planet is no longer coping. The next thing we need to do is put a price on pollution so that we can rapidly start to transition to a low-carbon future and send a clear price signal to the business sector that it's time to invest in the sustainability revolution already underway around the world.

According to a report released in May 2017 by the World Bank Group's Carbon Pricing Leadership Coalition, the most cost-effective way of fostering economic growth while reducing greenhouse gas emissions is to require countries to set a strong carbon price. This provides a financial incentive for industry to invest in clean energy and reduce their consumption of polluting fossil fuels. The commission's report stated that a strong and predictable carbon price provides a powerful signal to individuals and businesses that the future is low-carbon, inducing the changes needed in global investment, production and consumption patterns. It suggested that a $40–$80 range in 2020, rising to $50–$100 by 2030, is consistent with the core objective of the Paris Agreement of keeping temperature rise below 2°C. The report recognised that while carbon prices will vary across countries and be implemented at different times, the temperature target remains achievable with lower short-term carbon prices if complemented by other emission-reduction policies like Tradable Emission Permits, and followed by higher carbon prices down the track.

The scrapping of Australia's recently proposed Clean Energy Target in October 2017 is a sign of the political difficulty of putting a price on carbon, that has plagued the nation for over a decade. Following thirteen years of crippling drought, a carbon pricing scheme was actually introduced in Australia by the Gillard Labor government as the *Clean Energy Act 2011*, which came into effect on 1 July 2012. This was met by a very negative media campaign by Rupert Murdoch's News Corp, which called for a change of government. This eventually took place in September 2013, when Tony Abbott's Coalition government was elected, and the carbon price was revoked from July 2014. Australia is now in the dubious position of being the only country in the world to have successfully introduced a national carbon pricing scheme and then abandoned it with a change of government. The Abbott government strongly supported the coal industry, with Abbott himself stating that coal is 'good for humanity'. Despite another leadership change in mid-2015, when Abbott was removed as prime minister by his party and Malcolm Turnbull was elected, the climate policy war continues to rage on. The fossil fuel industry appears to have a stranglehold on the federal government, while the window for avoiding dangerous climate change rapidly closes. A decision to finally implement strong, bipartisan climate change policy will be a defining moment in Australian politics.

While some Australians might still have their heads in the sand, many people around the country, and the world, have moved on and are facing the fact that limiting the amount of global warming is a monumental challenge that effectively requires decarbonising the economy and our lifestyles. There is a growing literature on how the country can transition towards a 100 per cent Australian renewable electricity market; scenarios to achieve a 100 per cent reduction in Australia's greenhouse gas emissions from all sectors, including transport and agriculture; and scenarios to achieve 80–100 per cent reductions in global greenhouse gas emissions involving strong energy efficiency measures and the expansion of renewable energy production. According to ClimateWorks' 2014 report *Pathways to Deep Decarbonisation in 2050: How Australia Can Prosper in a Low Carbon World*, there are four pillars of decarbonisation: energy efficiency; low-carbon electricity; electrification of transport and a switch to low-carbon fuels, and the reduction of non-energy emissions through improvements in industrial processes and agricultural practices; and offsetting other emissions through carbon sequestration processes like replanting forests.

One of the low-hanging fruits is to set ambitious energy efficiency standards in buildings, industry and transport. This includes our homes, which are responsible for about one-fifth of Australia's greenhouse gas emissions. According to the 2015 Residential Energy Baseline study for Australia, heating and cooling accounted for a huge 40 per cent of household energy in 2014, with hot water heaters representing a further 23 per cent of total household emissions. After that, household appliances accounted for about 25 per cent of household energy use, with fridges, freezers and televisions typically the highest individual electricity users. Surprisingly, lighting only accounted for around 7 per cent of residential energy use. The good news is that these are all things you have the power to change today. You can choose to insulate your home, use reverse-cycle air-conditioning, and buy appliances with high energy and water efficiency star labels. Doing this will not only keep your energy bill down but also help you do your bit to reduce greenhouse gas emissions. Of course, government regulation is important for setting energy ratings and minimum standards, which should be reflected in the prices charged by retailers.

Another major decarbonisation pillar is the use of low-carbon electricity, either through 100 per cent renewable energy or a mix of renewables and other technologies, as we transition away from fossil fuels. Again, this is something that individual households can directly get behind by purchasing green electricity from quality renewable energy suppliers like Powershop or Diamond Energy, or by installing solar panels on their roofs. According to the Clean Energy Council, in 2016, 82.7 per cent of Australia's electricity was generated from coal and natural gas. Renewable energy made up the remaining 17.3 per cent, a record high, but only about half of what needs to be delivered under the federal Renewable Energy Target (RET) by 2020. The shortfall reflects industry uncertainty associated with the Abbott government's 2014 review of the federal renewable energy target that threatened to wind back or even scrap the scheme. The government sought advice from the Business Advisory Council, chaired by Maurice Newman, who has publicly called for the RET to be abandoned because he believes the scientific evidence for global warming and the economic case for renewable energy don't stack up. This uncertainty led to a 90 per cent drop in large-scale solar investments over an eighteen-month period.

Employment in the renewable energy industry dropped 15 per cent to just 11 150 jobs during the 2015–16 financial year following the Abbott government's RET review.

Luckily, this turned around in 2016, and now the renewable energy industry looks like it is on the cusp of a boom in Australia. It was a record-breaking year for the construction of major solar projects, and the trend is predicted to continue. Seven large-scale solar projects were completed in 2016 and over a dozen projects were to be built in 2017, as rapid advances in technology propel the industry forward. And in August 2017 came the announcement of the planned construction of the world's largest solar thermal plant in South Australia, beginning in 2018. Australia's Clean Energy Council says that renewable energy is now the cheapest kind of new power generation that can be built today—less than both new coal-fired and new gas-fired power plants. Large-scale solar is almost half the cost it was just a couple of years ago and is now set to play a significant role in meeting the national RET. Employment figures were set to increase substantially in 2017, with over thirty-five large-scale renewable energy projects either under construction or starting up that year, adding up to more than $7.5 billion in investment and more than 4100 additional direct jobs.

Despite all these promising signs, large-scale solar was responsible for only 1.2 per cent of the national energy mix in 2016. Renewable power generation from Australia's hydroelectricity plants was the biggest contributor, providing 42.3 per cent of total renewable energy, followed by wind (30.8 per cent) and small-scale solar (16 per cent). These modest figures don't reflect Australia's enormous potential to harness solar, wind, water and the other naturally occurring sources that are abundant across the country. According to the 2016 Australian Energy Update, wind and solar energy were continuing to grow, with wind accounting for one-third of renewable generation in Australia and one-third of total electricity generation in South Australia.

Unfortunately, only 3.2 per cent of Australia's electricity is currently generated by solar and 5.3 per cent by wind power. Because renewable energy sources like wind and solar power are known as intermittent energy sources, they need to be paired with storage for times when the sun isn't shining and the wind isn't blowing. Storage technologies like the lithium-ion Tesla 'Powerwall' solar batteries coming out of the United States, and the zinc bromide flow battery being developed here in Australia, are game-changing developments that promise to revolutionise 21st-century energy generation. In July 2017, a historic agreement was struck between

Tesla boss Elon Musk and the visionary South Australian Government to build the world's largest lithium-ion battery, which will have a staggering 100-megawatt (129 megawatt hours) capacity to store solar energy. It will be 60 per cent larger than any other large-scale battery storage system on the planet. With more investment and support, these batteries could prove to be the missing link needed to transition from fossil fuels to a clean energy grid. Another way to overcome an intermittent energy supply is by integrating renewable energy sources into an electricity grid like the National Electricity Market in eastern Australia. For example, this allows a house without its own storage batteries for a rooftop solar system to simply supplement its electricity after the sun has gone down from a source available elsewhere in the grid, like a wind farm or hydroelectricity plant in another state.

Government policy encouraging investment in renewable technology coupled with a strong carbon-pricing scheme would go a long way to making the renewable energy sector more competitive. Improved battery technology will make large-scale renewable energy more reliable and affordable. As these storage technologies come of age over the next decade or so, Australia's electricity system will need to be backed up by a fossil fuel like natural gas (the lesser of two evils). However, there are understandable concerns that new investment in gas might hold back the transition to renewables. In recent years, a number of very thorough and credible reports by a number of organisations, including the CSIRO, Beyond Zero Emissions, and Energy Networks Australia, have demonstrated that a 100 per cent renewable energy grid is possible. All concluded that 100 per cent renewable energy electricity in Australia is technically feasible between 2030 and 2050 at an economic cost similar to what it would take to keep the present network running (including the necessary replacement stations as old ones wear out).

Australia's clean energy industry looks like it is booming in line with the rest of the world. The International Renewable Energy Agency said in 2016 that there were 9.8 million jobs in the renewable energy sector globally. In the last four years alone, the number of jobs in the solar and wind sectors combined has more than doubled. The agency estimated that the number of jobs in the industry was expected to grow to 24 million by 2030 if countries moved to meet climate targets, which would more than offset expected job losses in the fossil fuel industries. Here in Australia, we are already starting to see this transition. According to a 2016 report compiled by the Climate Council and Ernst Young, around 12 900 people were employed in the renewable energy sector in Australia in the year 2013–14, compared with around 6500 jobs related to coal mined for local use. That is, renewables are already creating nearly double the number of jobs generated by the local coal-mining industry, suggesting that the tide has already turned in Australia's clean energy revolution.

The Australian renewable energy industry has warned that it needs policy certainty and support beyond 2020 if the growth trend is to continue. Unfortunately, there are worrying signs that the Turnbull government's review of its Direct Action climate policy could see an overhaul of the federal Renewable Energy Target and the rules governing the Clean Energy Finance Corporation (CEFC). The green energy fund is intended for investment in the development, commercialisation and use of clean energy technologies, and is currently prohibited from investing in carbon capture and storage and nuclear technologies. Under the current legislation, the CEFC is required to invest at least 50 per cent of its funds in renewable energy technologies, with the remainder left available for low-emission and energy efficiency technologies. In May 2017, the Turnbull government announced that it wanted to amend the rules to allow the green energy fund to support the coal industry in the form of investment in carbon capture and storage technology, to stave off the death of the fossil fuel industry.

In May 2017, Jim Barry, the global head of the world's largest infrastructure investment group, BlackRock, was quoted in the *Australian Financial Review* as saying that Australia is in effect 'denying gravity' by continuing to encourage coal investments, because renewable energy is now financially competitive with coal. He said that outdated opinions that renewable energy was too expensive and heavily subsidised had now been turned on their heads, as prices, particularly in solar energy, had fallen dramatically in recent years. Global investment in the renewable energy industry had soared to more than US$300 billion annually from just US$20 billion just over a decade ago. Barry went on to say: 'Coal is dead. That's not to say all the coal plants are going to shut tomorrow. But anyone who's looking to take beyond a 10-year view on coal is gambling very significantly'.

To give ourselves just a 50 per cent chance of staying within the 2°C Paris Agreement target, nearly 90 per cent of the world's existing coal reserves must be left in the ground. But the Turnbull government is still trying to cut a deal with Indian mining company Adani to dig the biggest coalmine in Australia. If it goes ahead, the burning of coal from Adani's massive Carmichael mine in Queensland's Galilee Basin will create billions of tonnes of carbon pollution, despite the overwhelming evidence that fossil fuels are killing the Great Barrier Reef and making many extreme weather events worse in Australia.

If it's built, the $21.7 billion mine will be one of the biggest in the world, including six open-cut pits and five underground mines across an area five times the size of Sydney Harbour. At peak production, the Adani Carmichael coalmine will generate up to 120 million tonnes of carbon dioxide annually—more than the annual emissions from fossil fuel burning in over 100 countries, or more than 2 per cent of the carbon we can put into the atmosphere if we hope to stay below 1.5°C of global warming. The Climate Council has estimated that if the Galilee Basin were a country, it would emit more than 1.3 times Australia's current annual emissions from all sources and rank in the top fifteen emitting countries globally. Over the course of the mine's estimated sixty-year lifespan, it would cumulatively generate a colossal 4.6 billion tonnes of planet-cooking carbon dioxide emissions.

Of huge concern to local farmers is the fact that the mine will use approximately 12 billion litres of water each year, which threatens to dry up the aquifers necessary for agriculture in the Great Artesian Basin. Once the coal has been dug up, it will be shipped to India. But first it needs to travel from the mine itself in central Queensland to a waterfront coal terminal at Abbot Point, 25 kilometres north of Bowen, via a new 388-kilometre rail link that will cost over $1 billion to construct. The giant mine will also generate so much extra coal that the terminal south of Townsville will need to be expanded to accommodate the massive volume. There are grave concerns that the enormous scale of the coal exports may damage the Great Barrier Reef, as the terminal is located on the coastline of the UNESCO-listed World Heritage Area. The threats of global warming, ocean acidification, dredging, ship strikes, noise pollution and coal dust all compound to further threaten our dying reef.

On top of this, Adani has a poor environmental record. In 2011, the mining company was fined $975 000 for failing to clean up the environmental damage after an unseaworthy ship carrying 60 000 tonnes of coal sank and caused an oil and coal spill along the coast off Mumbai. Considering the Adani Group's appalling track record, which also includes building without approvals, illegally clearing habitats and blocking access to local fishing communities, its plan to ship coal out of Abbot Point port over the fragile Great Barrier Reef clearly places the region at serious risk. As back-to-back bleaching has now killed 50 per cent of the reef, allowing the mine to proceed will effectively allow Adani to drag billions of tonnes of coal over its dead body for the next sixty years.

If it is possible to add further insult to injury, in June 2017 the federal parliament passed a controversial bill to amend the native title legislation, making it easier for companies like Adani to sign Indigenous Land Use Agreements with native title groups. Under the former legislation, all members of native title groups needed to approve an agreement for it to be valid. The government has now changed this so that only a majority of members have to agree, removing the last legal hurdle for the giant coalmine to go ahead, while leaving fractured Indigenous communities in its wake. Despite monumental opposition to the delayed project and doubts about whether Adani has secured the finance to proceed with the project, the mining company has said that construction work on the Carmichael mine will begin in late 2017, with coal exports beginning in 2020.

The approval of the Carmichael mine would also be a major step towards opening up the vast, coal-rich Galilee Basin region where a total of nine mining projects are planned. Former Greens senator Bob Brown has said that stopping the Adani coalmine is this generation's most urgent call to action, an event about which our grandkids will ask us: 'Where were you and what did you do?' In April 2016, Charlie Veron, former chief scientist at the Australian Institute of Marine Science, told *The Sydney Morning Herald*:

> It defies reason. I think there is no single action that could be as harmful to the Great Barrier Reef as the Carmichael coal mine … There is extraordinary disconnect between science and the political action. Politicians think the mine is good because it's good for [the] economy, but we are selling out the next generation of Australians as fast as we can go.

In his 2015 book *Atmosphere of Hope*, Tim Flannery said that 'for humanity to have the best chance of avoiding a world warmer than 2°C above the pre-industrial level, the burning of coal, oil and gas without carbon capture has to be a distant memory by 2050'. Opening new, colossal coalmines couldn't be further from this vision.

All the while, the cost of renewable energy is plummeting as manufacturers rush to meet exponential global demand, and efficient and increasingly affordable storage technologies surge ahead. These trends greatly increase the risk that any new coal developments like the Carmichael mine will become stranded assets as coal becomes increasingly obsolete in a low-carbon world. Even the financial sector can see the risk, with seventeen banks worldwide, including the 'Big Four' in Australia, ruling out any investment in the mine. Australian business leaders can see that the age of fossil fuels has come to an end.

We have already lost a decade of investment in crucial renewable energy infrastructure as our government has squabbled and back-flipped over energy policy in Australia. The only thing getting in the way of our renewable industry is a lack of political will. The people are ready and waiting for the clean energy revolution. Just like the community backlash against Trump's withdrawal from the Paris Agreement, it's now up to Australia's visionary business, community and scientific leaders to light the way to a better future.

41
WE ARE ALL IN THIS TOGETHER

In April 1967, one year before Martin Luther King Junior was assassinated, he delivered his famous anti–Vietnam War speech at Riverside Church in New York City. He spoke of the horrors of the war, saying, 'This madness must cease', and pleaded for peace and sanity to prevail. He famously went on to say:

> We are now faced with the fact that tomorrow is today. We are confronted with the fierce urgency of now. In this unfolding conundrum of life and history there is such a thing as being too late … We may cry out desperately for time to pause in her passage, but time is deaf to every plea and rushes on. Over the bleached bones and jumbled residue of numerous civilisations are written the pathetic words: too late.

Fifty years on, King's words perfectly capture the urgency of the ethical dilemma we now face with the global climate crisis.

The science is crystal clear: we are already committed to dangerous levels of climate change, and Australia is the most vulnerable nation in the developed world. Even if greenhouse gas emissions were stopped immediately, the Earth is locked in to further warming as the climate system establishes a new equilibrium over centuries to millennia. A 2017 study by Thorsten Mauritsen published in *Nature Climate Change* used temperature observations to estimate a committed warming of 1.1°C (0.7–1.8°C range) above pre-industrial (1850–99) levels by the end of the century, factoring in the buffering capacity of the ocean. That is, any further increases in greenhouse gases in the atmosphere will compound dangerous climate change already baked into the system from past emissions, and they will keep rising until emissions are actively removed. The urgent challenge is to stop releasing new greenhouse gases and begin to rapidly pull historical emissions out of our atmosphere and oceans.

There is a growing body of literature describing practical ways we can slow down global warming. A highlight is the 2017 book *Drawdown: The Most Comprehensive Plan Ever Proposed to Reverse Global Warming*, edited by Paul Hawken, which outlines 100 solutions that are already in place, based on peer-reviewed science, and expanding throughout the world. This impressive plan, which blends realism with vision, details how emissions can be reduced in the energy, food production, land use, transport, building, education and materials sectors. The simplicity and breadth of the solutions outlined in this groundbreaking book give me hope that we could actually figure this out.

Sunburnt Country has presented a diverse range of scientific and historical evidence that clearly shows that Australia's climate is changing beyond what our society has seen in the past, and much faster than anything we've experienced through our geologic history. Although global greenhouse emissions have stalled since 2014, the future is still uncertain. We can take steps to avoid the worst aspects of climate change by reducing our greenhouse gas emissions, but we need to act now. Once the world's governments decide to genuinely tackle the colossal issue of climate change, there will be an avalanche of scientific innovation and an unprecedented uptake of technological solutions that are already with us. It will create enormous economic opportunities and a real chance to achieve environmental sustainability.

In reality, moving towards a low-carbon economy represents the greatest business opportunity we have ever seen. The economic and social transformation urgently needed over the coming years is possible if the world goes into an emergency response, as it did during World War II. During that conflict, countries dedicated more than a third of their economies to the war effort and innovation flourished. In this early part of the twenty-first century, we're looking at a global transformation that's as huge as the one that took us from the days of horse-drawn carriages and gas lamps to the era of cars and incandescent light bulbs. In an interview with Fox News on 4 June 2017, former US vice-president Al Gore eloquently summarised the challenge, saying that 'we are in the midst of a sustainability revolution that has the magnitude of the industrial revolution but the speed of the digital revolution'. Perhaps the historic Paris Agreement is the sign that humanity is now witnessing the dawn of this global fight for an environmentally sustainable future on Earth.

In a world that has become increasingly addicted to screens and disconnected from nature, it's easy to feel like we've lost our way. Somehow we have lost touch with the Earth and we now tread heavily on it. British psychologist Sally Weintrobe has written extensively about the psychology of climate change. She has described the 'culture of uncare' that has accelerated during the rapid period of globalisation we've experienced since the late 1970s. She has argued that our culture of mindless consumerism and entitlement is driven by a powerful underlying notion that the Earth is here 'solely to provide endlessly for us and to absorb all our waste'. Weintrobe suggested that trillions of dollars have been spent on undermining our intrinsic human capacity to care for the environment through political framing and manipulation by the mass media and advertising. We have seen a shift towards a greater disregard for science, and have become a more materialistic and narcissistic throwaway society that values fulfilling an individual's immediate desires over safeguarding our collective future. During the 1960s, economist Garrett Hardin termed this the 'tragedy of the commons', where self-interest drives individuals to exploit collective resources in the short term, even to their long-term detriment. In a seminal 1968 paper published in *Science*, Hardin suggested that caring for humanity's shared future required a 'fundamental extension in morality'.

Weintrobe has explained how actively blocking feelings of empathy and concern to avoid psychological pain is a common human defence mechanism that is designed to protect us from becoming too emotionally overwhelmed. It's the part of us that changes the channel on television when horrifying images of war or a natural disaster jolt us out of the apathy that comes from living a relatively comfortable life in a privileged country like Australia. Endlessly distracting ourselves with mundane matters is a way of psychologically distancing ourselves from feeling conflicted and distressed by the realisation that we individually and collectively have an ethical dilemma around caring about each other and the future of life on the planet.

It's understandable that thinking about climate change can feel too overwhelming sometimes. Many of us are already trying to keep our heads above water: we have inner demons to battle, kids need to be dropped off at school, and bills don't pay themselves. There's absolutely nothing wrong with zoning out to trivial entertainment sometimes. But we need to be paying attention when it really matters most. The unprecedented challenges of our time now call for us to become active citizens, not just passive consumers. We are now living in the age of consequences, where the actions of every single person on the planet have the power to shape the future of life on Earth.

The good news is that we know that engaging with nature is a deeply fundamental part of being human. Nature has calming and restorative qualities that have been soothing frayed nerves for thousands of years. 'Nature deficit disorder' was a phrase coined by Richard Louv in his 2008 book *Last Child in the Woods* to describe the human costs of alienation from the natural world. Human beings, especially children, are now spending more time on electronic devices and less time outdoors, which has resulted in a wide range of behavioural issues. There is a growing body of evidence that suggests that playing outside in nature is linked to better mental health outcomes for kids. For example, psychological research has shown that a lack of exposure to natural environments is statistically linked with an increased likelihood of attention deficit disorder, and children with the condition exhibit fewer symptoms after spending time in green surroundings.

Adults also experience a multitude of mental and physical benefits from spending time outdoors. The Japanese practice of 'forest bathing', which is basically just being in the presence of trees, has been proven to lower heart rate and blood pressure, reduce stress hormone production, boost the immune system, and improve overall feelings of wellbeing. The benefits of spending time in nature are so clear that it became part of a national public health program in Japan in 1982, when the government promoted the practice as therapy. Even in this dazzling era of technology, nothing soothes the soul like some quiet time in nature, where we can hear our thoughts and feel part of something bigger.

In a country like Australia, we are blessed with magnificent natural landscapes that remind us that, as humans, we are deeply attached to nature. Of course, the First Australians already know this, which is why they have been instinctive guardians of the land for thousands of years. Deep down, we all know that we are not separate from nature and we intuitively feel an empathic affinity for other species. When we see what's really happening to the natural world, most of us feel a great deal of sadness, anxiety and fear. Our impulse is to run away from these difficult emotions, but it's critically important that we stay and face reality if we are to restore our care for the planet that sustains us.

Imagine what could be possible if we extended the care we express for the people we love most in our inner world, outwards to the rest of life on the planet? As American climatologist and psychologist Jeffry Kiehl explains in his beautifully insightful book *Facing Climate Change*:

> I feel we need to enter onto a path of compassionate action to avoid the worst consequences of human-induced climate change. We cannot

rely on technology alone to get us out of this situation; technology is only one aspect of the solution. If we open our hearts to the world's suffering and feel connection to the world, our actions will be true. Our path to a flourishing future will succeed through compassionate action rooted in care for others.

I talk to a lot of people who really care about climate change but feel overwhelmed and powerless to do anything about it. Many people realise that it's no longer enough to change a few light bulbs and recycle, but they tune out, thinking that someone else will figure this one out. Sally Weintrobe has said:

> Genuine hope, unlike false hope, is a trusted steadfast belief, strengthened by the part of us that cares, that we will find a way to face things truthfully, even when this brings difficult feelings and moral challenges, and even when we find ourselves stuck at times.

Given the immensity of what is at stake—our homes, our livelihoods, our future—it's important that we don't turn away and disengage at this critical time in human history.

Aside from caring about our future, the most powerful thing we can do is vote at the ballot box and with our wallets. Our politicians need to know that the community is concerned about what climate change will do to our jobs, lifestyles, health and ecosystems. If we don't help our energy sector transition smoothly into the clean energy revolution, business leaders will think that investing in Australia is still too risky. We need to let our politicians know that in a country like Australia that is drenched in sunshine, it's insane that only around 3 per cent of the country's electricity is generated from solar energy!

Australia's future depends on every person in this country voting for governments that will take strong, visionary policy action on climate change. We all need to make our voices heard by voting for local, state and federal politicians who are genuinely committed to implementing climate change policy that meaningfully addresses the largest intergenerational ethical challenge in human history. What we do now will shape future life in Australia and how much will be lost to future generations. Can we live with ourselves knowing that we are passing on an unsafe and unstable future to our young ones?

The good news is that Australia has a long history of communities taking a stand for environmental protection and social justice. Throughout our history we have stood up for what we believe in: we have fought for the restoration of dammed river systems like the Snowy, and against the logging of native forests, nuclear power, whaling, coal seam gas exploration and, most recently, the Adani coalmine in Queensland. On 22 April 2017, public concern about the risks of devaluing the role of science in our society culminated in millions of people in more than 600 cities around the world taking to the streets in 'March for Science' rallies, to defend the role of science in ensuring our health, economies, food security and safety. Thousands of people rallied across Australia, in cities and towns such as Sydney, Melbourne, Hobart, Perth, Brisbane and Townsville, calling on our political leaders to restore respect for the critical role that science plays in informing decisions that protect the public good.

In *Atmosphere of Hope*, Tim Flannery made special mention of the role of young people, saying: 'I want them to know that there is hope—that their new found voice is making a difference—and, whether through activism, community projects or building new green businesses, they will change the world'. I also want to add: All the technology we need to solve the climate crisis already exists! It takes people like you to step up and be the change you want to see in the world. Meet up with like-minded

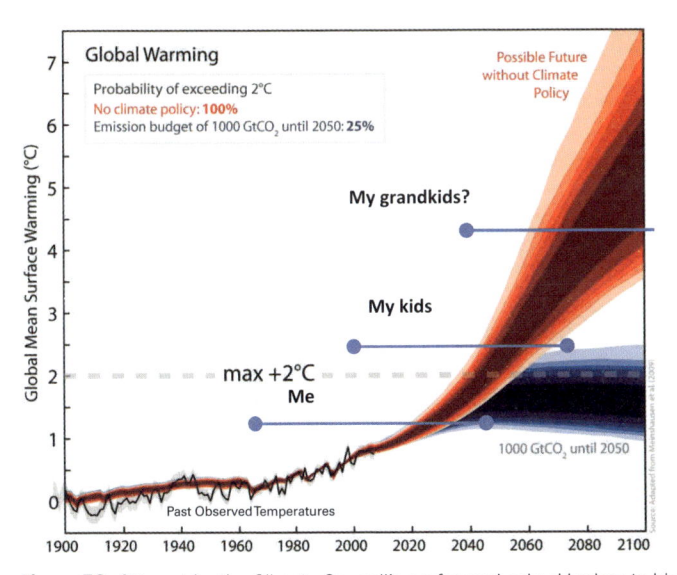

Figure 50. Attempt by the Climate Council's professor Lesley Hughes to highlight differences between the intergenerational experiences of climate change. It aims to make a connection between the numbers drawn from climate science and the personal motivations needed to drive action on climate change.

Source: Reproduced courtesy of Lesley Hughes, Macquarie University.

people who also care about climate change and realise that you are not alone with this. I know it's easy to feel disillusioned by the actions of the older generation, but remember that many of our elders are also fighting hard for a better future for everyone.

The battles being fought all over the world with increasing ferocity are a sign that the stakes are now higher than ever before. Growth in world carbon emissions stalled three years in a row in 2014, 2015 and 2016 while the global economy continued to grow. It's the first time that carbon emissions have not been tied to global economic growth, signalling that the great decline in emissions needed to stabilise the world's climate may finally be here. We are witnessing a pivotal moment in human history, one that may signal the end of the era of polluting fossil fuels and the dawn of the clean energy revolution. Although the challenges are colossal, so too are the opportunities and momentum that is underway to create a safer future. Change is inevitable: we can choose to face it with fear or courage. If we choose to engage positively with the processes of transformation, we have an opportunity to be a part of solutions that will benefit all of humanity.

The global backlash against Trump's abandonment of the Paris Agreement is a clear sign that the tide has turned. Here in Australia, we still have many battles against fossil fuel interests ahead of us, but awareness is now reaching critical mass. As a climate scientist, it comforts me to remember that we are living in historic times that are asking us to imagine that another world is possible, to try to believe that there is a fundamental goodness in people that will rise to meet the greatest moral challenge in human history.

History has taught us that politicians should never underestimate the power of people standing up for what they believe in. We are now at a turning point in human civilisation where everything we do really does make a difference. As we continue our fight against denial, inertia and apathy, be heartened by the wise words of anthropologist Margaret Mead: 'Never doubt that a small group of thoughtful, committed citizens can change the world; indeed, it's the only thing that ever has'.

Together, we've got this.

Acknowledgements

The process of writing this book started in 2007, during my time in the creative hotbed that is RMIT's Professional Writing and Editing program. I'd like to thank Sian Prior, Penny Johnson, Andrea McNamara and Di Websdale–Morrissey for teaching me the tools of the trade. I am very grateful for your encouragement to keep writing during such a formative time. Your belief in me as a writer and this manuscript sustained me through the decade it took to do the research distilled in these pages. This book is a testament to the fantastic work you do to help writers like me tell the important stories that need to be told.

Thanks to all of my fellow PWE writers for your feedback on my writing, especially Julie Perrin and Michael Green for your friendship and inspiration from the moment we crossed paths. Many thanks to Writers Victoria for supporting my work in the form of the Grace Marion Wilson Fellowship for an Emerging Writer in 2012. Glenfern was a safe haven at a time when I was coming under heavy attack from climate change sceptics. My fellowship was a timely affirmation that this book was worth writing, and that I had the support of the broader writing community behind me.

None of the research opportunities I've had to do this work would have been possible without the support of my mentor, the extraordinary David Karoly. I am deeply honoured to have worked with you over the past ten years, boss. Thank you for bringing out the best in me and for inspiring countless others to pursue this path. Your encouragement to write this book was invaluable. I would also like to especially thank my colleagues Raphael Neukom (University of Bern) and Ailie Gallant (Monash University) for their tireless support in developing the palaeoclimate reconstructions featured in this book. Thank you for your epic efforts and patience, especially through our gruelling ordeal with 'the paper'. Raphi, my most heartfelt thanks for your pure dedication to our field and everything you have done for me as a friend.

I would also like to thank the South Eastern Australian Recent Climate History (SEARCH) project team for contributing to the collaborative work that appears in this book. Huge thanks to David Karoly, Don Garden, Linden Ashcroft, Claire Fenby, Ailie Gallant, Raphael Neukom, Josh Staffield, Greta Harrison, Mitchell Black, and our Ozdocs citizen science volunteers for making the SEARCH project the success that it was. Special thanks to our partners: Margy Burn (National Library of Australia), Richard Neville (State Library of New South Wales), Janice van de Velde (State Library of Victoria), Kate Irvine (State and National Libraries of Australasia), Karl Braganza and Blair Trewin (Bureau of Meteorology), KS Tan and Bruce Rhodes (Melbourne Water), Rae Moran (former Victorian Department of Sustainability and the Environment), Jason Alexandra and Gemma Ansell (Murray–Darling Basin Authority), Nick Lomb and Matthew Connell (Powerhouse Museum), Rob Allan (UK Met Office), Neville Nicholls (Monash University) and Andrew Lorrey (New Zealand's National Institute for Water and Atmospheric Research). This work was made possible by funding by Australian Research Council fellowships associated with LP0990151 and DE130100668.

Sincere thanks to my colleagues Penny Whetton, David Karoly, Don Garden, Blair Trewin, Linden Ashcroft, Nerilie Abram, Claire Fenby and Tony Weir for making the time to provide expert reviews of this work. Your advice and help in checking all of the material contained in the book was invaluable. I am especially grateful to Penny Whetton for your fine-toothcomb and support during the final critical stages of the writing process. Special thanks also go to Blair Trewin for all of your technical checks and access to Bureau of Meteorology figures. Many thanks to Josh and Chris for making the time to take a final read of the manuscript for me.

Image permissions were kindly supplied by the National Library of Australia (Margy Burn), State Library of New South Wales, State Library Victoria, State Library of Queensland, Bureau of Meteorology (Blair Trewin), CSIRO (John Clarke, Paul Krummel and David Etheridge), Australian Antarctic Division (Tas van Ommen), Australian Institute for Marine Science (Eric Matson and Janice Lough), Australian Research Council Centre of Excellence for Coral Reef Science (Melissa Lyne and James Kerry), Victorian Department of Land, Water and Environment, Maitland City Council, University of Auckland's Tree Ring Lab, Climate

Council (Alexia Boland and David Alexander), Intergovernmental Panel on Climate Change (Sophie Schlingemann and Laura Biagioni), and Macquarie University (Lesley Hughes).

My most sincere thanks to Sally Heath and Louise Adler from Melbourne University Publishing for immediately recognising the potential of this project. Sally, it has been a privilege working with such an encouraging and engaged editor. I really appreciate all the time you have spent astutely bringing this book to life with me. It has been a pleasure working with you. Special thanks to Paul Smitz for your meticulous edit of my work, to Eugenie Bauch for her careful proofread, and to Louise Stirling and Tessa Connelly at MUP for your support.

Finally, I want to acknowledge the people in my inner circle who keep my world turning: Josh, Madeleine, Kimberley, Petra, Emma, Dave, Karen, Katy and Bec. Your love and friendship has restored my hope in the future of humanity. My deepest gratitude goes to Josh, for the blessing of a harmonious life; and Madeleine, for being a light in dark places. None of this would have been possible without the support and kindness you have both shown me—I dedicate this work to you.

References

Part I: Colonial Calamities

Allan, R. (1988). El Niño Southern Oscillation influences in the Australasian region. *Processes in Physical Geography 12*: 4–40.

Allan, R., Lindsay, J. and Parker, D. (1996). *El Niño Southern Oscillation and Climate Variability*. CSIRO, Melbourne, 416 pp.

Ashcroft, L., Gergis, J. and Karoly, D. J. (2014). A historical climate dataset for southeastern Australia, 1788–1859. *Geoscience Data Journal 1* (2): 158–178.

Bigge, J. T. (1823). *Report of the Commissioner of Inquiry on the State of Agriculture and Trade in the Colony of New South Wales*. Project Gutenberg Australia. Accessed at: http://gutenberg.net.au/ebooks13/1300241h.html

Bowes Smyth, A. (1790). *A Journal of a Voyage from Portsmouth to New South Wales and China in the Lady Penrhyn, Merchantman William Cropton Sever, Commander by Arthur Bowes Smyth, Surgeon—1787–1789*. State Library of New South Wales, Sydney. Accessed at: http://archival.sl.nsw.gov.au/Details/archive/110316318

Bureau of Meteorology (2008). *Climate of Australia*. Australian Bureau of Meteorology, Melbourne, 214 pp.

Bureau of Meteorology (2017a). Australian rainfall patterns during El Niño. Australian Bureau of Meteorology. Accessed at: http://www.bom.gov.au/climate/enso/ninocomp.shtml

Bureau of Meteorology (2017b). Australian rainfall patterns during La Niña. Australian Bureau of Meteorology. Accessed at: http://www.bom.gov.au/climate/enso/ninacomp.shtml

Bureau of Meteorology (2017c). El Niño Southern Oscillation (ENSO). Australian Bureau of Meteorology. Accessed at: http://www.bom.gov.au/climate/about/?bookmark=enso

Bureau of Meteorology (2017d). Indian Ocean Dipole (IOD). Australian Bureau of Meteorology. Accessed at: http://www.bom.gov.au/climate/about/?bookmark=iod

Bureau of Meteorology (2017e). Southern Annular Mode (SAM). Australian Bureau of Meteorology. Accessed at: http://www.bom.gov.au/climate/about/?bookmark=sam

Clark, C. M. H. (1950). *Selected Documents in Australian History 1788–1850*. Angus & Robertson Publishers, Sydney.

Clark, C. M. H. (1979). *The History of Australia Volume 1: From the Earliest Times to the Age of Macquarie*. Melbourne University Press, Carlton.

Clark, R. (1981). The journal and letters of Lt. Ralph Clark, 1787–1792. Australian Documents Library in association with the Library of Australian History, Sydney.

Coates, L. (1999). Flood fatalities in Australia, 1788–1996. *Australian Geographer 30* (3): 391–408.

Collins, D. (1804). *An Account of the English Colony in New South Wales: with Remarks on the Dispositions, Customs, Manners, &c. of the Native Inhabitants of that Country. To which Are Added; Some Particulars of New Zealand; Compiled, by Permission, from the Mss. of Lieutenant Governor King: and an Account of a Voyage Performed by Capt. Flinders and Mr. Bass; by which the Existence of a Strait Separating Van Diemen's Land from the Continent of New Holland Was Ascertained, Abstracted from the Journal of Mr. Bass.* Cadell and David, London.

Diaz, H. and Markgraf, V. (2000). *El Niño and the Southern Oscillation; Multiscale Variability and Global and Regional Impacts.* Cambridge University Press, Cambridge.

Fenby, C. D. (2012). Experiencing, understanding and adapting to climate in south-eastern Australia, 1788–1860. PhD thesis, School of Earth Sciences and School of Historical and Philosophical Studies, University of Melbourne, 321 pp.

Fenby, C. D., Garden, D. and Gergis, J. (2014). The usual weather in New South Wales is uncommonly bright and clear … equal to the finest summer day in England: climate and weather in New South Wales, 1788–1815. *Climate, Science and Colonization: Histories from Australia and New Zealand.* J. Beattie, M. Henry and E. O'Gorman. Palgrave Macmillan, New York: 43–60.

Fenby, C. D. and Gergis, J. (2013). Rainfall variations in south-eastern Australia, part 1: consolidating evidence from pre-instrumental documentary sources, 1788–1860. *International Journal of Climatology 33* (14): 2956–2972.

Foley, J. C. (1957). *Droughts in Australia: Review of Records from Earliest Years of Settlement to 1955, Bulletin No. 43.* Bureau of Meteorology, Melbourne.

Garden, D. (2009). *Droughts, Floods & Cyclones: El Niños that Shaped our Colonial Past.* Australian Scholarly Publishing Ltd, Melbourne, 428 pp.

Gergis, J. (2006). Reconstructing El Niño–Southern Oscillation; evidence from tree-ring, coral, ice and documentary palaeoarchives, A.D. 1525–2002. PhD thesis, School of Biological, Earth and Environmental Sciences, University of New South Wales, 305 pp.

Gergis, J. (2009). Leaping forward through the past: how historical documents can help scientists understand climate change. *University of Melbourne Collections 4* (June): 42–44.

Gergis, J. and Ashcroft, L. (2013). Rainfall variations in south-eastern Australia, part 2: a comparison of documentary, early instrumental and palaeoclimate records, 1788–2008. *International Journal of Climatology 33* (14): 2973–2987.

Gergis, J., Brohan, P. and Allan, R. (2010). The weather of the First Fleet voyage to Botany Bay, 1787–1788. *Weather 65* (12): 315–319.

Gergis, J. and Fowler, A. (2009). A history of El Niño–Southern Oscillation (ENSO) events since A.D. 1525: implications for future climate change. *Climatic Change 92* (3): 343–387.

Gergis, J., Garden, D. and Fenby, C. (2010). The influence of climate on the first European settlement of Australia: a comparison of weather journals, documentary data and palaeoclimate records, 1788–1793. *Environmental History 15* (3): 485–507.

Gergis, J., Karoly, D. and Allan, R. (2009). A climate reconstruction of Sydney Cove, New South Wales, using weather journal and documentary data, 1788–1791. *Australian Meteorological and Oceanographic Journal 58* (2): 83–98.

Gill, J. C. H. (1969). The Hawkesbury River floods of 1801, 1806 and 1809: their effect on the economy of the colony of New South Wales. *Journal of the Royal Historical Society of Queensland 8* (4): 706–736.

Harris, A. (1847). *Settlers and Convicts or Recollections of Sixteen Years' Labour in the Australian Backwoods.* C. Cox, London.

Hill, D. (2008). *1788–The Brutal Truth of the First Fleet.* Random House Australia, Sydney.

Hunter, J. (1793). *An Historical Journal of the Transactions at Port Jackson and Norfolk Island: Including the Journals of Governors Phillip and King, Since the Publication of Phillip's Voyage: with an Abridged Account of the New Discoveries in the South Seas.* John Stockdale, London.

Irvine, N. (1988). *The Sirius Letters: the Complete Letters of Newton Fowell, Midshipman and Lieutenant aboard the Sirius, Flagship of the First Fleet on Its Voyage to New South Wales.* Fairfax Library, Sydney.

Jevons, W. S. (1859). Some data concerning the climate of Australia & New Zealand. *Waugh's Australian Almanac for the Year 1859.* James William Waugh, Sydney: 47–98.

Jones, P. (2008). Historical climatology—a state of the art review. *Weather 63* (7): 181–186.

Karskens, G. (2009). *The Colony: a History of Early Sydney.* Allen & Unwin, Sydney.

Kington, J. A., ed. (1997). The voyage of the British First Fleet from Portsmouth to Port Jackson in 1787–1788 and its impact on the history of meteorology in Australia. *Colonial Observatories and Observations: Meteorology and Geophysics.* Department of Geography, University of Durham, United Kingdom.

Lamb, S. (1982). *Climate, History and the Modern World.* Routledge, London.

McAfee, R. J. (1981). *The Fires of Summer and the Floods of Winter: towards a Climatic History for Southeastern Australia, 1788–1860.* Macquarie University Library, Sydney, 379 pp.

Nash, D. J. and Adamson, G. C. D. (2014). Recent advances in the historical climatology of the tropics and subtropics. *Bulletin of the American Meteorological Society 95* (1): 131–146.

National Library of Australia (2017a). Trove. National Library of Australia. Accessed at: http://trove.nla.gov.au/

National Library of Australia (2017b). Trove Digitised Newspapers. National Library of Australia. Accessed at: http://trove.nla.gov.au/newspaper/

Nicholls, N. (1988). More on early ENSOs: evidence from Australian documentary sources. *Bulletin of the American Meteorological Society 69* (1): 4–6.

Phillip, A. (1789). *The Voyage of Governor Phillip to Botany Bay.* John Stockdale, Piccadilly.

Risbey, J. S., Pook, M. J., McIntosh, P. C., Wheeler, M. C. and Hendon, H. H. (2009). On the remote drivers of rainfall variability in Australia. *Monthly Weather Review 137*: 3233–3253.

Russell, H. C. (1877). *Climate of New South Wales: Descriptive, Historical, and Tabular.* Charles Potter, Government Printer, Sydney.

Russell, H. C. (1887). *Notes upon Floods in Lake George*, Charles Potter, Government Printer, Sydney.

SEARCH (2010). South Eastern Australian Recent Climate History (SEARCH) Project. The University of Melbourne. Accessed at: http://climatehistory.com.au

State Emergency Service (2017). About Us. State Emergency Service, New South Wales. Accessed at: https://www.ses.nsw.gov.au/about-us/

State Library of New South Wales (2011). Journals from the First Fleet. State Library of New South Wales. Accessed at: http://www.sl.nsw.gov.au/stories/terra-australis-australia/journals-first-fleet

Tench, W. (1789). *A Narrative of the Expedition to Botany Bay, with an Account of New South Wales, Its Productions, Inhabitants, &c.* Chamberlaine, Wilson, White, Byrne, Gruebier, Jones and Dornin, Dublin.

Tench, W. (1793). *A Complete Account of the Settlement at Port Jackson.* Nicol and Sewell, London.

Welbergen, J., Klose, S., Markus, N. and Eby, P. (2008). Climate change and the effects of temperature extremes on Australian flying-foxes. *The Royal Society 275*: 419–425.

Worgan, G. (1978). *Journal of a First Fleet Surgeon 1788.* Library Council of New South Wales in association with the Library of Australian History, Sydney.

Part II: Weather Watchers

Allan, R., Brohan, P., Compo, G., Stone, R., Juerg Luterbacher, J. and Brönnimann, S. (2011). The International Atmospheric Circulation Reconstructions over the Earth (ACRE) initiative. *Bulletin of the American Meteorological Society*: doi: 10.1175/2011BAMS3218.1.

Allan, R., Reason, C., Carroll, P. and Jones, P. (2002). A reconstruction of Madras (Chennai) mean sea-level pressure using instrumental records from the late 18th and early 19th centuries. *International Journal of Climatology 22*: 1119–1142.

Ashcroft, L., Gergis, J. and Karoly, D. J. (2013). Southeastern Australian rescued observational climate network, 1788–1859. *Zenodo*: doi: 10.5281/zenodo.7598.

Ashcroft, L., Gergis, J. and Karoly, D. J. (2014). A historical climate dataset for southeastern Australia, 1788–1859. *Geoscience Data Journal 1* (2): 158–178.

Ashcroft, L., Gergis, J. and Karoly, D. J. (2016). Long-term stationarity of El Niño–Southern Oscillation teleconnections in southeastern Australia. *Climate Dynamics 46* (9): 2991–3006.

Ashcroft, L., Karoly, D. J. and Gergis, J. (2012). Temperature variations of southeastern Australia, 1860–2011. *Australian Meteorological and Oceanographic Journal 62*: 227–245.

Ashcroft, L., Karoly, D. J. and Gergis, J. (2014). Southeastern Australian climate variability 1860–2009: a multivariate analysis. *International Journal of Climatology 34* (6): 1928–1944.

Ashcroft, L. C. (2013). Extending the instrumental climate record of southeastern Australia. PhD thesis, School of Earth Sciences, The University of Melbourne, 516 pp.

Australian Broadcasting Corporation (2003). The lost seasons. The Lab, Australian Broadcasting Corporation. Accessed at: http://www.abc.net.au/science/features/indigenous/

Australian Business Roundtable for Disaster Resilience and Safer Communities (2016). *The Economic Cost of the Social Impact of Natural Disasters.* Deloitte Access Economics, Sydney, 116 pp.

Australian Institute for Disaster Resilience (2017). Australian Disaster Resilience Knowledge Hub. Australian Institute for Disaster Resilience. Accessed at: https://www.emknowledge.org.au

Bates, D. (1992). *Aboriginal Perth and Bibbulmun Biographies and Legends.* Hesperian Press, Carlisle, Western Australia, 192 pp.

Bradley, W. (1969). *A Voyage to New South Wales, the Journal of Lieutenant William Bradley RN of HMS Sirius.* Ure Smith Pty Ltd, Sydney.

Bureau of Meteorology (2004). *Drought, Dust and Deluge: a Century of Climate Extremes in Australia.* Australian Bureau of Meteorology, Melbourne, 77 pp.

Bureau of Meteorology (2008). *Climate of Australia.* Australian Bureau of Meteorology, Melbourne, 214 pp.

Bureau of Meteorology (2016). Indigenous weather knowledge. Australian Bureau of Meteorology. Accessed at: http://www.bom.gov.au/iwk/

Bureau of Meteorology (2017a). Australian rainfall patterns during El Niño. Australian Bureau of Meteorology, Accessed at: http://www.bom.gov.au/climate/enso/ninocomp.shtml

Bureau of Meteorology (2017b). Australian rainfall patterns during La Niña. Australian Bureau of Meteorology. Accessed at: http://www.bom.gov.au/climate/enso/ninacomp.shtml

Bureau of Meteorology (2017c). El Niño—detailed Australian analysis. Australian Bureau of Meteorology. Accessed at: http://www.bom.gov.au/climate/enso/enlist/

Bureau of Meteorology (2017d). La Niña—detailed Australian analysis. Australian Bureau of Meteorology. Accessed at: http://www.bom.gov.au/climate/enso/lnlist/

Bureau of Meteorology (2017e). Long-term temperature record: Australian Climate Observations Reference Network—Surface Air Temperature. Australian Bureau of Meteorology. Accessed at: http://www.bom.gov.au/climate/change/acorn-sat/

Bureau of Meteorology (2017f). Previous tropical cyclones. Australian Bureau of Meteorology. Accessed at: http://www.bom.gov.au/cyclone/history/index.shtml

Bureau of Meteorology (2017g). *Special Climate Statement 61–exceptional heat in southeast Australia in early 2017.* Australian Bureau of Meteorology. Accessed at: http://www.bom.gov.au/climate/current/statements/scs61.pdf

Callaghan, J. and Power, S. (2011). Variability and decline in the number of severe tropical cyclones making land-fall over eastern Australia since the late nineteenth century. *Climate Dynamics 37* (3–4): 647–662.

Callaghan, J. and Power, S. (2014). Major coastal flooding in southeastern Australia 1860–2012, associated deaths and weather systems. *Australian Meteorological and Oceanographic Journal 64*: 183–213.

Clark, C. M. H. (1950). *Selected Documents in Australian History 1788–1850.* Angus & Robertson Publishers, Sydney.

Coates, L. (1999). Flood fatalities in Australia, 1788–1996. *Australian Geographer 30* (3): 391–408.

Coates, L., Haynes, K., O'Brien, J., McAneney, J. and de Oliveira, F. D. (2014). Exploring 167 years of vulnerability: an examination of extreme heat events in Australia 1844–2010. *Environmental Science & Policy 42*: 33–44.

Country Fire Authority (2012). About Us. Country Fire Authority, Australia. Accessed at: http://www.cfa.vic.gov.au

Fenby, C. D. (2012). Experiencing, understanding and adapting to climate in south-eastern Australia, 1788–1860. PhD thesis, School of Earth Sciences and School of Historical and Philosophical Studies, University of Melbourne, 321 pp.

Fenby, C. D. and Gergis, J. (2013). Rainfall variations in south-eastern Australia, part 1: consolidating evidence from pre-instrumental documentary sources, 1788–1860. *International Journal of Climatology 33* (14): 2956–2972.

Flood, J. (1995). *Archaeology of the Dreamtime: the story of prehistoric Australia and its people.* Angus & Robertson, Sydney, Australia, 328 pp.

Forest Fire Management Victoria (2017). Past bushfires: a chronology of major bushfires in Victoria from 2013 back to 1851. Forest Fire Management Victoria. Accessed at: https://www.ffm.vic.gov.au/history-and-incidents/black-friday-1939

Garden, D. (2009). *Droughts, Floods & Cyclones: El Niños that Shaped Our Colonial Past*. Australian Scholarly Publishing Ltd, Melbourne, 428 pp.

Garden, D. (2010). The Federation Drought of 1895–1903, El Niño and society in Australia. *Common Ground: Integrating the Social and Environmental in History*. G. Massard-Guilbaud and S. Mosley. Cambridge Scholars Publishing, Newcastle upon Tyne.

Gergis, J. (2009). Leaping forward through the past: how historical documents can help scientists understand climate change. *University of Melbourne Collections 4* (June): 42–44.

Gergis, J. and Ashcroft, L. (2013). Rainfall variations in south-eastern Australia, part 2: a comparison of documentary, early instrumental and palaeoclimate records, 1788–2008. *International Journal of Climatology 33* (14): 2973–2987.

Gergis, J. and Fowler, A. (2009). A history of El Niño–Southern Oscillation (ENSO) events since A.D. 1525: implications for future climate change. *Climatic Change 92* (3): 343–387.

Gergis, J., Karoly, D. and Allan, R. (2009). A climate reconstruction of Sydney Cove, New South Wales, using weather journal and documentary data, 1788–1791. *Australian Meteorological and Oceanographic Journal 58* (2): 83–98.

Gergis, J., Neukom, R., Gallant, A. J. E. and Karoly, D. J. (2016). Australasian temperature reconstruction ensembles spanning the last millennium. *Journal of Climate 29*: 5365–5392.

Green, D., Billy, J. and Tapim, A. (2010). Indigenous Australians' knowledge of weather and climate. *Climatic Change 100* (2): 337–354.

Jevons, W. S. (1859). Some data concerning the climate of Australia & New Zealand. *Waugh's Australian Almanac for the Year 1859*. James William Waugh, Sydney: 47–98.

Jones, D. A., Wang, W. and Fawcett, R. (2009). High-quality spatial climate data-sets for Australia. *Australian Meteorological and Oceanographic Journal 58*: 233–248.

Jones, P. (2008). Historical climatology—a state of the art review. *Weather 63* (7): 181–186.

Jones, P. (2016). The reliability of global and hemispheric surface temperature records. *Advances in Atmospheric Sciences 33* (3): 269–282.

King, A. D., Black, M. T., Min, S.-K., Fischer, E. M., Mitchell, D. M., Harrington, L. J. and Perkins-Kirkpatrick, S. E. (2016). Emergence of heat extremes attributable to anthropogenic influences. *Geophysical Research Letters 43* (7): doi: 10.1002/2015GL067448.

Lavery, B., Joung, G. and Nicholls, N. (1997). An extended high-quality historical rainfall data set for Australia. *Australian Meteorological Magazine 46*: 27–38.

McAfee, R. J. (1981a). *Dawes's Meteorological Journal, Bureau of Meteorology Historical Note No 2*. Australian Government Publishing Service, Canberra, 29 pp.

McAfee, R. J. (1981b). *The Fires of Summer and the Floods of Winter: towards a Climatic History for Southeastern Australia, 1788–1860*. Macquarie University Library, Sydney, 379 pp.

McCarthy, D., Rogers, T. and Casperson, K. (2006). *Floods in South Australia, 1836–2005*. Bureau of Meteorology, South Australian Regional Office, 252 pp.

McNamara, J. (2012). The Commonwealth response to Cyclone Tracy: implications for future disasters. *The Australian Journal of Emergency Management 27* (2): 37–41.

Murphy, B. and Timbal, B. (2008). A review of recent climate variability and climate change in southeastern Australia. *International Journal of Climatology 28*: 859–879.

Nash, D. J. and Adamson, G. C. D. (2014). Recent advances in the historical climatology of the tropics and subtropics. *Bulletin of the American Meteorological Society* 95 (1): 131–146.

National Library of Australia (2017a). Trove. National Library of Australia. Accessed at: http://trove.nla.gov.au/

National Library of Australia (2017b). Trove Digitised Newspapers. National Library of Australia. Accessed at: http://trove.nla.gov.au/newspaper/

Nicholls, N. (2014). FactCheck: Was the 1896 heatwave wiped from the record? The Conversation Australia. Accessed at: https://theconversation.com/factcheck-was-the-1896-heatwave-wiped-from-the-record-33742

Nicholls, N., Tapp, R., Burrows, K. and Richards, D. (1996). Historical thermometer exposures in Australia. *International Journal of Climatology* 16: 705–710.

Oderberg, I. M. (1980). Aboriginal tales retold. *Sunrise* (May). Accessed at: http://www.theosociety.org/pasadena/sunrise/29-79-80/my-imo8.htm

Peterson, T. C., Easterling, D. R., Karl, T. R., Groisman, P., Nicholls, N., Plummer, N., Torok, S., Auer, I., Boehm, R., Gullett, D., Vincent, L., Heino, R., Tuomenvirta, H., Mestre, O., Szentimrey, T., Salinger, J., Førland, E. J., Hanssen-Bauer, I., Alexandersson, H., Jones, P. and Parker, D. (1998). Homogeneity adjustments of in situ atmospheric climate data: a review. *International Journal of Climatology* 18 (13): 1493–1517.

Power, S., Casey, T., Folland, C., Colman, A. and Mehta, V. (1999). Inter-decadal modulation of the impact of ENSO on Australia. *Climate Dynamics* 15: 319–324.

Power, S. B. and Callaghan, J. (2016). Variability in severe coastal flooding, associated storms, and death tolls in southeastern Australia since the mid-nineteenth century. *Journal of Applied Meteorology and Climatology* 55 (5): 1139–1149.

Russell, H. C. (1877). *Climate of New South Wales: Descriptive, Historical, and Tabular.* Charles Potter, Government Printer, Sydney.

SEARCH (2010). South Eastern Australian Recent Climate History (SEARCH) Project. The University of Melbourne. Accessed at: http://climatehistory.com.au

State Library of New South Wales (2011). Journals from the First Fleet. State Library of New South Wales. Accessed at: http://www.sl.nsw.gov.au/stories/terra-australis-australia/journals-first-fleet

State Library of Queensland (2011a). 1893 Brisbane flood. John Oxley Library, State Library of Queensland. Accessed at: http://blogs.slq.qld.gov.au/jol/2011/11/18/brisbane-flood-of-1893/

State Library of Queensland (2011b). An overview of Brisbane River floods. John Oxley Library, State Library of Queensland. Accessed at: http://blogs.slq.qld.gov.au/jol/2011/01/27/an-overview-of-brisbane-river-floods/

State Library of Victoria (2017). *Victoria Government Gazette.* State Library of Victoria. Accessed at: http://gazette.slv.vic.gov.au

Timbal, B., Arblaster, J., Braganza, K., Fernandez, E., Hendon, H., Murphy, B., Raupach, M., Rakich, C., Smith, I., Whan, K. and Wheeler, M. (2010). *Understanding the Anthropogenic Nature of the Observed Rainfall Decline across South Eastern Australia.* Centre for Australian Weather and Climate Research (CAWCR) Technical Report No. 026, Melbourne.

Timbal, B. and Drosdowsky, W. (2013). The relationship between the decline of southeastern Australian rainfall and the strengthening of the subtropical ridge. *International Journal of Climatology* 33 (4): 1021–1034.

Timbal, B. and Fawcett, R. (2013). A historical perspective on south-eastern Australia rainfall since 1865 using the instrumental record. *Journal of Climate* 26 (4): 1112–1129.

Trewin, B. (2010). Exposure, instrumentation, and observing practice effects on land temperature measurements. *Wiley Interdisciplinary Reviews: Climate Change 1* (4): 490–506.

Trewin, B. (2013). A daily homogenized temperature data set for Australia. *International Journal of Climatology 33* (6): 1510–1529.

Trewin, B. and Fawcett, R. (2009). Reconstructing historical rainfall averages for the Murray–Darling Basin. *Bulletin of the Australian Meteorological and Oceanographic Society 22*: 159–164.

van den Honert, R. C. and McAneney, J. (2011). The 2011 Brisbane floods: causes, impacts and implications. *Water 3* (4): 1149.

Verdon-Kidd, D. and Kiem, A. (2009). Nature and causes of protracted droughts in southeast Australia: comparison between the Federation, WWII, and Big Dry droughts. *Geophysical Reasearch Letters 36* (22): doi: 10.1029/2009GL041067.

Webb, E. (1997). *Windows on Meteorology: Australian Perspective*. CSIRO Publishing, Melbourne, 432 pp.

Wells, K. (2015). Natural disasters in Australia. Australia.gov.au. Accessed at: http://www.australia.gov.au/about-australia/australian-story/natural-disasters

Williams, D. J. (1984). Sydney's climate since 1788—a preliminary investigation, BSc. (Honours) thesis, School of Earth Sciences, Macquarie University, Sydney, 184 pp.

Wilson, B. (1972). *Tales Told to Kabbarli: Aboriginal Legends Collected by Daisy Bates*. Angus & Robertson, Sydney, 101 pp.

Wragge, C. L. (1886). *Meteorological Inspection and Proposals for a New Meteorological Organisation: Report to the Colonial Secretary, Brisbane, Presented to the Queensland Parliament*, 14 pp.

Part III: Time Travellers

Abram, N. J., McGregor, H. V., Tierney, J. E., Evans, M. N., McKay, N. P., Kaufman, D. S., Thirumalai, K., Martrat, B., Goosse, H., Phipps, S. J., Steig, E. J., Halimeda Kilbourne, K., Saenger, C. P., Zinke, J., Leduc, G., Addison, J. A., Mortyn, P. G., Seidenkrantz, M. S., Sicre, M. A., Selvaraj, K., Filipsson, H. L., Neukom, R., Gergis, J., Curran, M. and von Gunten, L. (2016). Early onset of industrial-era warming across the oceans and continents. *Nature 536* (7617): 411–418.

Abram, N. J., Mulvaney, R., Vimeux, F., Phipps, S. J., Turner, J. and England, M. H. (2014). Evolution of the Southern Annular Mode during the past millennium. *Nature Climate Change 4*: 564–569.

Allan, R. (1988). El Niño Southern Oscillation influences in the Australasian region. *Processes in Physical Geography 12*: 4–40.

Allan, R., Lindsay, J. and Parker, D. (1996). *El Niño Southern Oscillation and Climate Variability*. CSIRO, Melbourne, 416 pp.

Allan, R. J. (1985). *The Australasian Summer Monsoon, Teleconnections, and Flooding in the Lake Eyre Basin*. Royal Geographical Society of Australasia, South Australian Branch, 47 pp.

Australian Antarctic Division (2017). About Antarctica. Australian Antarctic Division. Accessed at: http://www.antarctica.gov.au/about-antarctica

Boswijk, G., Fowler, A., Lorrey, A., Palmer, J. and Ogden, J. (2006). Extension of the New Zealand kauri (*Agathis australis*) chronology to 1724 BC. *The Holocene 16* (2): 188–199.

Bradley, R. and Jones, P. (1993). 'Little Ice Age' summer temperature variations: their nature and relevance to recent global warming trends. *The Holocene 3*: 367–376.

Brookhouse, M. (2006). Eucalypt dendrochronology: past, present and potential. *Australian Journal of Botany 54*: 435–449.

Brookhouse, M., Lindesay, J. and Brack, C. (2008). The potential of tree rings in *Eucalyptus pauciflora* for climatological and hydrological reconstruction. *Geographical Research 46* (4): 421–434.

Bureau of Meteorology (2008). *Climate of Australia*. Bureau of Meteorology, Melbourne, 214 pp.

Bureau of Meteorology (2017a). El Niño Southern Oscillation (ENSO). Australian Bureau of Meteorology. Accessed at: http://www.bom.gov.au/climate/about/?bookmark=enso

Bureau of Meteorology (2017b). Southern Annular Mode (SAM). Australian Bureau of Meteorology. Accessed at: http://www.bom.gov.au/climate/about/?bookmark=sam

Cook, E. and Kairiukstis, L. (1990). *Methods of Dendrochronology*. Kluwer Academic Publishers, Dordrecht.

Cook, E., Bird, T., Peterson, M., Barbetti, M., Buckley, B., D'Arrigo, R., Francey, R. and Tans, P. (1991). Climatic change in Tasmania inferred from a 1089 year tree-ring chronology of Huon Pine. *Science 253*: 1266–1268.

Cook, E., Bird, T., Peterson, M., Barbetti, M., Buckley, B., D'Arrigo, R. and Francey, R. (1992). Climatic change over the last millennium in Tasmania reconstructed from tree-rings. *The Holocene 2* (3): 205–217.

Cook, E., Woodhouse, C., Eakin, M., Meko, D. and Stahle, D. (2004). Long-term aridity changes in the western United States. *Science 306*: 1015–1018.

Cook, E., Buckley, B., Palmer, J., Fenwick, P., Peterson, M., Boswijk, G. and Fowler, A. (2006). Millennia-long tree-ring records from Tasmania and New Zealand: a basis for modelling climate variability and forcing, past, present and future. *Journal of Quaternary Science 21* (7): 689–699.

Cook, E. R., Anchukaitis, K. J., Buckley, B. M., D'Arrigo, R. D., Jacoby, G. C. and Wright, W. E. (2010). Asian monsoon failure and megadrought during the last millennium. *Science 328* (5977): 486–489.

Cook, J. (2017). CO_2 lags temperature—what does it mean? Skeptical Science. Accessed at: https://skepticalscience.com/co2-lags-temperature.htm

CSIRO and BoM (2015). *Climate Change in Australia—Information for Australia's Natural Resource Management Regions: Technical Report*, CSIRO and Bureau of Meteorology, 222 pp.

De'ath, G. (2009). Declining coral calcification on the Great Barrier Reef. *Science 323*: 115–119.

De'ath, G., Fabricius, K. E., Sweatman, H. and Puotinen, M. (2012). The 27-year decline of coral cover on the Great Barrier Reef and its causes. *Proceedings of the National Academy of Sciences 109* (44): 17995–17999.

DeLong, K. L., Quinn, T. M., Taylor, F. W., Lin, K. and Shen, C.-C. (2012). Sea surface temperature variability in the southwest tropical Pacific since AD 1649. *Nature Climate Change 2* (11): 799–804.

Diaz, H. F., Trigo, R., Hughes, M. K., Mann, M. E., Xoplaki, E. and Barriopedro, D. (2011). Spatial and temporal characteristics of climate in medieval times revisited. *Bulletin of the American Meteorological Society 92* (11): 1487–1500.

Dunbar, R. and Cole, J. (1999). *Annual Records of Tropical Systems (ARTS); Recommendations for Research*. IGBP Science Series, Geneva, 72 pp.

Dutton, A., Carlson, A. E., Long, A. J., Milne, G. A., Clark, P. U., DeConto, R., Horton, B. P., Rahmstorf, S. and Raymo, M. E. (2015). Sea-level rise due to polar ice-sheet mass loss during past warm periods. *Science 349* (6244).

Fowler, A., Palmer, J., Salinger, J. and Ogden, J. (2000). Dendroclimatic interpretation of tree-rings in *Agathis australis* (Kauri) 2: evidence of a significant relationship with ENSO. *Journal of Royal Society of New Zealand 30* (3): 277–292.

Fowler, A. M., Boswijk, G., Lorrey, A., Gergis, J., Pirie, M., McCloskey, S., Palmer, J. and Wunder, J. (2012). Multi-centennial tree-ring record of ENSO-related activity in New Zealand. *Nature Climate Change 2* (3): 172–176.

Frank, D., Esper, J., Zorita, E. and Wilson, R. (2010). A noodle, hockey stick, and spaghetti plate: a perspective on high-resolution paleoclimatology. *Wiley Interdisciplinary Reviews: Climate Change 1* (4): 507–516.

Fritts, H. (1991). *Reconstructing Large-Scale Climatic Patterns from Tree-Ring Data; A Diagnostic Analysis*. University of Arizona Press, Tucson.

Gergis, J. (2007). Lessons of the elders. *COSMOS Magazine 18* (Dec/Jan): 74–79.

Gergis, J. (2016). How a single word sparked a four-year saga of climate fact-checking and blog backlash. The Conversation Australia. Accessed at: https://theconversation.com/how-a-single-word-sparked-a-four-year-saga-of-climate-fact-checking-and-blog-backlash-62174

Gergis, J., Neukom, R., Gallant, A. J. E. and Karoly, D. J. (2016). Australasian temperature reconstruction ensembles spanning the last millennium. *Journal of Climate 29*: 5365–5392.

Gleckler, P. J., Durack, P. J., Stouffer, R. J., Johnson, G. C. and Forest, C. E. (2016). Industrial-era global ocean heat uptake doubles in recent decades. *Nature Climate Change 6* (4): 394–398.

Gouramanis, C., De Deckker, P., Switzer, A. D. and Wilkins, D. (2013). Cross-continent comparison of high-resolution Holocene climate records from southern Australia—deciphering the impacts of far-field teleconnections. *Earth-Science Reviews 121*: 55–72.

Great Barrier Reef Marine Park Authority (2017). Facts about the Great Barrier Reef. Great Barrier Reef Marine Park Authority. Accessed at: http://www.gbrmpa.gov.au/about-the-reef/facts-about-the-great-barrier-reef

Groveman, B. S. and Landsberg, H. E. (1979). Simulated northern hemisphere temperature departures 1579–1880. *Geophysical Research Letters 6* (10): 767–769.

Hansen, J., Sato, M., Kharecha, P., von Schuckmann, K., Beerling, D. J., Cao, J., Marcott, S., Masson-Delmotte, V., Prather, M. J., Rohling, E. J., Shakun, J. and Smith, P. (2016). Young people's burden: requirement of negative CO_2 emissions. *Earth System Dynamics Discussions 2016*: 1–40.

Hansen, J. E. and Sato, M. (2012). Paleoclimate implications for human-made climate change. *Climate Change: Inferences from Paleoclimate and Regional Aspects*. A. Berger, F. Mesinger and D. Šijački (eds). Springer, New York: 21–48.

Hawkins, E., Ortega, P., Suckling, E., Schurer, A., Hegerl, G., Jones, P., Joshi, M., Osborn, T. J., Masson-Delmotte, V., Mignot, J., Thorne, P. and Oldenborgh, G. J. v. (2017). Estimating changes in global temperature since the pre-industrial period. *Bulletin of the American Meteorological Society*: doi: 10.1175/BAMS-D-16-0007.1.

Hendy, E., Gagan, M., Alibert, C., McCulloch, M., Lough, J. and Isdale, P. (2002). Abrupt decrease in tropical Pacific sea surface salinity at end of Little Ice Age. *Science 295* (5559): 1511–1514.

International Geosphere–Biosphere Program (2012). Welcome to the Anthropocene. International Geosphere–Biosphere Program, Stockholm, Sweden. Accessed at: http://www.igbp.net/multimedia/multimedia/welcometotheanthropocenefilm andstillimages.5.1081640c135c7c04eb480001217.html.

International Union for Conservation of Nature, Laffoley, D. and Baxter, J. M. (2016). Explaining ocean warming: causes, scale, effects and consequences. International Union for Conservation of Nature, Switzerland. Accessed at: https://portals.iucn.org/library/sites/library/files/documents/2016-046_0.pdf

IPCC (2001). *Climate Change 2001: the Scientific Basis. Contribution of Working Group I to the Third Assessment Report of the Intergovernmental Panel on Climate Change.* J. T. Houghton, Y. Ding, D. J. Griggs, M. Noguer, P. J. van der Linden, X. Dai, K. Maskell and C. A. Johnson (eds). Cambridge University Press, Cambridge and New York, 881 pp.

IPCC (2007). *Climate Change 2007: the Physical Science Basis. Contribution of Working Group I to the Fourth Assessment Report of the Intergovernmental Panel on Climate Change.* S. Solomon, D. Qin, M. Manning, Z. Chen, M. Marquis, K. B. Avery, M. Tignor and H.L. Miller (eds). Cambridge University Press, Cambridge.

IPCC (2013). *Climate Change 2013: the Physical Science Basis. Contribution of Working Group I to the Fifth Assessment Report of the Intergovernmental Panel on Climate Change.* T. F. Stocker, D. Qin, G.-K. Plattner, M. Tignor, S. K. Allen, J. Boschung, A. Nauels, Y. Xia, V. Bex and P. M. Midgley (eds). Cambridge University Press, Cambridge and New York, 1535 pp.

Jacoby, G. and D'Arrigo, R. (1989). Reconstructed Northern Hemisphere annual temperature since 1671 based on high-latitude tree-ring data from North America. *Climatic Change* 14 (1): 39–59.

Jones, P., Briffa, K., Osborn, T., Lough, J., van Ommen, T., Vinther, B., Luterbacher, J., Wahl, E., Zwiers, F., Mann, M., Schmidt, G., Ammann, C., Buckley, B., Cobb, K., Esper, J., Goose, H., Graham, N., Jansen, E., Kiefer, T., Kull, C., Kuttel, M., Mosley-Thompson, E., Overpeck, J., Riedwyl, N., Schulz, M., Tudhope, A., Villalba, R., Wanner, H., Wolff, E. and Xoplaki, E. (2009). High-resolution palaeoclimatology of the last millennium: a review of current status and future prospects. *The Holocene* 19 (1): 3–49.

Jones, P. and Mann, M. (2004). Climate over past millennia. *Reviews of Geophysics* 42: 1–42.

Jouzel, J., Masson-Delmotte, V., Cattani, O., Dreyfus, G., Falourd, S., Hoffmann, G., Minster, B., Nouet, J., Barnola, J. M., Chappellaz, J., Fischer, H., Gallet, J. C., Johnsen, S., Leuenberger, M., Loulergue, L., Luethi, D., Oerter, H., Parrenin, F., Raisbeck, G., Raynaud, D., Schilt, A., Schwander, J., Selmo, E., Souchez, R., Spahni, R., Stauffer, B., Steffensen, J. P., Stenni, B., Stocker, T. F., Tison, J. L., Werner, M. and Wolff, E. W. (2007). Orbital and millennial Antarctic climate variability over the past 800 000 years. *Science* 317 (5839): 793–796.

Kotwicki, V. (2013). *Floods of Lake Eyre.* Dr Vincent Kotwicki's Lake Eyre Site. Accessed at: http://www.k26.com/eyre/index.html

Kotwicki, V. and Allan, R. (1998). La Niña de Australia: contemporary and palaeo-hydrology of Lake Eyre. *Palaeogeography, Palaeoclimatology, Palaeoecology* 144: 265–280.

Krummel, P. B. and Fraser, P. J. (2016). Southern hemisphere joins north in breaching carbon dioxide milestone. The Conversation Australia. Accessed at: https://theconversation.com/southern-hemisphere-joins-north-in-breaching-carbon-dioxide-milestone-59260

Lake Eyre Basin (2017). About the Basin. Lake Eyre Basin. Accessed at: http://www.lakeeyrebasin.gov.au/about-basin

Linsley, B., Wellington, G., Schrag, D., Ren, L., Salinger, J. and Tudhope, A. (2004). Geochemical evidence from corals for changes in the amplitude and spatial

pattern of South Pacific interdecadal climate variability over the last 300 years. *Climate Dynamics* 22: 1–11.
Lough, J. M. (2010). Climate records from corals. *Wiley Interdisciplinary Reviews: Climate Change 1* (3): 318–331.
Lough, J. M. (2011). Great Barrier Reef coral luminescence reveals rainfall variability over northeastern Australia since the 17th century. *Paleoceanography 26* (PA2201): doi: 10.1029/2010PA002050.
Lough, J. M. and Hobday, A. J. (2011). Observed climate change in Australian marine and freshwater environments. *Marine and Freshwater Research 62* (9): 984–999.
Lough, J. M., Lewis, S. E. and Cantin, N. E. (2015). Freshwater impacts in the central Great Barrier Reef: 1648–2011. *Coral Reefs*: 1–13.
MacFarling–Meure, C., Etheridge, D., Trudinger, C., Steele, P., Langenfelds, R., van Ommen, T., Smith, A. and Elkins, J. (2006). Law Dome CO_2, CH_4 and N_2O ice core records extended to 2000 years BP. *Geophysical Research Letters 33* (L14810): doi: 10.1029/2006GL026152.
Mann, M., Bradley, R. and Hughes, M. (1998). Global-scale temperature patterns and climate forcing over the past six centuries. *Nature 392*: 779–787.
Mann, M., Bradley, R. and Hughes, M. (1999). Northern Hemisphere temperatures during the past millennium: inferences, uncertainties, and limitations. *Geophysical Research Letters 26* (6): 759–762.
Mann, M. and Jones, P. (2003). Global surface temperatures over the past two millennia. *Geophysical Research Letters 30* (15): doi: 10.1029/2003GL017814.
Mann, M. E. (2012). *The Hockey Stick and the Climate Wars: Dispatches from the Front Lines*. Columbia University Press, New York.
Masson–Delmotte, V., Abe-Ouchi, A., Beer, J., Ganopolski, A., González Rouco, J. F., Jansen, E., Lambeck, K., Luterbacher, J., Naish, T., Osborn, T., Otto-Bliesner, B., Quinn, T., Ramesh, R., Rojas, M., Shao, X. M. and Timmermann, A. (2013). Chapter 5: Information from Paleoclimate Archives. *Climate Change 2013: the Physical Science Basis. Contribution of Working Group I to the Fifth Assessment Report of the Intergovernmental Panel on Climate Change*. T.F. Stocker, D. Qin, G.-K. Plattner, M. Tignor, S.K. Allen, J. Boschung, A. Nauels, Y. Xia, V. Bex and P.M. Midgley (eds.) Cambridge University Press, Cambridge: 383–464.
National Oceanic and Atmospheric Administration (2017a). The NOAA Annual Greenhouse Gas Index. NOAA, Earth System Research Laboratory, Global Monitoring Division, USA. Accessed at: https://www.esrl.noaa.gov/gmd/aggi/aggi.html
National Oceanic and Atmospheric Administration (2017b). Trends in atmospheric carbon dioxide. NOAA, Earth System Research Laboratory, Global Monitoring Division, USA. Accessed at: https://www.esrl.noaa.gov/gmd/ccgg/trends/index.html
Neukom, R. and Gergis, J. (2012). Southern Hemisphere high-resolution palaeoclimate records of the last 2000 years. *The Holocene 5*: 501–524.
Neukom, R., Gergis, J., Karoly, D., Wanner, H., Curran, M., Elbert, J., González-Rouco, F., Linsley, B., Moy, A., Mundo, I., Raible, C., Steig, E., van Ommen, T., Vance, T., Villalba, R., Zinke, J. and Frank, D. (2014). Inter-hemispheric temperature variability over the last millennium. *Nature Climate Change 4*: 362–367.
Neukom, R., Luterbacher, J., Villalba, R., Küttel, M., Frank, D., Jones, P. D., Grosjean, M., Esper, J., Lopez, L. and Wanner, H. (2010). Multi-centennial summer and winter precipitation variability in southern South America. *Geophysical Research Letters 37* (14): doi: 10.1029/2010GL043680.

Neukom, R., Luterbacher, J., Villalba, R., Küttel, M., Frank, D., Jones, P. D., Grosjean, M., Wanner, H., Aravena, J., Black, D., Christie, D., D'Arrigo, R., Lara, A., Morales, M., Soliz-Gamboa, C., Srur, A., Urrutia, R. and von Gunten, L. (2011). Multiproxy summer and winter surface air temperature field reconstructions for southern South America covering the past centuries. *Climate Dynamics 37* (1–2): 35–51.

PAGES 2k Consortium, Ahmed, M., Anchukaitis, K. J., Asrat, A., Borgaonkar, H. P., Braida, M., Buckley, B. M., Buntgen, U., Chase, B. M., Christie, D. A., Cook, E. R., Curran, M. A. J., Diaz, H. F., Esper, J., Fan, Z.-X., Gaire, N. P., Ge, Q., Gergis, J., Gonzalez-Rouco, J. F., Goosse, H., Grab, S. W., Graham, N., Graham, R., Grosjean, M., Hanhijarvi, S. T., Kaufman, D. S., Kiefer, T., Kimura, K., Korhola, A. A., Krusic, P. J., Lara, A., Lezine, A.-M., Ljungqvist, F. C., Lorrey, A. M., Luterbacher, J., Masson-Delmotte, V., McCarroll, D., McConnell, J. R., McKay, N. P., Morales, M. S., Moy, A. D., Mulvaney, R., Mundo, I. A., Nakatsuka, T., Nash, D. J., Neukom, R., Nicholson, S. E., Oerter, H., Palmer, J. G., Phipps, S. J., Prieto, M. R., Rivera, A., Sano, M., Severi, M., Shanahan, T. M., Shao, X., Shi, F., Sigl, M., Smerdon, J. E., Solomina, O. N., Steig, E. J., Stenni, B., Thamban, M., Trouet, V., Turney, C. S. M., Umer, M., van Ommen, T., Verschuren, D., Viau, A. E., Villalba, R., Vinther, B. M., von Gunten, L., Wagner, S., Wahl, E. R., Wanner, H., Werner, J. P., White, J. W. C., Yasue, K. and Zorita, E. (2013). Continental-scale temperature variability during the past two millennia. *Nature Geoscience 6*: 339–346.

Parrenin, F., Masson-Delmotte, V., Köhler, P., Raynaud, D., Paillard, D., Schwander, J., Barbante, C., Landais, A., Wegner, A. and Jouzel, J. (2013). Synchronous change of atmospheric CO_2 and Antarctic temperature during the last deglacial warming. *Science 339* (6123): 1060–1063.

Perkins-Kirkpatrick, S. E., White, C. J., Alexander, L. V., Argüeso, D., Boschat, G., Cowan, T., Evans, J. P., Ekström, M., Oliver, E. C. J., Phatak, A. and Purich, A. (2016). Natural hazards in Australia: heatwaves. *Climatic Change 139* (1): 101–114.

Power, S., Casey, T., Folland, C., Colman, A. and Mehta, V. (1999). Inter-decadal modulation of the impact of ENSO on Australia. *Climate Dynamics 15*: 319–324.

Raymo, M. E., Mitrovica, J. X., O'Leary, M. J., DeConto, R. M. and Hearty, P. J. (2011). Departures from eustasy in Pliocene sea-level records. *Nature Geoscience 4* (5): 328–332.

Rignot, E., Jacobs, S., Mouginot, J. and Scheuchl, B. (2013). Ice-shelf melting around Antarctica. *Science 341* (6143): 266–270.

Roberts, J., Plummer, C., Vance, T., van Ommen, T., Moy, A., Poynter, S., Treverrow, A., Curran, M. and George, S. (2015). A 2000-year annual record of snow accumulation rates for Law Dome, East Antarctica. *Climate of the Past 11* (5): 697–707.

Rubino, M., Etheridge, D. M., Trudinger, C. M., Allison, C. E., Rayner, P. J., Enting, I., Mulvaney, R., Steele, L. P., Langenfelds, R. L., Sturges, W. T., Curran, M. A. J. and Smith, A. M. (2016). Low atmospheric CO_2 levels during the Little Ice Age due to cooling-induced terrestrial uptake. *Nature Geoscience 9* (9): 691–694.

Russell, H. C. (1877). *Climate of New South Wales: Descriptive, Historical, and Tabular.* Charles Potter, Government Printer, Sydney.

Russell, H. C. (1887). *Notes upon floods in Lake George.* Charles Potter, Government Printer, Sydney.

Steffen, W. (2010). Observed trends in Earth System behavior. *Wiley Interdisciplinary Reviews: Climate Change 1* (3): 428–449.

Steffen, W., Broadgate, W., Deutsch, L., Gaffney, O. and Ludwig, C. (2015). The trajectory of the Anthropocene: The Great Acceleration. *The Anthropocene Review* 2 (1): 81–98.
van Ommen, T. D. and Morgan, V. (2010). Snowfall increase in coastal East Antarctica linked with southwest Western Australian drought. *Nature Geoscience* 3: 267–272.
Wernberg, T., Bennett, S., Babcock, R. C., de Bettignies, T., Cure, K., Depczynski, M., Dufois, F., Fromont, J., Fulton, C. J., Hovey, R. K., Harvey, E. S., Holmes, T. H., Kendrick, G. A., Radford, B., Santana-Garcon, J., Saunders, B. J., Smale, D. A., Thomsen, M. S., Tuckett, C. A., Tuya, F., Vanderklift, M. A. and Wilson, S. (2016). Climate-driven regime shift of a temperate marine ecosystem. *Science* 353 (6295): 169–172.
Wilson, R., Tudhope, A., Brohan, P., Briffa, K., Osborn, T. and Tett, S. (2006). Two-hundred-fifty years of reconstructed and modeled tropical temperatures. *Journal of Geophysical Research* 111 (C10): doi: 10.1029/2005JC003188.
Woodford, J. (2005). *The Wollemi Pine: The Incredible Discovery of a Living Fossil from the Age of the Dinosaurs*. Text Publishing, Melbourne, 222 pp.
Zinke, J., Rountrey, A., Feng, M., Xie, S. P., Dissard, D., Rankenburg, K., Lough, J. M. and McCulloch, M. T. (2014). Corals record long-term Leeuwin current variability including Ningaloo Niño/Niña since 1795. *Nature Communications* 5 (3607): doi: 10.1038/ncomms4607.

Part IV: History Repeating?
Allan, R., Lindsay, J. and Parker, D. (1996). *El Niño Southern Oscillation and Climate Variability*. CSIRO, Melbourne, 416 pp.
Arblaster, J., Jubb, I., Braganza, K., Alexander, L., Karoly, D. J. and Colman, R. (2015). *Weather Extremes and Climate Change: the Science behind the Attribution of Climatic Events*. Australian Climate Change Science Program, Canberra. Accessed at: https://www.climatescience.org.au/sites/default/files/Weather_Extremes_Report-FINAL.pdf
Arblaster, J. M., Lim, E.-P., Hendon, H. H., Trewin, B. C., Luo, G. and Braganza, K. (2014). Understanding Australia's record September heat in 'Explaining Extreme Events of 2013 from a Climate Perspective'. *Bulletin of the American Meteorological Society* 95 (9): S37–S41.
Australian Broadcasting Corporation (2009). 'Code red': bushfire warning system overhauled. ABC News, Australian Broadcasting Corporation. Accessed at: http://www.abc.net.au/news/2009-09-10/code-red-bushfire-warning-system-overhauled/1424150
Australian Bureau of Statistics (2010). Yearbook Australia 2009–2010: Australia's biodiversity. Australian Bureau of Statistics. Accessed at: http://www.abs.gov.au/AUSSTATS/abs@.nsf/Lookup/1301.0Feature+Article12009%E2%80%9310
Australian Business Roundtable for Disaster Resilience and Safer Communities (2016). *The Economic Cost of the Social Impact of Natural Disasters*. Deloitte Access Economics, Sydney, 116 pp.
Bao, J., Sherwood, S. C., Alexander, L. V. and Evans, J. P. (2017). Future increases in extreme precipitation exceed observed scaling rates. *Nature Climate Change* 7: 128–132.
Bereiter, B., Eggleston, S., Schmitt, J., Nehrbass-Ahles, C., Stocker, T. F., Fischer, H., Kipfstuhl, S. and Chappellaz, J. (2015). Revision of the EPICA Dome C CO_2 record from 800 to 600 kyr before present. *Geophysical Research Letters* 42 (2): 542–549.

Black, M. T. (2016). An attribution study of southeast Australian wildfire risk. PhD thesis, School of Earth Sciences, The University of Melbourne.

Bowman, D. (2016). Fires in Tasmania's ancient forests are a warning for all of us, The Conversation Australia. Accessed at: https://theconversation.com/fires-in-tasmanias-ancient-forests-are-a-warning-for-all-of-us-53806

Bradley, R. S. (1999). *Paleoclimatology: Reconstructing Climates of the Quaternary* (second edition). Academic Press, San Diego.

Brönnimann, S. and Krämer, D. (2016). *Tambora and the 'Year without a Summer' of 1816. A Perspective on Earth and Human Systems Science.* Geographica Bernensia, University of Bern.

Bureau of Meteorology (2008). *Climate of Australia*. Bureau of Meteorology, Melbourne, 214 pp.

Bureau of Meteorology (2009). *Special Climate Statement 17—the Exceptional January–February 2009 Heatwave in South-eastern Australia.* Australian Bureau of Meteorology. Accessed at: http://www.bom.gov.au/climate/current/statements/scs17d.pdf

Bureau of Meteorology (2012). *Special Climate Statement 38—Australia's Wettest Two-year Period on Record; 2010–2011.* Australian Bureau of Meteorology. Accessed at: http://www.bom.gov.au/climate/current/statements/scs38.pdf

Bureau of Meteorology (2013). *Special Climate Statement 43—Extreme Heat in January 2013.* Australian Bureau of Meteorology. Accessed at: http://www.bom.gov.au/climate/current/statements/scs43e.pdf

Bureau of Meteorology (2016). *Special Climate Statement 57—Extensive Early June Rainfall Affecting the Australian East Coast.* Australian Bureau of Meteorology. Accessed at: http://www.bom.gov.au/climate/current/statements/scs57.pdf

Bureau of Meteorology (2017). Previous tropical cyclones. Australian Bureau of Meteorology. Accessed at: http://www.bom.gov.au/cyclone/history/index.shtml

Bureau of Meteorology and CSIRO (2014). *State of the Climate 2014*. Australian Bureau of Meteorology. Accessed at: http://www.bom.gov.au/state-of-the-climate/2014/

Bureau of Meteorology and CSIRO (2016). *State of the Climate 2016*. Australian Bureau of Meteorology. Accessed at: http://www.bom.gov.au/state-of-the-climate/State-of-the-Climate-2016.pdf

Callaghan, J. and Power, S. (2014). Major coastal flooding in southeastern Australia 1860–2012, associated deaths and weather systems. *Australian Meteorological and Oceanographic Journal* 64: 183–213.

Chen, K. and McAneney, J. (2006). High-resolution estimates of Australia's coastal population. *Geophysical Research Letters* 33 (16): doi: 10.1029/2006GL026981.

Chen, X., Zhang, X., Church, J. A., Watson, C. S., King, M. A., Monselesan, D., Legresy, B. and Harig, C. (2017). The increasing rate of global mean sea-level rise during 1993–2014. *Nature Climate Change* 7: 492–495.

Clarke, H., Lucas, C. and Smith, P. (2013). Changes in Australian fire weather between 1973 and 2010. *International Journal of Climatology* 33 (4): 931–944.

Climate Commission, Steffen, W., Hughes, L. and Karoly, D. J. (2013). *The Critical Decade: Extreme Weather*. Climate Commission. Accessed at: http://www.climatecouncil.org.au/extreme-weather-report

Climate Council (2014). *Angry Summer 2013/2014*. Climate Council of Australia. Accessed at http://www.climatecouncil.org.au/angry-summer

Climate Council, Hughes, L. and Steffen, W. (2014). *Heatwaves: Hotter, Longer, More Often.* Climate Council of Australia. Accessed at: http://www.climatecouncil.org.au/heatwaves-report

Climate Council and Steffen, W. (2015). *Quantifying the Impact of Climate Change on Extreme Heat in Australia*. Climate Council of Australia. Accessed at: http://www.climatecouncil.org.au/quantifying-extreme-heat

Climate Council, Steffen, W. and Alexander, D. J. (2016). *Super-Charged Storms in Australia: the Influence of Climate Change*. Climate Council of Australia. Accessed at: http://www.climatecouncil.org.au/uploads/3ca765b1c65cb52aa74eec2ce3161618.pdf

Climate Council, Steffen, W., Hunter, J. and Hughes, L. (2014). *Counting the Costs: Climate Change and Coastal Flooding*. Climate Council of Australia. Accessed at: http://www.climatecouncil.org.au/coastalflooding

Cole-Dai, J. (2010). Volcanoes and climate. *Wiley Interdisciplinary Reviews: Climate Change 1* (6): 824–839.

Collins, M., An, S., Cai, W., Ganachaud, A., Guilyardi, E., Jin, F. F., Jochum, M., Lengaigne, M., Power, S., Timmermann, A., Vecchi, G. and Wittenberg, A. (2010). The impact of global warming on the tropical Pacific Ocean and El Niño. *Nature Geoscience 3* (6): 391–397.

CSIRO and BoM (2015). *Climate Change in Australia—Information for Australia's Natural Resource Management Regions: Technical Report*. CSIRO and Bureau of Meteorology, 222 pp.

Department of Climate Change (2009). *Climate Change Risks to Australia's Coast*. Australian Department of Climate Change. Accessed at: http://www.environment.gov.au/system/files/resources/fa553e97-2ead-47bb-ac80-c12adffea944/files/cc-risks-full-report.pdf

Diaz, H., Hoerling, M. and Eischieid, J. (2001). ENSO variability, teleconnections and climate change. *International Journal of Climatology 21*: 1845–1862.

Diaz, H. and Markgraf, V. (2000). *El Niño and the Southern Oscillation; Multiscale Variability and Global and Regional Impacts*. Cambridge University Press, Cambridge.

Dutton, A., Carlson, A. E., Long, A. J., Milne, G. A., Clark, P. U., DeConto, R., Horton, B. P., Rahmstorf, S. and Raymo, M. E. (2015). Sea-level rise due to polar ice-sheet mass loss during past warm periods. *Science 349* (6244).

Eddy, J. (1977). Climate and the changing sun. *Climatic Change 1*: 173–190.

Estrada, F., Botzen, W. J. W. and Tol, R. S. J. (2017). A global economic assessment of city policies to reduce climate change impacts. *Nature Climate Change 7* (6): 403–406.

Gallant, A. J. E. and Gergis, J. (2011). An experimental streamflow reconstruction for the River Murray, Australia, 1783–1988. *Water Resources Research 47* (12): doi: 10.1029/2010WR009832.

Gammage, B. (2011). *The Biggest Estate on Earth: How Aborigines Made Australia*. Allen & Unwin, Sydney, 384 pp.

Gao, C., Robock, A. and Ammann, C. (2008). Volcanic forcing of climate over the past 1500 years: an improved ice core-based index for climate models. *Journal of Geophysical Research 113* (D23): doi: 10.1029/2008JD010239.

Gergis, J., Gallant, A. J. E., Braganza, K., Karoly, D. J., Allen, K., Cullen, L., D'Arrigo, R., Goodwin, I., Grierson, P. and McGregor, S. (2012). On the long-term context of the 1997–2009 'Big Dry' in south-eastern Australia: insights from a 206-year multi-proxy rainfall reconstruction. *Climatic Change 111* (3): 923–944.

Gergis, J., Neukom, R., Gallant, A. J. E. and Karoly, D. J. (2016). Australasian temperature reconstruction ensembles spanning the last millennium. *Journal of Climate 29*: 5365–5392.

Gleckler, P. J., Durack, P. J., Stouffer, R. J., Johnson, G. C. and Forest, C. E. (2016). Industrial-era global ocean heat uptake doubles in recent decades. *Nature Climate Change 6* (4): 394–398.

Hegerl, G. and Zwiers, F. (2011). Use of models in detection and attribution of climate change. *Wiley Interdisciplinary Reviews: Climate Change 2* (4): 570–591.

Hegerl, G., Zwiers, F., Braconnot, P., Gillett, N., Luo, Y., Marengo Orsini, J., Nicholls, N., Penner, J. and Stott, P. (2007). Understanding and attributing climate change. *Climate Change 2007: the Physical Science Basis. Contribution of Working Group I to the Fourth Assessment Report of the Intergovernmental Panel on Climate Change.* S. Solomon, D. Qin, M. Manning, Z. Chen, M. Marquis, K. B. Averyt, M. Tignor and H. L. Miller (eds). Cambridge University Press, Cambridge and New York: 663–745.

Hughes, L., Hobbs, R., Hopkins, A., McDonald, J., Stafford–Smith, M., Steffen, W. and Williams, S. (2010). *National Climate Change Adaptation Research Plan for Terrestrial Biodiversity.* National Climate Change Adaptation Research Facility, Gold Coast. Accessed at: https://www.nccarf.edu.au/sites/default/files/attached_files_publications/NCCARF_terrestrial_biodiversity.pdf

Hughes, T. P., Kerry, J. T., Álvarez-Noriega, M., Álvarez-Romero, J. G., Anderson, K. D., Baird, A. H., Babcock, R. C., Beger, M., Bellwood, D. R., Berkelmans, R., Bridge, T. C., Butler, I. R., Byrne, M., Cantin, N. E., Comeau, S., Connolly, S. R., Cumming, G. S., Dalton, S. J., Diaz-Pulido, G., Eakin, C. M., Figueira, W. F., Gilmour, J. P., Harrison, H. B., Heron, S. F., Hoey, A. S., Hobbs, J.-P. A., Hoogenboom, M. O., Kennedy, E. V., Kuo, C.-y., Lough, J. M., Lowe, R. J., Liu, G., McCulloch, M. T., Malcolm, H. A., McWilliam, M. J., Pandolfi, J. M., Pears, R. J., Pratchett, M. S., Schoepf, V., Simpson, T., Skirving, W. J., Sommer, B., Torda, G., Wachenfeld, D. R., Willis, B. L. and Wilson, S. K. (2017). Global warming and recurrent mass bleaching of corals. *Nature 543* (7645): 373–377.

IPCC (2007). *Climate Change 2007: The Physical Science Basis. Contribution of Working Group I to the Fourth Assessment Report of the Intergovernmental Panel on Climate Change.* S. Solomon, D. Qin, M. Manning, Z. Chen, M. Marquis, K. B. Avery, M. Tignor and H.L. Miller (eds). Cambridge University Press, Cambridge.

IPCC (2013). *Climate Change 2013: the Physical Science Basis. Contribution of Working Group I to the Fifth Assessment Report of the Intergovernmental Panel on Climate Change.* T. F. Stocker, D. Qin, G.-K. Plattner, M. Tignor, S. K. Allen, J. Boschung, A. Nauels, Y. Xia, V. Bex and P. M. Midgley (eds). Cambridge University Press, Cambridge and New York, 1535 pp.

Jansen, E., Overpeck, J., Briffa, K., Duplessy, J., Joos, F., Masson-Delmotte, V., Olago, D., Otto-Bliesner, B., Peltier, W., Rahmstorf, S., Ramesh, R., Raynaud, D., Rind, D., Solomina, O., Villalba, R. and Zhang, D. (2007). Palaeoclimate. *Climate Change 2007: the Physical Science Basis. Contribution of Working Group I to the Fourth Assessment Report of the Intergovernmental Panel on Climate Change.* S. Solomon, D. Qin, M. Manning, Z. Chen, M. Marquis, K. B. Averyt, M. Tignor and H. L. Miller (eds). Cambridge University Press, Cambridge and New York: 433–498.

Jones, P. and Mann, M. (2004). Climate over past millennia. *Reviews of Geophysics 42*: 1–42.

Karoly, D. J. (2009). The recent bushfires and extreme heat wave in southeast Australia. *Bulletin of the American Meteorological Society 22* (1): 10–13.

Karoly, D. J. and Braganza, K. (2005). Attribution of recent temperature changes in the Australian region. *Journal of Climate 18*: 457–464.

King, A. D., Karoly, D. J., Donat, M. G. and Alexander, L. V. (2014). Climate change turns Australia's 2013 Big Dry into a year of recordbreaking heat, in 'Explaining Extreme Events of 2013 from a Climate Perspective'. *Bulletin of the American Meteorological Society 95* (9): S41–S45.

Lean, J. L., Beer, J. and Bradley, R. (1995). Reconstruction of solar irradiance since 1610: implications for climate change. *Geophysical Research Letters 22* (23): 3195–3198.

Lean, J. L. and Rind, D. H. (2008). How natural and anthropogenic influences alter global and regional surface temperatures: 1889 to 2006. *Geophysical Research Letters 35* (18): doi: 10.1029/2008GL034864.

Lewis, S. C. and Karoly, D. J. (2013). Anthropogenic contributions to Australia's record summer temperatures of 2013. *Geophysical Research Letters 40* (14): 3705–3709.

Lewis, S. C., King, A. D. and Perkins-Kirkpatrick, S. E. (2016). Defining a new normal for extremes in a warming world. *Bulletin of the American Meteorological Society 98* (6): 1139–1151.

McInnes, K. L., White, C. J., Haigh, I. D., Hemer, M. A., Hoeke, R. K., Holbrook, N. J., Kiem, A. S., Oliver, E. C. J., Ranasinghe, R., Walsh, K. J. E., Westra, S. and Cox, R. (2016). Natural hazards in Australia: sea level and coastal extremes. *Climatic Change 139* (1): 69–83.

Morrison, C. and Pickering, C. M. (2012). *Climate Change Adaptation in the Australian Alps: Impacts, Strategies, Limits and Management.* National Climate Change Adaptation Research Facility, Gold Coast. Accessed at: https://www.nccarf.edu.au/sites/default/files/attached_files_publications/Morrison_2012_Limits_Australian_Alps.pdf

National Aeronautics and Space Administration (2017). NASA, NOAA data show 2016 warmest year on record globally. NASA, Goddard Institute for Space Studies. Accessed at: https://www.giss.nasa.gov/research/news/20170118/

National Climate Change Adaptation Research Facility (2016). *Synthesis Summary 1: Heat and Heatwaves.* National Climate Change Adaptation Research Facility, Gold Coast. Accessed at: https://www.nccarf.edu.au/synthesis/synthesis-summary-1-heat-and-heatwaves

National Library of Australia (2017). Trove Digitised Newspapers. National Library of Australia. Accessed at: http://trove.nla.gov.au/newspaper/

PAGES2k-PMIP3, Bothe, O., Evans, M., Fernández–Donado, L., Garcia–Bustamante, E., Gergis, J., Gonzalez-Rouco, J. F., Goosse, H., Hegerl, G., Hind, A., Jungclaus, J., Kaufman, D., Lehner, F., McKay, N., Moberg, A., Raible, C. C., Schurer, A., Shi, F., Smerdon, J. E., Von Gunten, L., Wagner, S., Warren, E., Widmann, M., Yiou, P. and Zorita, E. (2015). Continental-scale temperature variability in PMIP3 simulations and PAGES 2k regional temperature reconstructions over the past millennium. *Climate of the Past 11* (3): 2483–2555.

Palmer, J., Cook, E., Turney, C., Allen, K., Fenwick, P., Cook, B., O'Donnell, A., Lough, J., Grierson, P. and Baker, P. (2015). Drought variability in the eastern Australia and New Zealand summer drought atlas (ANZDA, CE 1500–2012) modulated by the Interdecadal Pacific Oscillation. *Environmental Research Letters 10* (12): doi: 10.1088/1748-9326/10/12/124002.

Parrenin, F., Masson-Delmotte, V., Köhler, P., Raynaud, D., Paillard, D., Schwander, J., Barbante, C., Landais, A., Wegner, A. and Jouzel, J. (2013). Synchronous change of atmospheric CO_2 and Antarctic temperature during the last deglacial warming. *Science 339* (6123): 1060–1063.

Power, S., Casey, T., Folland, C., Colman, A. and Mehta, V. (1999). Inter-decadal modulation of the impact of ENSO on Australia. *Climate Dynamics 15*: 319–324.

Robock, A. (2000). Volcanic eruptions and climate. *Review of Geophysics 38* (2): 191–219.

Ruddiman, W. F. (2013). *Earth's Climate: Past and Future* (third edition). W. H. Freeman & Co Ltd, New York.

SEARCH (2010). South Eastern Australian Recent Climate History (SEARCH) Project. The University of Melbourne. Accessed at: http://climatehistory.com.au

Steffen, W. (2010). Observed trends in Earth System behavior. *Wiley Interdisciplinary Reviews: Climate Change* 1 (3): 428–449.

Steffen, W., Burbidge, A. A., Hughes, L., Kitching, R., Lindenmayer, D., Musgrave, W., Stafford-Smith, M. and Werner, P. A. (2009). *Australia's Biodiversity and Climate Change: a Strategic Assessment of the Vulnerability of Australia's Biodiversity to Climate Change.* CSIRO Publishing, Canberra.

Steinhilber, F. and Beer, J. (2011). Solar activity—the past 1200 years. *PAGES News* 19 (1): 5–6.

Stott, P., Gillett, N., Hegerl, G., Karoly, D. J., Stone, D., Zhang, X. and Zwiers, F. (2010). Detection and attribution of climate change: a regional perspective. *Wiley Interdisciplinary Reviews: Climate Change* 1 (2): 192–211.

Thomas, J. and Branley, A. (2017). Climate change could shrink Australia's ski season by 80 days a year by 2050, CSIRO says. ABC News, Australian Broadcasting Corporation. Accessed at: http://www.abc.net.au/news/2017-01-09/climate-change-could-shrink-australia-ski-season-csiro-says/8166372

Timbal, B., Arblaster, J., Braganza, K., Fernandez, E., Hendon, H., Murphy, B., Raupach, M., Rakich, C., Smith, I., Whan, K. and Wheeler, M. (2010). *Understanding the Anthropogenic Nature of the Observed Rainfall Decline across South Eastern Australia.* Centre for Australian Weather and Climate Research (CAWCR) Technical Report No. 026, Melbourne.

van den Honert, R. C. and McAneney, J. (2011). The 2011 Brisbane floods: causes, impacts and implications. *Water* 3 (4): 1149.

van Oosterzee, P. and Duke, N. (2017). Extreme weather likely behind worst recorded mangrove dieback in northern Australia. The Conversation Australia. Accessed at: https://theconversation.com/extreme-weather-likely-behind-worst-recorded-mangrove-dieback-in-northern-australia-71880

Verdon-Kidd, D. and Kiem, A. (2009). Nature and causes of protracted droughts in southeast Australia: comparison between the Federation, WWII, and Big Dry droughts. *Geophysical Research Letters* 36 (22): doi: 10.1029/2009GL041067.

White, N. J., Haigh, I. D., Church, J. A., Koen, T., Watson, C. S., Pritchard, T. R., Watson, P. J., Burgette, R. J., McInnes, K. L., You, Z.-J., Zhang, X. and Tregoning, P. (2014). Australian sea levels: trends, regional variability and influencing factors. *Earth-Science Reviews* 136: 155–174.

Wilderness Society, The (2015). Australia's biodiversity—a summary. The Wilderness Society Australia. Accessed at: https://www.wilderness.org.au/articles/australias-biodiversity-summary

Part V: The Age of Consequences

Arblaster, J. M. and Meehl, G. A. (2006). Contributions of external forcings to Southern Annular Mode trends. *Journal of Climate* 19 (12): 2896–2905.

Archer, D. (2016). *The Long Thaw: How Humans Are Changing the Next 100,000 Years of Earth's Climate*, Princeton University Press, New Jersey, USA, 200 pp.

Australian Bureau of Statistics (2010). Yearbook Australia 2009–2010: Australia's biodiversity. Australian Bureau of Statistics. Accessed at: http://www.abs.gov.au/AUSSTATS/abs@.nsf/Lookup/1301.0Feature+Article12009%E2%80%9310

Australian Government Department of Health (2017). National Notifiable Disease Surveillance System. Australian Government Department of Health. Accessed at: http://www9.health.gov.au/cda/source/rpt_3_sel.cfm

Australian Koala Foundation (2014). The economic value of the koala. Australian Koala Foundation. Accessed at: https://www.savethekoala.com/our-work/koala-worth-32-billion-30000-jobs

Australian Water Association (2017). Desalination. Australian Water Association. Accessed at: http://www.awa.asn.au/AWA_MBRR/Publications/Fact_Sheets/Desalination_Fact_Sheet.aspx

Bloomberg Philanthropies (2017). Mike Bloomberg doubles down to ensure America will fulfill the Paris Agreement. Bloomberg Philanthropies. Accessed at: https://www.bloomberg.org/press/releases/bloomberg-philanthropies-commits-15-million-fill-budget-gap-left-trumps-revoking-us-support-un-climate-treaty/

Brissenden, M., Fallon, M. and Davies, A. (2017). Power failure. *Four Corners*, Australia Broadcasting Association. Accessed at: http://www.abc.net.au/4corners/stories/2017/05/08/4663424.htm

Brown, B. (2017). The Adani mine is this generation's Franklin River. People power can stop it. *The Guardian*. Accessed at: https://www.theguardian.com/commentisfree/2017/mar/24/the-adani-mine-is-this-generations-franklin-river-people-power-can-stop-it

Bureau of Meteorology (2009). *Special Climate Statement 17—the Exceptional January–February 2009 Heatwave in South-eastern Australia*. Australian Bureau of Meteorology. Accessed at: http://www.bom.gov.au/climate/current/statements/scs17d.pdf

Bureau of Meteorology (2017a). Previous tropical cyclones. Australian Bureau of Meteorology. Accessed at: http://www.bom.gov.au/cyclone/history/index.shtml

Bureau of Meteorology (2017b). *Special Climate Statement 61—Exceptional Heat in Southeast Australia in Early 2017*. Australian Bureau of Meteorology. Accessed at: http://www.bom.gov.au/climate/current/statements/scs61.pdf

Canadell, P., Le Quéré, C., Peters, G. and Jackson, R. (2017). Fossil fuel emissions have stalled: Global Carbon Budget 2016. The Conversation Australia. Accessed at: https://theconversation.com/fossil-fuel-emissions-have-stalled-global-carbon-budget-2016-68568

Carbon Pricing Leadership Coalition (2017). *Report of the High-Level Commission on Carbon Prices*. Carbon Pricing Leadership Coalition. Accessed at: https://www.carbonpricingleadership.org/s/CarbonPricing_Final_May29.pdf.

Christoff, P. (2013). *Four Degrees of Global Warming: Australia in a Hot World*. Routledge, New York, 288 pp.

Clean Energy Council (2016). *Clean Energy Australia 2016 Report*. Clean Energy Council. Accessed at: https://www.cleanenergycouncil.org.au/dam/cec/policy-and-advocacy/reports/2017/clean-energy-australia-report-2016/CEC_AR_2016_FA_WEB_RES.pdf

Climate Commission, Hughes, L. and McMichael, A. (2011). *The Critical Decade: Climate Change and Health*. Climate Commision. Accessed at: http://www.climatecouncil.org.au/uploads/1bb6887d6f8cacd5d844fc30b0857931.pdf

Climate Council, Hughes, L. and Steffen, W. (2014). *Heatwaves: Hotter, Longer, More Often*. Climate Council of Australia. Accessed at: http://www.climatecouncil.org.au/heatwaves-report

Climate Council, Hughes, L., Hanna, E. and Fenwick, J. (2016). *The Silent Killer: Climate Change and the Health Impacts of Extreme Heat*. Climate Council of Australia. Accessed at: http://www.climatecouncil.org.au/uploads/b6cd8665c633434e8d02910eee3ca87c.pdf

Climate Council and Ernst Young (2016). *Renewable Energy Jobs: Future Growth in Australia*. Climate Council of Australia. Accessed at: http://www.climatecouncil.org.au/renewablesreport

Climate Council, Steffen, W., Bambrick, H., Alexander, D. and Rice, M. (2017). *Risky Business: Health, Climate and Economic Risks of the Carmichael Coalmine*. Climate Council of Australia. Accessed at: http://www.climatecouncil.org.au/uploads/5cb72fc98342cfc149832293a8901466.pdf

Climate Council (2017). *Unpacking the Finkel Review*. Climate Council of Australia. Accessed at: http://www.climatecouncil.org.au/unpacking-the-finkel-review

Climate Institute, The (2011). *A Climate of Suffering: the Real Cost of Living with Inaction on Climate Change*. The Climate Institute, Sydney. Accessed at: http://www.climateinstitute.org.au/verve/_resources/tci_aclimateofsuffering_august2011_web.pdf

Climate Institute, The (2015). *Sport & Climate Impacts: How Much Heat Can Sport Handle?* The Climate Institute, Sydney. Accessed at: http://www.climateinstitute.org.au/verve/_resources/Sport_and_climate.pdf

Climate Institute, The (2017). *Climate of the Nation 2017: Australian Attitudes on Climate Change*. The Climate Institute, Sydney. Accessed at: http://www.tai.org.au/sites/defualt/files/TCI0004_COTN_2017_final%20version.pdf

Climate Mayors (2017). 338 US Climate Mayors commit to adopt, honor and uphold Paris Climate Agreement goals. Climate Mayors. Accessed at: https://medium.com/@ClimateMayors/climate-mayors-commit-to-adopt-honor-and-uphold-paris-climate-agreement-goals-ba566e260097

ClimateWorks Australia (2014). *Pathways to Deep Decarbonisation in 2050: How Australia Can Prosper in a Low Carbon World: Technical Report*. ClimateWorks Australia. Accessed at: https://www.climateworksaustralia.org/project/national-projects/pathways-deep-decarbonisation-2050-how-australia-can-prosper-low-carbon

Coastal Risk Australia (2017). *Coastal Risk Australia: Predicted Coastal Flooding Resulting from Climate Change*. NGIS, Sydney. Accessed at: http://coastalrisk.com.au

Connor, N. (2015). 'The moment we finally decided to save our planet': US and China ratify Paris climate deal. *The Telegraph*, UK. Accessed at: http://www.telegraph.co.uk/news/2016/09/03/chinas-parliament-ratifies-paris-climate-change-agreement-ahead/

CSIRO (2017). Climate Change in Australia. CSIRO Australia, Accessed at: https://www.climatechangeinaustralia.gov.au/en/

CSIRO and Bureau of Meteorology (2015). *Climate Change in Australia—Information for Australia's Natural Resource Management Regions: Technical Report*. CSIRO and Bureau of Meteorology, 222 pp.

De'ath, G., Fabricius, K. E., Sweatman, H. and Puotinen, M. (2012). The 27-year decline of coral cover on the Great Barrier Reef and its causes. *Proceedings of the National Academy of Sciences* 109 (44): 17995–17999.

Deloitte Access Economics (2017). *At What Price? The Economic, Social and Icon Value of the Great Barrier Reef*. Deloitte Access Economics. Accessed at: https://www2.deloitte.com/content/dam/Deloitte/au/Documents/Economics/deloitte-au-economics-great-barrier-reef-230617.pdf

Department of Industry, Innovation and Science (2016). Australian Energy Update 2016. Department of Industry, Innovation and Science, Australia. Accessed at: https://www.industry.gov.au/Office-of-the-Chief-Economist/Publications/Documents/aes/2016-australian-energy-statistics.pdf

Department of the Environment, Water, Heritage and the Arts (2008). *Economic Activity of Australia's World Heritage Areas*. Gillespie Economics and BDA Group, Canberra.

Dunlop, I. and Spratt, D. (2017). *Disaster Alley: Climate Change, Conflict and Risk*. Breakthrough—National Centre for Climate Restoration, Melbourne. Accessed at: https://docs.wixstatic.com/ugd/148cb0_8c0b021047fe406dbfa2851ea131a146.pdf

Elliott, T. (2016). Decision on coal mine 'defies reason'. *The Sydney Morning Herald*. Accessed at: http://www.smh.com.au/federal-politics/political-news/decision-on-coal-mine-defies-reason-20160403-gnxbc6.html

Energy Consult (2015). *Residential Energy Baseline Study: Australia, Report Prepared for the Department of Industry and Science*. Energy Rating. Accessed at: http://www.energyrating.gov.au/document/report-residential-baseline-study-australia-2000-2030

European Parliament (2015). Negative greenhouse gas emissions: assessments of feasibility, potential effectiveness, costs and risks. European Parliament Think Tank. Accessed at: http://www.europarl.europa.eu/RegData/etudes/BRIE/2015/559498/EPRS_BRI(2015)559498_EN.pdf

Feldmann, J. and Levermann, A. (2015). Collapse of the West Antarctic Ice Sheet after local destabilization of the Amundsen Basin. *Proceedings of the National Academy of Sciences 112* (46): 14191–14196.

Finkel, A., Moses, K., Munro, C., Effeney, T. and O'Kane, M. (2017). *Independent Review into the Future Security of the National Electricity Market*. Department of Energy and Environment, Australia. Accessed at: https://www.environment.gov.au/energy/national-electricity-market-review

Flannery, T. F. (2015). *Atmosphere of Hope: Searching for Solutions to the Climate Crisis*. Text Publishing, Melbourne, 256 pp.

Frieler, K., Meinshausen, M., Golly, A., Mengel, M., Lebek, K., Donner, S. D. and Hoegh-Guldberg, O. (2013). Limiting global warming to 2°C is unlikely to save most coral reefs. *Nature Climate Change 3* (2): 165–170.

Garnaut, R. (2008). *Garnaut Climate Change Review Interim Report to the Commonwealth, State and Territory Governments of Australia*. Accessed at: http://www.garnautreview.org.au/2008-review.html

Garnaut, R. (2011). *The Garnaut Review 2011: Australia in the Global Response to Climate Change*. Cambridge University Press, Cambridge and New York.

Great Barrier Reef Marine Park Authority (2017). Great Barrier Reef tourist numbers. Great Barrier Reef Marine Park Authority. Accessed at: http://www.gbrmpa.gov.au/visit-the-reef/visitor-contributions/gbr_visitation/numbers

Hamilton, C. (2007). *Scorcher: the Dirty Politics of Climate Change*. Black Inc., Melbourne, 266 pp.

Hamilton, C. and Karoly, D. J. (2016). *The Climate Change Authority's Special Review on Australia's Climate Goals and Policies: towards a Climate Policy Toolkit—Minority Report*. Climate Council of Australia. Accessed at: http://www.climatecouncil.org.au/uploads/e11e0f33fae92ca7cc3239b91e0eb2ab.pdf

Hanigan, I. C., Butler, C. D., Kokic, P. N. and Hutchinson, M. F. (2012). Suicide and drought in New South Wales, Australia, 1970–2007. *Proceedings of the National Academy of Sciences 109* (35): 13950–13955.

Hannam, P. (2016). The 10 Sydney regions most exposed to bushfire risk. *The Sydney Morning Herald*. Accessed at: http://www.smh.com.au/environment/the-10-sydney-regions-most-exposed-to-bushfire-risk-20161107-gsk08y

Hansen, J., Sato, M., Kharecha, P., von Schuckmann, K., Beerling, D. J., Cao, J., Marcott, S., Masson-Delmotte, V., Prather, M. J., Rohling, E. J., Shakun, J. and Smith, P. (2017). Young people's burden: requirement of negative CO_2 emissions. *Earth System Dynamics* (8): 577–616.

Hansen, J. E. and Sato, M. (2012). Paleoclimate implications for human-made climate change. *Climate Change: Inferences from Paleoclimate and Regional Aspects.* A. Berger, F. Mesinger and D. Šijački (eds). Springer, New York: 21–48.

Harden Up (2017). Prepare your home for cyclones. Harden Up. Accessed at: http://hardenup.org/prepare-yourself/practical-preparation-advice/property-and-assets/prepare-for-cyclones/prepare-your-home-for-cyclones.aspx

Hardin, G. (1968). The Tragedy of the Commons. *Science 162* (3859): 1243–1248.

Hawken, P., Ed. (2017). *Drawdown: the Most Comprehensive Plan Ever Proposed to Reverse Global Warming.* Penguin Books, New York, 256 pp.

Hepburn, S. (2017). Adani gives itself the green light, but that doesn't change the economics of coal. The Conversation Australia. Accessed at: https://theconversation.com/adani-gives-itself-the-green-light-but-that-doesnt-change-the-economics-of-coal-78912

Hughes, L. (2011). Climate change and Australia: key vulnerable regions. *Regional Environmental Change 11* (1): 189–195.

Hughes, L., Hobbs, R., Hopkins, A., McDonald, J., Stafford–Smith, M., Steffen, W. and Williams, S. (2010). *National Climate Change Adaptation Research Plan for Terrestrial Biodiversity.* National Climate Change Adaptation Research Facility, Gold Coast. Accessed at: https://www.nccarf.edu.au/sites/default/files/attached_files_publications/NCCARF_terrestrial_biodiversity.pdf

Hughes, T. and Kerry, J. (2017). Back-to-back bleaching has now hit two-thirds of the Great Barrier Reef. The Conversation Australia. Accessed at: https://theconversation.com/back-to-back-bleaching-has-now-hit-two-thirds-of-the-great-barrier-reef-76092

Hughes, T. P., Kerry, J. T., Álvarez-Noriega, M., Álvarez-Romero, J. G., Anderson, K. D., Baird, A. H., Babcock, R. C., Beger, M., Bellwood, D. R., Berkelmans, R., Bridge, T. C., Butler, I. R., Byrne, M., Cantin, N. E., Comeau, S., Connolly, S. R., Cumming, G. S., Dalton, S. J., Diaz-Pulido, G., Eakin, C. M., Figueira, W. F., Gilmour, J. P., Harrison, H. B., Heron, S. F., Hoey, A. S., Hobbs, J.-P. A., Hoogenboom, M. O., Kennedy, E. V., Kuo, C.-y., Lough, J. M., Lowe, R. J., Liu, G., McCulloch, M. T., Malcolm, H. A., McWilliam, M. J., Pandolfi, J. M., Pears, R. J., Pratchett, M. S., Schoepf, V., Simpson, T., Skirving, W. J., Sommer, B., Torda, G., Wachenfeld, D. R., Willis, B. L. and Wilson, S. K. (2017). Global warming and recurrent mass bleaching of corals. *Nature 543* (7645): 373–377.

International Renewable Energy Agency (2017). Renewable energy and jobs: annual review 2017. International Renewable Energy Agency. Accessed at: https://www.irena.org/DocumentDownloads/Publications/IRENA_RE_Jobs_Annual_Review_2017.pdf

IPCC (2013). *Climate Change 2013: the Physical Science Basis. Contribution of Working Group I to the Fifth Assessment Report of the Intergovernmental Panel on Climate Change.* T. F. Stocker, D. Qin, G.-K. Plattner, M. Tignor, S. K. Allen, J. Boschung, A. Nauels, Y. Xia, V. Bex and P. M. Midgley (eds). Cambridge University Press, Cambridge and New York, 1535 pp.

IPCC (2014). Summary for policymakers. *Climate Change 2014: Impacts, Adaptation, and Vulnerability. Part A: Global and Sectoral Aspects. Contribution of Working Group II to the Fifth Assessment Report of the Intergovernmental Panel on Climate Change.* C. B. Field, V. R. Barros, D. J. Dokken, K. J. Mach, M. D. Mastrandrea, T. E. Bilir, M. Chatterjee, K. L. Ebi, Y. O. Estrada, R. C. Genova, B. Girma, E. S. Kissel, A. N. Levy, S. MacCracken, P. R. Mastrandrea and L. L. White (eds). Cambridge University Press, Cambridge: 1–32.

Jones, C., Hine, D. W. and Marks, A. D. G. (2017). The future is now: reducing psychological distance to increase public engagement with climate change. *Risk Analysis 37* (2): 331–341.

Joshi, K. (2017). Caring about climate change: it's time to build a bridge between data and emotion. *The Guardian*. Accessed at: https://www.theguardian.com/commentisfree/2017/jun/07/caring-about-climate-change-its-time-to-build-a-bridge-between-data-and-emotion

Kiehl, J. T. (2016). *Facing Climate Change: an Integrated Path to the Future*. Columbia University Press, New York.

King, A. D., Karoly, D. J. and Henley, B. J. (2017). Australian climate extremes at 1.5°C and 2°C of global warming. *Nature Climate Change 7*: 412–416.

Knaus, C. and Evershed, N. (2017). Great Barrier Reef at 'terminal stage': scientists despair at latest coral bleaching data. *The Guardian*. Accessed at: https://www.theguardian.com/environment/2017/apr/10/great-barrier-reef-terminal-stage-australia-scientists-despair-latest-coral-bleaching-data

Kolbert, E. (2014). *The Sixth Extinction: an Unnatural History*, Henry Holt & Company, New York, 336 pp.

Lewis, S. C., King, A. D. and Perkins-Kirkpatrick, S. E. (2016). Defining a new normal for extremes in a warming world. *Bulletin of the American Meteorological Society 98* (6): 1139–1151.

Louv, R. (2008). *Last Child in the Woods: Saving Our Children from Nature Deficit Disorder*. Algonquin Books, Chapel Hill, 416 pp.

March for Science (2017). March for Science April 2017. March for Science. Accessed at: https://satellites.marchforscience.com

Mauritsen, T. and Pincus, R. (2017). Committed warming inferred from observations. *Nature Climate Change 7*: 652–655.

Miller, W. (2014). How building codes save homes from cyclones, and how they don't. The Converastion Australia. Accessed at: https://theconversation.com/how-building-codes-save-homes-from-cyclones-and-how-they-dont-25550

Mora, C., Tittensor, D. P., Adl, S., Simpson, A. G. B. and Worm, B. (2011). How many species are there on Earth and in the ocean? *PLOS Biology 9* (8): e1001127.

Morrison, C. and Pickering, C. M. (2012). *Climate Change Adaptation in the Australian Alps: Impacts, Strategies, Limits and Management*. National Climate Change Adaptation Research Facility, Gold Coast. Accessed at: https://www.nccarf.edu.au/sites/default/files/attached_files_publications/Morrison_2012_Limits_Australian_Alps.pdf

National Aeronautics and Space Administration (2015). *NASA's Journey to Mars: Pioneering Next Steps in Space Exploration*. NASA, Washington DC. Accessed at: https://www.nasa.gov/sites/default/files/atoms/files/journey-to-mars-next-steps-20151008_508.pdf

National Oceanic and Atmospheric Administration (2017). *NOAA Technical Report NOS CO-OPS 083: Global and Regional Sea Level Rise Scenarios for the United States*. NOAA, Silver Spring, MA. Accessed at: https://tidesandcurrents.noaa.gov/publications/techrpt83_Global_and_Regional_SLR_Scenarios_for_the_US_final.pdf

Nicholls, N., Butler, C. D. and Hanigan, I. (2006). Inter-annual rainfall variations and suicide in New South Wales, Australia, 1964–2001. *International Journal of Biometeorology 50* (3): 139–143.

Palutikof, J. P., Barnett, J. and Guitart, D. (2013). Can we successfully adapt to 4 degrees of warming? Yes, no, and maybe. *Four Degrees of Global Warming: Australia in a Hot World*. P. Christoff (ed.). Routledge, New York: 216–34.

Parliament of Australia (2010). Carbon sequestration. Parliament of Australia. Accessed at: http://www.aph.gov.au/About_Parliament/Parliamentary_Departments/Parliamentary_Library/Browse_by_Topic/ClimateChangeold/responses/mitigation/carbon

Raftery, A. E., Zimmer, A., Frierson, D. M. W., Startz, R. and Liu, P. (2017). Less than 2°C warming by 2100 unlikely. *Nature Climate Change* 7: 637–641.

Readfern, G. (2017). 'It's a tragedy', Clive Hamilton says of Turnbull's climate transformation. *The Guardian*. Accessed at: https://www.theguardian.com/environment/planet-oz/2017/mar/10/its-a-tragedy-says-clive-hamilton-of-turnbulls-climate-transformation

Schurer, A. P., Tett, S. F. B. and Hegerl, G. C. (2014). Small influence of solar variability on climate over the past millennium. *Nature Geoscience* 7: 104–108.

Scopelianos, S., Fedorowytsch, T. and Garcia, S. (2017). Elon Musk's Tesla to build world's biggest lithium ion battery to secure power for South Australia. ABC News, Australian Broadcasting Corporation. Accessed at: http://www.abc.net.au/news/2017-07-07/sa-to-get-worlds-biggest-lithium-ion-battery/8687268

Selhub, E. M. and Logan, A. C. (2014). *Your Brain on Nature: the Science of Nature's Influence on Your Health*. John Wiley and Sons, Ontario, 256 pp.

Steffen, W. (2010). Observed trends in Earth System behavior. *Wiley Interdisciplinary Reviews: Climate Change 1* (3): 428–449.

Steffen, W., Burbidge, A. A., Hughes, L., Kitching, R., Lindenmayer, D., Musgrave, W., Stafford-Smith, M. and Werner, P. A. (2009). *Australia's Biodiversity and Climate Change: a Strategic Assessment of the Vulnerability of Australia's Biodiversity to Climate Change*. CSIRO Publishing, Canberra.

Tillet, A. (2017). Senate resolves native title concerns in boost for Adani coal mine. *Australian Financial Review*. Accessed at: http://www.afr.com/news/politics/senate-resolves-native-title-concerns-in-boost-for-adani-coal-mine-20170614-gwqonu—ixzz4lSm49twQ

Tourism and Events Queensland (2014). The Great Barrier Reef: A tourism story. Tourism and Events Queensland. Accessed at: http://teq.queensland.com/~/media/46970D8555BB4517B69C9501F96B46F6.ashx?la=en-AU

Tourism Research Australia (2017). International and national visitor survey results. Austrade. Accessed at: https://www.tra.gov.au/Research/View-all-publications/all-publications

Turton, S. M. (2014). Climate change and rainforest tourism in Australia. *Rainforest Tourism, Conservation and Management*. B. Prideaux. Routledge, New York: 70–86.

UNESCO World Heritage Center (2007). Gondwana Rainforests of Australia. UNESCO World Heritage Center. Accessed at: http://whc.unesco.org/en/list/368

United Nations Environment Programme (2016). *The Emissions Gap Report 2016*. UNEP, Nairobi. Accessed at: http://www.unep.org/emissionsgap/

United Nations Framework Convention on Climate Change (2014). First steps to a safer future: Introducing the United Nations Framework Convention on Climate Change. UNFCCC. Accessed at: http://unfccc.int/essential_background/convention/items/6036.php

United Nations Framework Convention on Climate Change (2017). The Paris Agreement. UNFCCC. Accessed at: http://unfccc.int/paris_agreement/items/9485.php

United States Conference of Mayors, The (2017). Mayors strongly oppose withdrawal from Paris Climate accord. The United States Conference of Mayors. Accessed at: https://www.usmayors.org/2017/06/01/mayors-strongly-oppose-withdrawal-from-paris-climate-accord/

Usher, K., Brown, L. H., Buettner, P., Glass, B., Boon, H., West, C., Grasso, J., Chamberlain-Salaun, J. and Woods, C. (2012). Rate of prescription of antidepressant and anxiolytic drugs after Cyclone Yasi in north Queensland. *Prehospital and Disaster Medicine* 27 (6): 519–523.

van den Hurk, A. F., Nicholson, J., Beebe, N. W., Davis, J., Muzari, O. M., Russell, R. C., Devine, G. J. and Ritchie, S. A. (2016). Ten years of the Tiger: *Aedes albopictus* presence in Australia since its discovery in the Torres Strait in 2005. *One Health* 2: 19–24.

van Hooidonk, R., Maynard, J., Tamelander, J., Gove, J., Ahmadia, G., Raymundo, L., Williams, G., Heron, S. F. and Planes, S. (2016). Local-scale projections of coral reef futures and implications of the Paris Agreement. *Scientific Reports* 6: 39666.

Victorian Department of Human Services (2009). *January 2009 Heatwave in Victoria: an Assessment of Health Impacts*. Victorian Government Department of Human Services, Melbourne. Accessed at: https://www.parliament.vic.gov.au/vufind/Record/82439

Webb, C. (2015). Is climate change to blame for outbreaks of mosquito-borne disease? The Conversation Australia. Accessed at: https://theconversation.com/is-climate-change-to-blame-for-outbreaks-of-mosquito-borne-disease-39176

Webb, C. (2016). New mosquito threats shift risks from our swamps to our suburbs. The Conversation Australia. Accessed at: https://theconversation.com/new-mosquito-threats-shift-risks-from-our-swamps-to-our-suburbs-56350

Webb, L. B. and Hennessy, K. (2015). *Projections for Selected Australian Cities*. CSIRO and Bureau of Meteorology. Accessed at: https://www.climatechangeinaustralia.gov.au/media/ccia/2.1.6/cms_page_media/176/CCIA_Australian_cities_1.pdf

Weintrobe, S. (2012). *Engaging with Climate Change: Psychoanalytical and Interdisciplinary Perspectives*. Routledge, London.

Wells, K. (2013). The Australian desert—the outback of Australia. Australia.gov.au. Accessed at: http://www.australia.gov.au/about-australia/australian-story/austn-desert-outback

Wiggins, J. (2017). BlackRock says coal is dead as it eyes renewable power splurge. *Australian Financial Review*. Accessed at: http://www.afr.com/business/mining/coal/blackrock-says-coal-is-dead-as-it-eyes-renewable-power-splurge-20170524-gwbuu6—ixzz4lSipWpuz

Zorthian, J. (2017). Stephen Hawking says humans have 100 years to move to another planet. *TIME*. Accessed at: http://time.com/4767595/stephen-hawking-100-years-new-planet/

Index

Note: Page numbers in bold indicate images or captions.

Abbott, Tony, 250, 252, 256
Abbott government, 229, 256, 257–8
Aboriginal people, 33, 59
 culture of, 116, 117, 119–20; cultural memory, 118; Dreamings, 120
 dynamic equilibrium with landscape, 174; as guardians, 267
 and European diseases, 49
 and frontier violence, 45, 49, 50, 60
 native title: and land use agreements, 262
 peoples: Bibbulmun, 118; Ngunnawal, 147; Tharawal, 119; Yarralin, 119–20
 population decline in last ice age, 117
 Sydney region: food sources of, 14; impact of drought, 45; relations with early Europeans, 36, 60; and seasons, 119
 weather knowledge, 35, 59, 115, 120, 123; and belief, 119–20; and climate extremes, cycles, 114, 120; and oral storytelling, 58, 116, 118; reading the environment (plants, animals), 58–9, 116, 118, 119, 174; and seasons, 119; and shifts in climate over millennia, 116, (last ice age), 117, 118
Abram, Nerilie, 139, 167
Adani. *See* coal
Adelaide, 58
 flooding, **84**
 heatwave of 2009, 195
 weather records, 72–3
agriculture, 36, 90
 and Adani coalmine project, 261
 and climate change, 113
 and diseases, 39
 farmers, communities, 233–4; and suicide, 234
 and flood-prone areas, 42
 good crops, harvests, 39, 49, 74
 impact of climate, 219; bushfires, 83–4; drought, 44, **45**, 47, **93**, 94, **95**, 98, 99, 100, 234, (properties abandoned), 100–1, (suicides), 101, 234; erratic rainfall, 19, 20–1, 33, 34, 39, 45; floods, 35, 37, 38, 39–40, 70, 82, (devastation), 81; pest outbreaks, 35, 234
 importance of weather records, 71, 85
 and land use, 80; land clearing, 174; misplaced optimism, 85, 86
 see also Murray–Darling Basin
Allan, Rob, 61, 62, 65
Antarctica, 127, 138
 Casey Station, 138, 142
 and climate history, 35; and Law Dome, 138–9, 140, 204
 and global warming, 167–8; basal melting, 168; ice-sheet instability, 225
 and weather, 24, 31, 138
Arblaster, Julie, 190
Archer, David, 216
Arrhenius, Svante, 182
Ashcroft, Linden
 historical climate research, 70, 76, 80, 90
Atkins, Richard, 69
Attenborough, Sir David, 244
Australia
 as dry continent, 24, 108; fire prone in south, 192
 economic development: of agriculture, 90; to 1850s, 80; gold rushes, 80, 82; Great Depression, 94; recession, 80

300

environmental protection, social justice: history of community action, 268–9
and fossil fuels: coal exports, generation, 250, 251, 252, 260; industry, lobbyists, 250, 256, 270
immigration, 80
population in coastal zone, 209–10
sport, 228; and warming climate, 228–9
world wars, 94
see also climate history of Australia; agriculture
Australian Institute for Disaster Resilience, 13

Banks, Joseph, 13
Barry, Jim, 260
Bass, George, 33
Bates, Daisy, 118
Bigge, John Thomas, 46
biodiversity of Australia
  alpine regions, species, 197, 198, 199; impact of warming climate, 199; and snowfall, 198 and tourism, agriculture, 197–8, 199
  ecosystems, 144, 236; and agriculture, 236; and tourism, 237, 239
  endemic species, 199, 237
  eucalypts, 130–1, 239, 240
  impact of climatic conditions on, 237–8
  and landscape, 23, 24, 56, 267; ancient, 4; and land use, 174; and settler knowledge, 83; and soil erosion, 99
  as 'megadiverse', 199, 237
  and rainforests, 199–200, 239; global conservation value of Gondwana Rainforests, 239–40; habitat losses, 239; and fire, 199–200
  species extinction rate, 240; and ecological changes, 240–1
biodiversity of Earth, 236
  and ecosystems, 236
  and extinctions, 240–1
Black, Mitchell, 195
Bloomberg, Michael, 246, 247
Bowes Smyth, Arthur, 4, 5–6, 7, 12–13
Bowler, Jim, 117
Bradley, Raymond, 149, 150, 151, 152
Bradley, William
  watercolours, **15**, 63
  weather observations on First Fleet, 63, **64**, 65
Braganza, Karl, 189, 194

Brisbane
  floods, 1893, 86, **87**, 88, 89, 109; 1974, 88, 109, **110**; 2011, 88; and mitigation measures, 88–9, 109
  21st century: record temperature, 222
Brisbane, Thomas, 70–1, 75
Brodie, Jon, 244
Brookhouse, Matthew, 131
Brown, Bob, 262
Byron, Lord, 177

Carter, Bob, 162
China
  drought and famine, 90
Chirnside, T, 76
Christoff, Peter et al.
  Four Degrees of Global Warming, 253–4
Churchill, Winston, 215
Clark, Manning
  Select Documents in Australian History, 76
Clark, Ralph, 6, 12
Clean Energy Council, 257, 258
Clean Energy Finance Corporation, 260
climate of Australia
  bushfires, 8, 34, 53, 83, 92, 164, 183, 192; Ash Wednesday 1983, 53, 78; Black Friday 1939, 95, **96**, 97, 193, 195; Black Thursday 1851, 77, **78**, 83, 193; impact of, 78, 83–4, 193, (devastation), 96
  bushfires, recent: 192; Black Saturday 2009, 20, 181, 192, 194, 227, (and comparison, FFDI index), 192, 193, (ferocity and impact), 181, 192, 193, 227; conditions for, 193, 195
  climate defined, 56
  and climate zones, 23, 85, 118–19, 146; tropical north, 132
  cyclones, tropical, 16, 24, 27, 86–7, 89, 104, 105, 108, 224; Althea, 108; Debbie, 212, 224, 233, 243; Dora, 108; impact of cyclones, 105, 108, 109, 110–11, **112**, 224, 233, 243; Larry, 233; Tracy, 110–11, **112**, 224; Yasi, 203, 233; Wanda, 109
  and disease, 111; Murray Valley encephalitis, 104; Ross River virus, 106, 108
  drought, 8, 20–1, 27, 33, 34, 36, 43, 44, **45**, 48, 50, 70, 71, 108, 204; and desalination plants, 223–4; Federation Drought, 91, **92**, **93**, 94, 127–8, 204; impact of droughts, 19, 21, 33, 44, 47,

98, 99, 100–1, 228–9; Millennium Drought 'Big Dry', 91, 100, **101**, 156, 193, 203, 204, 205, 206, 223; World War II Drought, 91, 94–100, 203, 204, 228; severe, 53, 91–3; widespread, 49, **92**

dust storms, 53, 77, 92, 93, 98, 195, (widespread), 99

extremes of, 8, 36, 50, 53, 66, 70, 89, 97, 114, 181, 184–5, 186, 203, (becoming more common), 97, 148, 182–3; and coastal populations, 105; factors in, 23–5, 27, 28, **29**, **30**, 31–2, 113; and impact on people, society, 9, 11, 35–6, 86–7, 89–90, 97, 105, 109, 110–11, (and public response), 88, 111; of temperature, 18, 27, 182, **183**, 184, 222

and farming practices, 45, 46, 80; rethinking, 50

floods, 8, 17, 27, 34–5, 36, 37, 39–40, **41**, **42**, 48, 70, 80, 83, **84**, 85–6, (1950s), 104–6, 224, (1970s), 104, 108, 109–11, 203, (from 2000), 202–3, 210, 211, 224; causes, 103, 202–3; impact, 35, 37, 40, 41, 80, 82, 83, 84, 85, 86, 87, 103, 105–6, 109, 203; range of, 103; and rescues, 40, 82, 83, 105, 106; and river floodplains, 104, 109

heatwaves, 8, 18, 19, 20, 21, 34, 53, 65, 69, 77, 83, 92, 97, 184–5, 195, 227, 228; deaths, 97, 181, 227; increased frequency, 183, 184, 185, (and cities), **185**; and wildlife, 19–20, 44, 65

storms, lightning, 12, 13, 16, 93; storm surges, **210**, 211, 212

variability, 3, 7, 8, 16, 39, 44, 45, 46–7, 48, 50, 70, 80, 194, 209, 216, 237; and climate records, 54, 57, 68, 204; human influence, 211, 212, 216, 265; and 'normal' range, 54, 183, 191, 219

and warning systems, 89

see also climate change; future climate change; rainfall history; temperature

climate change

burning of fossil fuels, 174, 179, 270; Australia, 250, 253, 261; impact of, 140, **142**, 151, 181, 182, 194, 208, 216, 261

carbon dioxide concentrations, emissions: history of, 140, 173; and ocean acidification, 135, (increase and impact), 135, 142–3; and natural variability, 138, 143, 174, 176–7; recent levels, 140, 141, **142**, 143, 167, 174, 180, 181, 208, 255, 270; symbolic level recorded, **142**

climate change policy, Australia, 160, 217, 226, 263, (under Paris Agreement), 247, 251; and carbon pricing scheme, 151, 161, 250, (*Clean Energy Act 2011*), 256; and clean coal, 251, 252; and Clean Energy Target, 252, 256; Direct Action, 260; and 'National Energy Guarantee', 252–3; as political poison, 250, 256; political support for coal, 251, 256, 260, 262; public opinion, 250–1, (and voter input needed), 268; Renewable Energy Target, 257–8, 260

climate change politics, history: Paris Agreement, 168, 243, 246–7, (aims of), 245–6, 247, 256, 260, 265, (and weak collective emissions targets), 248; UN Conference on Environment and Development, 245; UN Environment Programme, 247; and UN Framework Convention on Climate Change, 217–18, 245

crisis: Earth's climate equilibrium disturbed, 180, 215; and risk of destabilisation, 141–2

and early weather observations, 61, 67, 68; comparisons with modern day, 64

and environmental change: Anthropocene era, 153, 166–7, 181, (and rate of change), 153, 174; and resilience of ecosystems, 153

global warming: human-induced, 150–1, 152, 154, 175, 178, 180, 181, 186, 189, 194–5, (beginning), 167, 168, (and influence on climate), 186, 187, **188**, 196, 208; impact of cities, 180–1; and natural range of climate variability, 61, 131, 158, 159, 167, 168, 171–3, 175, 179, 188, 189, 196, (factors in), 176–8, 181, 187, (rate of natural warming), 173; recent, 152, 158, 163–4, (extent and rate), 168, 173, 189, 208, 215

greenhouse gases, 136, 181; changes over millennia, 140, 141; nineteenth century, 168; recent rise in emissions/ concentration, 140, 141, 143, 146, 150, 154, 164, 166, 167, 176, 178, 180, (to continue), 142, 186, (impact of), 134, 139, 146, 151, 191, 223, (stalled), 217, 265, 270

living in a shifting climate, 182–6
and ocean warming, 134, 136, 179; around Australia, 134, 135, 136–7, 163, 164; factors in, 209; marine heatwaves, 134, 137; tropical, 136
and ozone depletion, 139, 166, 167, 223
sceptics, 68, 141, 153–4, 161, 257; attacks against scientists, research, 151, 161–2, 164–5; and hockey stick curve, 150, 151, 163; and human activity, 173, 189; opposition to regulation of greenhouse emissions, 151
and sea level rise, 143, 172, 209; around Australia, 209, **210**, 212; causes, 209
speed of change, 196; warming, 201
threat posed, 10, 134, 135, 137, 139, 151, 159, 162; breakdown in climate relationships, 207, 253; to developing countries, 219; to ecosystems, 146, 153, 218; to human societies, 153, 185, 215, (of sea-level rise), 209–10, 212; with 2°C temperature rise, 143
warming in Australian region: change in atmospheric circulation, 222, 223; changes in hot extremes, 182, **183**, 208–9; since 1910, 113–14; since 1950, 97, 160, 162, 163–4, 193, 195, 197; Tasmania, 130
and warming planet, 137, 140, 151, 164, 165, 180, 201, 208; implications for Australia, 114, 137, 153, 189–91, 219, (as vulnerable nation), 105, 111, 114, 219, 238, 254, 264; receding ice sheets, 141; temperature change and positive feedback loop, 140–1, 217
and the water cycle, **201**
see also climate science; future climate change
Climate Change Authority, 251, 252
Climate Council, 212, 229, 260
climate cycles, natural (and Australia)
El Niño, 25, **26**, 28, **29**, 53, 56, 70, 77, 90, 108, 164, 179, 180, 195, 208, 209, 211; and droughts, 27, 34, 91, 94, 98, 127–8; and monsoons, 132; Ningaloo Niño, 136–7; and sea temperatures, 241
El Niño–Southern Oscillation (ENSO), 25, 28, 175, 178–9; and Australia's regional climate, 25, **26**, 27, 28, 80, 106, 127, 128, 190, 202; and Kauri tree-ring record, 128; and the SOI, 25, 28; and variability, 134, 135; and warming planet, 179–80
Indian Ocean Dipole (IOD) events, 28, **30**, 31, 80, (negative), 145, 202
interaction of atmosphere and Indian, Pacific and Southern oceans, 178
Inter-decadal Pacific Oscillation (IPO), 94, 135; positive and negative phases, 106, 108, 113, 135–6, 206–7
La Niña, 25, **26**, 28, **29**, 33, 43, 70, 77, 94, 103, 104, 105, 113, 134, 135, 144, 145, 179, 202, 209, 224, 253; and floods, 25, 27, 39, 80, 85, **106**, **107**, 108, 109, 110, 134, 202, 203; and monsoons, 132; and ocean warming, 136, 203; weak, 98
monsoon systems, 25; in Australia, 27, 28, 103, 109, 132–3, 202
solar activity, 175–6
Southern Annular Mode (SAM), **31**, 32, 139
and volcanic eruptions, 76, 153, 175, 176–7
climate history of Australia
climate records, 56–7, 71–2, 80, 91; limits of, 54; and prehistory, 58–9, 116–17; and projections of future climate, 54, 59
key weather events: bushfires, catastrophic, 77–8, 95–7; Cyclone Tracy, 110–11, **112**, 224; droughts, 76–7, 90, 91–101, 205–6; floods, 80–2, 86–9, 103, 104–6, 108–9; heatwaves, 97, 184, **185**, 195; and national response to disasters, 112–13; snow, frost in Sydney, 75–6
scientific sources, observations, 11, 28, 39, 50, 53, 68, 70, 72–3, 75, 77, 78, 147, 190, 206, (gaps), 69, 70; Bureau of Meteorology, 9, 10, 53–4, 55–6, **57**, 59, 68, 76, 80, 89, 91, 104, 142, 184, 216, 217, 222; collating observations, 56; and comparisons, 64, 65, 66, 67; early decades of settlement, 54, 60, 61, **62**, 63, 64, 65, 66, (and quality of data), 67–8, 69, 70, (outside Sydney), 70, 71, 72; observatories, weather stations, 61, 71, 72, 75, 79, 90, 91, 142, 184–5, 189, 222; and (standardised) measurement practices, 55–6, 58, 64, 67
social, archival sources, 3, 4, 8, 11, 44, 45, 49, 73, 74, (range of), 58; colonial, 9,

10, 13, 14, 16, 17, 18, 19–20, 21–2, 33, 34, 37, 38, 39, 40, 41, 45, 46, 47, 48, 49, 55, 65, 66, 69, 70, 71–2, 74, 77–8, 123, 204–5, (and accuracy), 75; and interpretation, 10–11
  see also Aboriginal people; climate science; SEARCH project; temperature
Climate Institute, 228, 233, 251
climate science, 157
  climate models, 127, 159, 160, 164, 196, 216, 217; and rainfall in warmer climate, 202; and simulations, 139, 187, **188**, 190
  collaborative nature of, 157
  detection and attribution studies: of fire events, 195–6; natural climate forces and human influences, 167, 187, 189; and recent warming, 187–8; and rainfall, 202; using palaeoclimate records, 190
  palaeoclimatology, 10, 76, 123, 168; applying scientific method, 124–5, 151, 161, 163, 164–5; and calibration, 124; challenges, 131; coral records, 70, 76, 123, 124, 131, 133–4, 150, 160, 204, (and frequency of major floods), 134, (and ocean temperature rises), 135, 136, 137; ice cores, 28, 123, 124, 139, **140**, 150, 176, (and carbon dioxide concentrations), 140, 141, **142**, 143, 173, 174, (and greenhouse gases), 138, 150; sediment layers, 150 (and rainfall), 144, 204; tree-ring records, 28, 70, 76, 123–4, 128, 129–30, 139, 144, 149, 204, (and recent warming), 130, 150, 160
  and public and political respect for role of science, 266, 269
  research on climate history of Australia and region: colonial period, 10, 39, 43, 44, 45, 49, 77, 78, 79; twentieth century, 113, **114**, (warming), 162, 163–4
  see also climate change; rainfall; temperature
Climate Works
  Pathways to Deep Decarbonisation …, 256–7
coal
  global demand declining, 251–2; new coal developments as stranded assets, 262–3

political support in Australia for, 251, 256, 260
  proposed Adani Carmichael coalmine, 260–1, 262–3; impacts of, 261; and native title legislation, 262; opposition to, 269
Coastal Risk Australia, 226
Cochrane, Tom, 246
Collins, David, 4, 13, 14, 16, 17, 19–20, 21, 34, 35–6, 38
Cook, Ed, 130
Cook, Gary, 75
Cook, Capt. James, 3, 13, 38
coral reefs
  bleaching, 134, 208
  calls for urgent protective action, 243
  see also Great Barrier Reef

D'Arrigo, Rosanne, 149
Darwin
  and Cyclone Tracy, 110–11, **112**
  rebuilding of, 113
Dawes, William
  and Aboriginal people, 60
  weather records (journal), 60, 61, **62**, 63, 64–5, 66, 67, 69
De'ath, Glenn, 135, 241
DeLong, Kristine, 136
Dibbs, Sir George, 87
Dunlop, James, 71

Earth
  orbit and effect on climate, 171–2, 175, 181, 194
  population, 173; and demand for resources, 181
Emergency Management Australia, 112–13
Estrada, Francisco, 180
European settlement, early decades
  exploration, 145; and search for new pastures, 44, 74, 80
  First Fleet, 7; celebrations on arrival ashore, 13; conditions on board, 3, 4, 6 (and animals), 5; and weather, seas, 3, 4–6, 8, 12–13, 63, **64**, 65, 66
  government policies, 21; grain purchases, 44, 45; water infrastructure, regulation, **21**, 22, 47
  grog, 39; and alcoholism, 39
  industry in, 39
  new colony (NSW): and clothing, 18–19, 36; expansion, 33, 44, 45, 48, 49, 70, 72; and knowledge of local

conditions, 4; on life support, 36; population, 37; problems, shortages, 13–14, 15, 16–17, 18, 19, 34, 36, 37, 38, 40, 41, 43, 45, 47, 48; settlement and conditions, 13, 14, (isolation), 14, 16, 18

Norfolk Island penal colony, 15, 16, 17

Second Fleet, 18

and weather conditions, 3, 13, 14, 16, 17, 22, 28, 32, 50; drought, 8, 20–1, 27, 33, 34, 36, 39, 43, 46, 48, 74; floods, 8, 17, 27, 34–5, 37, 38, 39–41, 42, 48, 74; heatwaves, 8, 18, 19, 20, 21, 34, 69; observatories, weather stations, 61, 71, (and measurement using instruments), 60, 61, **62**, **63**, 64, 65, 70–1

see also Aboriginal people; rainfall history

Eyre, Edward John, 145

Fahrenheit, DG, 54
Fenby, Claire
  climate research of, 10, 39, 43, 44, 45, 49, 77, 78
Finkel, Alan, 252
Flannery, Tim
  Atmosphere of Hope, 244, 262, 269
Flinders, Matthew, 33
Foley, James, 9
forests, 95, 96, 97, 130, 194
  rainforests, 199–200, 238, 239–40
Fowell, Newton, 4–5
Fowler, Anthony, 128
future climate change (and Australia)
  and action on climate change, 186, 198, 218; and carbon capture and storage, 248; cutting greenhouse gas emissions, 226, 248, 253, 270, (practical ways), 265, (and strong political commitment), 255, 265, 268; and future technological breakthroughs, 248, 268; Paris Agreement, 245–7, 249, 260, 265, (and averting disaster), 247–8, 255; to stabilise warming below 2°C, 248, 249, 251, 262, (end fossil fuel use), 255, 260, 265, (price on pollution), 255–6, (transition to renewable energy), 256–7, 259; urgency of, 265
  and adaptation, 202, 249, 254, 255; building codes, 224; desalination plants, 223–4; environmental health indicators needed, 232; and sport, 228–9

and agriculture, 222; decreased rainfall, 234
and the Anthropocene, 181, 240–1
biodiversity, alpine landscapes: impact of future climate change, 143, 146, 199–200, 241, (on species, ecosystems), 164, 238, 240, 243, 253
and challenges, 11, 179; avoid releasing new greenhouse gases, 265; citizen action, 266, 267–8, 270; ethical, 226, 264, 266, 267–8, **269**, 270
and cities: Brisbane, 221; Darwin, 225; and fire risk, 222; Hobart, 225; Melbourne, 222, 225; Perth, 229; and sea level rise, 225–6; Sydney, 221, 222, 225
climate extremes, 113, 148, 186, 220, 234–5, 253; droughts, 202; fire weather, 193–4, 195, 222; floods, 222; and rainfall, 202, 222, 223, 225, 253; sea level rise and flooding, erosion, 212, 218, 225; temperatures, 184, 185, 186, 220–1, 222, 225, 227
and developing nations, 219, 246
energy and infrastructure, 222, 224
factors determining future climate, 216, 253
greenhouse gas emissions, concentrations, 186, 215–16; continued impact, 264; rising, 253; scenarios, 216–17, 264–5, **269**; and unpredictability of climate, 220
and human health: heat stress, 227, (outdoor workers), 229–30, (and sport), 228; mental health impacts, 232, 233; spread of infectious diseases, 230–1, 232
impacts: at 2°C of global warming, 253; at 4°C of global warming, 254
and natural disasters, 111–12, 113, 196; bushfires, 194
'new normal', 218, 225
projections, CSIRO/Bureau of Meteorology: for monsoonal north, 224, 225, 230; for rainfall in arid zone, 146; rainfall, 202, 225, (southern Australia), 234; for snowfall, 198, 199; warming in Australia, scenarios, 216–17, **218**, 220, **221**, 225, 238; warming and drying in southern, eastern Australia, 193–4, 222–3
projections, research, 194; hotter, wetter climate, 231; sea level rise, 225–6;

warming, global, 215, 217, 247, 248, 253, 254
  redrawing our maps, 220, 226; cyclones, 224–5; eastern regions, 221–2; inland Australia, 220, (and liveability), 220; tropical zone, 232
  and tipping points, 234–5; and chain reaction, 235; climate feedbacks, 253; irreversible impacts, 153, 168, 253
  and tourism industry, 198–9, 221
  see also renewable energy

Gallant, Ailie, 204
Gammage, Bill
  The Biggest Estate on Earth, 174
Garden, Don, 9, 90, 93
  Droughts, Floods & Cyclones, 80
Garnaut, Ross, 219
Gergis, Joëlle
  as climate scientist, 61, 167, 203–4, 211, 270; Kauri and tree-ring record, **127**, 129; rediscoveries, 61–3, 65; as target of climate sceptics, 151, 161–2, 164
  leads PAGES Australasian working group, 154, 156, 157, (1000-year temperature reconstruction), 151, 160, 161–2, 163, 164, 190–1; and politics, 160–1
  leads SEARCH project, 9, 58
Gill, JCH, 40
Gillard, Julia, 250
Gillard government, 160–1, 256
Gipps, George, 72
Gleckler, Peter, 179
Gold Coast, 105, 109
Gore, Al, 265
Goyder, George, 84–5
Great Barrier Reef, 204
  damage from Cyclone Debbie, 243
  impact of global warming on, 261; bleaching, death, 164, 180, 243, (catastrophic), 208, 241, **242**, 243, 253, 254, 261
  and growth of coral reef communities, 132; decline in calcification, 135; reading growth bands, **133**
  scale of, 132
  temperature and ocean water history, 136, 241
  threats to, 164, 261, 262
  and tourism, 237, 243
Great Dividing Range, 23, 147
Grenville, Kate
  The Lieutenant, 60

Groveman, Brian, 149
Gulf of Carpentaria
  dieback of mangrove forests, 180

Hamilton, Clive, 251
  Scorcher, 250
Hardin, Garrett, 266
Harris, Alexander
  Settlers and Convicts, 19
Hawken, Paul (ed.)
  Drawdown, 265
Hawkesbury River
  and drought, 99
  farming: and diseases, 39; good harvests, 39
  floods, 34–5, 37, 38, 39–40, 41, **42**, 48, 70
  settlement on, 33, 37
Hawking, Stephen, 241
Hendy, Erica, 136
Hobart
  drying trend, 222
  original meteorological register, **71**
Hoffmann, Johann Peter, 177
Hughes, Lesley, 240, **269**
Hughes, Malcolm, 150, 151, 152
Hughes, Terry, 241, 243
human health
  and disease, 222; infectious diseases, 166, (mosquito-borne), 230–2
  and impact of weather conditions, 72, 181; heatwaves: (heatstroke), 185, 229, (sport), 228
  mental health: and connection with nature, 267; impact of changing climate, 192, 228, 232–3
  see also future climate change
Hunter, John, 5, 6, 14–15, 21–2, 33, 37
Hunter region, 48, 49, 105, **106**
Hunter River, 99

India
  drought and famine, 90
Indian Ocean, 28, 29, **30**, 32, 103, 108, 113, 134, 139
Industrial Revolution, 136, 175
  human activities, development, 166, 180; and global warming, 167, 168; impact on climate, ecosystems, 153, 166; land use changes, 180, 181
IPPC, 162
  global climate reports: *Third Assessment Report*, 150, 188; *Fourth Assessment Report*, 152, 188, 189; *Fifth Assessment Report*, 152, 162, 163, 189, 216

Jacoby, Gordon, 149
Jevons, William Stanley, 8, 9, 33, 40, 48
  climate study, 79
Jiawei Bao, 202
Jones, Phil, 149, 150
journals. *See* newspapers and journals

Karoly, David, 164, 203, 251, 252
  work of, 164, 189, 194
Karskens, Grace
  The Colony, 45
Kiehl, Jeffry
  Facing Climate Change, 267–8
King, Andrew, 190, 253
King, Martin Luther Jr, 264
King, Philip Gidley, 4, 6, 16, 38, 41
Kolbert, Elizabeth
  The Sixth Extinction, 240

Lake Eyre (Kati Thanda–Lake Eyre), 109, 145, 146
  rainfall and floodwaters, 145, 146; and wildlife, 145–6, (threat of future climate change), 146
  and Kati Thanda–Lake Eyre Basin, 145, 146
Lake George (Weereewa), **147**
  'disappearing lake', 147
  water levels, 46, **47**, **48**, 147–8
Lake Mungo, 117
Landsberg, Helmut, 149
Lang, Rev. John Dunmore, 49
Lewis, Sophie, 183, 189, 218
Lough, Janice, 134
Louv, Richard
  Last Child in the Woods, 267

McAfee, Robert, 9, 61, 63
McAneney, John, 88, 109
McIntyre, Stephen, 161
Mackellar, Dorothea, 8, 192
Macquarie, Lachlan, 43, 44, 45
Mann, Michael, 150, 151, 152
  and climate sceptics, 158, 162, 163
Mauritson, Thorsten, 264
Mead, Margaret, 270
Melbourne, 58
  drying trend, 222
  dust storms, 53, 195
  flooding in CBD, **81**, 82
  heatwave of 2009, 181, 195, 227
  observatories in, 79, 195
  population growth, 82

meteorology in Australia
  growth in, 79; climate studies, 79–80; observatories, weather stations, 79, 90, 91
  and role of climate scientists, 80
  see also climate history of Australia
Milanković, Milutin, 171
Murdoch, Rupert, 256
Murray–Darling Basin
  drought, 94, 100, 128; and Murray–Darling Basin Authority, 94; record low water flows, 100, 206; and water-use regulation, 94
  ecosystems of, 236
Musk, Elon, 259

National Library of Australia, 75
National Oceanic and Atmospheric Administration (US), 225
Neukom, Raphael, 156–7
Newman, Maurice, 257
New South Wales
  and Cyclone Debbie, 212, 224
  droughts, 74, 76, **95**; Federation Drought, 92, 94; World War II Drought, 94–5, **98**
  dust storms, 94–5, 98–9
  floods, 82, 85, 104, 105
  suicides, rural, 234
  see also European Settlement; Hawkesbury River
newspapers, journals
  Argus, 81, 88
  Asiatic Journal, 49
  Australian, 162
  Australian Financial Review, 260
  Clarence and Richmond Examiner, 82
  on droughts, 47, 90
  on floods, 41, 81, 82
  Guardian, 244, 251
  Geelong Advertiser, 77
  Geophysical Research Letters, 149
  Gippsland Times, 83
  government gazettes, 73, 78
  Holocene, 157
  Journal of Climate, 160, 189
  Monitor, 75
  Nature, 150, 167, 243
  Nature Climate Change, 128, 157–8, 180, 247, 264
  Nature Geoscience, 155, 162
  New South Wales Advertiser, **69**
  and paper shortage, 70
  Portland Guardian, 82

Science, 266
Sydney Bulletin, 93
Sydney Gazette, 39, 41, 43–4, 46, 48, 48–9, **69**
Sydney Morning Herald, 75, 82, 85–6, 197, 262
and temperature and rainfall records, 71–2, 74, **75**, 197
New Zealand, 15
  European settlement, 129
  SEARCH project in, 126; Kauri, 126, **127**, 128–9, (and rings), 129, (samples from entombed trees), 129; and Māori, 126, 128
Nicholls, Neville, 9, 234
Northern Hemisphere
  and environmental history, 129
  temperature history, 149–50, 152, 153, 167; not global, 158, 159
Northern Territory (Top End), 109
  Kakadu, 116, 119
  seasons in, 116, 118, 119
  see also Aboriginal people; Darwin

Pacific Ocean, **26**, 32, 77, 103, 105, 127, 134, 139
  trade winds of, 25, 27, 178, 179
PAGES network, 152
  Australasian working group, 154, 156, 157, (1000-year temperature reconstruction), 151, 160, 161–2, 163, 164, 190–1; and hostility, 161–2, 163, 164–5; and politics, 160–1
  and review, 162, 163
  work of, 154, 156, 158, 163
Palmer, Jonathan, 206
Palutikof, Jean, 254
Paris Agreement. *See* climate change
Parkes, Sir Henry, 87
Parrenin, Frederic, 141
Patyegarang (young girl), 60
Peacock, Edward, 72
  The Heads of Port Jackson, **72**
Perth
  drying trend, 222; linked to human activity, 223; record dry years, 98
Phillip, Arthur, 4, 6, 7, 12, 14, 20–1, 33, 60
photography
  and weather events, 87
Polidori, John William
  The Vampyre, 177
Power, Scott, 108

psychology of climate change
  and blocking feelings of empathy, care, 266, 268
  'culture of uncare', 266; separation from nature, 267

Queensland
  cyclones, 27, 86–7; Debbie, 212, 224, 233, 243; Yasi, 203
  droughts: Federation Drought, 92, 93
  floods, 27, 82, 85, 86–7, **110**, 134; 2010–11, 103, 109, 203; and government response, 87, 109; inland, 109
  Galilee Basin and coalmines, 260, 261, 262
  settlement, 49
  tropical north, 132, 134

Raftery, Adrian, 247
rainfall, global, 202
rainfall history, Australia, 10
  colonial period, early decades: good rains, 33, 39, 46, 48–9; storms, heavy rains, 14, 16, 18, 34, 35, 39–41, 42, 44, 74, 76
  colonial period, later decades: storms, heavy rains, 80–2, 83, 84, 85, 86, 88, 89, 103
  rainfall: erratic, 20, 22, 144, 146; natural factors influencing, 144, 202; and variability, 103, 202
  rainfall record, 56, **57**, 67, 74, 86, 88; palaeoclimate reconstruction of, 156, 204, **205**, 206; inland–coastal divergence, 74; quality of, 91
  storms and First Fleet, 12–13
  in tropical north, 132; increasing, 134, **222**
  twentieth century: heavy rain, 98, 104, 105; rainfall deficits, decline, **92**, 94, **98**, 100, **101**, 139, 148, 222–3; wet periods, 100, 104–6, **107**, 108, 109–10, **111**, 113, 205
  21st century, 222; deficits, decline, 203, 205, 206, 222; record-breaking rains, 202, 203, 211
  see also climate of Australia
religion, 49
renewable (clean) energy, 252
  and Australia, 252, 259; and government policy, 259, 260, 263; potential in, 258, 268; SA Government, 259; and

transition to renewable-electricity
market, 256–7, 259
business investment, 255, 257–8, 260;
and cost, 258, 260, 262
and Carbon Pricing Leadership
Coalition, 255–6
and global transformation, 265
revolution in, 248, 252, 259, 270;
employment, 258, 259–60; and
technology, 258–9, 262, 269
Rignot, Eric, 168
Royal Society of London, **62**, 63, 71
Royal Society of New South Wales, 80
Rudd, Kevin, 250
Rumker, Charles, 71
Russell, Henry Chamberlain (HC), 9, 39,
41, 44, 47, 48, 63, 147
Climate of New South Wales, 79–80

Schwabe, Heinrich, 175
Shelley, Mary
Frankenstein, 177
science, history
and Age of Reason in Europe, 54
and meteorological instruments, 54, 60;
and systematic observations, 54–5
and old records, 61, 65, 124
and instruments, 54
SEARCH project, 9
and climate reconstructions back to
European settlement, 9, 10, 58, 71–2,
153
Eureka Prize, 10
method, 10, 11, 58, 70
OzDocs citizen science project, 75
partners, 9–10, 58, 73, 206
see also New Zealand
ships
exploration: and weather records, 54
Endeavour, 3–4, 6
Golden Grove, 15
Justinian, 18
Lady Juliana, 18
Lady Penrhyn, 4
Porpoise, 38
Prince of Wales, 5
Scarborough, 5
Sirius, 4, 5, 6, 12, 14, **15**, 60, 63; lost, 17
Supply, 4, 6, 17
snow, 24
in alpine regions since 1950s, 198,
238
and future climate change, 238

in Melbourne, 153
in Sydney, 75–6, 153, 197
Somerset, Henry, 89
South Australia, 49
bushfires, 53
drought, 84
heavy rains, 84; floods, 82, **84**
inland–coastal divergence in conditions,
84; and Goyder Line, 84–5, 86, 220
meteorological records: early, 72
warming and drying trend in, 85
Waste Lands Alienation Act (1872), 86
Southern Hemisphere, 28, 31, 125
climate history, 130, 149, 156, 158;
delayed warming in, 168; paleoclimate
records, 156–7; and temperature
reconstruction, 156, 157–8
tree species, 124
wind systems, 24, 168
Southern Ocean, 3, 4, **15**, 25, 31, 32, 85,
103
as buffer, 130, 167
and climate variability, 139
and subtropical ridge, 24
State of the Climate report (BOM), 184
Stretton, Leonard, 95
Sturt, Charles, 74
Sydney
Botany Bay, 3, 4, 6–7, 13
drought, 49, 74
meteorological observations, 60, 61, **62**,
63, 64–5, 66, 67, 69–70, 71, 74, 91;
observatories, 61, 71, 72
Port Jackson/Sydney Cove, 3, 6, 7; early
days, 13–14, 15, 16–17, 19–20, 33, 34,
58, 72
snow, 75, 153, 197
water supply, 19–20, 48; and regulation,
21, 22
weather in 21st century, 197; heatwave,
222
see also European settlement
Sydney, Lord, 6

Tank Stream, **21**, 22, 43
Tasmania/Van Diemen's Land, 49, 58, 71
ancient forests, 130; Huon pine tree-
ring record, 130; rainforests, 199–200
bushfires, 164, 199–200
floods, 85, 108, 211
snow, 24; in summer, 5
technology
and vision of natural disasters, 106

temperature
  global temperature, scientific research:
and ice age cycles, natural, 172–3; last
ice age, 117; Pliocene, 143, 173; recent
warming, global, 137, 149, 150–1, 154,
155, 158, 164, 165, 166, 201, 216, (run
of above average temperatures), 208,
(temperature increases not uniform),
216; reconstructions of, 149–50, 156,
('Little Ice Age', 76, 77, 150, 152–3,
166, 176, (Medieval Climate Anomaly;
NH), 150, 152, 153, 155, 158; record
breaking, 183, 208, 218, 253; regional
temperatures (reconstructions), 152,
154–5, 156, 157–8, 164, (and hockey
stick curve), 150, 151, 152, 158; *see
also* temperature history of Australia
and region
  measurement, records, 54, 55
  ocean temperatures, **26**, 27, 28, 29, **30**,
31, 117; in Southern Hemisphere,
168; warming, **114**, 134, 136–7, 179,
201
  temperature changes: and greenhouse
gases, 154; and positive feedback loop,
140–1
  temperature history of Australia
and region, 10, 20, 65, 69, 74, 83;
cold, 75; and comparisons, 66, 67;
and greenhouse gas emissions,
anthropogenic, 146, 160, 164, 189,
190; reconstructions, 117, 151, 156,
160, 161–2, 163, 164, 190, 204; and
records, monitoring, 55, 56, **57**, 67,
76, (early), 63, **64**, 65, 66, (quality
of), 91; sea surface temperatures,
114, (record), 197, 211, (rise), 134,
135, 136–7, 163, 164, 168, 184,
203, (warm), 208; warming, recent
decades, 97, 160, 162, 163–4, 180,
182–5, 189, 190, (temperature
records), 184, 185, 189, 190, 195, 197,
208–9, 222
Tench, Watkin, 13, 14, 15, 16–17, 18, 19,
21, 69
  Narrative of the Expedition to Botany Bay,
8
tourism, 166
  and economy, 237
  and global warming, 137, 238

Townsville, 99
Trump, Donald, 246, 247, 263, 270
Turnbull, Malcolm, 250, 251
Turnbull government, 252, 260, 262
Turner, JMW (William), 177

United States
  and Paris Agreement, 245, 246–7, 263,
270

van den Honert, Robin, 88, 109
van Ommen, Tas, 138
Verdon-Kidd, Danielle, 94
Veron, Charlie, 262
Victoria, 49, 53, 72
  bushfires, 20, 53, 77–8, 83, 181; Black
Friday, 95, **96**, 97, (royal commission),
96, 97; impact, 78, 83, 95, 181,
(devastation), 96
  dust storms, 93, 94–5, **99**
  flooding, 104
  forests in, 95, 96; and management, 97
  Forests Act, 97
  gold rush in, 78, 80, 81
  high country: climate variations in, 131
  independence, 78
  as Port Phillip, 72
  see also climate of Australia

Watchorn, Robert, 77
Weintrobe, Sally, 266, 268
Wentworth, William, 39
Western Australia, 49, 92
  and rainfall, 139
  waters of, 136–7
White, John, 5, 6
wildlife
  and bushfires, 96
  and heat stress, 19–20, 44, 65
  and Kati Thanda–Lake Eyre Basin,
145–6
Williams, Serena, 228
Wilson, Rob, 136
Worgan, George, 6, 12
World Meteorological Organization, 56
World War II, 215, 265
Wragge, Clement, 55
Wyatt, William, 72–3

Zinke, Jens, 136